African-American Philosophers

17 Conversations

edited by
George Yancy

ROUTLEDGE
New York and London

Published in 1998 by
Routledge
29 West 35th Street
New York, NY 10001

Published in Great Britain in 1998 by
Routledge
11 New Fetter Lane
London EC4P 4EE

Copyright © 1998 by Routledge
Angela Davis interview copyright © 1998 by Angela Davis
Joy James interview copyright © 1998 by Joy James

Printed in the United States of America on acid-free paper
Design: Jack Donner

Library of Congress Cataloging-in-Publication Data

African-American philosophers : 17 conversations / edited by George Yancy.
   p.   cm.
Includes bibliographical references.
ISBN 0–415–92099–X (alk. paper). — ISBN 0–415–92100–7 (pbk. : alk. paper)
   1. Afro-American philosophy. 2. Afro-American philosophers—Interviews.
3. Philosophers—United States—Interviews. I. Yancy, George.
B944.A37A37 1998
191'.089'96073—dc21   98–15201
                                                   CIP

African-American Philosophers

For Adrian B. Yancy

Contents

Acknowledgments

I wish to first and foremost express appreciation concerning the cooperation of the African-American philosophers interviewed for this project. It is their philosophical agency and rigorous insights that make this text possible. I would particularly like to thank Howard McGary for his helpful comments on my introduction. Adrian Piper is to be especially thanked for her confidence and encouragement that I pursue this project. She is also to be tremendously thanked for her impassioned persuasiveness beyond my expectations. In this regard, Joyce Cook is to be thanked for her decision to join this particular textual and extratextual conversation. Cook is a formidable philosopher and I might add a delightful person of profound integrity. I would like to thank Lewis Gordon and Leonard Harris, two of the first persons with whom I shared this project, for their early show of enthusiasm and interest. Ann Longo and Stefanie Kelly for their making my conversations with Angela Davis such an organized success. Stefanie Kelly is to be particularly thanked for her contextual and historical insights concerning certain aspects of Angela Davis's life and academic career. And Julius Bailey and David Kim for making my conversation with Cornel West a success. Transcriptionists Susan Hadley, Sheryl Owen-Ogburn, Beth Hayes, and Angela Murphey for their endurance. And Renee Crouse for her helpful suggestions. James G. Spady for his incredible intellectual rigor and his rich historical and philosophical insights. It is through Spady, as a Black scholar of uncompromising ethical and intellectual integrity, that I have learned the true value of critical philosophical *engagement*. To Ruth Yancy, my mother, I thank you for your positive obsessions, passionate drive, and truly unconditional love. George Yancy, El, your natural critical mind exposed me early on to a spirit of philosophical criticality. Adrian Yancy, thanks for your love, curiosity, and sheer existential presence. Uncle William, thanks for your scholarly leadership and support. Artrice McGill, Trae, Shemika, and Michael Snead, Georgie and Shavone Yancy, thanks so very much for just the love and support. Charles Williams for his insights into the implications of the interviews as material for object relations theory. Melvin Rogers for his narrative insights and patience. I would also like to thank several early philosopher-mentors: W. Sellars, A. Grunbaum, N. Rescher, A. Nehamas, John McKenney, and Eugene Fitzgerald. Also, I am very grateful to William Germano, Gayatri Patnaik, Lai Moy, and Nick Syrett of Routledge for their enthusiastic work and valuable suggestions at all levels concerning the publication of this book. Lastly, to Susan Hadley, a burgeoning intellectual in the field of music therapy, I wish to extend a warm thanks. She was there from the inception of the conceptualization of this project. Not only did she unselfishly devote many hours of labor to this text, with all of the predictable personal and interpersonal frustrations, but she was also an insightful critic and encouraged me to continue when at times I felt so deeply alone in my intellectual endeavor to bring this project to fruition. It is her faith, confidence, emotional support, friendship, and above all these, love, for which I am indebted. Susan, I greatly appreciate your collaborative intellectual labor. Thanks for being my Friedrich Engels.

Introduction

Philosophy and Moving
the Center of Conversation

George Yancy

> The most intellectually underdeveloped state of academic philosophical articulation among marginal peoples may be that of Afro-Americans and Africans—owing to severe conversational exclusion and societal oppression.
>
> —Cornel West

Lewis Gordon, the African-American philosopher, articulates a compelling paradox: In attaining a life-project, everything before it becomes read into it. This process of making narrative sense of the past as it stands in relationship to the present, and vice versa, stems from a desire for our lives to be thematically intelligible and existentially meaningful. Otherwise vague, inchoate, and disparate experiences are eventually reshaped into a unified plot. One's life is understood not as a series of episodic and disconnected set of events, but as an interconnected whole replete with rich and profound personal hermeneutic possibilities.

African-American Philosophers, 17 Conversations is intimately linked to my own pre-reflective experiences in the academy while studying philosophy formally; my reading of mainstream philosophical texts; and my own humble attempt to "move the center." Speaking within the context of European literature, the Kenyan writer Ngugi Wa Thiong'o maintains, "It was not a question of substituting one center for the other. The problem arose only when people tried to use the vision from any one center and generalize it as the universal reality."[1] Ngugi's metaphor of moving the center, with all of its deconstructive and democratizing force, is germane within the context of this volume. Indeed, this volume attempts to move the center of mainstream Euro-American philosophical conversation to include other, equally legitimate, philosophical conversational streams. In particular, it explores how these streams are generated, sustained, and discursively configured by African-American philosophers—and within the context of African-American philosophical thought more generally.

African-American Philosophers, 17 Conversations explores, through conversational interviews, the identities and diverse philosophical positionalities of seventeen contemporary African-American philosophers. One central aim of this volume is to deconstruct the boundaries between what is deemed "marginal" versus what is deemed "mainstream" philosophical conversation. As sites of African-American philosophical presence, agency, and embodied critical subjectivity, these interviews challenge the totalizing tendencies of (white male) Western philosophy's will to philosophic conceptual and institutional hegemony.

Another goal is to offer a diversity of African-American philosophical voices in order to illustrate the wide range of philosophical concerns that African-American philosophers continue to grapple with. Hence, areas discussed include Black existentialism, feminist thought, critical race theory, philosophy of science and epistemology, legal philosophy, philosophy of religion, social and political philosophy, moral theory, metaphysics, etc.

But what is the genesis of this text? In terms of my own personal archaeology of knowledge, I can remember first coming upon the formal use of the term *philosophy* while reading through *The World Book Encyclopedia* under the letter *P* and feeling extraordinarily excited by the idea that one could actually choose a profession grounded in the love of wisdom (*philosophia*). As I voraciously read through the entire encyclopedic overview, I came across such names as Socrates, Plato, Aristotle, Montaigne, Aquinas, Descartes, Spinoza, Locke, Berkeley, Kant, Hegel, Russell, James, Dewey, and others. The encyclopedic overview also came replete with some of their images: all white male faces, studious and pensive.

I also recall seven categories that listed under each the names of various philosophers. The seven categories included American, British, French, German, Greek, Roman, and Other Philosophers.

But even under the "Other" category, the names of African-American philosophers were nowhere to be found. Pre-reflectively, what residual impact did this have on my own self-perception, racially, culturally, and philosophically? Hardly seventeen, I recall the distinct feeling of being utterly unique, perhaps even the only African-American interested in philosophy and in becoming a philosopher. Both my white and Black high school teachers reinforced this feeling, for they themselves had studied little or no philosophy and not one of them, at least those who were asked, could provide for me the name of a single African-American philosopher, living or dead.

However, feeling compelled to read more, I engrossed myself in three introductory texts on philosophy: Bertrand Russell's *The History of Western Philosophy*, Will Durant's *The Story of Philosophy: The Lives and Opinions of The Greater Philosophers*, and Robert Paul Wolff's *About Philosophy*. This last text had on its cover the faces of Socrates, Plato, Kant, John Stuart Mill, Jean-Jacques Rousseau, Kierkegaard, Descartes, and Leibniz. This was clearly an example of the philosophical canon as pictorial text. Again, more studious and pensive white male faces. African-American philosopher Leonard Harris describes a similar situation as follows:

> The Society for the Advancement of American Philosophy's (SAAP) *Newsletter* is adorned with the pictures of ten archetypal American philosophers: Emerson, Thoreau, Peirce, James, Dewey, Royce, Whitehead, Santayana, Suckiel, and Dooley. Olaudah Equiano (Gustavus Vasa, the African), author of a slave-narrative form of ethical and social critique; David Walker, author of the impassioned call to arms by the enslaved; Alexander Crummell, Cambridge-educated Platonist and a moral suasionist; Alain Locke, critical relativist and radical pragmatist; do not adorn its cover.[2]

The associations, presumptions, and implications were all there. As African-American philosopher John Pittman writes, "'Philosophy' is usually introduced to college audiences by displaying the writings of some select group of 'dead white men,' all European or Anglo-American. This is traditional, and it is here that the weight of tradition is heaviest."[3]

Hence, the history of Western philosophy is the history of white men engaged in conversation with themselves, a narrative tale steeped within a certain white male discourse of value—culturally preserved, reproduced, and disseminated. The "aboutness" of philosophy has historically had nothing to do with Black people; rather, philosophy was *about* "Othering," silencing, muting, and effectively invisibilizing. But these significant metaphilosophical observations, and the weight of their pervasive political implications, did not crystallize for me; European/Anglo-American philosophy as a site of racialized normativity did not occur to me for years.

As an undergraduate at the University of Pittsburgh, I took philosophically rigorous courses with Wilfrid Sellars (theory of knowledge), Nicholas Rescher (Kant), Annette Baier (modern philosophy), Alexander Nehamas (ancient Greek philosophy), and Adolf Grunbaum (tutorial on Freud). Also I had very stimulating informal discussions with Carl Gustav Hempel. It was Hempel who encouraged me to rethink certain metaphysical assumptions. In short, each of these philosophers affected my philosophical maturation in positive and indispensable ways. Still, the dynamics of race and the cultural and institutional power of the Euro-American philosophic canon formed the unspoken backdrop of my early philosophical educational experience. From the first moment of having read the encyclopedic overview of philosophy, on through the University of Pittsburgh, and throughout my graduate studies at Yale, the continuity and reinforcement of Euro-American philosophy made itself felt and seen.

Though none of my mentors discouraged me from pursuing advanced philosophic studies, I nevertheless experienced a feeling of estrangement and discouragement that was felt as a result of being unable to identify racially and culturally with other African-American philosophers in the academy.

In terms of the categories that African-American philosopher Anita Allen has generated, there were no role models to act as ethical templates for the exercise of adult responsibilities, symbols of special achievement, or nurturers providing special education services. But surely, I reasoned, African-Americans wondered about the existence of God, theorized about the distinction between mind and body, speculated about the nature of time, tackled the problem of appearance and reality, thought about the nature of beauty, thought about the nature of justice and the requirements for an ethical life, and developed sophisticated philosophical worldviews. But where were they to be found? Could it be that the notion of an African-American philosopher, like a rectangular circle, was a contradiction in terms, or perhaps an ontological aberration? As African-American philosopher Robert Birt has written:

Philosophy is often regarded as among the highest of human intellectual activities and manifestations of human intellectual excellence, a superior endeavour suited for "superior" (i.e. "white") minds—hardly an endeavour for which blacks are deemed capable or which would fit them for their "natural" function as useful labourers. To this day a "black philosopher" is commonly regarded as a contradiction in terms, an anomaly or an undesired intruder into a realm that does not concern him or her. That any but whites can be masters in the intellectual realm, that blacks might actually have something of value to contribute to American or world philosophical culture is an idea at best tolerated "with a grain of salt" or simply rejected and/or ridiculed as ludicrous.[4]

But, for me, even in terms of philosophical "at homeness," as it were, there was a sense of tension. The socioeconomic matrix of my Black North Philadelphia experience, having been raised in Richard Allen Projects, had a concreteness and social realism that tended to explode the value and pertinence of Kant's concern as to whether we can know synthetic propositions a priori or Plato's realm of perfect Forms. Within certain urban enclaves of poverty, there are many traditional philosophical concerns, solipsism, for example, which compete for conceptual space. There are certainly tight links between one's context of being-in-the-world and what is deemed a relevant or intelligible province of concern.

During the end of my undergraduate training at the University of Pittsburgh, aspects of my previous philosophical training and thinking radically changed. These conceptual "paradigmatic shifts," so to speak, occurred through systematic and critical conversational *engagement* with the African-American historian and cultural theorist James G. Spady over a period of several years. Spady has consciously and conscientiously worked to find and create categories and illuminating equations, often indigenous to regions of the Black lifeworld itself, which help explain the multivariant levels of meaning within the Black experience. Whether critically interpreting the thought of Cheikh Anta Diop, Larry Neal, Dr. Martin Luther King, Jr., or exploring surrealism, hip-hop culture, or the cultural semiotics of sports, Spady's insights have critically impacted the discourse of African-American cultural scholarship and have contributed toward shaping historical memory.

In fact, it was Spady who first brought to my attention the work of African-American philosopher Eugene C. Holmes (1907–1980) who had done work on the philosophy of time and taught at Howard University. Again, Spady brought to my attention Leonard Harris's *Philosophy Born of Struggle: Anthology of Afro-American Philosophy from 1917*. For the first time, I experienced a profound feeling of affirmation, validation, and a communal organic sense of participating within a historically rich tradition of African-American philosophical thought. Was this feeling not an aspect of what the African scholar Edward Wilmot Blyden (1832–1912) called the feeling of "people with whom we are connected"?[5] From Harris's text I was led to the ethical and aesthetic writings of Thomas Nelson Baker (1860–1940), the first African-American to receive a Ph.D. in philosophy from Yale University (in 1903). It would take sixty-two years, until 1965, before the first African-American woman, Joyce Mitchell Cook, received a Ph.D. (also from Yale) in philosophy.

I soon became aware of the fact that there were several African-Americans who had written complex philosophical dissertations, before the 1950s, for a Ph.D. in philosophy: Thomas Nelson Baker ("The Ethical Significance of the Connection Between Mind and Body"); Gilbert Haven Jones ("Lotze und Bowne: Eine Vergleichung ihren Philosophischen Arbeit"); Alain Leroy Locke ("The Problem of Classification in Theory of Value"); Forest Oran Wiggins ("The Moral Consequences of Individualism"); Cornelius Lacy Golightly ("Thought and Language in Whitehead's Categorical Scheme"); William Thomas Fontaine ("Fortune, Matter and Providence: A Study of Ancius Severinus Boethius and Giordano Bruno"); Eugene Clay Holmes ("Social Philosophy and the Social Mind: A Study of the Genetic Methods of J. M. Baldwin, G. H. Mead, and J. E. Boodin"); Albert Millard Dunham ("The Concept of Tension"); Frances Hammon ("La Conception Psychologique de la Societe chez Gabriel Tarde"); and others.[6]

As I conducted my original research on Baker, the paucity of information on his life and thought became painfully evident.[7] So many questions went unanswered. What led Baker, born enslaved, to pursue the study of philosophy? What made him a lover of wisdom? Who impacted his thinking? Were his parents instrumental in shaping his intellectual growth more generally? What was it like for a Black male studying philosophy at Yale in the late 1800s and early 1900s? Which philosophy courses did Baker take while at Yale? How was Baker personally affected by racism at Yale?

It was during this time that the idea occurred to me of bringing together a collection of conversational interviews of African-

American philosophers, but not just out of a sense of fulfilling a sociopolitical or ethical obligation. Rather, the project was and is motivated by a more genuine obligation to the practice of philosophy itself; that is, the recognition that contemporary African-American philosophers have a great deal to say that is of unequivocal *philosophical value*. Hence, through the modality of conversational interviews, despite the current preoccupation with deconstructing and reducing the subject-author to an ad infinitum play of linguistic codes and conventions, these thinkers would speak for themselves in the richness of their own authorial voices.

The interviews provide an opening into the narrative *epistemic* and *meaning* constructions of each thinker. And it is through such a dialectical conversation (etymologically, "wandering together with") that the genesis of the identities of these thinkers take narrative and dynamic shape, and that the unity of their narrative identities, philosophical cognitions, and respectively adopted *Weltanschauungen* can be metaphilosophically glimpsed.

Dialectical conversations, after all, are complex sociolinguistic interactions that function as sites of fecundity, richness, openness, tension, and contestation. And, as is well known, there are many instances of dialectical conversation in the history of Western philosophy. One can find this in Plato's dialogues, in the correspondences between Descartes and Elizabeth of Bohemia, and in exchanges between Bertrand Russell and Frederick Copleston. And in his seminal work, *Dialogue, Dialectic, and Conversation: A Social Perspective on the Function of Writing*, Gregory Clark observes the following:

> Martin Heidegger, for example, wrote, "our being . . . is founded in language" and language "only becomes actual in conversation," an activity he defined as "speaking with others about something for the purpose of bringing about "the process of coming together." From this definition, Heidegger could argue, "conversation and its unity support our existence" and, indeed, "we . . . are a conversation." And although this is the process Martin Buber described as dialogue, he used the term *conversation* to suggest his notion of the ideal dialogue. For Buber, "genuine conversation" is a dialogue in which each participant "has in mind the other or others in their present and particular being and turns to them with the intention of establishing a living mutual relationship between himself and them."[8]

In light of the relatively poor numerical representation of African-Americans in the professional field of philosophy, *African-American Philosophers, 17 Conversations* is a long overdue text. In an essay published in the early 1970s, African-American philosopher William Jones matter-of-factly wrote about the "ominous gravity" and "desperate urgency" of the problem of the paucity of African-Americans in the professional field of philosophy. He observed:

> Although blacks constitute more than 10% of the general population, they comprise less than 1/100 of the personnel in philosophy. Accordingly, to approximate their proportion in the general population black representation in philosophy must be increased ten-fold. To date fewer than 35 blacks with the terminal degree in philosophy have been identified—this figure also includes Africans and West Indians—or about 1 black Ph.D. in philosophy for every million black citizens. The picture is not significantly brighter if we consider the number of black undergraduate majors and graduate students in philosophy. To date fewer than 100 blacks in graduate schools have been isolated and only 170 undergraduate majors.[9]

And as late as 1995, Leonard Harris noted that "there are no Blacks on the faculty in the Philosophy Department at any of the eight Ivy League universities and no Blacks on the faculty in the Philosophy Department at nine of the eleven Big Ten universities."[10] Harris goes on to note the following:

> In 1990, there were 8,792 members of the American Philosophical Association (APA). Assuming they were all employed, 202 persons of color took home pay checks while 8,590 whites took home pay checks (approximately 2.3 percent of the APA was minority, of which 1.1% were Black, 1.2% Hispanic, 0.1% Native American).[11]

Lastly, he observes, "An average of 250 doctoral degrees per year have been awarded in philosophy since 1949. Approximately 274 philosophy Ph.D.'s were awarded in 1993, of which six were awarded to Blacks."[12] Both Harris and Jones link these statistics principally to larger issues of institutional racism and oppression.

African-American Philosophers, 17 Conversations works with the assumption that much of (white) Western philosophy, despite its many thoughtful and brilliant contributions, and despite our own training within this tradition, functions as a site of white cultural hegemony, sustained and perpetuated in terms of the particularity of race and gender related institutional power.

There is no suggestion here to attempt to bring closure to the philosophic discourses of Euro-American philosophers per se; rather, there is the need to de-center Euro-American philosophy, with all of its associated normative implications, in terms of what gets defined as philosophically important and to expose its philosophically dominant discourses and practices as forms of colonial expression and cultural arrogance. Moreover, there is the need to *recognize*, with transformative intent and action, the discourses, sentiments, intuitions, analyses, insights, concerns, and culturally informed illuminations that African-Americans philosophically bring to the profession of American philosophy in terms of what gets defined as philosophical, philosophically relevant, textually significant, etc. As African-American philosopher Lucius Outlaw argues:

> We mislead ourselves if we require that there be something more than "family resemblances" common to all the instances we recognize as instances of "philosophy," where the common feature is more or less systematic *reflection* on various aspects, in various areas, of experience to the end of facilitating ordered, meaningful existence. There are no transcendental rules a priori that are the essential, thus defining, feature of "philosophy."[13]

There are serious issues here concerning the maintenance and continual nurturance of an African-American philosophical identity; the need for coequal philosophic representation; the contestation of philosophic literary hegemony as this is expressed in canonical exclusionary power; the restructuring of philosophical syllabi and curricula; and the power to define and institutionalize African-American domains of philosophical concern, interest, and value. William Jones writes:

> What is at stake here is the power and authority to define. Is the white philosopher to be the sole definer of reality? Is his perspective alone to be afforded philosophical merit? With this understanding of what is at stake, it is unobscure that blacks dehumanize themselves if they do not insist upon the right to make their history the point of departure for their philosophizing. Blacks announce their own inferiority if they do not force the established philosophies to revalidate themselves and reconstruct their normative apparatus in light of the black perspective.[14]

Indeed, during the early 1970s Jones founded the first formal Committee on Blacks in Philosophy and during this time encountered the oppressive institutional rigidity of the American Philosophical Association. He reflects:

> The response of the APA was predictable. We have found that oppressors go through three denials. They would describe the present situation such that the labeling of oppression is inaccurate or inappropriate. You can use internal criticism to have them relinquish the first denial. But then they're going to move to the second denial, "Well, I'm not the cause." But then, again, through internal criticism, we get them to relinquish that claim. So, they admit that there is oppression, that they are culpable, and that there is something that must be done to correct this oppression. But this is where the third denial emerges. The oppressor will select a method of correction that will *not* correct. The APA did not see the oppression in their structures or in their policies because they were not looking at it from the angle of analysis that would reveal such things as oppression.[15]

The interviews in *African-American Philosophers, 17 Conversations* are similarly structured according to a set of questions relating to early biography, formative influences, and significant contributions provided by the interviewee's areas of special philosophical concern. As the African-American philosopher Alain Locke has written, "All philosophies, it seems to me, are in ultimate derivation philosophies of life and not of abstract, disembodied 'objective' reality; products of time, place and situation, and thus systems of timed history rather than timeless eternity."[16]

Hence, there is the recognition that each interviewee represents an embodied *Cogito* and a dynamically relational mode of existence. Not disembodied Cartesian thinking substances but thinkers having concernful positionalities as shaped by historical, cultural, familial, and racial mediation. But there is also no pretense that I have discerned an ontological essentialist foundationalism that forms the sine qua non of African-American philosophical identity and thought. Instead, what emerges is a complex set of philosophical positionalities and thoughts exhibiting areas of commonality and diversity broadly informed by, though not simply reduced to, African-American culture. Indeed, one might say that there are "family resemblances" among the cadre of African-American philosophers represented in this text. And, unlike white philosophers, African-American philosophers, within the context of American racism, share a certain *Othered* experiential reality, one might say social ontology, that shapes aspects of their being-philosophically-in-the-world. Hence, within the body of each conversational interview, the motif of race, its historical reality, its cultural dimensions, its heinous weight, its political importance, and its philosophical problematicity, is both explicitly and implicitly operative.

Also within the body of this text, I've attempted to create, through the strategy of asking similar thematic questions, an intertextual dialectic between the interviewees. Whether it concerns the nature of race construction, the importance of the concept of race, what it means to be an African-American philosopher, whether there is something straightforwardly termed "African-American philosophy," the reader will find varying degrees of both shared and conflictual philosophical responses. There is no single monolithic philosophical voice. Indeed, what is also unique about this text is its inclusion of womanist African-American philosophical voices. One simply cannot find a single text that takes seriously and includes so many diverse African-American women's voices under the rubric of philosophy. In this way, the text also functions as a site of contestation in relationship to the male (Black or white) philosophical hegemonic voice. Indeed, within this volume the reader gets a clear sense of how African-American women philosophers critically assess a variety of philosophical concerns and their status within the larger academic institutional practices of philosophy. As African-American intellectual and activist Mary Church Terrell observed, "Nobody wants to know a colored woman's opinion about her status or that of her group. When she dares express it, no matter how tactful it may be, it is called 'propaganda.'"[17]

The interviews in *African-American Philosophers, 17 Conversations* were conducted between early 1996 and the middle of 1997. The text is self-consciously steeped in the politics of recognition and the hermeneutics of suspicion. Indeed, it is a text which helps to de-marginalize philosophical discursive spaces and domains of philosophical meaning as constituted and critically shaped by African-American philosophical agency and *Geist*.

Notes

1. Ngugi Wa Thiong'o, *Moving the Center: The Struggle For Cultural Freedoms* (London: James Currey, 1993), 4.

2. Leonard Harris, "The Horror of Tradition or How to Burn Babylon and Build Benin While Reading 'A Preface to a Twenty Volume Suicide Note,'" in *African-American Perspectives and Philosophical Traditions*, John P. Pittman, ed. (New York: Routledge, 1997), 110.

3. Pittman, "Introduction to the Routledge Edition," in *African-American Perspectives and Philosophical Traditions*, xi.

4. Robert E. Birt, "Negation of Hegemony: The Agenda of *Philosophy Born of Struggle*," *Social Science Information* 26, no. 1 (March 1987): 116.

5. Howard Brotz, *Negro Social and Political Thought 1850–1920* (New York: Basic Books, 1966), 197.

6. Harry Washington Greene, *Holders of Doctorates Among American Negroes: An Educational and Social Study of Negroes Who Have Earned Doctoral Degrees in Course, 1876–1943.* (Newton, MA: Crofton Publishing Corporation, 1974), 202–12.

7. George Yancy, "Thomas Nelson Baker: Toward an Understanding of a Pioneer Black Philosopher," *The American Philosophical Association Newsletter on Philosophy and the Black Experience* 95, no. 2 (spring 1996): 5–9.

8. Gregory Clark, *Dialogue, Dialectic, and Conversation: A Social Perspective on the Function of Writing* (Carbondale and Edwardsville: Southern Illinois University Press, 1990), 33.

9. William Jones, "Crisis in Philosophy: The Black Presence," in *Radical Philosophers' News Journal* (August 1974): 40.

10. Leonard Harris, "'Believe it or Not' or the Ku Klux Klan and American Philosophy Exposed," in the *APA Proceedings* 68, no. 5 (May 1995): 133.

11. Ibid., 134.

12. Ibid.

13. Lucius T. Outlaw, Jr., "African, African American, Africana Philosophy," in *African-American Perspectives and Philosophical Traditions*, 73.

14. William R. Jones, "The Legitimacy and Necessity of Black Philosophy: Some Preliminary Considerations," *The Philosophical Forum* 9 (winter-spring, 1977–78): 157.

15. From an unpublished interview with Jones conducted during the spring of 1997.

16. Leonard Harris, *The Philosophy of Alain Locke, Harlem Renaissance and Beyond* (Philadelphia: Temple University Press, 1989), 34.

17. Mary Church Terrell, *A Colored Woman in a White World* (1940; reprint, New York: Arno Press, New York Times, 1980), 224.

[one]

Angela Y. Davis

Angela Y. Davis is an internationally renowned activist-scholar who is currently professor of history of consciousness at the University of California at Santa Cruz. She earned her B.A. in French literature from Brandeis University, graduating magna cum laude and Phi Beta Kappa. She earned her M.A. from the University of California at San Diego, where she also completed work for her Ph.D. in philosophy. Davis also studied philosophy at the Sorbonne in Paris and at Johann Wolfgang von Goethe University in Frankfurt, Germany. In 1972 she received an honorary doctorate in philosophy from Lenin University; however, she never received her Ph.D. in the States because her research and writings were stolen by the FBI in 1970. Her dissertation work has never been returned to her.

Davis first came to international attention in 1969, when she was fired from her teaching position in the Philosophy Department at the University of California at Los Angeles as a result of her membership in the Communist Party U.S.A. She soon began work on the case of the Soledad Brothers, three Black inmates who had been unjustly accused of murdering a prison guard. Although she eventually had her job restored, she began receiving numerous death threats. Her daily departure from the UCLA campus entailed having a security officer start her car in case a bomb had been planted there. Once off campus, however, she was responsible for her own security; she purchased two guns—which she registered in her name—for this purpose, and among her body guards was seventeen-year-old Jonathan Jackson, younger brother of Soledad Brother George Jackson.

In August 1970, unbeknownst to Davis, Jonathan took the two guns she had purchased and traveled to the Bay Area. He, along with a prisoner who was on trial, took a judge, a district attorney, and several jurors hostage, demanding a public hearing for the Soledad Brothers via the radio airwaves. However, when police opened fire indiscriminately, Jonathan was killed, along with prisoner James McClain and Judge Harold Haley. The district attorney was critically injured. Dramatic news photographs of the judge leaving the courtroom with a shotgun strapped to his neck were circulated nationwide, and Davis, who had been in Los Angeles at the time, was charged with murder, kidnapping, and conspiracy. Realizing that her life was in danger, she went underground. Two months later, she was arrested in New York. She subsequently spent sixteen months in jail before her case went to trial. Acting as her own cocounsel, she was acquitted in June 1972.

Former California Governor Ronald Reagan vowed that Davis would never again teach in the University of California system. Yet today, along with her tenured professorship, she holds the distinction of having been named in 1994 the University of California's prestigious teacher and writer specializing in race and gender studies, philosophy, critical theory, prison abolitionism, and Black feminism. Her work has been published in numerous journals and anthologies, and her five books include her autobiography, *Women, Race and Class*; and the forthcoming *Blues Legacies and Black Feminism: Gertrude "Ma" Rainey, Bessie Smith and Billie Holiday* (Pantheon, 1998). Davis has been the subject of numerous biographical sketches, scholarly essays and books, films, and sound recordings. (A selection of Angela Davis's most recent publications are found at the end of the interview.)

Angela Y. Davis
University of California at Santa Cruz

George Yancy: When and where were you born?
Angela Y. Davis: I was born January 26, 1944, in Birmingham, Alabama.

Yancy: How did the pervasiveness of segregation in Birmingham, Alabama, impact your early childhood consciousness?
Davis: Fortunately, I learned how to challenge the ubiquitous segregation in Birmingham at a very young age. I am very thankful to my parents for having reared me for as long as I can remember to think in a critical way about the conditions of our lives. My mother and father

always pointed out that while we might have been living in circumstances within which Black people (or Negroes, as we were called then) were deemed inferior, that was not, in fact, the way it was supposed to be. So, in a sense, I grew up with an awareness of the need to contest, rather than simply accept, the given. I have often been asked to describe my path to political activism. I usually point out that there was no one pivotal event in my life. My activism is how I learned to live in the world.

Yancy: While at Carrie A. Tuggle Elementary School, I understand that you were introduced to the works of Frederick Douglass, Sojourner Truth, and Harriet Tubman. How did these figures impact your consciousness early on?

Davis: Living in a segregated environment, attending segregated schools, I imagine our teachers sought ways to transform conditions that were destined to have a negative impact on the students into experiences and lessons that were affirmative. I am thankful that I had the opportunity to participate at a very early age in what we eventually came to call Black History Month. From the time I was in the first grade we celebrated what we then called Negro History Week. We were always required to do projects, which meant doing some kind of minimal research on prominent Black figures, contemporary and historical. Whenever we sang the "Star Spangled Banner," we also sang the "Negro National Anthem." So I learned "Lift Every Voice and Sing" when I was three or four years old. I think this attempt to build community within the context of segregation was what motivated many people to fight back. It certainly played a role in *my* early motivation to protest racism. As children, we knew that people like Frederick Douglass and Sojourner Truth and Harriet Tubman fought for Black people as a whole, which helped to give us a sense of community. Within this stringently segregated environment, we acquired a sense of "our people," and of freedom as our people's destiny.

Yancy: Talk about the shaping of your early critical consciousness.

Davis: When I was very young I had the opportunity to visit New York during the summers, to move in and out of the South. My mother was doing graduate work at New York University for her M.A. degree, and she would take all of us—her four children—to New York every summer. In New York we had the opportunity to get to know and make friends with people of all different ethnic and racial backgrounds. Traveling back and forth also gave me a consciousness of possibilities that went beyond what was deemed possible in Birmingham, Alabama. So I decided to seek ways of moving beyond those restrictive conditions—and by the time I was in high school I investigated concrete possibilities of continuing my schooling outside the South. Also—and this was important in shaping my consciousness—my mother was very close friends with a number of people who were involved in radical politics, Black people who were members of the Communist Party. She had worked with these individuals in organizations in the South prior to the McCarthy era. During these trips to New York, we spent time with Black people who by that time had really put their lives on the line. This was during the late '40s and early '50s, during the McCarthy era. My parents' friends were in great danger on a daily basis, and I remember being aware of this, and knowing that it was a result of their work for racial and economic justice. These experiences helped to arm me with a vision of what it meant to be in active opposition to an unjust society.

Yancy: So, it was the early political praxis of your mother and father that really helped to shape your consciousness early on?
Davis: Yes, absolutely.

Yancy: Given that your mother and father were both teachers, I assume that you were exposed to books at a young age.
Davis: My father was a teacher for quite some time until the challenges of supporting a family led him to look for more lucrative employment. We all grew up, my sister, brothers, and I, in a learning environment. In a sense, books were the most important toys we received. There was one book that I remember I found particularly fascinating. It was a dictionary—a huge book for a child—that my parents bought for me. I remember reading every single page of that dictionary when I was about four years old. My mother encouraged all of us to read. She began teaching me to read when I was three or so. By the time I was four I had a regular reading schedule. When I went to school at five, I was much more advanced than any of the other children in my class. My mother was actually quite astounding in that respect. Under her tutelage, my sister's daughter began to read when she was two. I think that this is probably a testament to my mother's perseverance and ability [more] than anything else.

Yancy: Would you say that you evidenced a philosophical disposition early on?

Davis: In the sense that we all have potential to engage philosophically with the world, I would say yes. I explain this philosophical disposition as a consequence of my parents' encouragement to think critically about our social environment, in other words, not to assume that the appearances in our lives constituted ultimate realities. Our parents encouraged us to look beyond appearances and to think about possibilities, to think about ways in which we could, with our own agency, intervene and transform the world. In this sense my own philosophical disposition initially expressed itself not so much as a specific mode of thought, but rather as a quotidian way of living in the world.

Yancy: Why did you want to be a physician and what led you to give up this ambition?

Davis: I wanted to do something that was unique at that time, something that was extraordinary, something that was not generally offered to Black people—especially Black women—as a possibility during the '40s and '50s. I became very fascinated at an early age with the children's hospital adjacent to the nursery school I attended. I wanted to help others, I felt moved by a deep desire to heal. I don't think that I've abandoned that vocation. Rather, I've found other ways of carrying it out.

Yancy: Hence, this theme of healing is still in place.

Davis: Yes. Anti-racist activism, for example, is very much about social healing. Education and the production of knowledge can also be motivated by a desire to heal. I should also mention, in this context, that I have been working with the National Black Women's Health Project for over ten years. This is the way I have come to think about and work toward healing today.

Yancy: And how we come to think about things differently is often mediated by distance.

Davis: Absolutely.

Yancy: While attending Elisabeth Irwin High School, though at this time you did not understand scientific socialism, you became acquainted with the idea that there could be an ideal socioeconomic society. What factors shaped your consciousness such that you were even receptive to this notion?

Davis: My receptivity to Marxism is very much related to the way I was reared. If I learned as a very young child that racism was fundamentally wrong and that it was possible to recreate a world in which racial justice prevailed, I also was encouraged to think critically about what we now call whiteness. As difficult as it may have been to separate racism from an essentialist notion of whiteness, I do remember struggling hard as a child to understand how white people might extricate themselves from the racism that infected their attitudes. As a child, what I learned from my peers was that white people were evil, that the reason we were treated the way we were was because white people were inherently bad. But my mother constantly urged me to think about white people and racism in very different terms. I think she drew upon a universalistic vision. I actually remember that I would say, "Mother, there's a white man at the door," or "There's a white woman on the telephone who wants to speak with you." And my mother would always say, "There's a *man* at the door," or "There's a *woman* who wants to speak with you."

I would problematize that now, but it was very helpful, at that age, in making me think more deeply about what it meant to engage in oppositional practice against racism. When I eventually lived in New York with a white family of prominent progressives—William Howard and Mary Jane Melish—and was attending a school that was overwhelmingly white, I struggled with this more universal vision of humanity and with ways of thinking about the project of making things better in the South. I discovered the notion of a working class— a multiracial working class—serving as an historical agent of changing the world. At the same time, as I have already mentioned, many of my mother's friends were members of the Communist Party. Consequently many of my own friends in New York—the children of my mother's friends—were politically active at fourteen or fifteen: Bettina Aptheker, for example, who is the daughter of Herbert and Fay Aptheker; Mary Lou Patterson, the daughter of William L. and Louise T. Patterson; Margaret Burnham, who is the daughter of Louis M. and Dorothy Burnham. Herbert Aptheker is the prominent historian who wrote pioneering texts in Black studies; William Patterson defended the Scottsboro Nine and, with Paul Robeson, presented the Petition Against Genocide to the United Nations; Louis Burnham was the editor of the *Guardian*, the newspaper which was at that time connected to the Party. So my social life, as it took shape in relation to the friends I already had, was very much a political life. I eventually became involved in what was the youth organization of the Communist Party. At the same time, I was attending a progressive high school where we were able to study Marx and read the *Communist*

Manifesto in the eleventh grade. I make these points because I don't think my own political vision came from within as much as it was shaped by external forces, by the particular historical conjunctures where I fortunately found myself.

Yancy: What was it about the *Communist Manifesto* that "hit you like a bolt of lightning," as you state in your *Autobiography*?

Davis: Well, you know, "Workers of the world, unite! You have nothing to lose but your chains." It gave me a way to think about the world, about my experiences growing up in the South, that made a great deal of sense. It provided me with a way to conceptualize and yet to transcend much of the pain I had experienced. It is very hard to think about one's past except through the lens of one's present insights, so I guess today I would say that it gave me some basic conceptual tools with which to think about what we now call intersectionality, or the relationship between race and class. Gender was something that we had not yet learned to think about back then. But from a very early age I was struggling with a way of thinking about white people that did not universally demonize whiteness. My exposure to the *Communist Manifesto* gave me some fundamental conceptual tools with which to think about social change in a way that moved beyond an exclusive focus on race.

Yancy: Had you remained in the South, what would have been the trajectory of your sociopolitical consciousness?

Davis: I think that I probably would have become involved in the Civil Rights Movement as it unfolded in the South from 1960 onward. I went to New York in September of 1959, and I remember very vividly the moment of the first sit-ins in February of 1960. I had been in New York just a few months, and I desperately wanted to go back home. I had the feeling that somehow I had made a wrong decision to leave Birmingham—wrong in a world historical sense. I felt that I had given up my chance to be a part of these earthshaking, historical events. I can remember telephoning my parents, talking to my mother and crying because I wanted so much to return. From the moment of the first sit-ins, I would often think about the way my life might have unfolded had I not gone to New York. I don't know whether things would have been substantively different. Indeed, I might have been shaped by a different set of circumstances, but I like to think that I would have pursued a similar political vocation even though some things in my life probably would have been very different.

Yancy: While in high school had you encountered any books by African-American authors?

Davis: Yes. I think that the most influential work I encountered was James Baldwin's *Fire Next Time.* It helped me to think more deeply about the way that the Civil Rights Movement exploded. I went on to read as many of his works as I could find. Later, when I went to college, I had the opportunity to hear Baldwin speak. He has always been a model for me in the way he related his work as an artist and as a writer to the social movements emerging around him.

Yancy: You heard him speak while you were at Brandeis University, right?

Davis: Yes. I heard him speak in the middle of the Vietnam War. As a matter of fact, I heard him and Herbert Marcuse speak during the same critical period of the U.S. troop buildup in Vietnam. These were two individuals who clearly used their knowledge to illuminate and contest political injustices—and to encourage people to engage in collective struggles for change. I think of both Baldwin and Marcuse as mentors who helped me to conceptualize a relationship between theory and practice, a challenge that I continue to struggle with today.

Yancy: Before coming to Herbert Marcuse to ask him to help you to draw up a bibliography on basic works in philosophy, what got you initially interested in philosophy?

Davis: I became interested in French literature in college. As a matter of fact, my initial interest developed in high school when I was compelled to do a very intensive program in French in order to catch up with my classmates who had already taken two years of French by their junior year in high school. In my junior year, I took an intensive tutorial which required me to basically learn three years of French in one year, so that I could take the regular courses with my classmates during my senior year. That was a very serious challenge, particularly since I had never given a great deal of thought to learning a foreign language—this was not encouraged in the high school I attended in Birmingham, Alabama. But by the time I finished that tutorial I had become deeply interested in French literature and, as a matter of fact, I decided to major in French literature when I entered Brandeis University.

During my third year, I participated in a junior-year-abroad program that allowed me to study at the Sorbonne. The focus of my studies was contemporary French literature, which meant that I took a course on the novel, one on the theater, a course on contemporary

French poetry, and a course on contemporary French ideas. It was in that course on contemporary French ideas that I was introduced to the philosophical works of Sartre and the works of phenomenologists like Merleau-Ponty. By the time I completed that year in France I realized that I was most interested in the realm of ideas. This is what led me to philosophy. When I returned to Brandeis the following year to complete my studies there, I also began an intensive study of Western philosophy with Herbert Marcuse.

Yancy: I imagine that your philosophical predisposition was reinforced as a result of reading philosophically oriented French literature.
Davis: Absolutely.

Yancy: While studying philosophy at Johann Wolfgang von Goethe University in Frankfurt, Germany, under Theodor Adorno and Jurgen Habermas, in what philosophical manner did each of these thinkers shape your own philosophical reflections?
Davis: Because I had, during the previous year, done work with Marcuse, I had an established interest in the German idealist tradition, in particular. That's why I decided to go to Germany to study. What I hoped to learn from Adorno was the way in which one can draw productively on the tradition of German idealism in order to develop the basis for a critical theory of society. I was most interested in ways in which philosophy could serve as a basis for developing a critique of society and how that critique of society could figure into the development of practical strategies for the radical transformation of society. Of course, Adorno at that point had assumed a somewhat more conservative posture, particularly with respect to the relationship between theory and practice.

I have to point out that this was a period of intense student activism in Germany as well as in other parts of Europe—in France, for example. And it was a period during which the student movement was taking shape in the United States, the antiwar movement was developing, and of course the Black Liberation Movement was moving into a different phase. And all of these dynamics were very much connected with my own philosophical interests. I never saw philosophy as separate from a social critique or from social activism. Oscar Negt, as a young professor at the time, was involved in the work of the German Socialist Student Organization, SDS (*Sozialistischer Deutscher Studentenbund*), the organization with which I was working. From Negt's example, I was able to understand how one could do academic work and at the same time connect one's scholarly research to the struggle for radical social transformation.

I also attended lectures by Habermas, who by that time had become quite critical of the student movement. Although previously he had written on the emergence of the German student movement, during this period—which one might characterize as the most militant phase of that movement—he began to express extremely conservative criticisms of the SDS. So what I found most interesting about my stay in Germany was the way in which it was possible to develop very interesting ways of mediating organizing work and scholarly work.

Herbert Marcuse visited Europe on several occasions, and the most important reason I eventually decided to return to the United States and work closely with him was because he maintained a sense of the connectedness between emerging social movements and his larger philosophical project. At that time, Adorno wasn't very interested in such a project. Adorno took the position that if in fact the revolution had not occurred, it was an indication of a flaw that was deeply rooted in the theoretical process and that the critical question was not so much how to continue the organizing or activist work, but how to examine the theoretical weaknesses. He therefore called for a retreat into theory. Since this was an era of international uprisings and new social movements, I found myself fundamentally at odds with Adorno and all the more drawn to Marcuse.

Yancy: How does critical theory offer a philosophical framework helpful to Black struggle here in America?

Davis: Critical theory envisions philosophy not so much as an abstract or general engagement with questions of human existence; rather, it envisions a productive relationship between philosophy and other disciplines—for example, sociology, cultural studies, feminist theory, African-American studies—and the use of this knowledge in projects to radically transform society. Critical theory, as formulated and founded by the Frankfurt School—which included Horkheimer and Marcuse—has as its goal the transformation of society, not simply the transformation of ideas, but social transformation and thus the reduction and elimination of human misery. It was on the basis of this insistence on the social implementation of critical ideas that I was able to envision a relationship between philosophy and Black liberation.

Yancy: Within the context of the academy, what is the role of the African-American female philosopher?

Davis: That is a very broad question, particularly since philosophy has a
vast range of definitions in the United States. I can talk about the philosophical project of attempting to bring together feminist theory and
Black studies, and employing philosophical ideas in ways that place
African-American women as much at the center of liberatory discourse
and praxis as African-American men, etc. I am not suggesting that every
Black woman philosopher would see this as her project. But I do think
that it is important to insist on gender analyses within Black philosophical projects, as well as in organizing efforts in Black communities.

Yancy: How can African-American philosophers come to see their
departments as sites for struggle?

Davis: I think that is an important question in the U.S., particularly in
philosophy departments where race is not always considered an
appropriate subject for philosophical inquiry, especially given the
popular philosophical emphasis on color blindness in contemporary
U.S. society. I think that African-American philosophers as well as
other philosophers of color—and white philosophers who consider
themselves socially progressive—need to insist upon integrating into
the curriculum courses that foreground race and courses that focus on
African-American historical interests. When I first began to teach
philosophy at UCLA, there was not a single course that had anything
to do with African-American ideas. So I designed a course entitled
"Recurring Philosophical Themes in Black Literature," in which, for
example, I asked students to read Frederick Douglass's depiction of
the master-slave relationship and to compare it with the relevant
passages in Hegel's *Phenomenology.* I also encouraged students to
identify philosophical themes in the work of Ann Petry and other
Black women writers. This was prior to the emergence of critical studies of African-American literature. I found that it was extremely important to legitimate the production of philosophical knowledge in sites
that are not normally considered *the* philosophical sites. And, of
course, this was in 1969, nearly thirty years ago. Today, there has
been some progress, but it's clear—especially in philosophy departments where faculty and students struggle to legitimize philosophical
knowledge that is produced in places that aren't considered essentially philosophical—that there is an ongoing struggle to legitimize alternative sites of knowledge production.

Yancy: Do you privilege your Marxist identity over your racial identity?

Davis: No. I've never been able to figure out how one goes about making those decisions about which part of one's identity should take precedence. Marxism has assisted me in developing clarity regarding the relationship between race, class, and gender. So I see these identities as very much interconnected and wouldn't want to develop a hierarchical approach to them.

Yancy: And I assume that you also nonhierarchically integrate your feminist identity as well?
Davis: Absolutely.

Yancy: In what direction should Black feminist theory move?
Davis: I would respond to that question by arguing that Black feminist theory is not a unitary theory, that there is no such thing as Black feminist theory. Patricia Hill Collins in her pathbreaking work, *Black Feminist Thought,* does create this sort of encyclopedic approach to Black feminist thought, but I don't know if we can simply argue that every Black woman who has produced important knowledge can be considered a Black feminist. I really do appreciate her effort to identify nonscholarly or nonacademic sites for the production of important Black feminist ideas. I would say that one of the challenges for Black feminist theories is to engage the category of class in a way that allows us to understand the production of Black feminist insight in the workplace and in organizing efforts—particularly in the latter '90s with the demise of so many social movements. I think that it's extremely important to rehabilitate the role of the organizer. And, therefore, I like works like Joy James's *Transcending the Talented Tenth,* in which she offers an innovative analysis of the Black intelligentsia. I really like the way she looks at women like Ella Baker and Charlene Mitchell as having produced important knowledge for Black communities. I think this is one of the directions in which Black feminist theories need to move.

Yancy: What are some of the difficulties preventing the formation of a united women's movement?
Davis: I don't think that we need a united women's movement because I think that there are political questions and issues that can't be reconciled by deploying a universal category of "womanhood" or "sisterhood." Historically, there has been a rather naive approach to women's unity, just as there has been a rather naive approach to Black unity. I don't think that it's possible to ground unity solely in race or gender. Unity needs to be produced politically, around issues and

political projects. So I would suggest that we need to do a lot of work not only around coalition building—which is the approach that is most often taken—but around, for example, women of color formations that have emerged on the grassroots level and on college campuses, that demonstrate how unity can be produced around political projects. I don't think that unity should be sought simply for the sake of unity.

Yancy: Did you find the American Communist Party just as sexist as you found the Black Panther Party?

Davis: When I joined the Communist Party, which coincided with my activism in the Black Panther Party, the women's movement was just beginning to take shape, and I guess I would say that both of these organizations were probably equally influenced by sexist and patriarchal ideas. I wouldn't say that one was more sexist than the other, although patriarchal influences may have been differently expressed. I was initially impressed by the fact that women did achieve leadership positions in the Black Panther Party, although that in itself was very complicated. After the publication of Elaine Brown's book, *A Taste of Power*, stories that I had not heard about the organization at the time came to light. Within the Communist Party U.S.A., on the other hand, there was a continuous struggle to legitimize the leadership of women and to find ways to integrate a gender approach into the class analysis of the party. At the same time, many women's leadership positions were gendered as female. For example, women tended to be organizational secretaries rather than district organizers. Within both the CPUSA and the BPP, extremely important contestations over gender took place. This is how I see that history through the conceptual prism of the present. In other words, we did not then possess the conceptual tools for gender analysis that we possess today, and we couldn't benefit from the history of social movements around gender as we can today. So, I would characterize both organizations as sites of extremely intense, passionate, and often productive contestations over gender.

Yancy: You have critiqued the Million Man March in terms of its masculinist and hierarchical structure. How do Black women challenge such a structure without themselves creating their own feminist and hierarchical structure? In short, how do we best merge both Black male and female discourse and action?

Davis: I should point out that the critique that I represented of the

Million Man March was one that was formulated by an ad hoc group of Black women and men. It was not meant to be a critique proposed solely by women. It was meant to be a feminist critique. The men who participated in our ad hoc committee—and who have gone on to become involved in a loosely knit network that we call African-American Agenda 2000—argued as much for the inclusion of women as the women did. As a matter of fact, drawing from my own involvement with feminist struggles, I would say that the most interesting and productive battles have never been gender wars—not struggles between women and men—but rather struggles over the *role* of women and struggles over the acknowledgment of gender. Men and women have positioned themselves on both sides of those struggles.

In terms of the Million Man March, we were not simply concerned with the explicit exclusion of women. We were most concerned, I think, with the representation of the March as providing a strategy of salvation for the Black community, which positioned men in the privileged role. This led to the marginalization of issues like the impact of the criminal justice system on women, the impact of drugs on women, etc. The masculinist approach prevented us from engaging in a national conversation around the gendered character of our struggles in Black communities. And, at the same time, many of us were concerned that the politics of the March did not place the struggle for the emancipation of the Black community within a global context. In particular, the organizers of the March did not acknowledge the extent to which transnational capitalism plays a structural role in the impoverishment of Black communities. The March did not attempt to encourage, for example, an awareness of the relationship between capitalist globalization and the rising numbers of Black men and women consigned to live out their lives within the prison industrial complex.

Yancy: I have a question related to your essay "Black Women and Music: A Historical Legacy of Struggle." Do you see Sister Souljah and Queen Latifah as operating within the same discursive space as such singers as Ma Rainey, Bessie Smith, and Billie Holiday?

Davis: That's a complicated question because historical conditions have changed. During the 1920s—the classic blues era—the recording industry was at an embryonic stage. Therefore, the process through which decisions were made regarding which songs got to be recorded, how they were distributed, etc., was very different from the contemporary process of the production and distribution of popular music. What I find most interesting about the work of the early blues women is that at a time when there were few public discourses on gender, women's blues served as a site for explicit and provocative conversations about Black gender politics. I argue in my forthcoming book on this issue (*Blues Legacies and Black Feminism*) that Black women blues singers allow us to see the emergence of a politics of gender produced by Black working-class women at a time when research on Black feminist traditions generally relies on written texts produced by figures such as Mary Church Terrell and Ida B. Wells. I argue that through music an aesthetic community was forged, which allowed for the development of a Black working-class discourse on gender and sexuality.

Today, however, things are quite different, particularly because hip-hop artists are forced to contend with a very different process of production. Moreover, the commodification of their work happens through a process that is far more complicated than during the early stages of the recording industry when people basically could record what they wanted to record. The audience for that music was almost exclusively a Black audience. The records were sold in community places like barbershops and hair salons. Precisely because of the segregation of the music, far fewer market-driven restrictions intervened. But I do think that in hip-hop culture today, the political consciousness of young people, particularly young Black people, is shaped much more through the cultural politics of hip-hop than through social movements.

So, I think that it is important to look at the contributions of artists like Latifah and Souljah. But it is also important to recognize the way that some of these aesthetic struggles are staged. When one recognizes that Yo Yo, for example, who served as a feminist counterpart to Ice Cube—and who responded to the misogynist pronouncements in his work—was "discovered" by Ice Cube, and that their conversation was largely motivated by market considerations, one must question the implications of that exchange, even though on the surface it may have had some value. Cultural politics are far more complicated today. Nevertheless, rap music is an important site of political struggle, and it is essential to take it seriously rather than simply to advocate discarding it because of its misogyny or its oftentimes naive nationalism. Look at artists like Michael Franti, for example, who used to be with the Disposable Heroes of Hiphoprisy and now leads Spearhead. He is a wonderful artist who does a remarkable job contesting misogyny and homophobia, along with racism. So I do think that cultural politics, as Stuart Hall argues, must be taken seriously.

Yancy: Since the collapse of the U.S.S.R., have you thought about the work of Karl Marx or Marxism any differently?

Davis: Well, since the collapse of the Soviet Union and of the European socialist countries, I have become even more convinced of the importance of studying the work of Karl Marx and developing the kinds of anticapitalist analyses that will hopefully push us beyond this historical period during which capitalism is assumed to be hegemonic. Because the socialist experiment in countries like the Soviet Union and the German Democratic Republic did not work, this does not mean that socialism is no longer a part of the historical agenda, and it certainly does not imply the historical triumph of capitalism. As a matter of fact, I would argue that in the aftermath of the collapse of the socialist countries, the expansive globalization of capital has led to a predicament in which the everyday lives of people are even more directly and intimately affected by capital than, say, twenty years ago. The project of developing explicitly anticapitalist theories and practices is of greater importance now than ever before.

Yancy: Briefly, what are some of the psychological dimensions of being hunted by the State?

Davis: Well, first of all, it was a very difficult situation to find oneself in. And I can't say that I wasn't extremely afraid. Fear was something that I had to deal with daily during that period. I imagine that I was able to overcome that intense fear for my life by focusing on *why* the state was conducting this massive search for me. It didn't make sense that they were hunting me for the threat that I posed as an individual. I realized that there was a symbolic value to their focus on me, which turned the FBI hunt into a generic assault on potentially radical Black women. This insight came later when I discovered how many thousands and thousands of Black women had been stopped or arrested by police.

The circulation of my photograph on the FBI wanted poster helped to create a generic image of the radical Black woman with the large "Afro," which made vast numbers of African-American women vulnerable to the State. I always tend to deal with my deeply individual and personal fears by attempting to understand the larger implications. The fact that so many people did organize around my case assisted me to move beyond that fear, which otherwise might have become all-consuming.

Yancy: As an African-American woman philosopher, who is Angela Y. Davis?

Davis: That is a question that I am constantly working on. I think I can say, however, that for many decades the theme of my work, of my life, has been the attempt to use whatever knowledge, skills, and wisdom I may have acquired to advance emancipatory theory and practice. As I've already said, my philosophical inclination was a gift that resulted from the conditions of my childhood. It emerged from the way in which I was compelled to learn how to be critical of the environment in which I grew up and, at the same time, to seek ways of transforming that critique into political practice. I don't think that part of me has changed over the last fifty years. But I also need to acknowledge that whatever I am and whatever I become is always related to developments outside of myself. I see myself and my work as connected with a collective effort to bring about radical social change.

As a teacher, for example, I work with as many students of color as possible, both undergraduates and graduates. We don't have a Black studies program at UC Santa Cruz, so I often end up serving as adviser for undergraduates who want to create an independent Black studies major. Of course I also work with a number of organizations. In the National Black Women's Health Project, I have helped develop a political framework for the conceptualization of Black women's health as physical, psychological, emotional, and spiritual. I also work with organizations like the Prison Activist Resource Center—and I currently am involved in organizing a national conference on the prison industrial complex that will be held in the fall of 1998. For at least thirty years, I have worked collectively in defense of prisoners' rights and to challenge racism and political repression in the criminal justice system as well as in the larger society.

At the end of the day, I am not so much concerned about my own personal influence as I am concerned with carrying out a legacy and doing my best to guarantee that that legacy lives on with future generations. I see myself, along with many other people, as a part of a tradition of struggle, and this is what I try to convey to students, workers, and prisoners. Therefore I am most concerned with how my ideas and experiences can be productively used within collective contexts. I'm far less interested in claiming ownership of my ideas and experiences than I am in ensuring that this tradition remains a vital one, and that it is transformed in productive and progressive ways by each new generation.

A Selection of Published Works of Angela Y. Davis

Books

Blues Legacies and Black Feminism: Gertrude "Ma" Rainey, Bessie Smith and Billie Holiday (New York: Pantheon Books, 1998).

Women, Culture and Politics (New York: Random House, 1989).

Women, Race and Class (New York: Random House, 1981).

Angela Davis: An Autobiography (New York: International Publishers, 1974).

If They Come in the Morning: Voices of Resistance (New York: Third Press, 1971).

Articles

"Fighting for Her Future: Human Rights and Women's Prisons in the Netherlands," coauthored with Kum-Kum Bhavnani, *Social Identities* 3, no. 1 (February 1997).

"Race and Criminalization: Black Americans and the Punishment Industry," in *The House That Race Built*, Wahneema Lubiano, ed. (New York: Random House, 1997).

"Incarcerated Women: Transformative Strategies," coauthored with Kum-Kum Bhavnani, in *Psychology and Society: Radical Theory and Practice*, Jan Parker and Russell Spears, eds. (London: Pluto Press, 1996).

"Gender, Class and Multiculturalism: Rethinking 'Race' Politics," in *Mapping Multiculturalism*, Avery Gordon and Christopher Newfield, eds. (Minneapolis: University of Minnesota Press, 1996).

"Afro Images: Politics, Fashion and Nostalgia," in *Picturing Us: African American Identity in Photography*, Deborah Willis, ed. (New York: The New Press, 1994).

"Surrogates and Outcast Mothers: Racism and Reproductive Rights," in *It Just Ain't Fair: The Ethics of Health Care for African Americans*, Annette Dula and Sara Goering, eds. (Westport, CT: Greenwood Publishing Group, Inc., 1994).

"Black Nationalism: The Sixties and the Nineties," in *Black Popular Culture*, Gina Dent, ed. (Seattle: Bay Press, 1993).

"Clarence Thomas as 'Lynching Victim': Reflections on Anita Hill's Role in the Thomas Confirmation Hearings," in *Reflections on Anita Hill: Race, Power and Gender in the United States*, Geneva Smitherman, ed. (Detroit: Wayne State University Press, 1993).

"Remembering Carole, Cynthia, Addie Mae and Denise," *Essence* magazine, September 1993.

"Meditations on the Legacy of Malcolm X," in *Malcolm X in Our Own Image*, Joe Woods, ed. (New York: St. Martin's Press, 1992).

"Nappy Happy: A Conversation with Ice Cube," *Transition*, no. 58 (1992).

[two]

Cornel West

Cornel West is the most prominent contemporary African-American philosopher. Henry Louis Gates, Jr. has described West as the "pre-eminent African-American intellectual of our generation." West is currently professor of philosophy of religion and Afro-American studies at Harvard University. He has taught at Union Theological Seminary (1977–1984), Williams College where he was visiting Henry Luce Professor of Religion (1982), Yale University Divinity School (1984–1987), University of Paris (1987), and in 1988, was professor of religion and head of Princeton University's Afro-American studies program. As is reflected in the sheer diversity and intricate, provocative style of his thick, historicist and prophetic discourse, with its synoptic moral, philosophical, and sociopolitical implications, West appears to be at home in a variety of areas: history of Western philosophy, African-American philosophy, contemporary American philosophy, philosophy of religion, contemporary Marxist and post-Marxist philosophy, critical race theory, social and political philosophy, critical theory, postmodernist and deconstructionist thought, critical legal studies, etc. Indeed, in an *Essence* magazine article (1993) he states, "There are intellectuals who grapple with one idea for years, but that's not my style. I want to be a provocative intellectual who writes about many issues." West received his undergraduate training at Harvard University (1973), where he completed the program in Near Eastern languages and literature in just three years. He graduated magna cum laude and was recognized as a student leader. He obtained his Ph.D. in philosophy from Princeton University in 1980. West's work, which is broadly constituted by a prophetic vision and a deep and probing attempt to understand the contingent, tragic, and joyful in human existence, has generated many scholarly essays and commentaries, and has been published in numerous distinguished journals and anthologies. West has written and cowritten a number of books, including *Race Matters* (1993), which was a best-seller; a two-volume work entitled *Beyond Eurocentrism and Multiculturalism,* which was awarded the 1993 American Book Award; *Breaking Bread: Insurgent Black Intellectual Life* (with bell hooks, 1991); and *The American Evasion of Philosophy: A Genealogy of Pragmatism* (1989). (A selection of his publications follows this interview.)

Cornel West
Harvard University

George Yancy: When and where were you born?
Cornel West: In Tulsa, Oklahoma, June 2, 1953.

Yancy: Given that your father was a civilian Air Force administrator, your family moved around quite a bit. How did eventually growing up in a segregated part of Sacramento, California, shape your early consciousness?

West: Well, in one sense, of course, it was inescapable because it was segregated, Jim Crowed in its own unique Californian way, but in another sense it meant that from early on whiteness was really not a point of reference for me because the world was all Black. So much of my life was spent where I didn't interact with white brothers and sisters at all. And I think, in the end, that was a very positive thing because it gave me a chance to really revel in Black humanity, and when it became time to interact with white brothers and sisters I could really see them just as humans. I didn't have to either deify them or demonize them, I didn't have to put them on a pedestal or put them in the gutter. I could just view them as human beings, and I think that was quite a contribution of my own context.

Yancy: I see. So what was it specifically about your experience of the absurd, at the age of thirteen or fourteen, that made the work of Søren Kierkegaard so attractive to you at such an early age?

West: I think early on I was just in some sense seized by a certain kind of terror that struck me as being at the heart of things human and a profound sadness and sorrow that struck me as being at the core of the human condition. And so in reading Kierkegaard from the Book-mobile, and here was someone who was seriously and substantively wrestling with a certain level of melancholia, I was struck by his very honest and candid—I want to stress honest and candid—encounter with what he understood to be this terror, this suffering, and this sad-ness and sorrow. It resonated deeply with me. Brozier Hall Fry used the wonderful phrase "the tragic qualm" to describe this encounter. It is a kind of vertigo, a dizziness, a sense of being staggered by the darkness that one sees in the human condition, the human predica-ment.

Yancy: And how did reading Kierkegaard at such an early age impact your later philosophical development?

West: I think that it was decisive. It gave me a profoundly Kierke-gaardian sensibility that required then that philosophizing be linked to the existentially concrete situations, wrestling with decision, commit-ment, actualized possibility and realized potential. And so I tended then to have a deep suspicion of what Arthur Schopenhauer calls "university philosophy" or "academic philosophy" that tended to be so much concerned with abstract concepts and forms of universaliz-ing and always in track of necessity as opposed to the concrete, the particular, the existential, the suffering beings, and the loving beings that we are and can be. You have to realize that I was coming out of the church, and so there was always Job sitting there, Daniel sitting there, and even Christ, especially the Christ between Good Friday and Easter, the Christ during that very dark Saturday, which struck me as highly illuminating of what it meant to be human. How do you really struggle against the suffering in a loving way, to leave a legacy in which people would be able to accent their own loving possibility in the midst of so much evil? So in that sense I think that the Black church and its profound stress on the concrete and the particular—wrestling with limit-situations, with death, dread, despair, disappoint-ment, disease, and so on—has been influential on my Kierkegaardian outlook.

Yancy: How influential were your parents in terms of your early intel-lectual development?

West: Fundamental. They gave the greatest gift I could receive—unconditional love. They also exemplified such love in their dealings with others. They also encouraged my intellectual curiosity and energy yet always put it in a Christian perspective—understanding and changing the world is but sounding brass and tinkling cymbal without genuine love and compassion.

Yancy: I've had the opportunity to see you teach at both Princeton and Harvard and there is often this preacherly, although critical, style that you use. How has African-American homiletics shaped your peda- gogical approach within the walls of academia?

West: Well, I've always wanted to be myself, and, of course, that is a perennial process. I did not in anyway want an image of Union or Yale or Princeton or Harvard to shape me. I wanted to shape my own image in those contexts, and to be myself meant to be involved, engaged, passionate, and so forth. I do think though that we have to make a very important distinction between passionate rhetoric that tries to communicate and the sermonic or the preacherly, because passionate rhetoric is simply a way of exemplifying a certain level of self-involvement and self-investment in what one is talking about, and I think the sermonic or the homiletic or the preacherly has no monop- oly on that kind of self-involvement and self-investment. It's true that the Black homiletical tradition in certain forms, (and there are homil- etical forms, of course, that are not passionate), particularly those forms coming out of Baptist churches and Pentecostal churches, tend to be self-involved and self-invested. I am no doubt influenced by a number of those styles, but, for me, it's much more just a question of acknowledging anytime you're engaged in serious philosophical reflection that so much is at stake, your whole life, the structures of meaning that you try to create, the structures of value that you hold, your mode of being in the world. So, in questioning yourself at such a deep level and at such a fragile and delicate level, I can't but help, at least in my case, overflow with passion.

Yancy: Although you switched to Near Eastern languages and literature at Harvard University, talk about what led you to pursue philosophy proper.

West: Well, as I've said, I read Kierkegaard, but I also read Will Durant's *The Story of Philosophy* about five times, and I had read some other popular histories. For example, I was reading in and out of Bertrand Russell's *The History of Western Philosophy* early on. When I went to Harvard, I talked with Bob Nozick, who was my tutor and was actually quite wonderful, and I told him what I was reading and he said, "Well, that's wonderful, Cornel, but we are going to introduce you to some high-powered philosophy so you'll be able to build on what you've read." But it was clear to me, I think, because I did have Sartre with me at the time, that I was being introduced to analytical philosophy at Harvard. Analytical philosophy was very interesting. It always struck me as being very interesting and full of tremendous intellectual curiosities. It is wonderful to see the mind at work in such an intense manner, but, for me, it was still too far removed from my own issues. There were such issues as the problem of evil, suffering, misery, and how to engage in struggle, how do you talk about courage, how do you talk about joy, etc. For me, such issues were much more at the center of things. So even as an undergraduate, I was taking biblical Hebrew, Aramaic Old Testament, and Koine Greek, classical Greek, as a way of being able to read some of the religious literary texts that were of interest to me. In that sense it was a kind of antidote to a lot of the analytical philosophy.

Yancy: Who were some of the high-powered philosophers that Nozick had in mind?

West: Oh, I would think beginning with Gottlob Frege, Bertrand Russell, Rudolf Carnap, Willard Quine, and then probably on to Burton Dreben and himself. There were some wonderful folk at Harvard at the time. Harvard was experiencing a kind of golden age in philosophy. I was really lucky to be there.

Yancy: Do you see yourself as a professional philosopher?

West: No, not at all. I think that my concern has always been just trying to make sense of the world and trying to leave the world a little better than I found it. I think that if I were to call myself anything it would be a man of letters who's deeply immersed in philosophical texts, in literary texts, deeply concerned also with scientific texts, but science much more as one element in the quest for wisdom rather than science as a way of gaining knowledge in order to dominate nature. So, in that sense, I have an intellectual curiosity that is quite broad, but I've never viewed myself as an academic or professional philosopher in a narrow sense.

Yancy: Would you say that departments of philosophy are just too limiting for your rather variegated and broad intellectual project?

West: Well, not necessarily. You have to find someplace to gain a foothold. I could be in a philosophy department and still do what I want to do. You know, my aim was always to teach at Union Seminary, which I was able to do in '77. That was quite a breakthrough because Union Seminary, for me, was the real institutional site that brought together all of my interests. It was a Christian seminary, it was deeply shaped by progressive politics, Marxism, feminism, antihomophobic thought, and Black liberation theology. It was in New York and it was where the great Paul Tillich and Reinhold Niebuhr, who were two of my heroes early on, had spent so much of their careers.

Yancy: If you had to trace your philosophical identity, provide a short list of names and texts.

West: That's a very good question. Well, with respect to the modern period, I would begin with Pascal's *Pensees*, and from there I would go to Hume's "Skepticism with regard to the senses" and "Skepticism with regard to reason," those two chapters in book one of his *Treatise on Human Nature*. I would then go on to Kant's 1791 piece called *On the Failure of All Modern Philosophical Theodicies*. It's an essay that is really pivotal. Now this essay goes hand in hand with Schelling's 1809 treatise on the essence of freedom. Schelling lived another forty-five years but he never published anything else, which is quite interesting. I would then go to Schopenhauer and Kierkegaard, two fundamental figures. From there, I would then go to Nietzsche, *The Genealogy of Morals*. I would then go to literary figures, both novelists and playwrights, like Ibsen, Strindberg and Chekhov, Thomas Hardy, Tolstoy, and then Kafka, Eugene O'Neill, *The Iceman Cometh*, Tennessee Williams's *A Streetcar Named Desire*, and then to Toni Morrison's *Beloved*. I think that there you would capture at least a crucial part of my own intellectual lineage, as it were.

Yancy: Why is Kant's theodicy piece so pivotal?

West: Well, because it showed that the problem of evil could not be theoretically resolved at all. It was a question of coping, he argued, with artistic wisdom and negative wisdom. It was through the wrestling of a Kant, who we associate with a kind of obsession with rationality and autonomy, that I was able to see his other side, which is his artistic wisdom, his negative wisdom, and his reading of the Book of Job in that essay, which I think is quite fascinating, rarely talked about by scholars of Kant. The Book of Job, of course, becomes linked to the great tradition of modern drama that one sees in an O'Neill.

Yancy: Is there a Black musical motif that shapes your writing? I'm thinking specifically of your short story entitled "Sing a Song."

West: That short story was published in *Prophetic Fragments*. I had worked on novels and short stories early on, over twenty years ago, but I've only published one short story. But it's true that Black music, especially the Blues, is one fundamental source or creative lens through which I view the world. There is no doubt about that. It's a profoundly tragic-comic, neither sentimental nor cynical, stress on struggle. Keep keeping on, trying to hold the blues at arm's length by means of singing the blues or enacting the blues. And most importantly, I think, always viewing oneself as embedded and embodied and also indebted to those who came before. So there is that sense of radical conditionness on the one hand and, on the other, a sense of freedom, but still within that context of radical conditionness, especially to oneself. There is the sense of trying to muster the courage to be oneself, the courage to wrestle with the truth about oneself, the truth about America, the truth about the world and the courage to fight for justice. Those notions of freedom, courage, and joy would probably be the three fundamental motifs in my work, and I think that they are probably best enacted in the best of the Black musical tradition.

Yancy: What shapes your synoptic style of writing?

West: Part of it, for me, has to do with a sense of history, which is very important. Anytime that you have a sense of history then you are always talking about the very complex relations of the present to the past and ways in which futures are not embedded in the present. And anytime that you talk about history it usually takes some narrative form, there is some story likeness, and that tends to be easier to follow oftentimes. I think that is probably one factor that shapes my synoptic style of writing. Also, there is a certain kind of openness about one's own self such that people can see that you're being self-critical and they can see how you are complicitous with some of the very things that you talk about. In other words, it's not a matter of simply pointing fingers or calling names, but really showing that you are in the very mess that you are trying to grasp. Moreover, this tends to open people up a little bit. If you're willing to take a risk and become vulnerable, then it tends to open others to take a risk and become vulnerable with regard to listening to what you're saying.

Yancy: Is there anything that can be called "African-American philosophy"?

West: So much would hinge upon what we mean by "philosophy." If we understand philosophy as a type of autonomous discourse that somehow transcends history, I would say "no," because I don't think that there is such a thing in general. If, however, we understand it as a certain cultural response to the world and trying to come up with holistic views, synoptic visions, and synthetic images of how things hang together, then certainly there is an Afro-American philosophical tradition, I believe, most definitely. But also I tend to be rather Jamesian in my understanding of philosophy. I think that philosophy is in one sense connected to certain temperaments and that we see those temperaments through images of the world. In this case, the notion of an image has to do with philosophical articulation, a *Weltanschauung*, a worldview, and so forth. Art, for example, can be viewed as an image of the world through which we see a certain temperament of the artist. But I also believe that philosophy and art are really intimately interlinked because it has to do with the nature of our articulation. The last line of Federico Garcia Lorca's play entitled *Blood Wedding* is significant. That last line, "the dark root of the scream," is so very important; for it is a question of how we take that scream, that cry, that guttural cry that we make and transform and transfigure that scream, that cry, into linguistic articulation, into a way of understanding the world, a way of trying to make the world in some sense intelligible. I never want to lose sight of that scream and that cry, because I think that really fits at the center of any serious philosophy that's grappling with life.

Yancy: Why is there such a paucity of African-American professional philosophers?

West: Well, we haven't reached a point where we've convinced enough young Black brothers and sisters that to engage in philosophical discourse in academic spaces is desirable, attractive, appealing, or just hip or cool. There is a great deal of philosophical reflection going on in Black America, no doubt about that, from barbershops to hip-hop music, to mainstream rhythm and blues, and so on. The singer Babyface has his own philosophical sensibility with his conceptions of life and so on. Stevie Wonder certainly does. In academic philosophy we simply haven't made it attractive enough. But it also has much to do with the image of a philosopher, which is primarily dominated by the analytical philosopher who is clever, who is sharp, who is good at drawing distinctions, but who doesn't really relate it to history, struggle, engagement with suffering, how we cope with suffering, how we overcome social misery, etc.

Yancy: So, one way of making philosophy attractive to African-Americans is to link it to these larger historical processes.

West: Absolutely right.

Yancy: What does the "Black experience" have to offer American philosophy that is of philosophical value?

West: A profound sense of the tragic and the comic rooted in heroic efforts to preserve human dignity on the night side of modernity and the underside of modernity. In short, a deep blues sensibility that highlights concrete existence, history, struggle, lived experience and joy.

Yancy: Do you think that African-American philosophers have failed to fulfill the role of organic intellectual?

West: I don't think that all of them should. I think that we've got to have a variety of different paradigms of philosophizing. For example, some would be linked to a community that would involve overcoming the "gown-town" distinction and some would not. So, I don't think that there has been a failure per se. I would like to see more, but I think that we have to have a division of labor, and we have to have a certain tolerance for plurality and diversity of roles and functions among Black philosophers.

Yancy: Talk about the specific impact of Richard Rorty's thought on your own philosophical reflections.

West: It's on two levels. On the one hand, he is just a very good personal friend and colleague, and as a young person it's so nice to have a figure to take interest in your work and your mind, to be such a fascinating and challenging interlocutor and conversational partner. But that's a very personal thing and that is what I encountered at Princeton in 1973, six years before he wrote *Philosophy and the Mirror of Nature* and became famous. He remains a very, very good friend and colleague. On the other hand, intellectually, I think that Rorty was tremendously liberating for me because from my readings of Kierkegaard, Nietzsche, Gadamer, Heidegger, and the later Wittgenstein, which I had read before I went to Princeton, I was already predisposed toward the kind of antifoundationalism, contextualism, and deep thoroughgoing historicism that he was putting forward. Now he couched it within a certain self-styled pragmatism, and I had already actually been predisposed to pragmatism, having studied pragmatism under Israel Scheffler at Harvard. But he was able to couch it in such a grand worldview that he could really show how things hang together, and that is what I think I was able to acquire from him more than anything else. It was this deep historicist sensibility of always trying to show how things hang together, along with antifoundationalism and contextualism that he was putting forward. So in that regard, his work was pivotal. There is no doubt about it, even given my disagreements, Rorty is pivotal, both at the personal level as well as the intellectual level.

Yancy: In a *Transition* essay, Rorty argues that you are "still enamored of the idea that your own academic discipline, namely, philosophy, is somehow more closely linked to prophetic vision than are, say, anthropology, literary criticism, or economics, or art history."

West: No, I don't think that is true. I think that brother Rorty makes such a claim because of my own influences coming out of the Marxist tradition where the role of social theory is highlighted. I really do believe that we've got to be able to give some fallible yet persuasive explanations of wealth, power, and the State, as weapons in our institutional and individual struggles to overcome forms of social misery. But I don't think that philosophy is any closer. If I were to go out on a limb, I would probably make a case for art, but I'm not sure that I want to go that far. I think that Schelling and Schopenhauer make the strongest cases in the modern Western philosophical tradition as to why art illuminates more than other forms of cultural production. Actually, I think that there is something to that. I think that when you look at a Chekhov, a Coltrane, a Tolstoy, or a Toni Morrison, you actually see deep, deep, existentially deep, sea diving taking place. That is not the case in most texts in anthropology, most texts in sociology, and so on. But, on the other hand, it is also true that there are some sociologists, like my own favorite, Georg Simmel, who gets very deep. They tend to be those who are highly suspicious of their profession, but they are using certain insights of professional sociologists as springboards to engage in deep sea diving. Very much so.

Yancy: Again, in the same *Transition* piece, Rorty argues that "it will be easier to encourage such protest [where we're talking about social protest] if we toss aside the last remnants of Marxist thought and in particular the desire for a general theory of oppression."

West: Well, I disagree with the first part and agree with the second part.

I think that the Marxist intellectual tradition remains indispensable in order to keep track of certain forms of social misery, especially these days in terms of the oligopolies and monopolies that take the form of transnational corporations that have a disproportionate amount of wealth and power, not just in America but around the world. You need some Marxist theoretical insights in order to keep track of that. At the same time, I am against general theories of oppression, and therefore, for me, my particular stand within the Marxist tradition is linked primarily to that of Gramsci, which always places stress on historical specificity, on concrete circumstances and situations. This does not require a general theory of oppression per se. And in that regard I think that one can talk about a Gramscian strand in the Marxist tradition that is suspicious of general theory, which resonates with Rorty's suspicion of general theory, but it's still not a question of eliminating the remnants of Marxism per se. Not at all. I don't see how, in fact, we can understand the market forces around the world and the fundamental role of transnational corporations, the subordination of working people, the tremendous class conflicts going on around the world at the marketplace between management and labor without understanding some of the insights of the Marxist tradition.

Yancy: In his controversial essay in *The New Republic*, Leon Wieseltier claims that you maintain that the abolition of transcendence is necessary for religion and that you don't realize the dire contradiction that you've created. What's your response?

West: I never knew what Leon was talking about. I've never rejected transcendence per se. There are many, many different varieties and versions of transcendence. You can reject certain forms of transcendence while you defend other forms. But I certainly would never want to reject transcendence per se. Paul Ricoeur has taught us that you have to have some distanciation, some critical distance from an object of investigation in order even to engage in reflection, and that is a certain kind of transcendence right there. And certainly anybody like myself who talks about struggle, who comes out of a Christian tradition, which includes some kind of overcoming, to use the Hegelian term, *aufhebung*, which is a kind of transcendence, would never really want to call into question transcendence per se. Also keep in mind that there are many Hegelian forms of transcendence, but they're always involved in an interplay with transcendence and immanence, with some verticality and some horizontality.

Yancy: Staying with the concept of transcendence, what does a "West-ian," as it were, conception of God look like?

West: Well, I don't think that we have such a thing as a "Westian" any-thing, really. There are certain lenses through which I look at the world, but, for me, any God-talk is so inextricably linked to talk about so many other things that it would have to do with the nature of the stories and narratives where God is invoked as an agent in order to provide illuminations about what it means to be human. And so I tend to side with those in the Christian tradition of putting a high premium on Christ. So I'm a kind of Christocentric thinker in that regard and therefore following Karl Barth, the greatest Christocentric thinker of the twentieth century, I think that our concrete images of God are best rendered in the various narratives told about Christ as loving, strug-gling, sacrificing, suffering, and overcoming. And so in that regard, I probably would want to send somebody to certain Barthian texts or make certain links to James Cone, who, of course, was a very close student of Karl Barth.

Yancy: In terms of your Christocentric perspective, what value do you place on a priori and a posteriori arguments for the existence of God?

West: I don't believe that any arguments for or against the existence of God have much weight one way or the other. Not at all. I think that particular way of couching the question is already impoverished, and it reflects a certain kind of ahistorical way of understanding God-talk of which I am highly suspicious. I think that it's interesting that there has been these fascinating attempts—St. Augustine, St. Anselm, and a whole host of others—to wrestle with the question in that way. But that strikes me as just a kind of cultural practice that is relatively impoverished in terms of engaging in a form of God-talk that has played a certain role in philosophical reflection. But I can't think that way at all. It is not my way of being oriented to understanding what it means to be human in relationship to a religious tradition, or Christian tradition in this case.

Yancy: Do you believe that there is a "salvific" role for you to play vis-à-vis Blacks here in the United States?

West: No. I never use the word "salvific" in that sense. I don't think that salvation is anything that we humans have anything to do with. Cer-tainly, I would use the language of betterment, amelioration, break-through, progress, trying to overcome and trying to alleviate and attenuate the hell that we are catching. I certainly want to play some role, but I think that one plays that role whether you are a philosopher, carpenter, musician, mother, father, or uncle. That's just a human endeavor. It's really a question of trying to serve, and that is something that each and every human being can do. For me, it's linked to my coming out of the Christian tradition, you know, "Knowest ye the greatest among you will be your servant." In that regard, it is not salvific at all, but it's certainly one of rendering service, which to me is the finest, is the highest, honor that one can have in relationship not just to Black people but human beings as a whole.

Yancy: Speaking of rendering service, Du Bois seems to add a gendered spin on this activity of rendering service in terms of his belief that the Negro race, as he put it then, would be saved by its exceptional *men.*

West: I think that we have to weaken the claim and say that to those to whom much is given, much is required if they are willing to serve. And so for those who have had a certain kind of privilege, for those who have been able to benefit from the struggles of so many other people, they have some obligation and duty to serve others to make some contribution to a cause much bigger than that of themselves or their own personal careers. I agree with that weaker version. Unfortunately, Du Bois's claim was deeply ensconced within a profoundly elitist conception of culture. He was actually following Matthew Arnold in so many ways. And one has to separate the elitism from the honest acknowledgment that some people have more opportunities than others, some people have more privileges than others. And the question becomes how do you use, deploy, those privileges, and how do you use your privilege in such a way that it is in some way enhancing and empowering for those who are less privileged than you. Du Bois would agree with the weaker claim and there, I think, we would both be on common ground.

Yancy: Do you see the category of race as the dominating discourse in the United States?

West: Oh, absolutely. Whenever you have a civilization that is shaped by 244 years of chattel slavery, enslavement of African people, and eighty-one years of Jim Crow, minstrels as the first national pastime, jazz as its highest art form, you can't claim that race has not been a fundamental construct that has shaped how we've gone about making sense of the world. And as constructed as the concept of race is, its effects and consequences through culture have been immense and will continue to be immense far into the twenty-first century.

Yancy: And, of course, you're also pushing for an emphasis on class, yes?

West: You can't talk about the vicious legacy of white supremacy without talking about the legacies of economic inequality, class inequality, and also the pernicious practices of male supremacy and heterosexism, homophobia, ecological abuse, losing sight of the humanity of disabled people, and so forth. All of these have to be part and parcel of the various evils in American civilization and ultimately, of course, evils in human civilization across the board in modern times.

Yancy: Continuing with this issue of racism, as a postmodernist and historicist you are skeptical of epistemological foundations. Therefore, how do you convince, let's say, a KKK member that his/her respective racist ideology is *false*, that he/she has actually *gotten the world wrong*?

West: I think that your question is a good one, but I'm not sure that I am a postmodernist. I've never really described myself that way. For me, Kierkegaard is about as antifoundationalist as they come, and I would never call him a postmodernist. I would talk about John Dewey in the same way. He is about as antifoundationalist as they come, but I would not call him a postmodernist. I mean, we've got the most thoroughgoing antifoundationalists around and yet they would not be considered postmodernists. And so I'm not so sure that I would want to accept that adjective, though I do recognize that postmodernists do highlight antifoundationalism.

Yancy: But you do embrace a contextualist and revisionist thesis.

West: Absolutely! And I think that this is both Christian, coming out of Pascal and Kierkegaard, and modern, coming out of Dewey and later Wittgenstein. However, I think that your question is still a good one. In terms of your question, it would have to do with context, it would have to do with the language of the Ku Klux Klan to whom I was speaking. When you want to constitute a dialogue with the KKK or whomever, you have got to be able to communicate with them. First, what sort of narratives are they using? Second, how do you engage in immanent critiques of their narratives to get them to see that they're actually involved in a deep contradiction or a major blindness in terms of downplaying certain elements of those narratives and high-lighting other elements of those narratives?

Now if the KKK is, as more than likely, Christian, then you've got to wrestle over their understandings, renderings, or interpretations of certain Christian narratives and how in fact they become tied to a white supremacist perspective. We know that modern Christianity is thoroughly shot through with white supremacy like every other insti-tution in modernity early on: science, journalism, right across the board, churches, including mosques, synagogues, and so on. White supremacy cuts through and saturates and permeates every institu-tional nook and cranny of modernity. Hence, how then do you muster resources based on the tradition out of which they come, that serves as the basis for criticizing the white supremacy to which they are cap-tive? It's a question of how you weave narratives and how you reweave them in such a way that a person would be open to a critique of white supremacy.

Now that's just the intellectual level. Then you've got the matter of certain interests. For example, why is it that they're so invested in white supremacy? What are the wages of whiteness that they accrue, given the investment? And that becomes psychocultural and psycho-sexual and all of these different dimensions: the intellectual, the argu-ment in relation to self-interest, the psychocultural and psychosexual anxieties associated with Black bodies or brown bodies or red bodies. All of these elements must go into the conversation if you're trying to convince and persuade a person that they're wrong. And at that point I don't think that it's at all a question of epistemic skepticism or epistemic foundationalism. That is just an impoverished way of pos-ing the question, which, unfortunately, tends to be rather typical of all of the courses in morality. They don't have that thicker historical con-text as part and parcel of the understanding of moral discourse and ethical exchange. But even after all of this, of course, one may still be unsuccessful.

Yancy: You commented that you would not describe yourself as a post-modernist. Would you elaborate on this?

West: I am first and foremost a modern Christian person of African descent in America trying to love my way through the darkness of an advanced capitalist global system and the thunder of postmodern market-driven culture. The complex interplay of scepticism and hope, doubt and faith—in Pascal, Montaigne, Kierkegaard, and Coltrane—is shot through my work. Yet the centrality of compassion and love in

my view locks me into premodern figures (like Jesus) and modern
writers (like Chekhov and Hardy). Postmodern is an adjective that
highlights certain features of our culture—it is not a school of thought
or descriptive term for a philosophical position. In fact, Pyrrho's scepticism is much more radical than Derrida's—at the existential level,
which is where late moderns like me begin and, if possible, linger.

Yancy: Was the New York Society of Black Philosophers instrumental
in terms of helping to create a critical mass of African-American
philosophers?

West: Well, for me, it was crucial. It was monumental in terms of facil-
itating a context in which persons concerned with philosophical
reflections of the Black experience, all of whom were not Black,
though large numbers were, could meet regularly at Al Prettyman's
place there in New York. Howard McGary, Lucius Outlaw, and many
others—I guess it must to have been about ten or twelve of us—who
met there all the time. Actually, David Dinkins [New York City's former mayor] used to stop in every once in a while. He was a friend of
Blumsberg's. There was also Frank Kirkland, who came later on, and a
host of other people. We gave papers, encouraged reflection, gave
each other encouragement, and, most importantly, we took each
other seriously, which meant giving each and every one of us the benefit of being wrong. That, to me, is probably the most enabling and
ennobling form of support that one can give another human being,
whether an intellectual or not. That's what we were able to do. We
really constituted an intellectual neighborhood, a real community of
inquirers wrestling with the construct of race to philosophical traditions. And though it is still active, I haven't been part of it for years.
However, I can't imagine myself without it.

At the same time, I was part of the *Social Text* collective, Fredric
Jameson, Stanley Aronowitz, Rick Wolf, Steve Resnick, and others. I
was also part of the *Boundary 2* collective, Paul Bove, William
Spanos, Joseph Buttigieg, Jonathan Arac, Donald Pease, Margaret
Ferguson, and others. I was actually lucky to be part of a number of
different high-powered, highly engaging, highly challenging subcul-
tures, really, that were far removed from the academy, but were as
intellectually challenging as anything in the academy.

Yancy: Out of all of the African-American philosophers, you're the
most visible.

West: That's true. Well, you know, part of it has to do with the fact that for twenty years I've been lecturing almost 150 times a year. And so I get a chance to meet a lot of people, a lot of people get to hear me in so many different contexts. One becomes thoroughly multicontextual in terms of one's language, in terms of how one communicates with people. And, of course, there is television, which is another context that really projected my image. I've oftentimes been misunderstood, but that's often the case with television. But I think that the multicontextualism, the traveling, the engagement in so many different milieus more than anything else accounts for my visibility.

Yancy: Before we conclude, briefly talk about how your opinion of Minister Louis Farrakhan has changed since your audience with him.

West: Before I met him, of course, all that I knew him by was his own deep commitment to Black freedom and his deep love for Black people, both of which are expressed within his own very limited vision of how you achieve Black freedom. And I never had a chance to sit down with him and break bread. And after sitting down and breaking bread and exchanging over time this rather intense dialogue, it was clear to me that he, like any other human being, is open to being convinced, persuaded, had his own views, arguments, perspectives, etc. And so from the beginning, I approached him like I approach anybody, which is first an act of charity, to see in fact what openness, what positive elements are part of his view where I can resonate with him, and then of course to highlight the negative ones and the highly objectionable ones. But, over time, I've definitely seen a change in him, no doubt about it.

Yancy: What is your overall philosophical project?

West: It's hard to say. I think that fundamentally it has to do with wrestling with the problem of evil in modernity, especially as it relates to people of African descent in particular. And all human beings catch hell in general, but it has very much to do with the dark side, the underside of the human predicament. That's why it cuts across, I think, so many disciplines. How do you preserve some compassion in the face of the absurd, some sense of joy in the face of the nullity and nothingness that characterizes so much of our human endeavors?

Yancy: As an African-American intellectual, who is Cornel West?

West: I think that I'm just a brother who comes out of the Black church on the block, trying to make sense of the world, and making a blow for freedom in the short time that I'm here, and having fun in the meantime. I would also say that I'm one-half of the person my brother is and one-third of the person my father was, and then hope that I can actually resonate and keep alive in some sense the depths of my mother, and the determination of my sisters!

A Selection of Published Works of Cornel West

Books

Restoring Hope: Conversations on the Future of Black America (Boston: Beacon Press, 1997).

The Future of the Race, with Henry Louis Gates, Jr. (New York: Random House, 1997).

Jews and Blacks: A Dialogue on Race, Religion, and Culture in America, with Michael Lerner (New York: NAL/Dutton, 1996).

Jews and Blacks: The Hard Hunt for Common Ground, with Michael Lerner (New York: The Putnam Publishing Group, 1995).

Jews and Blacks: Let the Healing Begin, with Michael Lerner (New York: A Grosset/Putnam Book, 1995).

Keeping Faith: Philosophy and Race in America (New York: Routledge, 1993).

Beyond Eurocentrism and Multiculturalism, Volume One: Prophetic Thought in Postmodern Times (Monroe, ME: Common Courage Press, 1993).

Beyond Eurocentrism and Multiculturalism, Volume Two: Prophetic Reflections: Notes on Race and Power in America (Monroe, ME: Common Courage Press, 1993).

Race Matters (New York: Random House, 1993).

Breaking Bread: Insurgent Black Intellectual Life, with bell hooks (Boston: South End Press, 1991).

The Ethical Dimensions of Marxist Thought (New York: Monthly Review Press, 1991).

The American Evasion of Philosophy: A Genealogy of Pragmatism (Madison: University of Wisconsin Press, 1989).

Prophetic Fragments (Grand Rapids: William Eerdmans Publishing Company, 1988).

Post-Analytic Philosophy, with John Rajchman (New York: Columbia University Press, 1985).

Prophesy Deliverance! An Afro-American Revolutionary Christianity (Westminster: John Knox Press, 1982).

[three]

Adrian M. S. Piper

Adrian M. S. Piper is professor of philosophy at Wellesley College. She earned an A.A. in fine arts from the School of Visual Arts and her B.A. in philosophy from City College of New York. Her M.A. and Ph.D. degrees in philosophy were both earned from Harvard University. She has also taught at the University of Michigan, Stanford University, Georgetown University, and the University of California at San Diego. She is the first African-American woman tenured philosopher in the United States. Her areas of specialization are metaethics, moral psychology, history of ethics, Kant's metaphysics, Kant's ethics, and Kant's aesthetics. Her articles and reviews have appeared in *Ethics*; *Political Theory*; *The International Library of Legal and Political Philosophy*; *Midwest Studies in Philosophy VII: Social and Political Philosophy*; *Nous*; *American Philosophical Quarterly*; *The Journal of Philosophy*; *Social Theory and Practice*; *Identity, Character and Morality*; *The Philosophical Forum*; and more. She has also received two honorary degrees, a D.L. and a D.A. from the California Institute of the Arts and the Massachusetts College of Art, respectively. She is also the author of numerous works in the areas of art and art criticism. (A more complete citation list of Adrian M. S. Piper's published works in philosophy can be found at the end of the interview.)

Adrian M. S. Piper
Wellesley College

George Yancy: When and where were you born?
Adrian Piper: September 20, 1948, in Harlem, New York.

Yancy: What was it like growing up in Harlem?
Piper: Well, when I was a kid it was actually pretty nice. We lived at
150th Street between St. Nicholas and Edgecombe Avenue. It is in an
area called Washington Heights but we know what that means. The
architecture was very beautiful and there are a lot of old mansions
even now. And at that time the neighborhood was quite nicely kept
up. And so there were parks. For example, there was Edgecombe
Avenue Park, which was very clean and pretty, and I used to play
there when I was a kid. When I was younger I had friends in the
neighborhood. Most of the middle-class Blacks who were my friends
and friends of my parents moved out and we were one of the few middle-class Black families left there. And then it was more complicated
because I and my folks are very often mistaken for white and were
mistaken for white in that neighborhood as well. So, as I got older it
became progressively more uncomfortable. The neighborhood
became more dangerous. We moved to Riverside Drive and 145th
Street when I was, I think, fourteen.

Yancy: So, it became personally dangerous for you?
Piper: Well, I was attacked once. And unpleasant epithets were slung
my way by people who assumed I was white.

Yancy: How did the fact that you phenotypically looked white, and as
a result received so much hostility from your peers, impact your early
understanding of your own racial identity?
Piper: Well, it made it more confusing. I think that such things made it
take a lot longer for me to figure out what to think about all of it. I just
got very different and conflicting responses from people. And, you
know, there's this sense in which when you present someone with an
anomaly that they're not use to, the first thing they try to do is to place
you, they try to put you in your place and also identify you for their
purposes of classification. And since I was being identified by lots and
lots of different people and classified in lots and lots of different ways,

I had a lot of trouble defining my identity for myself. There really wasn't any preconceived identity that I could rely on.

Yancy: So, you didn't experience what Malcolm X talks about where he stresses that he hated the white blood in his body, his light skin, etc.?

Piper: No, I really didn't. I've actually done a bit of introspection on this very matter and I don't think that I have the problem of being consumed with self-hatred. That's not a major issue for me. I would have to say that I have a great deal more of a feeling of pride in my Black heritage, in my identity as a Black woman, because I think that African-Americans have just been heroic, saintly, in terms of what they've had to cope with in living in this country. So, I feel much more strongly about that aspect of my identity. But I have never divided things up along racial lines within my own background.

Yancy: Provide a sense of the formative years, where you went to elementary school and so on.

Piper: Well, first, I went to Riverside Church, nursery and kindergarten. I then went to New Lincoln from first grade through twelfth grade. New Lincoln was basically a private prep school of a very progressive sort. And a lot of kids of people from the theater and art worlds went there. Zero Mostel's kids went there. Larry Gelbart's kids went there. Arthur Sackler's kids went there. He was someone who did a lot in the arts. Faith Ringgold's and Susan Sontag's kids also went there. So, it was a liberal and progressive milieu.

Yancy: Do you remember any particular teachers at that time who may have had a formative influence?

Piper: Yes I do. Mrs. Catherine Moore was my teacher in fourth grade and she was absolutely wonderful. She was really a very demanding and also a very personable Black woman. I believe she was the only Black teacher I had. And she was just terrific. I think she was the person who turned around my math scores. When I went into Mrs. Moore's class I was really doing badly in math and when I left I was doing great. So, I think she was responsible for that.

Yancy: What about in high school?

Piper: I remember I had Marva Spellman in the ninth grade who was a dancer. Then in the tenth grade I think I had William Beiser, who was a very nice man. And actually I had occasion to think about him recently because there is now a new edition out of Herman Melville's *Pierre, or, The Ambiguities* which is getting a lot of attention because it has been edited in some unusual ways. And Mr. Beiser assigned me a three-part presentation that I had to give to the class on that book. And it was really one of the most demanding and also the most interesting things I had read at that point. And I really enjoyed that a lot.

Yancy: And were your parents instrumental in shaping your early intellectual growth?

Piper: Yes they were. I think both of my parents really had a lot of philosophical skills. My dad, who was born in West Virginia, was a lawyer but he was trained as a Jesuit and of course there is a strong philosophy connection there. And my mother, who was born in Port Antonio, Jamaica, was just very philosophical in her reasoning and very analytical in the way she argued. And let me add that I grew up in an extended family because my maternal grandmother and my maternal uncle also lived with us. And I was an only child. So I was basically around these four adults all the time and I think I learned very early on that the way for me to defend myself and gain status among these four huge people was through being rational and logical. That was something that I think I learned at a pretty young age. Yes, my parents were very strong in terms of their intellectual role in my life. My dad came from a family of strong and educated women. And he was always very, very clear about the importance of education. I mean he was a really great dad. I remember once we were all going somewhere and it was raining and there was a taxi strike. I might've been ten or eleven at the time. We were standing outside getting soaked by the rain trying to find a cab and I was grousing and whining about the strike. And my dad started explaining to me that the cabbies were right to go on strike, that they didn't make a decent living, that they had families to support, etc., etc. I mean, he's standing there getting soaked by the rain, no cab in sight, and telling me that the strike was perfectly justified! I was completely flabbergasted. I'd never heard anyone argue against their own immediate self-interest before, appealing to general principle even though it meant they had to sacrifice. It really blew me away. He was an important role model for me, both ethically and philosophically. I argued with him, and I talked philosophy with him. And I also talked philosophy and argued with my mother. One of the earliest memories that I have is of my mother raising her voice to me and saying something like, "Does there have to be a reason for everything?" And I would say, "Yes!" That's something that probably happened when I was maybe four or five years old. My parents were both absolutely formative. They were just very, very encouraging. I guess the only thing is that my mother wanted me to be an English professor. She really loved literature herself and she wanted me to do that. But she was quite happy when I chose philosophy. And I do like novels and poetry very much, but it's not something that I've studied academically.

Yancy: Were there any formal or informal institutions such as the church that may have shaped your philosophical identity at that time?

Piper: I went to Riverside Church. My parents were both Catholic. But because, I think, the priest whom they wanted to marry them thought that they were a mixed marriage—that my father was white and my mother was not—he refused to marry them. So they married in a Protestant church and raised me as a Protestant. So, I basically got a Protestant upbringing and actually remember in junior high school and high school going to Sunday school and having lots of philosophical discussions with my teachers about God, the existence of God, and all that great stuff. I remember that happening actually quite a lot. And then also when I was in high school Mr. Beiser taught a philosophy course and I remember studying Benedictus de Spinoza. And we did Bertrand Russell. You know his little book *The Problems of Philosophy*? We did that and I loved it. I just absolutely loved it.

Yancy: What was it specifically about Spinoza that attracted you?

Piper: Well, during this time, and I couldn't have been any more than fifteen, I loved the rigor and the globalness, the kind of all-encompassing totality of what he was trying to do. We read the *Ethics*. And I loved the idea of being able to give, as it were, a unified field explanation of everything in terms of substance.

Yancy: What got you interested in the visual arts?

Piper: I've just always painted and drawn and sculpted since I was a wee tot. My mom worked at City College. She was the administrative assistant in the English Department. So my Grandmother was home all the time and she took care of me. And she was always encouraging me to draw and paint and put together little things. And I just always did that and so that was a given.

Yancy: What was the experience like at the School of Visual Arts in New York?

Piper: Oh, that was wonderful. After New Lincoln, which was pretty demanding intellectually, the School of Visual Arts was a completely different kind of experience because it was demanding artistically. And I just worked so hard. I just thought about art all the time. It is so different from academia. If you have never been inside an art school, it's kind of hard to describe. You just work all the time. The teachers come around and they critique your work and you have class meetings where everybody critiques everybody else's work. Then you go to galleries or you read art magazines and then you critique what you have seen and what you have read. And so it is a total immersion experience. And for three years it was wonderful.

Yancy: What took place such that you went from the School of Visual Arts on to City College of New York to study philosophy?

Piper: Well, a number of things. I had started actually showing my work internationally before I got out of art school. I was doing conceptual art and showing in these group shows in the States and also outside the States, for example, Germany, Sweden, Amsterdam, and other places. Also, while I was in art school, Jasper Johns, who is a major artist, was reading Wittgenstein. And so Wittgenstein became someone that everyone thought they should read. And I indeed read Wittgenstein and got very interested in German at that point. The text of *The Investigations* has the English translation on one side and the original German on the other side. And so I started looking at German and studying a little bit of German at that point. And then, I guess, for me, the formative thing that happened when I was about twenty was that I had been asked to show in this group show in New York. I had written an essay about my work which was at that point about space and time and forms of perception and how objects change when you walk around them. And a friend of mine, who was in philosophy, read it and said to me, "Look, if you are really serious about this you need to read Kant's *Critique of Pure Reason.*" And so I did. And I just absolutely loved it. I was sure that I really understood what Kant was saying.

Yancy: Since Immanuel Kant does come to play such a significant philosophical role for you, what exactly was it about his *Critique of Pure Reason* that made you love it so early on?

Piper: Well, I think that there were a few things. My friend who recommended the *Critique of Pure Reason* actually recommended specifically the Transcendental Aesthetic where Kant talks about the transcendental ideality of space and time as forms of perception. And that was, in fact, just exactly the way I was thinking about my relation to sculptural objects that I was making and the sense of perceiving things differently depending on the perspective I was taking on them and so forth. So, I think that that part of the *Critique* really sort of just clicked right into what I was thinking about anyway, and, of course, did it at such a deep level and with such profundity. Also, and this is going to sound very peculiar, I found Kant to be very accessible. You know, obviously the level of abstraction on which Kant is working is very, very high. But he has a way of using technical terminology, of coining technical terms, using words to mean a certain thing, which he is fairly consistent about from one context to the next. And he has a way of using that terminology with the kind of precision that made it possible for me to actually follow or think that I was following points that he was making. There are actually arguments in the Transcendental Aesthetic and they're not all terrific, but they all give you a very strong intuitive sense of what Kant was trying to get at by making this claim about space and time. I found that it really spoke to me. And then afterward when I started studying philosophy in college, I spent a lot of time on the Transcendental Deduction and that spoke to me in a very different way and about slightly different issues. Also, I just felt a very natural affinity for the way Kant was thinking. I feel completely programmed by the *Critique of Pure Reason.*

Yancy: Do you feel that philosophy constituted a drive for you, a tremendous passion, if you will?

Piper: Yes. Yes, it was something that I just needed to do. It's really hard to explain. In a way it felt so familiar, it felt so much like what I had always done when I was talking to my parents or talking to my relatives. When I started reading philosophical texts and particularly when I started reading *The Critique of Pure Reason*, I just knew I had to do this. I *had* to do it.

Yancy: When did you decide that you wanted to study philosophy at Harvard?

Piper: See, it's complicated because City College at that time was a fast-track type place. They did really quite well in placing their students in graduate school. I remember one guy a year before me who went to Princeton and another guy who was in my year, if I remember correctly, went to MIT. And then one person went to Pitt. So it was a given that if you were a serious philosophy major you were going to go on. And I was a serious philosophy major and I just never questioned that assumption. And at some point my advisor said something about the fact that I needed to start thinking about taking the GREs. And I said, "Yes, I'd better do that." And he asked me if I had all of my applications for graduate school. And I said, "Well, yes I'd better do that." And it was all just part of the process.

Yancy: So, you find yourself at Harvard. What courses did you take and with whom?

Piper: I took Willard Quine's "Word and Object" seminar, I took John Rawls's social philosophy, I took Roderick Firth's epistemology, and I took a seminar on Gottlob Frege with Burton Dreben. I took another philosophy of language course with Linda Foy. I took a course in Kant's moral philosophy with Terry Irwin, and I took a course in ethics with Bob Nozick for which I got the only B+ I ever received. And I also took a seminar on Kant's Transcendental Deduction with Dieter Henrich.

Yancy: How was Bob Nozick as a teacher, and why do you think that it was in his course that you received your only B+?

Piper: Well, he was a very dynamic teacher. He was very lively and quick and covered a great deal of material at a very rapid rate. He was just going through lots of different kinds of readings, not all of which were in philosophy. So, it was a very exciting course. I think that I got a B+ because I had actually been doing quite well up until that point, and so I had the stupid idea that I could write a final paper for that course over a weekend. I sat up all night Friday, Saturday, and Sunday. Now, of course, by Monday morning I was completely incoherent and the paper was a shambles and I just handed it in. So, it was a sad misjudgment. I mean, I should have given his course the same attention and care that I gave all of my other courses. I just didn't do it.

Yancy: As for Dieter Henrich's seminar, was it very influential in terms of shaping your reading of Kant?

Piper: Well, actually, by the time I took Henrich's course I was starting to develop my own views about Kant. But one of the things that I liked so much about that course was that Henrich's knowledge of the text of the *Critique of Pure Reason* was just astounding. I mean, he just knew everything, line by line. It was possible to argue with him about Kant on a level which I have not found possible with anyone else. I mean, you could quote back and forth specific sentences, specific passages in the *Critique* in support of your view, and you wouldn't even have to elaborate at great length what your view was and why you were quoting that passage, and because his knowledge of the text was so extensive he would get it immediately. So, it was possible to discuss and argue with him at a very precise and rigorous level. It was a wonderful experience for me. And I don't know if I mentioned this, but in this course we spent the entire semester on about ten pages of the *Critique*.

Yancy: Who impressed you most at Harvard in terms of teaching style and philosophical rigor?

Piper: Well, I think different people impressed me in different ways. Rawls was a very, very impressive teacher. I mean he was not charismatic. But he was extremely careful in his formulation of issues. He was very careful with the texts. Every now and then he would branch into discussions of other fields that were important to what he was talking about, such as social choice theory or decision theory. When I taught for him afterwards he actually said he did that on purpose because he wanted people to know that there was always so much more to learn. I thought that was a terrific thing to do. I think I really got my understanding of what it meant to be a serious philosopher and scholar from working with him. He taught this course in which he covered really just about everybody. We did Marx and social contract theory and utilitarianism and Kant and just everybody. And he was so respectful of the texts and at the same time so willing to share his own ideas about what they meant and their importance. At the same time he was really quite self-effacing about his own work in that context. He was a very impressive teacher.

Yancy: What about Quine and Linda Foy?

Piper: Linda was a wonderful teacher. She was a very responsive and also a very careful philosopher. I think I learned a lot about rigor and precision from taking her philosophy of language course. Quine, I enjoyed very much as a teacher. I took two courses with him. I took a logic course and then his "Word and Object" course. He is a personage. He's so much of a personage that it is hard to think of him as an "ordinary" person. I remember presenting a paper which was quite critical of some basic views of his. It was critical essentially of behaviorism and he was very displeased. Very, very displeased.

Yancy: How did your fellow grad students treat you as a Black woman studying philosophy? Was there ever any tension?

Piper: Well, most of them I think did not know I was Black. And I was at that point too naive to realize I had to announce it. What did sometimes happen was that the context would be appropriate in which I would refer to myself as a Black woman or someone would find out through some third person that I was Black and then there would be some period of disbelief and searching stares and that kind of thing. But I do very often, virtually all the time, have this experience of being mistaken for white. I was at that time much too young to realize what was involved. I had been raised on this idea that race was not important, that people were to be treated as individuals and I believed all that. And so it wasn't really an issue, I think.

Yancy: At this juncture when you were at Harvard doing your graduate studies in philosophy were you still pursuing the visual arts?

Piper: Yes, I was.

Yancy: How did these two pursuits square with one another?

Piper: Well, they really didn't. I kept them separate. That was something that I had done since I was an undergraduate at City College. You see, I had these experiences of having my artwork reviewed say in *The Village Voice* or the local newspaper and then my philosophy professor would read about it and then explain to me why what I was doing wasn't art and then we'd get into a long discussion about what art was. It was not a promising discussion. So I just basically never discussed my artwork.

Yancy: Do you construct yourself as an African-American philosopher?

Piper: Yes.

Yancy: Do you see yourself as doing African-American philosophy?

Piper: I don't know what that is. I work on Kant's metaethics and metaethics more generally. I mean, I just do philosophy.

Yancy: Then what for you constitutes African-American philosophy?

Piper: I would think that African-American philosophy would take as its subject matter African-Americans. Now I could think of a variety of ways in which that subject matter might enter into or overlap with more traditional areas of philosophy. For an example, questions of social justice, obviously; questions of personal identity; personal continuity; and strategic issues in action theory and applied social philosophy. That's the way I would think about it. And of course there is historical African-American philosophy having to do with Du Bois or Alain Locke and others.

Yancy: Are there specific obstacles that a Black woman must confront if she intends to do well in philosophy or more generally in the academy?

Piper: Oh definitely, yes. I think the primary problem is that everybody assumes that Black women are basically maids or prostitutes and so you have a lot to get over when you go into a department.

Yancy: How can we get more Black women in the profession of philosophy?

Piper: I think about this a great deal and I think that the problem about getting Black women into the profession is that if you tell them what it is really like, no rational Black woman would want to go into it.

Yancy: Would you elaborate on this?

Piper: Well, let me start with a general characterization of the problem and then talk specifically about Black women. The general problem is that philosophy is the arena of idealism. You know, that's what we do in philosophy. We discuss and are preoccupied with truth, beauty, and goodness. That's really what it's all about and so I think that it tends to draw people who are very idealistic, who have very high expectations of themselves, other people, the world, etc. And when you discover that the field of philosophy is no different from any other field in basically being structured and governed by relationships of power and status, it's tremendously disillusioning. It's not only that you yourself have to be subject to these power plays, Machiavellian schemes of one-upmanship, back stabbing, and all of that, and that's bad enough, but it really destroys your ability to believe that the field is about what it says it's about. That's really very disillusioning I think for everybody. And when you see such things at work in the field, in order to survive in the field, it's very important to draw a sharp distinction between the activities of doing philosophy, thinking, writing, discussing, teaching, etc., and the professional practices of the field. And that really becomes very essential. Now, I think that the problem specifically for Black women is that when doing the activity of philosophy it's very important to be able to focus in on the question that you're dealing with. So, if you're dealing with the nature of the good then you have to think about that particular thing. If you're dealing with metaphysical questions about the status of substance, you have to be really prepared to just think hard about that. And see, I think that what happens for Black women very often is that the quantity, the sheer quantity of abuse, the sheer quantity of harassment that we experience in the field makes it almost impossible to think about philosophical questions or about philosophy without having these extremely negative associations. And so, if you are not very, very careful it can poison your love of the activity of philosophy. That in my opinion is the reason why it's so hard, not necessarily to get Black women interested in philosophy, but to keep them in the field. They are just so overwhelmed, they just start feeling so incredibly damaged by the experiences that they have with their colleagues and with the profession and so they just drop out.

Yancy: Do you think that Black males have similar experiences?

Piper: Well, on the basis of sheer numbers I would say that the experiences are not as bad. My understanding is that there are just a little over a hundred Black men in the field. At this time, to my knowledge, there are only three tenured women in the field, Michele M. Moody-Adams, Georgette Sinkler, and myself. And the total number of women who are either in graduate programs or in junior positions or somewhere in the field is somewhere between fifteen and twenty. So, on the basis of statistics I would have to infer that it can't possibly be as bad for Black men.

Yancy: Within the context of African-American women and the profession of philosophy, how have you been able to personally combat racism and sexism?

Piper: I think that there are basically two ways. The most instinctual way is for me to just try and remove myself from those toxic contexts as much as possible. I have a number of very good friends, people that I've known for years, that I can count on the fingers of one hand. I choose my friends very carefully because I don't want to be around people who are infected with this kind of noxious sensibility that I find in the profession. So, I don't actually have much personal contact with my colleagues for the most part. Now, that's one thing and I think that's something everybody does. Everyone chooses their context in a manner that is life-affirming and supportive. The other thing, at least for me, that has been so incredibly important is my artwork. The fact that I've had another context that I can refer to and escape to in order to salvage my sense of self-respect and my sense of well-being is so very important to me. I think that if I were trapped within the context of professional philosophy and had no recourse, no outside resource, I would have been dead in the water long ago.

Yancy: What do you think enabled you to become the first Black woman tenured philosopher in the United States?

Piper: I think that my having been the only tenured Black woman philosopher for a long time has a lot to do with how I look. I think that the fact that I do not look so different from what the primarily white profession is used to seeing has been an advantage. You know the fact that I've been perceived to fit in, in many ways has been an advantage.

Yancy: Are you suggesting this whole notion of white skin privilege and so on?

Piper: Well, I think yes. I think that's an important part of it.

Yancy: Moving on to issues of rationality, how do you define rationality differently from Richard Rorty or someone like Paul Feyerabend?

Piper: I think my definition of rationality is very weak and traditional. It's basically being able to reason according to the rules of logic and observe the law of noncontradiction.

Yancy: Do you see any value in terms of some feminists, Sandra Harding, for example, who argue that our Western conceptions of knowledge and rationality are saturated with patriarchal prejudices?

Piper: I'm familiar with Sandra's work and I find it extremely interesting. I think that it can never hurt to critique Western conceptions of anything, including rationality most centrally. As it happens, I disagree with that particular argument. I in fact do not think that Western conceptions of rationality have the character that they do because they are saturated with patriarchal presuppositions. I actually think that the Western conception of rationality is just fine, thank you very much.

Yancy: Is it possible to have a culture where the conception of the self does not involve a highest order disposition to rationality?

Piper: I can't imagine what one would look like. I mean, there isn't any culture that we know of that doesn't attempt to explain itself and its existence in terms of certain very comprehensive and broad-based cosmological assumptions. Sometimes it becomes religion, sometimes it becomes mythology, sometimes it becomes science but there's always some attempt to maintain coherence and consistency.

Yancy: But one culture may use mythology whereas another culture may use science to provide them with coherence and intelligibility. Given this, how do we talk about the metacultural superiority of one culture over that of another?

Piper: Well, if you had asked me this question thirty years ago, I would have said that the proof of superiority is in the pudding and that the culture whose methodology bears the most fruit in practice, that is, enables the mastery of nature, enables the development of sophisticated technology, etc., is clearly the superior one. I think it is now clear that we have Western technology, based on Western, I guess you might say, mythology, to thank for the destruction of the natural environment and the social environment as well. We have Western technology to thank not only for toxic waste dumps but the atom bomb, new weaponry, etc. It seems to me that just about all the things that we find wrong at this point in time with human existence on the planet can be ascribed to Western technology. So, my answer at this point would be to say that it probably is possible to find some criterion according to which one culture's mythology might be considered superior to another's. But I would no longer have any idea what that criterion was. I think that it would have to be something that talked about how spiritually and psychologically evolved a community was. I don't think, however, that Western society would stack up very well along those criteria.

Yancy: This brings me to Kant. Given his views on Blacks can he be called a racist?

Piper: Yes, sure.

Yancy: Is he himself guilty of a form of pseudorationality and pseudo-coherence, as you use these terms in several of your essays, to the extent that the African was perceived as the "Other" which threatened his European sense of identity, integrity, and self-preservation?

Piper: Yes, I think that's true. I think that what is to be gained from reading Kant is to be gained from reading those works of his in which he speaks from what he takes to be a broadly universal perspective and I think there is a great deal of value in what he has to say and I think it is equally applicable to African-Americans as well as to everybody else. But I think that Kant's own prejudices do come up in some of his minor writings and he turns out to be just as flawed and human as everybody else.

Yancy: Which minor works are you referring to?
Piper: Well, I'm thinking about his *Anthropology from a Pragmatic Point of View* and I'm thinking about that long and rather embarrassing section in the middle part of *Religion Within the Limits of Reason Alone* in which he explains why Judaism isn't a real religion and Catholicism doesn't do too well either. I mean there are places where he lets it rip and what he allows to be seen of his own views is really not particularly appealing. On the other hand, what he says about the capacities of the human mind and the nature of subjectivity and the self, as he develops these in the *Critique of Pure Reason,* I think has a great deal of validity.

Yancy: Kant's views on Black people are highly conceptually distorted. So, would you also say that such devices as rationalization, dissociation, and denial, as you've used these in some of your essays, were clearly operative in his views on Black people?
Piper: Yes, I would. And I think that they are operative in everybody's views about something. I mean, I don't think that anyone is free of having to basically employ those devices in order to maintain the coherence of themselves and their views.

Yancy: Do you take such devices to be ontologically constitutive of what we are?
Piper: Yes, I do. In fact, I would almost be prepared to say that it has to be true by definition if you take the amount of incoming anomalous information available to us on a sensory level to be potentially unlimited. There's simply no way we can process all of it. There's no way we can make sense of all of it. And so we have to impose selective filtering mechanisms, or devices.

Yancy: Did Kant really think that the categorical imperative applied to Blacks such that they should not be treated as a means?
Piper: That I can't say.

Yancy: I guess I'm sort of drawing an implication, right?
Piper: Well, draw it.

Yancy: In other words, given his views on Blacks, and hence, one might say his condoning slavery and so on, it might follow that for him this particular category of people may not in fact fall within his kingdom of ends.

Piper: Well, women don't either. Kant was very provincial in a way that I think most philosophers are in terms of the applicability of their universalizations. But I don't think that that makes him different from any other philosopher.

Yancy: Now when does xenophobia, which, in your view, is based upon such devices, become racism?

Piper: Racism like sexism and homophobia and all of those "isms" is ultimately completely arbitrary. It happens to be the color of people's skins. It could just as easily be the color of their eyes. It could just as easily be whether someone has red hair or not or whether they have freckles or not. I do think there is an arbitrary quality to all cases of xenophobia. It's simply a question of what someone is used to and what is unfamiliar to them. And so I think xenophobia becomes racism in those cases where people simply do not have much information about what Black people are really like.

Yancy: The racist seems to lack the desire to move beyond his/her one-dimensional conception of the "reality" of Black people. Does the racist lack what you refer to as a modal imagination, particularly as you discuss this concept in your essay "Impartiality, Compassion, and Modal Imagination"?

Piper: Well, not about some things. I think they lack the modal imagination to understand what it is like to be a Black person—but that is because they lack information about that—and that's because they don't want that information, they prefer ignorance. It's not as though the information isn't available.

Yancy: In the 1970s you did a lot of street performances, for example, where you changed your physical appearance and so on. Can you elaborate on this?

Piper: Basically I treated my physical form as a sculptural object and manipulated it in all sorts of ways with respect to shape and smell and texture. I used balloons, castor oil, etc. You know, various odd kinds of materials. I did all sorts of things.

Yancy: What was the connection of this to philosophy?

Piper: I never try to think about the connection between art and philosophy. I mean, I think there are connections but there are connections that I really prefer to discover rather than try to forge. And so the connections are always retrospective. In point of fact, in retrospect, I think that there were some connections but they were not connections that I thought about consciously at the time. I was very interested in the problem of solipsism and the problem of other minds and the idea of making oneself intelligible as a recognizable person rather than as a coat stuffed with straw as Descartes put it. So, those were some of the things that I was thinking about at the time. I would not have tried to give my performance work a philosophical underpinning. I just did it.

Yancy: Can you elaborate on the influence of the artist Sol LeWitt on your approach to art?

Piper: Yes, Sol's work was absolutely formative for me. I had read the essay "Notes On Conceptual Art," which was just a revelation in terms of what art making could be and in terms of what the process and the product of art could be. I also saw a show in 1967 which was "Forty-six Variations on Three Different Kinds of Cubes." And that was a show I think the importance of which even now has not been fully appreciated. In my view, Sol is to art what Bach is to music.

Yancy: Sol's "Forty-six Variations on Three Different Kinds of Cubes" suggests the idea of exhausting all the combinations of a thing. You've related this notion of exhausting the combinations of a thing to music and literature, specifically in relation to Johann Sebastian Bach, and Samuel Beckett, respectively.

Piper: Well, you see, both Beckett and Bach use the concept of a permutation or a variation. For Bach, there are numerous pieces, canons, three-part variations, and sonatas. Lots of Bach's compositions involve this notion of beginning with a motif and then doing variations on it. And similarly with Beckett where he will start out with a description of some very minimal, pared down existential situation and then literally lists all the variations on that description that one can imagine, given certain constraints of course. And the result of that, within a Beckett novel, is that it highlights the existential character of the situation even more because essentially the function of listing all of these permutations is to exhaust all possible meanings of particular situations. And then finally, what you're confronted with is simply the fact of these situations themselves as existential dilemmas without further implications. So, one way of connecting all of this to philosophy is to

focus on philosophical imagination. Part of what we try to train people to do when we're teaching philosophy, and I think part of the way
that we are trained, is not simply to articulate and develop some view,
but also to learn to anticipate possible criticisms of it. And at the
beginning it is very important that we engage in dialogue with other
philosophers in order to figure out what the range of possible
responses might be. But in the end, we have to learn to do that for
ourselves. We have to learn to figure out all the variations on the arguments that we are giving, anticipate them and qualify our own arguments in light of them and try to refine the arguments accordingly so
that they're not susceptible to certain objections. A very important
part of the philosophical process involves producing a sophisticated
and considered philosophical argument.

Yancy: Are there any particular philosophers that have generally
shaped your philosophical consciousness?

Piper: Well, Kant is really my great influence. I really don't believe that
I will be capable of thinking an original thought now that I've been so
thoroughly programmed by Kant's *Critique of Pure Reason* and
Groundwork. There are a lot of people whose work I like. Obviously,
I'm a great fan of John Rawls, although I don't always agree with what
he says.

Yancy: Is there a relationship between your philosophical ideas and
your identity?

Piper: Well, I think so. I mean I take metaethics very seriously and I
take questions of the self very seriously and I think that rationality is
the only thing that gets me through the day despite how flawed and
imperfect it is. So, I take those things very personally and they are of
personal importance to me. I guess what I would say is that I do not
regard my work merely as an intellectual game.

Yancy: What are some of your current philosophical projects?

Piper: Well, I'm still finishing up this three-volume monster called
Rationality and the Structure of the Self.

Yancy: Would you provide a summary of what this work will philosophically involve?

Piper: There are basically three volumes. The first volume is dedicated
to complaining about other people. The second volume is devoted to
giving a textual interpretation of Kant's *Critique of Pure Reason,*

Groundwork of the Metaphysic of Morals, and his *Critique of Practical Reason.* And then the third volume is devoted to developing a Kantian interpretation of the self, rationality, and of the issues that lead me to criticize all those thinkers in the first volume. Now, the Kantian interpretation is based on the reading of Kant I have given in the second volume. So, basically volume one is critical, volume two is exegetical, and volume three is substantive.

Yancy: Say something about the actual critical content of the work.

Piper: My criticism is of what I call the Humean conception of the self, which is the prevailing model of the self. A conception of the self as I define it contains two parts. There is a model of rationality and a model of motivation. The model of rationality describes the conditions of internal coherence and equilibrium within the self and consistent principles for acting on the conditions that obtain within the self. And then the model of motivation describes what actually gets the self to move, to transform selfhood into agency. So, that's going to be true no matter what your conception of the self is. For the Humean conception of the self, the model of rationality is the expected utility-maximizing conception of rationality. In other words, it is basically an instrumental conception of rationality, cost-benefit analysis. Now, the model of motivation is the belief-desire model. According to this model, all actions are motivated by desires for certain ends and the actions reflect our beliefs about how best to achieve those ends. Now, what I argue in the first volume is not that these models are wrong, it's simply that they are incomplete and it is because they are incomplete that they can't do the work that they are supposed to do. First of all, there are internal inconsistencies in the expected utility-maximizing model of rationality. There are also internal inconsistencies in the belief-desire model of motivation, let alone how such models are used. They are used by many moral and political philosophers as a foundational, metaethical conception to ground a conception of human nature, human agency, etc., and thereby justify a broader conception of what we ought to do and how we ought to live. And not only can these models not perform that function because of the internal inconsistencies, they can't perform that function because the models themselves do not contain all that is true and relevant about the self for human beings.

Yancy: Within this context whose work will you critique?

Piper: Well, it is within this context that I critique John Rawls, Thomas

Nagel, Allen Gewirth, Richard Brandt, Bernard Williams, Harry Frankfurt, David Lewis, and others.✓

Yancy: Say something more about the exegetical aspect, volume two.

Piper: In the second volume I turn to what is really the substantive attempt to argue for the Kantian conception of the self, and since it is grounded in Kant, I have to first say what I think it is that Kant is doing. Also, in volume two I try to show that Kant exegesis has taken a very peculiar turn in this country. Here we tend to think that Kant's moral philosophy has nothing to do with his metaethics and epistemology. So, Kantian moral philosophers begin their study of Kant with the *Groundwork* and they move forward to his *Doctrine of Virtue, Religion Within the Limits of Reason Alone,* and on to his later writings; whereas students of the first *Critique* will focus on the first *Critique* and Kant's writings in science, and very often they are those philosophers who also have an interest in the philosophies of science, language, and mathematics. And so that's considered to be a completely separate area of inquiry. What I try to show first is that it's not possible to make sense of what Kant says in his moral writings if you do not presuppose the background which he has laid out in the *Critique of Pure Reason.* And the technical terms transfer pretty straightforwardly. There are, of course, changes in Kant's views as he writes his works through the years, but the essential metaphysical and epistemological assumptions are always operating and always active in all of his writings. So, if you don't begin with the *Critique of Pure Reason,* a great deal of the moral writings will seem like it's been pulled out of a hat. Now, that's the first part of what I try to show in the second volume. And then the second thing is that because the *Critique of Pure Reason* has been ignored, Kantian moral philosophers very often do not have viable and potent conceptions of the self and rationality to work with because all of that is developed in the *Critique of Pure Reason.* In fact, what you find is that the models of rationality and the self that Kant provides are useful and incredibly potent in providing the kind of underpinning we need, the metaethical underpinning, for a substantive, normative moral theory.

Yancy: Now, what about the third volume?

Piper: Well, in this volume I try to provide this metaethical underpinning with some attention at the end to its normative implications. And I argue that the basic model of rationality in Kant is this very weak, very general, and really quite innocuous model of rationality. You know, observing the law of noncontradiction, attention to the basic axioms of logic, etc. It basically comes to rationality as logic, but here there needs to be lots of qualification because, though this is also Kant's model of rationality, Kant was working with anachronistic conceptions of logic. He was working with Aristotelian logic, basically tinkered with in all sorts of idiosyncratic ways and so you have to throw all of that out. Once you do that, you get a very streamlined notion of rationality that can do a great deal of work. You can use this notion of rationality not only to explain the basic requirements for internal coherence and consistency of the self, you can also use this notion of rationality to explain human motivation. So, it's even more streamlined than you might think because from this notion of rationality you get both your model of rationality and also your model of motivation. These two models, however, do not displace the Humean conception, they incorporate it. So, my strategy here is the same as Kant's strategy was in response to Hume, that is, not to deny the truth of anything Hume said but basically to incorporate it within a more comprehensive model. That's what I try to do in the third volume. And then toward the end, I talk about the implications of this Kantian conception of the self for various ways of conceiving what moral theory is and what it can do and I then draw some normative implications at the very end. Since the project is essentially metaethical, I mostly confine my attention to metaethical issues.

Yancy: How do you think Kantian scholars will respond to this particular work?

Piper: Well, I have actually tried out some of this material among Kant scholars and I am happy to say in a tentative sort of way that the response so far has been pretty good. In fact, it has been just the kind of response that I most like. One Kant scholar actually said, "I don't agree with you, but I can't prove you're wrong." You know, grudging respect is definitely the best response.

Yancy: Lastly, how does Adrian Piper see herself as an African-American woman philosopher?

Piper: Well, to tell you the truth I don't think about it much unless somebody makes me think about it. There are all sorts of things that I really like. For example, I like philosophy, I like music, I like yoga, and I like studying German. There are all sorts of things that I like. And the only time that I think about race is when someone brings it to my attention, when someone tries to put me in my "place," or when someone feels the need to bring it up because of discomfort that they need to resolve for themselves or because of some political issue or because it's a topic that needs to be addressed in some philosophical context. It is within such contexts as these that I am reminded of how I appear to other people and who I am in this race-divided society. But it's not something that I want to carry home with me. And I feel that I've had a bad day if it's something that I have to carry around with me inside. You know, when I have those days in which I'm just smarting from various remarks and actions and betrayals and just all of the usual things that we know about. When I have to carry that around with me I feel that there is work to be done, so I simply don't carry such things around. For me, the worst thing of all is to have my own consciousness and my own love of what I do invaded by those questions.

A Selection of Published Works of Adrian M. S. Piper

Articles

"Kant on the Objectivity of the Moral Law," *Reclaiming the History of Ethics: Essays for John Rawls*, Andrews Reath, Christine M. Korsgaard, and Barbara Herman, eds. (New York: Cambridge University Press, 1997).

"The Form of Self-Knowledge in Kant's Metaethics," *Diskursparadigma: Form*, Georg Schollhammer, ed. (Vienna: Springer Verlag, 1997).

"Making Sense of Value," *Ethics* 106, no. 2 (April 1996): 525–37.

"Two Kinds of Discrimination," *Yale Journal of Criticism* 6, no. 1 (1993): 25–74.

"Xenophobia and Kantian Rationalism," *Philosophical Forum XXIV*, no. 1–3 (fall-spring 1992–93): 188–232.

"Government Support for Unconventional Works of Art," *Culture and Democracy: Social and Ethical Issues in Public Support for the Arts and Humanities*, Andrew Buchwalter, ed. (Boulder: Westview Press, 1992).

"Impartiality, Compassion, and Modal Imagination," *Ethics* 101, no. 4, Symposium on Impartiality and Ethical Theory (July 1991): 726–57.

"'Seeing Things'," *Southern Journal of Philosophy* XXIX, *Supplementary Volume: Moral Epistemology* (1990): 29–60.

"Higher-Order Discrimination," in *Identity, Character and Morality*, Amelie O. Rorty and Owen Flanagan, eds. (Cambridge, MA: MIT Press, 1990), 285–309; reprinted in condensed form in the monograph series, *Studies on Ethics in Society* (Kalamazoo, MI: Western Michigan University Press, 1990).

"Hume on Rational Final Ends," *Philosophy Research Archives* XIV (1988–89): 193–228.

"Pseudorationality," in *Perspectives on Self-Deception*, Amelie O. Rorty and Brian McLaughlin, eds. (Berkeley and Los Angeles: University of California Press, 1988), 297–323.

"Personal Continuity and Instrumental Rationality in Rawls' Theory of Justice," *Social Theory and Practice* 13, no. 1 (spring 1987): 49–76.

"Moral Theory and Moral Alienation," *The Journal of Philosophy* LXXXIV, no. 2 (February 1987): 102–18.

"Instrumentalism, Objectivity, and Moral Justification," *American Philosophical Quarterly* 23, no. 4 (October 1986): 373–81.

"Two Conceptions of the Self," *Philosophical Studies* 48, no. 2 (September 1985): 173–97, reprinted in *The Philosopher's Annual VIII* (1985): 222–46.

"Critical Hegemony and Aesthetic Acculturation," *Nous* 19, no. 1 (1985): 29–40.

"The Rationality of Military Service," in *Conscripts and Volunteers: Military Requirements, Social Values, and the All-Volunteer Force*, Robert Fullinwider, ed., Maryland Studies in Public Philosophy (Totowa, NJ: Rowman and Allenheld, 1983): 126–47.

"A Distinction Without a Difference," *Midwest Studies in Philosophy VII: Social and Political Philosophy* (1982): 403–35.

"Property and the Limits of the Self," *Political Theory* 8, no. 1 (February 1980): 39–64; reprinted in *The International Library of Legal and Political Philosophy*, Thomas Campbell, ed. (London: Dartmouth Press, 1992).

"Utility, Publicity, and Manipulation," *Ethics* 88, no. 3 (April 1978): 189–206.

[four]

Howard McGary, Jr.

Howard McGary, Jr. is professor of philosophy at Rutgers University. He earned his B.A. in philosophy from California State University at Los Angeles and his Ph.D. in philosophy from the University of Minnesota. He has taught at the Center for African Studies, Jesus College, Oxford University. He has also taught at the University of Arizona and the University of Illinois at Chicago Circle. His areas of specialization are African American philosophy and social and political philosophy. His articles and reviews have appeared in *The Journal of Ethics*; *Existence in Black: An Anthology of Black Existential Philosophy*; *The Philosophical Forum*; *Alienation and Social Criticism*; *APA Newsletter on Feminism and Philosophy*; *The Underclass Question*; *Exploitation and Exclusion: Race and Class in Contemporary US Society*; *The Journal of Philosophy*; *American Philosophical Quarterly*; *The Journal of Value Inquiry*; *Philosophy Born of Struggle: Anthology of Afro-American Philosophy from 1917*; *Nous*; *Ethics*; and more. He is also coauthor of *Between Slavery and Freedom: Philosophy and American Slavery*. (A more complete citation list of Howard McGary, Jr.'s published works can be found at the end of the interview.)

Howard McGary, Jr.

Rutgers University

George Yancy: When and where were you born?

Howard McGary: I was born on July 22, 1947, in Texarkana, Texas, though I only lived there until I was about a year and a half old. After that I moved to Los Angeles, California.

Yancy: What was it like growing up in Los Angeles?

McGary: I grew up in South Central, L.A., where I went to John C. Fremont High School, which was a predominantly Black and Hispanic high school. It was named after the explorer. My father owned a restaurant and so I grew up in a pretty close-knit community with a lot of friends and a lot of support from my parents.

Yancy: Provide a sense of your early formative educational experiences before college.

McGary: For elementary school, I went to 75th Street School, which was pretty enjoyable. Most of the kids were from my neighborhood so I knew them all well. For junior high I went to Edison Junior High School. That experience was a little different because I was out of my immediate community. So when I went to junior high school I had to meet a new set of people and so that involved a little more, I would say, stress, and I had to use a little more ingenuity in order to be able to create a kind of environment that I felt comfortable in. Now, high school was a little bit different because in high school there were gangs. Los Angeles has a long history of street gangs. And so in Los Angeles, everyday life involved that kind of environment. So you couldn't sort of stand on the sidelines in that sort of environment. You had to have associates. You had to sort of make it, right? So almost everyone at that point was either directly involved in a street gang or had some close association with people who were.

Yancy: Did your family tend to insulate you from this kind of thing?

McGary: They tried to but it just was not something that they could really successfully do. In L.A. at that particular time it was really kind of a way of life. There were a number of street gangs and a male growing up in that environment could not really be protected from it. You had to leave the home so it was virtually impossible to be immune to it.

Yancy: During this early formative period which teachers impacted you most?

McGary: There was a woman in my elementary school by the name of Mrs. Jones. She had a great impact on me and a number of other students. She always stressed the idea of the importance of self-determination and the importance of doing your best and the importance of not being led astray by things and other people. She had a real impact on me. I can't say that I recall that the impact was so much an academic one but I think she had a real impact on my character development. Now, in high school I had a Spanish teacher by the name of Mr. Brown who I found to be really important in my academic development because he was a person who encouraged me to read, he was a person also who encouraged me to see the value of learning about other cultures. He was also a person who was very much willing to sit and listen. He had a real ability to hear others. So when I think back I think he had a tremendous impact, although at the time I didn't realize that.

Yancy: So by the end of high school what was it that you wanted to do?

McGary: I always, from the very beginning, wanted to be a teacher.

Yancy: Who influenced you in this direction?

McGary: I think it was because of the influence of my mother. Before she began to work in the restaurant when she was in Texas, she had been a teacher. As a result, we read a variety of things in the home. In particular, in the home, I was aware of Booker T. Washington and Du Bois and these figures as a kid growing up. Also, I have a sister who always wanted to be a teacher and in childhood games would always play classroom. So I always remember while growing up I was really taken by that. She was very sensitive and thoughtful and this in a lot of ways helped to open me up to learning as well. I can't think of anything else I wanted to be other than a teacher.

Yancy: Did your father impact your educational development in any way?

McGary: My father was not a person who really emphasized education but he was a person who always thought that you'd be better off in having one than not. But I can't say that he was a person who really stressed and pushed education. My father was very much concerned with being able to make a living and provide for your family, though an education was seen as an instrument for that. So he didn't see edu-

cation as a good in itself but as an instrument for personal and economical advancement. So to that extent he was clearly supportive of
education.

Yancy: So when did you first decide that you wanted to study philosophy?

McGary: Well, I went to undergraduate school at California State, Los
Angeles, and while there I was interested in math and also interested
in history and I took a philosophy course sort of on a whim. And I
took the course and I really liked it but I just didn't see philosophy as
something that one would major in. You know, it was good to take a
course in it, I enjoyed the course very much, but it wasn't a field or a
subject that would be conducive to my being able to make a living.
And then of course my father was in the restaurant business and of
course he hoped that one of his children would continue to build
what he had started. So philosophy wasn't something that I was hot
on at first. But I took one course and I had a very good teacher. He
was an old man by the name of Ritter from L.A. City College and he
wrote the introductory textbook that we were using.

Yancy: How did this initial exposure to philosophy impact you?

McGary: I think that philosophy gave me the occasion to be able to
think about things and wonder about things in a way that I had not
been able to do before. I mean, to explore topics and issues and to
think deeply about things, not to look at things on a surface level. To
look at the nature of things. That had a real impact on me. But at that
point I must admit that I just didn't see this as being something that
one would do and certainly not something that one would devote
one's life to. So I took Ritter's course and then I left philosophy alone
for a while but then I decided that I wanted to try another course. So I
took an introductory course in logic with a woman named Sharon
Bishop-Hill. And I enjoyed that course as well. So, I said, "Boy, I'm
really enjoying this!" And I was learning a lot and I was finding that
philosophy was also assisting me in my other courses. I took a history
of philosophy course and that put me in greater stead in my literature
courses and also in my history courses. So I just found that philosophy
sort of provided a way for me to get into various subjects in ways that
I never imagined that it would.

Yancy: So when exactly did you decide that you wanted to major in
philosophy?

McGary: Actually, I guess it was about in my junior year. At that point I decided I wanted to study philosophy and so I graduated with a B.A. in philosophy. So I was wondering what I was going to do. So I talked with my father. I did some student teaching for a while at Jefferson High School in Los Angeles and I enjoyed that but I still had this longing for philosophy. I missed it. I was still reading philosophy but I was not pursuing any courses in philosophy. So I applied to graduate school. I applied to UCLA and the University of Minnesota and I also applied to law school. I got accepted into law school and I got accepted into UCLA and the University of Minnesota in philosophy. So I thought, I'd go to law school but then at the last moment I thought, "No! I really, really like philosophy." So I decided that I would take a chance and pursue it. So I went and talked to people at UCLA and I talked on the phone with people at Minnesota and I was very much impressed with the people at Minnesota in terms of how open they were and how responsive they were to my questioning. Not that UCLA wasn't open and responsive, but I felt that Minnesota was a place where I could flourish and I also thought that it might be good to get away from Los Angeles. So I went to Minnesota.

Yancy: During the time that you were deciding between studying law and philosophy and you decided upon philosophy, would you say that it constituted a passion for you?

McGary: Yes, I think it was. It was something that I took a lot of delight in. And I felt that it was a way for me to express myself. I saw it as a medium for self-expression, as a way of understanding things about the world.

Yancy: Who at Minnesota influenced you most?

McGary: John Dolan. He taught philosophy of language and logic primarily, but he was also interested in social and political philosophy. His area of specialization was philosophy of language and he taught the logic sequence.

Yancy: What was it about him? Was it his teaching style?

McGary: I think it was his teaching style but even more so than that he was a person I think that had a great deal of integrity and I was very much taken by that. He was a person who had strong convictions and was willing to stand behind those convictions. And I think that's what most impressed me about him. And also he was willing to explore various ideas and explore them in some great depth.

Yancy: And who else besides John Dolan?

McGary: And also another person who I think was very influential was a person by the name of Homer Mason who was at that time the chairperson of the department. He did political philosophy and he was very supportive and always willing to try to help me to accommodate to my new setting and graduate school. This was particularly important when I first came to Minnesota and did not know anything about the Midwest, coming from California, and having to adjust to a change in environment and change in culture.

Yancy: Were you typically the only Black person in your philosophy classes?

McGary: Yes.

Yancy: Did you ever feel discouraged because you were the only Black presence in your philosophy classes?

McGary: Yes, I did. Numerous times I think I felt discouraged and I felt that some of the things that I had an interest in I could not fully develop, not just academic interests but also cultural interests, etc. I always felt that those things sort of went undeveloped.

Yancy: So, what sustained you during this period?

McGary: Well, I think that what sustained me was that I had a roommate, who was in the psychology department, whom I was extremely close to. His name is Lionel Greene and he and I spent a lot of time studying and a lot of time together. We drew upon each other and I think we nurtured each other. And he had a very good sense of humor. And also too I developed a good friendship with John Dolan. And so I think that that was very important. And I'll tell you what else helped there. We formed a Black Graduate Student Association. At that time, in the 1970s, Minnesota recruited a number of Black graduate students in various departments. And so we formed an association and so what we did was that we had academic gatherings as well as informal social gatherings. That helped out a great deal. And so once a month, or once every two months, people would meet and give presentations.

Yancy: Do you understand your identity to be that of an African-American philosopher?

McGary: Yes, I do.

Yancy: Would you provide a sense of the nature of that identity?

McGary: Well, I always perceived that when you do philosophy, it is not done above history and culture. So philosophy is always done within a social and political context and it is always done with people drawing on certain intuitions. So, I believe that the intuitions that I have, have been shaped by my racial identity and my cultural identity. And I have always been self-conscious about that. I always drew upon those experiences in my philosophical work.

Yancy: Provide a sense of the scope of African-American philosophy.

McGary: Well, I view African-American philosophy very broadly. I think that some people who do African-American philosophy are people who would argue that their race and their culture have nothing to do with their philosophy. But I just don't think that is true because I think that those experiences do shape our ideas and the way we think about things. So even though we may self-consciously adopt a method, nevertheless many of our insights, many of our intuitions about things will be shaped and contoured by those experiences. I know that often when I have spoken to Laurence Thomas, for example, he might produce an essay in ethics and then I'll read that essay and say, "Well, Laurence, did you know that this particular issue that you are discussing here seems to come directly from the African-American experience?" And then we'll talk about it. And even though he might not have seen that, right, and self-consciously produced the essay in that way, I think that he has on a couple of occasions come to see that such an insight was derived from those experiences.

Yancy: So, would you say that there is a new crop of African-American philosophers who are coming up who don't see themselves as doing African-American philosophy, who don't really want to identify themselves with that kind of genre?

McGary: There have always been people that way. I think there have always been philosophers who have felt that their race or culture has nothing to do with the doing of philosophy.

Yancy: But is there any sense to the notion of a philosopher qua philosopher?

McGary: Well, I think that when you talk about this you are speaking about method. And a lot of people believe that they have a certain type of methodology and that if they employ this methodology then it is irrelevant whether or not they are Black, or white, or whether or not they were raised in this or that environment. It is still the whole idea of the method. But philosophers just don't operate on the basis of methodology. You have to focus on what the content is that you are using the particular method on. Philosophers are going to start with certain sorts of assumptions and intuitions. Now even though they want to challenge and question those assumptions, we still have to begin at some place. Now I think that our experiences certainly have a bearing on that. Now race, being such a crucial identification in American life, and it's not like race is insignificant in American life, is one of the primary ways that people identify themselves. Even with people who claim that they don't notice race, it's not clear to me that they are being honest. So I tend to question the idea that you are just a philosopher who employs a particular method.

Yancy: What kind of response would you have for Naomi Zack, or Anthony Appiah, or even Skip Gates for that matter who seem to want to de-essentialize this notion of race?

McGary: See, there are two questions. One question is to ask does race have any meaning at all? Or is race a meaningless concept? Now when talking about race as having a biological meaning or a genetic meaning I would agree with Appiah. But I do think that race does have a social meaning and a social significance. And I think that when Du Bois talked about the sociohistorical meaning of race then I think that he was right, that it does have such a meaning. I don't think it is a natural kind but I do think that it is a social kind. Appiah certainly wouldn't say that if you went into a classroom and picked out a person and said, "That is a Black person," that that would be a meaningless concept. He might ask whether I can give a coherent biological or genetic account of what that means. One may not be able to do that but certainly that concept would have meaning for us in our society. So if this nonessentialism is supposed to mean that race has no social and moral significance, and that it's totally morally and socially irrelevant, I think that would be a mistake.

Yancy: How has this new crop of African-American philosophers impacted the development of a critical community of African-American philosophers?

McGary: You see, what I think is that when I first started out in philosophy there was this whole issue about whether or not one could use the African-American experience and African-American texts as sources of philosophical illumination and people were very closed to that idea. So, consequently, as you know, as you are working your way through a graduate program, if you are interested in the African-American experience, then you are going to need mentors. You are going to need people who are going to tell you, for example, that "This is an important problem," or "This is an important issue," or "These are important texts where some philosophical light can be shed." And I'm saying, that in most places, I don't think people were provided with that opportunity to explore African-American texts as a source of philosophical examination. But I was lucky in that regard because, as I said, my professor, John Dolan, was very open to that idea of using and drawing upon such texts as a source of philosophical examination. And that is not to say that it wasn't important to learn the major figures in Western philosophical thought. But also, Dolan was aware of Du Bois and others and the importance of these figures. So it wasn't as though I had to make a case that these people had important things to say. Also, in my second year of graduate school, I met Irving Thalberg, Jr., who is now deceased and he was very influential, extremely influential. I think after John Dolan he was the most influential person in my development. Thalberg was someone who knew both the philosophical literature as well as the literature coming out of the African-American experience. So, that I found extremely valuable.

Yancy: Has African-American philosophy really changed since the days of such African-American philosophers like Eugene Holmes, Cornelius L. Golightly, Broadus N. Butler, Winston K. McAllister, and others?

McGary: Yes, I think it has. I mean, I think that we are now at a point where people can study and do and write African-American philosophy without feeling, I think, that they have to first make a case for the legitimacy of it. So the idea of using the African-American experience in philosophical illumination or examination is something that I think the present generation can do and do without having to feel that they're doing something that is totally out of whack.

Yancy: Tommy Lott sees African-American philosophy as being in the process of canonization. Do you share this view?

McGary: It is. I think that is the important thing. When we first started out you couldn't point to a text that was drawing upon the African-American experience and where the author of that text was designated as a professional philosopher. But that's not totally true. You could point to Alain Locke. But Locke was pretty much the only person that at that particular time could be pointed to as having produced a major body of work in philosophy. You had people like Cornelius Golightly, you had people like Berkley Eddins, but these people didn't have, at the time I first started, a major body of work out there to point to. So, if during that time you were talking about doing graduate studies or exploring texts, then people were somewhat concerned about whether or not there was anything for you to research. And so I'm saying that now that is not the case for people who want to work on African-American issues and African-American concerns philosophically. There are texts and numerous articles out there. So there is a body of literature, there is a canon that is being developed. So I think Tommy Lott is exactly right about that. So, for example, if a student wanted to do a dissertation then there are people out there now whose work could be used as a basis for that. And so that makes a huge difference. You see, I think one of the mistakes that we made as African-American philosophers or people who were using the African-American experience as a source of philosophical illumination, is that we spent too much time debating the issue of whether or not there was something called African-American philosophy when we should have focused on producing a body of philosophical literature. I see myself as using the African-American experience as a source of philosophical illumination. I don't think that my method is distinctively African-American, that's not the way I conceive of what I'm doing. So I'm not a person who's saying that I have an Afrocentric way of approaching things. But what I do, though, is that I do use the African-American experience along with other experiences. I use African-American texts along with other texts as a way of trying to gain some understanding about the nature of things.

Yancy: So the error is not in drawing upon African-American experiences so as to illuminate one's philosophical worldview, but it is the idea of looking at the methodology as being distinctively African-American.

McGary: Right. So I think, say for example, that the logic I use is the logic that everyone uses. But I do think that there are certain insights, that there are certain ways that problems present themselves, and certain experiences, that might enable us to gain greater insight into human understanding, or the nature of morality, or the nature of the way in which political institutions ought to operate. So, I think in the past all too often these experiences have been excluded and as a consequence I think we haven't gotten a full picture. And so in my work what I've tried to do is to draw upon African-American texts and African-American history as a way of examining more general philosophical concerns.

Yancy: So, you wouldn't want to *racialize* the law of the excluded middle?

McGary: No, definitely not.

Yancy: What would you say to a young African-American thinking about going into the field of philosophy?

McGary: I would say that it is an excellent time to go into the field of philosophy because I know now that there are people who are willing to be on a conference in their program in African-American philosophy now where they would have never been willing to do that before. So I think people perceive that there are real opportunities and I think there are real opportunities for people who are working in this field. So I would encourage people if they have any interest to develop that interest because I think that there are opportunities. We at Rutgers have been doing a number of things to try to encourage African-Americans and other people of color to enter the field of philosophy. We put on a conference in 1995 entitled "Race: It's Meaning and Significance," as a way of trying to attract scholars and students to philosophically examine race and also as a way of trying to get people who are interested in Black studies to see that history and the social sciences are not the only fields that have something to contribute to the study of the African-American experience. And we also had a summer institute in 1995 where we brought eleven undergraduate students of color from around the country and they spent a week at Rutgers and they interacted with Rutgers's faculty members who came in and talked about their specific experiences as philosophers and their particular work. We also had visitors from other universities to come in as well and do the same thing and I think the students really enjoyed it and we really enjoyed them and I think it had an impact. And I think that some of those students are going to go on and probably pursue a career in philosophy.

Yancy: Have there been many African-American graduate students who have come through the philosophy department there at Rutgers?

McGary: I have been at Rutgers for nineteen years and in my time we have had four.

Yancy: And did they all successfully complete the program?

McGary: Of the four, only one will successfully complete the program. His name is Paul Taylor and he is about to receive his Ph.D. He has taken a job at the University of Kentucky.

Yancy: How do we best create a greater Black presence in the field of philosophy?

McGary: Well, I think we do so in part by creating literature. I think that is the best way to do it. I think if we create interesting and important literature you will attract people to the field. And I think that's the best way to go. Again, to reemphasize what I have said earlier, I think we spent too much time in the '70s arguing about whether or not there was an African-American philosophy. I think we would have been better off just writing and producing a body of literature. And I think that is what is having a real impact now because kids can now point, if they have an interest in African-American philosophy, to various texts and that has a definite impact.

Yancy: Briefly, talk about the importance of the New York Society for the Study of Black Philosophy.

McGary: It started out as a group called the New York Society for the Study of Black Philosophy. It is now The Society for the Study of Africana Philosophy. But this group actually started in the early eighties. And a number of people, Cornel West, Lucius Outlaw, myself, Bernard Boxill, and many others, were involved in that group in some way. And it was a group where people could come and give papers and many books and chapters of books were tried out in that forum. But there were also very important African-American philosophical conferences that were held. There were two at Tuskegee, one at Haverford College, and the early one at the University of Illinois at Chicago. These were important historical events and I think that they played a significant role in shaping the course of history with regard to people of color concerning the study of philosophy.

Yancy: Out of the New York Society for the Study of Black Philosophy, how has Cornel West shaped African-American interest in philosophy?

McGary: Well, I think that the important thing that Cornel has done is to be found in the chapter "The Four Traditions of Response" in his book *Prophesy Deliverance*. This was a paper that, I think, really encouraged a number of African-American students to see philosophy as something that can connect and does connect with their immediate experiences. This chapter was also published in a different form in the special issue of the *Philosophical Forum*, 1977/1978 issue, which was devoted to philosophy and the Black experience. But I know that that had a great impact on a number of students. And I think that Cornel's presence, you know, given that he is such an articulate and thoughtful and learned person, has really encouraged Black students to take a look at philosophy.

Yancy: How do you feel that the American Philosophical Association has helped to increase the number of Blacks in the profession.
McGary: I think that the APA has done very little as an organization. Very little.

Yancy: Is this because its white male hegemony is still very much in place?
McGary: Yes, I think that that is true. And I also think that the APA has not been very creative. So, even where I think it might have had the will and the motive and the inclination to do something, it has not been very creative in attempting to try and put some of that goodwill into action. So I don't see a lot of concrete things that the APA has done to bring about any significant change. Most of the work and most of the initiatives have come out of the APA Committee on Blacks in Philosophy and those things have not always been met with hostility but they have not really fully been embraced and there hasn't been a real effort to bring about real change. No resources have really been provided to do anything. For example, this summer institute was something that has been discussed for years and years and Rutgers University made that institute real. I think the APA has had the resources to do something like this, and I think the APA thinks that it is a good idea, but nothing came of it.

Yancy: What do you think can be done in terms of getting the APA to be more supportive of these things?
McGary: Well, I think that, as with many of these types of organizations, you don't pressure them from the outside. So, I think that any pressure has to come from within the body. And I think academics in general feel uneasy, since we pride ourselves on freedom of thought and expression, about any sense of being coerced into doing something. So I think any initiative has to come from within. So, I think it is extremely important for people of color or for people who see these

issues as important to get actively involved in the APA and then on the committees of the APA. I think that's the way to get the organization moving in a direction that it ought to go.↙

Yancy: Talk about your interest in the philosophical implications of slavery.

McGary: Well, I got interested in that because when I was in graduate school I was a teaching assistant for one semester in the African-American Studies Program and as a part of the course dealt with slavery. So I began to read a lot of commentaries on slavery. At that particular time there was a big debate about the nature of slavery. For example, what was slavery like? So I was really made fully abreast of that through my teaching experience in that course. And I also, at that particular time, had a close association with a friend of mine named Ralph Crowder, who is an historian now at UC Irvine. And he and I used to talk for hours and hours about slavery and slave narratives. I began at that point to read slave narratives and was just fascinated by them. At that time though, I didn't see a connection between the reading of these slave narratives and philosophy. I saw these things as being sort of separate. But then as I began to read more and more political philosophy and looked at attempts by analytic philosophers to explain the nature of freedom, I thought "Wow, there is an intimate connection between what is going on in these narratives and what people are trying to do in these so-called philosophical texts." And so I began to try and bridge that gulf, because, you know, no gulf really existed there. So I found that these slave narratives were extremely important to me in coming to understand certain concepts and so that is how I got into it.

Yancy: What kinds of philosophical conceptual issues do you feel need to be explored with respect to the slave experience?

McGary: I think there are a host of things. For example, the whole concept of freedom really needs to be reexamined. And I think the slave experience can really shed light there. You know, Angela Davis has a paper, "Unfinished Lecture on Liberation—II," which is in Leonard Harris's *Philosophy Born of Struggle*, where she begins to try and tease out an understanding of freedom from the slave narratives. But she doesn't go very far with it. I think that that work really deserves further attention. And also I think that when we look at other concepts like, for example, integrity as a moral notion or as a virtue, I think that the slave experience has a lot to tell us about that concept.

Yancy: So slavery constitutes a crucible in terms of which we can understand these concepts.

McGary: Right. I think so. Often people talk about integrity in terms of being willing to stand by one's principles in some sort of Kantian way, let's say, and that makes a lot of sense. But it's not just being able to stand by one's principles, I think it's revealed in being able to stand by one's principles in a certain type of context. So I think slavery can tell us something about that. Also I think slavery can tell us something about courage and friendship. I think that all of these concepts could benefit from a close reading of that human experience.

Yancy: What for you constitutes the range of forms of resistance during slavery?

McGary: I think that there are various types of resistance. What I try to show in one of my chapters in the book *Between Slavery and Freedom* is that in order to distinguish resistance from other things like compliance you cannot do this without looking at a particular social context. So I am saying that in order to understand whether or not a particular act counts as an act of resistance you just can't focus on the agent's beliefs or the agent's intentions but you have to look at the contexts in which those beliefs and intentions are located and the social practices surrounding those beliefs and intentions. So an action in one situation may not be able to be described as an act of resistance but in another context that act may be described as an act of resistance, even though the particular *actor* did not have the belief that he was doing this in order to, let's say, overcome oppression. What I have in mind, for example, is that if you read slave narratives one of the things that you find is that slaves would break farm tools and one would question why all these farm tools were being broken. Even if you went to the slave and said, "Well, why are you breaking these farm tools?" it wasn't even clear in their minds that they were directing this at bringing down the institution of slavery. But there is a pattern of this and I think that act, from the perspective of a third party, from the perspective of a social scientist, could be described as an act of resistance. Likewise, there were games that slave children would play that were taught to them by their parents which had a consequence of setting back slavery, working against the institution of slavery. But the games were taught to the children as games. And this was a very nice procedure because even if the children were interrogated about what they were doing they couldn't reveal anything because they didn't know anything. They were actually bringing down the institution of slavery and this had some design. I would want to describe these as being acts of resistance even though the people who were actually performing these acts did not have the actual intention of bringing down the institution of slavery.

Yancy: It's interesting that the nineteenth-century infamous pseudoscientist, Samuel Cartwright of Louisiana, accounts for the tendency for slaves to break tools or to run away as really being symptoms of some disease of some sort. The former he referred to as *Dysaethesia AEthiopica* and the latter he referred to as *Drapetomania.*

McGary: Exactly. His seems to be a very far-fetched explanation of these acts of resistance.

Yancy: In your chapter "Resistance in Slavery" you agree with Orlando Patterson, where he argues that stealing was a way that slaves asserted their humanity, and you go on to say, "I would add that it was a way of resisting the oppressive characterization of themselves as non-persons." Is it possible that contemporary Blacks who feel that they are characterized as non-persons engage in resistance through acts of stealing?

McGary: I think that in certain contexts it is. Because to be called a thief is to be called a person. And I think that is probably right. Because I know that even in the latter part of the twentieth century there is, and I don't have to tell you this, a real affront upon the humanity of African people. And we see it in a variety of sources and it is presented through a variety of mediums and so I think under certain conditions stealing is an assertion of resistance. However, it is an assertion, I think, that has very bad consequences, social consequences and personal consequences. But I think nevertheless that it is a cry for recognition in some cases.

Yancy: How should we then characterize, let's say, the violence within Black urban spaces? Should we look at it as an example of nihilism as Cornel West seems to suggest?

McGary: Well, I don't think that nihilism explains it all. I think that it does have something to say about the phenomenon of violence but I don't think it captures it fully. I think that there are some people who are not hopeless. There are people who do believe that there are values and that these values are worth holding on to, but I think that they see their situation as desperate. I mean, there is a difference between having no hope and having lost all sense of value, and feeling that you are in a desperate situation and that desperate situations call for desperate measures. I think in a lot of situations many young people feel that they're in a very, very desperate situation and that it requires desperate measures. So I guess that I don't think that the appeal to nihilism explains that phenomenon. I think it requires a closer look at what African-American people are up against. For example, in Bill Lawson's book *The Underclass Question*, one of the things that I try to show in that book is that there is an inaccurate description of what many African-American people are morally up against, who are in the so-called underclass. So today many people will say that Black people in the underclass are lacking strength of character. And this characterization can cut in many ways. You know, you can say that they don't have the right values, they don't have the correct morals, or they don't have the right drive and don't have enough determination, etc. And I try to show, in Lawson's book, that you can ask too much of people. I guess the best way to put it is as Aristotle said, that there are pressures that no person can bear. And so sometimes people can be put into contexts that we couldn't expect any human being really to bear up under, certainly not feel that they should be obligated to bear up under. I mean, if they did, we would think that would be great. That would be wonderful. But I think it is unreasonable to expect and to demand that people ought to achieve certain things when certain odds are really stacked against them.

Yancy: And what Black people are up against you see as far more systemic.

McGary: I see it as certainly more systemic than people are willing to realize. Say, for example, if you just look at housing in the United States. It is *extremely* more difficult for Black people, independent of their economic status, to acquire housing than it is for whites. Typically Black people pay more for their housing than whites do. So, for example, you could go into any university town and a Black person typically will have a narrower range of housing opportunities than the typical white person. So that means, typically, that we are directed toward housing, if it is going to be safe and secure, that is typically more expensive than it is for the typical white student. And we don't even have to talk about loan practices. In fact, there was a wonderful special on PBS which talked about the unfair loan practices in South Central, L.A. It detailed how Black people are just not given the same opportunities. It amazes me that people could argue that it is clear that there is nothing systemic going on when the evidence is quite the

contrary. The claim, I guess, is that Black people should be superhu-
man. And I think that morality doesn't require that of people. I mean,
of course, we would say that would be great, that would be good, if
you did that, but I don't think that we can have those types of expectations of people. I mean, I think it would be better to make the system
just than to leave the system unjust and expect people to achieve in
spite of it. I think that is what people are saying. The system is unjust
and the system is stacked against you but if you work hard and if you
put your nose to the grindstone you can achieve in spite of it. Well,
that's a difficult thing to motivate and especially motivate young people to achieve *in spite of.* That's a hard thing. It is not impossible. But
you shouldn't be surprised when many people fail.

Yancy: Now, what got you interested in issues concerning alienation?
McGary: Well, I guess it just seems as though the Marxist analysis
    really did not fully capture the estrangement that I think that African-
    Americans feel.

Yancy: So Marx's analysis does not conceptually capture the levels of
    alienation felt by Black people.
McGary: I don't think it does because I don't think that the levels of
    alienation experienced by Black people are rooted primarily in eco-
    nomic relations. I think that the sense of alienation experienced by
    Black people in the U.S. is also rooted in the whole idea of what it
    means to be a human being and how that has been understood. So it
    is not simply that people are estranged from the product of their labor,
    it is not simply that people are estranged from each other because of
    capitalism. I think it has more to do with the whole idea of estrange-
    ment relative to the culture being set up in such a way with the belief
    that certain people can be used in ways that other people can't be
    used. So, I think due to slavery and Jim Crow, in this country, that cer-
    tain norms and practices have developed such that there is a belief
    that African-Americans in the culture, still, I think, can be used as
    tools, as human tools. And I think that this has a consequence of
    estrangement because I think that our full humanity is not being rec-
    ognized by the institutional and social practices that surround us. In
    an essay that I have written for a book entitled *Exploitation and Exclu-
    sion: Race and Class in Contemporary U.S. Society,* edited by
    Leonard Harris, Abebe Zegeye, and Julia Maxted, I tried to show how
    if you just focus on economics that you are going to miss the full
    implications of estrangement for Black people. And I tried to show

that through the idea of exploitation, what it means to use another person, that Black people have been used in ways that white people have not. And that this is the sense of estrangement that the Marxist analysis is unable to get at.

Yancy: Now, say something about how your identity relates to your overall philosophical project?

McGary: Well, I think that what it does is that it shapes and calls my attention to certain problems. I mean, I think the fact that I am a Black person and grew up in South Central, L.A. makes the underclass a problem that I am interested in. It is something that grabs me. So, I think that my identity shapes my projects to the extent that it makes certain things real to me perhaps in a way that they are not as real and as urgent to other people. It is not that I can say that I am only concerned with race and African-American culture but my experience as an African-American growing up in South Central, L.A. has had an impact on the things that I see as being important problems in need of clarification or illumination.

Yancy: What do you see as instructive for African-American philosophy?

McGary: I can't emphasize enough that what I think is crucial now is that African-American philosophers spend the time creating the canon. I think that that is going to have the most significant impact in terms of attracting people of color to the field. Because I know that this work is now making its way into classrooms, so people are now using these articles and these books in courses and this is beginning to have an impact. I now have students coming to me to work on issues of race and racism, at the graduate level. And it is not just Black students. I have a white student who is very good and she is working on issues of race, racism and has published a couple of pieces and she is at the point of getting ready to write her dissertation on racial oppression. So, I think that African-American philosophy is not something that can be done and should be done only by African-Americans. If that is one's view then I think it is wrong. And I think we do a disservice to the subject if that is the way it is conceived. I see it as involving certain texts, an examination of texts. There are historical texts that people are now mining. For example, Bernard Boxill is doing some excellent work on Frederick Douglass and Delany. He is going to come out with a book on nineteenth-century social and political philosophy where he examines in a rigorous way, like someone would examine John Locke's work, going through with a fine tooth comb. More of that work needs to be done. So, we are now producing these texts and what we want is to engage people in an examination of the ideas contained in these texts. That is my hope and I think we are off to a good start. I am very optimistic about where things can and will go.

A Selection of Published Works of Howard McGary, Jr.

Books

Between Slavery and Freedom: Philosophy and American Slavery, with Bill Lawson (Bloomington: Indiana University Press, 1992).

Articles

"Race, Racism, and Interracial Coalitions," *The Journal of Ethics* 1 (1996).

"Physical Violence, Psychological Violence, and Racial Oppression," *Existence in Black: An Anthology of Black Existential Philosophy*, in Lewis R. Gordon, ed. (New York: Routledge, 1996).

"Alienation and the African American Experience," *The Philosophical Forum* 24, nos. 1–3 (1992–93): 282–96, and reprinted in Richard Schmitt and Thomas Moody, eds., *Alienation and Social Criticism* (Atlantic Highlands, NJ: Humanities Press, 1994), 132–46.

"The Inclusion of African-American Materials into Philosophy Courses," *APA Newsletter on Feminism and Philosophy* 92, no. 1, (1993): 51–55.

"The Black Underclass and the Question of Values," in *The Underclass Question*, Bill Lawson, ed. (Philadelphia: Temple University Press, 1992), 55–70.

"Power, Scientific Research, and Self-Censorship," in *Rethinking Power: Theories and Applications*, Thomas E. Wartenberg, ed. (Albany, NY: SUNY Press, 1992), 225–39.

"The Moral Status of Groups," in *Encyclopedia of Ethics*, Lawrence C. Becker and Charlotte B. Becker, eds. (New York: Garland, 1992), 422–25.

"Race and Class Exploitation," in *Race and Class Exploitation in the Twentieth Century-Patterns of Exploitation in Capitalistic Societies*, Abebe Zegeye, Leonard Harris, and Julia Maxted, eds. (London and New York: Hans Zell, 1991), 14–27.

"Friedman on Impartiality and Practicality," (abstract) *The Journal of Philosophy* 86, no. 11 (1989): 657–58.

"Forgiveness," *American Philosophical Quarterly* 26, no. 4, (1989): 343–51.

"The Concept of Resistance: Black Resistance During Slavery," in *Freedom, Equality and Social Change: Problems in Social Philosophy Today,*

Yeager Hudson and James Sterba, eds. (Lewiston, NY: Edwin Mellen Press, 1989), 359–71.

"South Africa: The Morality of Divestment," *The Philosophical Forum* 18, nos. 2–3 (1987): 203–12.

"Morality and Collective Liability," *The Journal of Value Inquiry* 20, no. 2 (1986): 157–65, and reprinted in Larry May and Stacey Hoffman, eds., *Collective Responsibility: Five Decades of Debate in Theoretical and Applied Ethics* (Lanham, MD: Rowman and Littlefield, 1991), 77–87.

"Teaching Black Philosophy," *Teaching Philosophy* 7, no. 2, (1984): 129–37.

"Reparations, Self-Respect, and Public Policy," *The Journal of the Society for the Study of Black Philosophy* 1, no. 1 (1984): 15–26, and reprinted in *Ethical Theory and Society: Historical Texts and Contemporary Readings*, David Theo Goldberg, ed. (New York: Holt, Rinehart and Winston, 1989), 280–90.

"Racial Integration and Racial Separatism: Conceptual Clarifications," in *Philosophy Born of Struggle: Anthology of Afro-American Philosophy from 1917*, Leonard Harris, ed. (Dubuque, IA: Kendall/Hunt, 1983), 199–211.

"Justice and Reparation," *The Philosophical Forum* 9, nos. 2–3 (1977–78): 250–63.

"Social Justice and Public Policy," with Robert Mier, *Educational Studies* 8, no. 4 (1978): 383–93, and reprinted in Robert Mier, *Social Justice and Local Development Policy* (Newbury Park, CA: Sage, 1993), 20–31.

"Reparations and Inverse Discrimination," *Dialogue* (Journal of Phi Sigma Tau) 17, no. 1 (1974): 8–10.

[five]
Lewis R. Gordon

Lewis R. Gordon is professor of Afro-American studies, religious studies, and modern culture and media at Brown University, where he also is Presidential Faculty Fellow of the Pembroke Center for the Study and Teaching of Women. He earned a B.A. degree, magna cum laude and Phi Beta Kappa, in philosophy, political science, and ancient literature as a member of the Lehman Scholars Program, Lehman College. He earned his M.A., M.Phil., and Ph.D. degrees, with distinction, in philosophy from Yale University where he was a Danforth-Compton Fellow. He also has taught at Purdue University, where he was an associate professor of philosophy and African-American studies and a faculty member of the English and philosophy doctoral programs. Gordon's areas of specialization are Africana philosophy and religion, philosophy of existence, phenomenology, philosophy of human studies (especially sociology, anthropology, economics, and cultural studies), social and political philosophy, literary and musical theory, and postcolonial thought. His articles and reviews have appeared in *Sartre Studies International*; *The C.L.R. James Journal*; *Sophia*; *Political Affairs*; *The Black Scholar*; *Nineteenth Century Context*; *The APA Newsletter on Philosophy and the Black Experience*; *Canadian Philosophical Reviews/Revue Canadienne de Comptes rendus en philosophie*; *Social Identities*; *Social Text*; and more. He is the author of *Fanon and the Crisis of European Man: An Essay on Philosophy and the Human Sciences*; *Bad Faith and Antiblack Racism*; and *Her Majesty's Other Children: Sketches of Racism from a Neocolonial Age*. He is coeditor of *Fanon: A Critical Reader*. He is the editor of *Existence in Black: An Anthology of Black Existential Philosophy*.

He also is editor of *Radical Philosophy Review: A Journal of Progressive Thought* and coeditor of the Cornell University Press book series, *Studies in Africana Thought*. This interview took place in April 1996, during Gordon's last semester as associate professor of philosophy at Purdue University. (A selection of Lewis R. Gordon's published works can be found at the end of the interview.)

Lewis R. Gordon
Brown University

George Yancy: When and where were you born?
Lewis Gordon: I was born on May 12, 1962, in Kingston, Jamaica.

Yancy: What was it about where you were born that may have shaped your philosophical tendencies?
Gordon: I'm not really sure that the place had much to do with it, and yet I'm sure that it did. One reason that I put it in that strange way is because there is something interesting about attaining a life-project in which everything before it is read into it. And it wouldn't be a fallacious reading to do so because in many ways one's place and one's life are connected. It's paradoxical. In one sense, there is something about being born on an island, although I left Jamaica when I was nine years old. There was this consciousness of being surrounded by a world within a world that may have raised certain questions for me as a child. The other thing is that there are important sociological factors that we may bring into focus. In my case, I first lived in my maternal great-grandparents' home. There are not many people who get to have their great-grandparents around until they are sixteen years old, as I had. And in that context my great-grandfather and great-grandmother had many children. By the time I was born, many of their grandchildren were having children and it was like an African compound system. It was a large home with different compartments. So, as a child, there I was, with many aunts and a few uncles here and there. It was a huge family setting, which afforded a great deal of communal security. Right after that, my mother and I moved on and we lived in different parts of the island where I was more isolated. But I think that the context of first being in a large community of people and then being an isolated child trying to develop some sense of community develops a sense in which one begins to think of the world in very different ways. In my case, there was a period when I lived in an

area in Jamaica called the Saint Andrew's Province. That was a particularly lasting experience for me. At the time, my paternal granduncle, Jack Gordon, popped up. He was dying from many diseases. I was a child with lots of time on my hands, since my grandfather refused to pay for my schooling. So Jack and I spent a year together. Jack spent a lot of time taking me on long walks in which we talked about many things. He taught me how to read better. He taught me how to write better and how to do things like build kites and make glue out of flour and water. He was also, in terms of his theological position, a Rastafarian. So it was one of those things where there was a constant approach to reading books like the Bible in a more critical way. For instance, in many households children are introduced to the Bible as "The word of God and how to follow it!" His way of introducing me to the Bible was: "This is what people *say* is the word of God, and here are some problems raised by it, and here are how some of us have tried to resolve them."

Yancy: Did the Church or any other formal or informal religious institution play a role in creating an early interest in your philosophical concerns?

Gordon: Although for me, the Rastafarian was the image of the "deep" thinking person, I would say that the lasting influence was what it was like to be outdoors looking at the sky and thinking, "Good Lord, how large the world really is." C. I. Lewis talks about a similar experience in *The Library of Living Philosophers* volume on him. He talked about what it was like living in Massachusetts as a child and spending summers looking at the sky. When you look up at the stars and you really think about how daunting it all is, it's something that can stimulate you into a consciousness that says "Why am I here?" And interestingly enough, you even find it in Euro-philosophers like Kant, who talks about it in terms of the sublime. You know the heart of philosophy in the normative sense is the experience of wonder and in many ways that's a childhood experience of moving through, constantly looking, looking around us, asking ourselves, "Isn't it amazing that we can be conscious of being here, but we cannot quite grasp what it means to be?"

Yancy: Talk about your early consciousness in the United States.

Gordon: It was more of a consciousness of being in a world where there were so many whites. My home in the United States was the South Bronx for quite a while. We lived in a building that has since been demolished. In that area, I was in a community where it was mostly Black, but there were also Puerto Ricans, and the school I attended, the elementary school, was right on the borderline of an Italian neighborhood. But the main experience was that at school I was in this world of just so many white people in contrast to my experience in Jamaica. When I was on the island of Jamaica there were white-looking Jamaicans but the school teachers were Black, the headmaster or principal was Black. When you turned on the television, the prime minister was Black. There was constant representation of accomplished Black people. And suddenly there I was in this circumstance in which there was just so many white people. So many white people who hated Black people. In fact, one of my first negative experiences was when I sat next to a boy who kept calling me a "nigger" and I had never heard the word "nigger" before. True, in Jamaica there is the word *neayga* but the connection didn't quite come through to me. I don't want to make it sound like there isn't this crap in the Islands. There is, but people from the islands are often less aware of it, perhaps so in bad faith. Anyway, I finally started asking about this word and all the white kids laughed and a Black kid explained it to me and I went back and the white kid said it again and I grabbed him by the throat and beat the crap out of him. Later that day I beat him up again. And from that point on I began to understand the racial reality of this country, though it was still perplexing to me. I just couldn't accept what was up with white folks here.

Yancy: Were there any teachers here in the United States during your formative years that had an impact on you philosophically or just intellectually, more generally?

Gordon: I would say that there were quite a few. Two of the teachers in the elementary school were very good. One teacher, Miss Detucci, had me read my stories every week in front of the class. Miss Detucci was a totally caring person. She was really together. It is something else when you find that it's nine in the evening in the South Bronx, and people are out there playing congas and all that in the street—you know everybody's out, it's festive in the summer—and suddenly you go outside and you'd see this woman pop up and she would be Miss Detucci. She wasn't a person who simply taught us in the day. She actually took the time to get to know people in the area. Another teacher, my sixth-grade teacher, Miss Domini (folks who read Latin would see that as an interesting name in this context), not only worked out for me to get a writing award but she also gave me a set of encyclopedias. She had me write more than most kids had to write, and she constantly brought fiction for me to read.

Yancy: Any male teachers?

Gordon: Sure, there was a fellow by the name of Cirqua who taught me in the ninth grade. He was an amusing, unusual fellow. He wanted us to read the *New York Times* every morning as part of our social studies requirement. But I was too poor. I was in a situation where my mother had to walk a mile in the morning and evenings because she could not afford to take the bus to the subway to ride to work. I could not afford to buy regular copies of the *New York Times*, so the agreement was that I would come into school forty-five minutes early in the morning to read his copies. As I came in and read the paper, we got to talk more and our conversations went on to Hegel and Marx. In fact, one of the subjects that we ended up spending a lot of time on was Hegel's philosophy of history. I was fascinated by both Hegel's and Marx's conception of dialectical thought and practice—especially its significance for our understanding of history. Another person who was very interesting and had nothing to do with theory in that sense was my high school music teacher. His name was Mr. Seltzer. I was part of the concert wind and percussion ensemble. I played percussion for them—drums, tympanies, xylophones, the whole shebang. Seltzer had an adult way of dealing with students. Basically, from the moment that you were in that class and straight through to graduation, you behaved as a professional musician. He had all kinds of requirements and credos about being on time, about how you approach your music, and so on. I excelled in musical theory. In fact, very quickly: I learned within a few weeks all the music theory they could offer. It got to a point where I was actually able to make money teaching musical theory and teaching folks how to read music generally—all this while a high school student.

Yancy: When did you realize that you wanted to study philosophy?

Gordon: Well, that is connected to that point I made earlier, that there is a point of reflective realization but a reflective realization that brings you back to a point where you've always realized it was such. On the one hand, the reflective realization came when I decided to pursue my Ph.D. But by then I had already taken many philosophy courses. Now the unreflective part was in high school. I recall wondering about the permanence of abstract reality and the fleetingness of the present. I had asked my music teacher about the permanence of aesthetic creation, which designated me, from my classmates' perspective, "weird." Then there was college. I only took courses that interested me. So, I wasn't thinking that I wanted to be a philosopher or do philosophy; I just thought the subjects were interesting and took the courses. It was a consequence of doing that that I accumulated several courses in that area, and in two others (political science and classics), so when it was time to choose a major, I chose two in which I had sufficient courses. But it wasn't as if I said, "I want to be a philosophy major or a political scientist," and so forth. The background in ancient literature emerged the same way. Again, on an unreflective level, I was pursuing what I liked, which was also what I wanted, which were those subject matters.

Yancy: Where did you do your undergraduate work?

Gordon: I did it at Lehman College, City University of New York, under a special program called the Lehman Scholars' Program. I hadn't planned to go to college, I was a jazz musician, but my girlfriend was going to college and I wanted to spend more time with her. She's now my wife, Lisa. I went to college to spend a semester with her and I took courses that I liked.

Yancy: Which courses?

Gordon: These were courses on logic and reasoning, philosophy of law. I had to take the required writing course and I had a good time with that. I also took a course on political theory. But what happened was that I was doing very well and one of the professors, Bernard Baumrin, said that there was a new experimental program there and that I should try it. It turned out that this fellow from Cambridge University and Columbia University decided that he wanted to put together a special kind of scholars' program in the Bronx through the City University of New York. And I said, "No, I'm playing jazz, I'm just here for the semester." But as I was walking through one of the buildings one day I heard someone playing *Bird* [Charlie Parker] *at the Roost.* So, I went into his office and I said "Hey, this is *Charlie Parker at the Roost!*" and it turned out to have been the fellow who was organizing the scholars' program. He and I spent about two hours talking. I was very impressed by him, and apparently he was by me. His name is Gary Schwartz, and he has been a wonderful friend and source of inspiration over the past decade and a half of my life. Gary is a truly wonderful human being. Anyway, I went home that day and wrote an essay for admission to his program and got in. The program

turned out to have been wonderful. This was a special honors program where faculty who were doing cutting-edge research were
drawn from different parts of the university. The deal was that they
would get to teach their research to a small seminar of five to six students. (Budgetary demands have now made these seminars large—
about twenty-five students.) The requirements were the honors
seminars, the construction of our majors, a minimum of two years of
the sciences, a minimum of two years of a foreign language, and an
honors thesis.

Yancy: Where did you do your graduate work and why there?
Gordon: Well what happened was that after I completed my study at
Lehman College I became a high school teacher. But I didn't do that
immediately. I did some music for a while. I also spent a semester at a
law school primarily because I hadn't expected to graduate from college so quickly. I tried to do some other things as well. While I was a
college student I did a lot of political work, particularly with regard to
the struggle against Apartheid and the advocacy for immigrant education. So, I decided to go back to doing something like that in New
York and became a per diem high school teacher.
   To remain a high school teacher, there were two requirements. One
is that I had to get a minimum of twelve credits in education to receive
my regular license. The second was that if I were going to keep that
license I had to get a master's degree. So, I decided that rather than
continue in education I would go and look into some graduate work
at Columbia University. I ended up studying aesthetics with Mary
Mothersill and epistemology with Sidney Morgenbesser. Mothersill is
a famous aesthetician at Columbia University. Morgenbesser held the
John Dewey chair there. After that I ran a dropout prevention program
at Lehman high school in the Bronx. And then I decided I was going to
do my Ph.D. I thought carefully about it. I realized that my unortho-
dox learning style continued from my childhood. I was not comfortable in the more narrow environment. As I see it, a problem with a
great deal of humanities education in the United States is that the
universities ultimately only teach us to do good book reviews. I
wanted to write and explore greater things. So, as I thought it through,
many of my educated friends had suggested that Yale had an unortho-
dox way of approaching graduate education. I was particularly interested in the intersection of literature and philosophy (for which Yale
was well known at that time), and I was interested in trying to build
connections with problems of education. Because the program I was

coordinating in New York was a program where although many of the students were very bright, they were kids the system had gave up on. I was particularly interested in human derailment and the question of developing or strengthening ethical relations among human beings. So I decided I'd go to Yale. Yale focused more on the essay with an eye on the book as the medium of philosophical expression. It was a university that focused more on whether the individual was creative and I thought that would be the place at which to be.

Yancy: And who influenced you most at Yale?

Gordon: I initially went to Yale to do work on Aristotle so the person I was most intensively related with the first year was Sarah Brodie. When I showed up there she was director of graduate studies and she suggested that, because I had predominantly an analytic background, perhaps I should at least familiarize myself with some of the "other stuff." So, she suggested I take Maurice Natanson's course on Sartre's *Being and Nothingness.* Maurice Natanson completely— completely—floored me, turned me around, and I ended up working as his teaching assistant. He eventually became my advisor. I would have to say frankly that no teacher has affected my philosophical development as much as Maurice Natanson. He is number one. He is the primary influence on who I am now.

Yancy: In your book *Fanon and the Crisis of European Man* you quote Emmanuel Hansen who says that Fanon's "life and personality were inextricably linked with his ideas." In what ways are your life and personality inextricably linked with your ideas?

Gordon: My life and personality are inextricably linked with my ideas because for the most part I am in the category of what is called a praxis intellectual. I did much community work in New York and New Haven. I worked in about sixteen organizations and it was in a context where we were dealing with an ongoing struggle to deal with everything from the question of not only poverty in those cities but also, in some cases, its effect on how the resources for indigent victims of AIDS were constructed and distributed. But even before that, there was this link. Throughout my childhood I wrote incessantly, and my experience and struggles with writing are such that the writer as a model of the philosophical worker has had an impact on my way of doing philosophy. Right now I'm making a mark in what's called "existential phenomenology," which is the position that ultimately human reality cannot be looked at in terms of an essence and that, fundamentally, a strong or a proper philosophical anthropology is one in which the understanding of the human being emerges from how the human being lives. So, it's one of those things where the constant interaction with not only fellow individuals, who may be called activists, but also the teaching situation, the constant sense of communicating and dealing with bringing out human potential, that played a role in my philosophical positioning of how various lack of options or various structural impediments can have an impact on how we understand the human being. I think that what we could also say is this: If you look at all I've told you, almost every instant dealt with trying to understand not only my relationship with another human being but groups of human beings. And right now if you look at most of my writings from my first book, even my articles, most of what I've written can be considered a contribution to philosophical anthropology and problems of social reality.

Yancy: How would you define existentialism and is there a specifically Black existentialist orientation? If so, what are some of its philosophical elements?

Gordon: Well, I would argue that the moment one decides to take racism seriously as a philosophical subject one is compelled to consider Black existentialism. One of the reasons I make this claim is that if you look at history, from even nineteenth-century thinkers like Frederick Douglass and Anna Julia Cooper, what you would find is that the moment one raises the question that some human beings have not been treated like human beings at all, one is forced to dig more deeply into the question of what it means to be a human being. Now the problem is that for racism to work, one has to have a notion of the preclusion of a concept of a particular category of humanity before that humanity can live or "be" who or what it is.

In its formal structure, the classical existentialist statement is that the human being's existence precedes its essence. Now, if you look at a great deal of African-American, African, and Africana thought on the question of racism, almost all of them take two forms. They take an existential identity form and an existential liberation form. The reason the existential liberation form begins to emerge is that for liberation to be possible means that the particular condition of oppression must not be an essential, necessary, permanent condition of oppression. Oppression must be capable of change. It has to, in other words, have within it the possibility of its no longer being there. That creates a "catch-22" for many people. Many individuals would like to formulate certain questions of liberty. For example, how can we achieve a certain level of liberty without dealing with the question of responsibility? What is advanced by existentialism, well, I don't even want to say "existentialism," let's just say "philosophy of existence." What is advanced by philosophy of existence is that there is no way for the human being to have liberty without responsibility. What this means, then, is that in philosophy of existence a distinction is made ultimately between liberty and freedom. Now, if you look at the works of Frederick Douglass, particularly his fight with [the slave-breaker Edward] Covey in his three autobiographical narratives, he points out that although there were periods in which he may have had some modicum of liberty, those were periods in which he did not have freedom. Yet, when Frederick Douglass began to argue about his freedom, he argued about it primarily in terms of his resistance to Covey. Now the idea was that Covey would break him. And that meant instead of making him structurally or institutionally a slave, Covey attempted to make him existentially a slave. The struggle against being reduced existentially to a slave has been a hallmark of many Black liberation theologians' texts. It has been the hallmark of nearly everyone from W. E. B. Du Bois onward, as well. If you look at the way in which he articulates it in *The Souls of Black Folk*, he says that ultimately the fundamental question you have to pose, if you want to cut through the bull around racism, is to ask, What does it mean to be a problem? Now, what he means is that in those cases one is pathologized; one is literally and essentially the meaning of "problem." What he also was saying was that if one is going to do a proper form of theorizing around Black folk, one has to understand the distinction between people having problems and people being, and in fact *meaning*, problems. The question of being a problem is an existential point. Its meaning is a hermeneutical existential one. Literally, if you are a problem, how can you justify your right to exist? At this point, then, the question of who you are in terms of its justifying categories becomes an existential question. You'll find this also in Fanon. Fanon puts it in a different way.

In *Les Damnés de la terre*, Fanon says, Look, fundamentally what colonial domination is, what racism is, is ultimately compelling a particular category of human beings to ask every day, in reality, not only "Who am I?" but "*What* am I?" Now the moment you begin to raise that question in a philosophical sense, the conceptualization of yourself becomes post-you in an alienated way, which raises the question of your existence. Similarly, you look at someone like Anna Julia

Cooper, where she says when all is said and done the question is: What are we worth? There is something incoherent in asking a human being, ultimately, "What are you worth?" She hits the core of something that you find later in Fanon, you even find it in Euro-philosophers like Sartre. Sartre pointed out, and Fanon points this out too, that ultimately it is one thing to ask a person in a particular context, where there are certain norms available, to justify what he or she has done, but there is no way a human being can justify why he or she exists. Now, in many ways if you look at the structure of racism, it raises the question: Do Black people deserve to exist? But the problem is, once you do exist, if you cannot offer your very existence itself as a right, then that means that your existence is already subordinated in the very question. But in many ways, if you look at the whole history of racist literature that asks questions such as, "Well, gee, how did Black people come about?" you will find yourself in an effort to persuade the white population that Black people are worth keeping around. Again, you'll find this throughout the history of racist literature—and a good deal of so-called "legitimate" and "orthodox" literature. I've edited a volume of essays entitled *Existence in Black: An Anthology of Black Existential Philosophy*. This is where Black existential philosophy becomes a field of its own. In this volume, I had twenty authors all explore the question of the relationship between Blackness and existence. What's interesting about it is that although many of these existential questions I just raised had emerged in every essay, if you speak to each contributor individually, each one thinks that he or she is very different from the others. The interesting thing about all of the essays is that all of them featured arguments (1) rejecting essence as a feature of human being and (2) supporting the importance of recognizing the sociohistorical context in which we theorize. Now that becomes the hallmark of Black existentialism and the reason it is the hallmark—and this is something you find in Fanon's *Black Skin, White Masks*—is because you cannot even raise the question of a Black person without raising the question of sociohistorical circumstances, what Fanon calls "sociogenic" factors.

Yancy: How do you speak of "race" within an existentialist frame of reference that takes seriously Sartre's thesis that existence precedes essence? And here I'm thinking about this whole notion of man as *homo absconditus* (man as an open and inscrutable question). Doesn't that concept explode the notion that we are to divide individuals along an essentialist racial axis?

Gordon:　Well, we have to understand the very important concept in phenomenology called the problem of constitution. The problem of constitution is that in meaningful reality there are passive and active elements. In other words, every effort to try to understand something puts us in an active relation to something that is going to be understood as already having been there. So what this means is that when we raise the question of what the human being *is*, we always raise the question of the situation and context in such a way that the human being seems to have always been. Sartre uses terms such as "transcendence," "facticity," and "metastability" to illuminate this concept. You can think about it in this way. The very fact that human beings are constituting creatures means that almost all identities will have some room in which they can be questioned to create a sense of the responsibility of the human being in terms of his or her relation to that identity formation. But the problem with that is that because it's always raised within an intersubjective framework, what happens is that that concept begins to function in what we may call "social reality"— what is sometimes referred to by anthropologists as the world of language and psychodynamics. In other words, it has a very meaningful and real impact on the lives of people in a shared world. So, race itself may be understood in terms of a form of constructivism. You could consider, for instance, how human beings constitute a concept called "race." The fact of the matter is that the way race is lived, the way it is actually lived, has, as a form of social reality, an impact in terms of the way we can understand ourselves normatively. And this is something that Fanon tries to do in *Black Skin, White Masks* and a classic essay entitled "Racism and Culture." First, he exploded the notion of race with regard to Blacks by pointing out that the Black is ultimately a white construct. He says this right in the introduction of *Black Skin*. But then he goes through the ways in which Blacks have tried to overcome that construction through semiotics (discussion of language, symbols, and signs), through sexual relations (questions of love), and through certain forms of political relations without trying to deal with a revolutionary systemic critique. What Fanon shows is that all of those failed. Fanon showed, by the time he arrives at the fifth chapter, what is the lived experience of being Black. The lived experience of being Black is that of being embedded in a sociohistorical structure. No matter how constructed it may be, being Black is a reality that has an impact on a Black person's existential core.

Yancy:　I'm wondering, does Fanon or Sartre give credence to the sociohistorical situatedness of a Black identity that takes place in a precolonial context? In other words, can we talk about Black identity without talking about it within a white hegemonic context?

Gordon: I don't think you can and neither do they. And here is one reason. They would argue that you can talk about what we would call today Black ethnicities. I must say, however, that the racist contact with Africa is actually precolonial although many recent scholars try to reduce it to the modern colonial period. It makes sense in this pre-white–Black connection to speak of Akan, Ibo, Zulu, etc., to speak of what we now call ethnic groups. Now the thing about it is that some people say: "Well, you know, does it mean that whites had to have been on top and Blacks had to be on the bottom?" But the problem is that it becomes a very silly exercise. Let's just suppose that there is a time when Blacks were the top and whites were the bottom. The problem is since they are functioning in terms of their reference exactly in terms of high and low, it just means that we will be stuck with the same question. Those people on the bottom would be those we call the Black. So, it's one of those things where analytically it doesn't work in addressing the heart of the problem. On a different level, there is something else that Fanon hinted at in *Les Damnés,* and it is something that I am developing right now. Blacks are not the Other in Western society. Fundamentally, the self–Other dichotomy is across ethnic, class, or gender lines. But what the Black is, is the not-Other and not-self. To put it differently, in the Western framework the only way the Other can emerge is if there were some notion that the Other can be a human being. Racism, properly understood, reduces Blacks below the human. Speaking of what was also conquest, Fanon says, in *Les Damnés,* that when the French took Algeria they saw themselves as taking nothing more than the land. And in a context like that it is the Hegelian thesis that there is no *Geist* there, there is no human being there—and consequently no "experience." And literally if there is no *Geist,* then one cannot even get into the dialectics of recognition. So, one of the things that Fanon has hinted at, which I've been trying to develop, is that the reason that we get into lots of error in contemporary race theorizing is that we're structuring it so much in terms of the thesis of self-and-Other, which creates a form of human-nature view of how racists have behaved toward Blacks.

Yancy: In relationship to your theory of bad faith as a theory of racism, what do you think about Frances Cress Welsing's theory of color confrontation, which grounds white anti-Black racism in a psychological core of melanin envy, or the Nation of Islam's Theory of Yacub's History?

Gordon: Yes, many of those positions again slip into some notion of human nature. And by the very fact that I'm using the Bad Faith argument, I'm really compelled to push the issue of racism as a choice that is made. Already that puts me diametrically opposed to those positions. Those arguments, particularly, are rooted in the Negritude movement and the rationalizations and mythopoetics on which it and similar Manichaean theories are based. One of the problems with them is that they ultimately depend upon some notion of essential Blackness that can create this problem. But the problem is that, as we know, it is not really a question of morphology. There are Black people who are light. A racist may think that lighter persons may have a little white in them and therefore are a little smarter or superior. But the bottom line is that the racist is going to have a visceral response there. So it's one of those things where those arguments again just evade the issue. All you have to do is find some white people and change their birth certificates and suddenly you're going to find the emergence of a causal language of blackness. For example, suppose there is a white woman or a white guy who has a lot of fun going out, dances well, and everything is fine and one day you change his/her birth certificate. In other words, list that he/she had Black parents. Suddenly, the dancing is going to be causal, it's going to be linked to some mythical Black gene. This slip of a person into necessity begins to emerge and that becomes the ontological core of racism. And in fact, one thing that some authors are pointing out (e.g., Paget Henry, Clevis Headley, Marilyn Nissim-Sabat, Paul Gilroy, and others) about my argument is that race has to be understood through ontology, that is, existential ontology, not through epistemology. Literally, racism is not about people's beliefs about people, it's the content of those beliefs. The content of those beliefs is about what people are, that is, the whole question of the being of groups of people. Once we shift to the question of being, at that point, we have to deal with these ontological dimensions. And, once we make this shift into ontological questions, for example, "Who are Black people?" that is, what Black people are, we begin to realize what happens when a racist begins to think in terms of a Black and white category. In other words, we understand how a person who is morphologically white begins to shift into a language of necessity that is going to bring that person into a realm of destiny about who he/she is.

Yancy: How does the concept of Negritude have any relevance for Blacks in the United States today?

Gordon: The concept of Negritude has relevance simultaneously as part of our history and as something whose seduction we must resist. It's part of our history in the sense that there was not only the Negritude writers but the fact that racially, whatever one's position on race is, we are Black people. So the question of a Black consciousness is relevant to us. That's what Negritude is about. The problem with Negritude is that we have to be careful of structuring a Black consciousness simply as the antithesis of a white one because then we fall into these reactionary problems where we become *affect* and whites become *rationality*. The danger that we face is creating ourselves as the essential negation of whites. We have to recognize that we are historically structured as the essential negation of whites. But we're not in our being the essential negation of anybody.

Yancy: Well, concerning the issue of bad faith, can one also talk about misogyny as a form of bad faith?

Gordon: Yes. In the book on bad faith, I draw a link between anti-Black racism and misogyny. And one of the things about misogyny is that not only does it create a language where one begins to create a world—in the face of contradictory evidence—that looks upon women as inferior, but also, ultimately, one of the things about misogyny is that it questions the humanity of women. And ultimately, one of my arguments about bad faith is that it is, in one of its variations, misanthropic. One of the reasons it is misanthropic is because it is connected to the effort to deny humanity in others.

Yancy: What can be done to get more young African-Americans in the field of philosophy?

Gordon: There are many things that can be done. One thing that really struck me that is very unusual about myself, which I didn't think was unusual until I got the position at Purdue University, is that one of the reasons I decided to go out to Purdue was because the *Newsletter on Philosophy and the Black Experience* is located there. Also Leonard Harris is there and he's a full professor of philosophy and African-American studies, so I knew he would be someone with whom I could learn a lot about the history of the subject. In addition to that, with the wealth of information and the fact that people tend to visit the African-American Studies and Research Center at Purdue, I could glean a sense of who is in this area of specialization. To make a long story short, most of the philosophers of African descent around my age, and my age would be people between twenty-five and thirty-four, are not from a background like mine. For the most part, they are from a prestigious private secondary school background. For the most part, they are individuals who were in a more middle-class setting. And, for the most part, they are individuals who may have had far, far better training to go on to college from high school than I had. In addition, when I was living in the South Bronx, I lived in a one-bedroom apartment with seven people. And it is a situation where, to this day, my mother does not make over $15,000 a year. So it is a very different background.

I say all that to point out that what I think would be rather important would be a concerted effort to introduce philosophy into public schools and to earlier levels of education where there tends to be a greater concentration of Black students. Also, to put it straightforwardly, right now there need to be some far more significant forms of institutional economic resources for students to be able to pursue things like summer education programs and intellectual summer camps. Also, there need to be fellowships and scholarships that are readily available for people to get through graduate school. Now, those are structural things that need to be in place. I think another thing that is seriously needed is a changed understanding of what philosophy is in the United States. That, however, is going to be a tough fight. And the reason I say this is because most philosophy departments with Ph.D. programs consist of many mediocre white people, who, in order to protect themselves from admitting their mediocrity, hide not only behind a welcomed veil of ignorance—usually under pompous appeals to value-neutral "objectivity"—but also behind a veil of false excellence. They pretend they are better than they really are. They have an interest in mainstream philosophy's continuing to be a boring, ahistorical, and nonpolitical enterprise. Now, what that means is that there is priority placed not only on certain institutions for publication, but also on the very framework of how philosophical questions are raised. These attitudes and practices are not only alienating for many Black people who are philosophically minded, but in many ways, even if they try to get through many of these places, they are also genuine obstacles for them, genuine obstacles posed by these gatekeepers. I'll give you an example of what I mean. My tenure at Purdue has enabled me to find out the background of many individuals who have pursued degrees in philosophy or related areas. Now here's the thing. A place where you'd find most Black people who do philosophy, but are not listed as philosophers, will be in religion. Another place would be education. Black studies, American studies, and political theory (rather reluctantly) are next. Philosophy departments are near, if not at, the bottom of the list.

Now the prejudice of the profession is such that we treat professionally people as philosophers who have Ph.D.'s in philosophy—although the experience of many Black philosophers is to have been treated otherwise. Among the white folks, an exception is the J.D. Ronald Dworkin and Bruce Ackerman are respected philosophers without Ph.D.'s in philosophy but with J.D.'s. There are, however, people who have Ph.D.'s in philosophy of education who do philosophy, but they are not recognized as philosophers at least in their treatment by most of the folks in the American Philosophical Association. Here's another place where many Black philosophers come through: When Cornel West was at Princeton there was a program called Ethics, Religion, and Politics. Now, quite a number of Black Ph.D.'s came through that program. What do they work on? In their work, they take on Nietzsche, Heidegger, Wittgenstein, and Habermas; they look into Jameson, they look into Cone; they look into Black theology, and they look into problems of ontology and the philosophy of langauge. In other words, they look at everything that an African-American *philosopher* who's getting a Ph.D. in philosophy looks at. In short, they work on those things that someone like Cornel West works on. Yet they are not even considered, by many philosophical associations, as philosophers. But they do philosophy.

In fact, it is interesting that when the works of these individuals come out, it is their books that nearly all of us who are on the editorial board of the *Newsletter on Philosophy and the Black Experience* request for review by philosophers. If you look at the background of a lot of these people, they've got B.A.'s or M.A.'s in philosophy. Why, then, with a B.A. or M.A. in philosophy, do they decide to go on to get a Ph.D. in religion, religion and ethics, education, literature, or political theory for that matter? Well, the answer is very simple. In those fields, they are encouraged to address issues that concern people of African descent. Outside those fields, they are left with few options. The situation is the same on the hiring level. At one university, for an example, the chair of the African-American studies program had wanted to invite me to join their faculty. The problem was that African-American studies appointments are joint appointments. He asked the philosophy department to consider my candidacy. There has never been a Black person at all on the faculty of the philosophy department there. And, consequently, one has to ask why. Well, as it turns out, they see themselves as doing simply logic and epistemology. Even if there were a Black philosopher doing epistemology and logic—and there are Blacks who do logic and epistemology—if they found out that the person is also raising the question of what it means to be a person of African descent living under conditions as we do in this country, then that person is automatically not going to be considered at that institution in the department of philosophy. (Barnard college had momentarily entertained my candidacy when I was completing my degree in 1992 but they, in a similar vein, decided I was "too continental," which I supposed was more politically correct than admitting that I was too Black.) Anyhow, what immediately happened at the institution with interest in me was that the department of religion, in which there are philosophers as well, said they were interested in my joining their department. Now you can see how these things often operate, right? Look at Princeton. Where did Cornel West teach? He was in religion and African-American studies at Princeton. I have had experiences where, after a faculty voted to hire me as a full professor, an influential faculty member intervened and blocked the vote on the grounds that I would attract "too many Black people." So, what's going to be needed is what I call a *Geist* war; there has to be a war at the ideological level. That is, raising the question of whether philosophy has been responsible to itself in terms of what it is. For my part, I consider my work to be both philosophy and beyond philosophy. In some of my writings, I call my work *radical theory*, which involves a metatheoretical critique of our disciplines, including philosophy.

Yancy: Do you feel that you've had to adjust personally to fit into the academy?

Gordon: I haven't had to. But I think for me it has been a different experience. I came out of graduate school with the position that I also specialize in Africana philosophy. I specialize in philosophy of existence, phenomenology, social and political philosophy, philosophy of human studies, and aesthetics, and I have no problem with seeing myself as a Black philosopher. Now, given my position, there were certain things I expected to encounter, so I decided that my philosophical project was the most important issue to focus on. I didn't expect to ascend as quickly as I have in the academy, though. It turned out fine because I had confidence and faith in what I wanted to do and I wasn't worried about "playing it safe," as they say. You know, usually when you're a new scholar, scholars on every level advise you on the safest ways to move through the profession. What I did when I completed graduate school was not to follow the advice of many of those people. Instead, I spoke to my advisor, who himself was a wonderful risk-taker. My advisor, Maurice Natanson, is a very unusual man. He got his Ph.D. from the University of Nebraska. He got his B.A. from a small college in Tennessee. He got a doctorate in social sciences from the New School for Social Research. And he was a professor of philosophy at Yale. He is one of the world's most famous phenomenologists and among the founders of American phenomenology.[1] Well, the man has written over ten books and God knows how many articles, many of which changed the face of scholarship in the profession. The advice he gave me was that when all is said and done, you simply have to do good work and have faith in the philosophical integrity of the questions that you ask. And that is what I do, or at least try to do. I did not come out thinking of what is the most prestigious this or that. Here is an example: I chose my journals not according to whether they were the so-called best in the field, but according to whether I read them—some of which, as it turned out, were among the best in my areas. I chose my book publishers not according to their prestige, but according to whether I have been reading the books they publish. I know Routledge and Blackwell are prestigious publishers, true, but for me that wasn't the issue. The issue was that the way I was presenting Fanon challenged some of the postmodern cultural studies interpretations of Fanon, and cultural studies folks read Routledge books. Given that, that was a place to publish my book. The critical reader on Fanon was sent to Blackwell because of the excellent job they did on a volume devoted to C. L. R. James. When I published *Bad Faith* with Humanities Press, it was because I was dealing with an existential and phenomenological positioning according to a left and Africana standpoint. The Humanities Press publishes works by C. L. R. James, Hegel, Merleau-Ponty, Husserl, Buber, and Sartre. So, given that approach I just simply concentrated on myself as a philosopher and a writer rather than on some sort of careerist view of what I was about.

Yancy: Are there specific responsibilities that an African-American philosopher has that a Euro-American philosopher does not have?

Gordon: I would argue that on a basic ethical level we all have these responsibilities. For example, there is the question of treating students with integrity, the question of trying to encourage a healthy space through which, for instance, a Black female student could get into philosophy, etc. I think white or Black you have that resposibility. But there are realities we face as Black people, realities that we cannot leave to white people to do because history tells us that they won't. So, I would argue that all Black faculty have the responsibility to sit on job committees. I, for instance, have personally played a role in the hiring of over seven Black people at Purdue. It's not simply looking for candidates. It's also about scoping out the political terrain to make sure that there is an environment conducive for hiring those candidates. There are many phony jobs out there for Black people. You know, simply to put it on the books that Black people have been interviewed is enough to satisfy some legal guidelines. We also have a responsibility for the ideological war. The fact of the matter is there are right-wing forces in the United States that are investing tons of money and time in cultivating an ideological program against the existence of Black people in the academy. It is just irresponsible for me to be a Black person in the academy and not take a position on that war.

Yancy: Does jazz provide a philosophical framing for you?

Gordon: Yes, it does. In fact, you know it's funny, I receive letters on the books and articles that I write, and quite a lot of commentators have observed that the actual structure of my sentences and my paragraphs remind them of jazz. So, that connects to the earlier question you had about whether our life experiences play a role in what we do. I would say that it does that stylistically with me. You may notice that aspect even in the *Bad Faith* book. For example, I write short chapters instead of long chapters. Some of my paragraphs are just one sentence long and in the middle of a complex philosophical argument I'll break into dialogue or stories. All of that is connected to jazz. And also jazz, by the way, I would argue, is strongly connected to Black existentialism. Why? Because in jazz you do not follow what is absolutely written in advance. All that the written music does is to set the context for improvisation. So, literally, the jazz musician doesn't even know what will be played until he or she performs it. That is existential.

Yancy: Is philosophy for you a kind of inner urging or calling?

Gordon: Absolutely both! It's like Sartre's notion of Kafka's Gate. You know the story of the guy who goes to the gate. "Open the gate, open the gate!" he yells. He's there for a long time and he finally asks,

"Who's gate is this?" And the watchman says "It's yours." Well, in many ways as I look back on it, philosophy becomes the configuration of what I ultimately do. For me, philosophy is not the way it's looked at, for instance, in the analytical tradition where it is simply a method of analyzing concepts toward some sense of scientific understanding. For me, philosophy is a normative enterprise. It's ultimately trying to deal with the very core of not only who we are and how we are responsibly related to being here, but also the question of what it means simply to be. Once we begin to think of it that way philosophy is connected to what it means to be alive.

Yancy: Finally, what are some of your current philosophical projects?

Gordon: I will be working on a treatise entitled *Essence and Social Theory*, where some of these questions you've asked me are going to be developed in terms of a full-scale theory of how we can have a view of essence without essentialism. I also connect these concerns to questions of social theory. There is a hint of this in the third chapter of my book on Fanon where I talk about anonymity and Schutz's view of typification. Then I'm going to develop those ideas into another book entitled *Portraits: An Essay on Human Reality*. This is going to be a focused exploration of the question of the human being, in spite of Foucault's insistence that the human being will be one day washed away like an inscription in the sand. There are a few other works, too.

One of my other projects, philosophically, in terms of the history of philosophy, is the whole question of Africana philosophy. In other words, philosophy across the African diaspora. And you can see how the book on Black existentialism relates to that end. I'm also doing something for Blackwell Publishers entitled *Key Figures in African-American Thought* and that's going to bring out some of those issues. In addition to some of the philosophy of human sciences material I will edit something entitled *Communicating Differences: Essays in Philosophy and Communicative Praxis* with a colleague of mine, Jacqueline Martinez, in communications. She and I are constructing a theory of how one can continue to theorize about the human being given the arguments I put forth in the bad faith and the Fanon books. One thing that has been intriguing some of my readers, and which they are beginning to explore, is the argument that I advance that in poststructuralism the appeal to social constructivism is evasive primarily because sociality itself is a constructed reality but reality nevertheless. So, for instance, many people who appeal to social construction like Anthony Appiah tend to appeal to it with the effort of trying to articulate certain forms of human reality as fictitious. But what I point out in my response is that something's being socially constructed does not mean that it is fictitious. For instance, language, communication, and sociality themselves are constructed, but they are very real. They have real truth conditions. It is an error, it seems to me, to take the position that a category, like race, for example, is automatically fictitious simply because it is constructed. There is a question that emerges here: What would happen to certain realities like communication given the fact that social constructivism is redundant? So, Martinez and I are putting together, with a collective of individuals who have been looking at works in phenomenology and communication, a work that will begin to explore the implications of that thesis. So, you can see that everything I just told you about really connects to the core questions of consciousness, the human being, and ontology.

Note

1. This interview was conducted in late spring 1996. Maurice Natanson died shortly thereafter, on August 16, 1996.

A Selection of Published Works of Lewis R. Gordon

Books

Black Texts and Black Textuality: Constructing and De-Constructing Blackness, with Renée T White. (Lanham, MD: Rowman and Littlefield, 1999).

Philosophy of Existence. Volume of the *Edinburgh Encyclopedia of Continental Philosophy*, Simon Glendinning, general editor (Edinburgh: Edinburgh University Press, 1998).

Her Majesty's Other Children: Philosophical Sketches of Racism from a Neocolonial Age (Lanham, MD: Rowman and Littlefield, 1997).

Existence in Black: An Anthology of Black Existential Philosophy (New York and London: Routledge, 1996).

Fanon: A Critical Reader, with T. Denean Sharpley-Whiting and Renée T. White (Oxford: Blackwell Publishers, 1996).

Fanon and the Crisis of European Man: An Essay on Philosophy and the Human Sciences (New York and London: Routledge, 1995).

Bad Faith and Antiblack Racism (Atlantic Highlands, NJ: Humanities Press, 1995).

Articles

"Theorizing the Epidermal Schema: Fanon, Philosophy, and Racism," in *Philosophy and Racism*, Susan Babbit, ed. (Ithaca: Cornell University Press, 1998).

"Three Perspectives on Gays in African-American Ecclesiology and Religious Thought," in *Sexual Orientation and Religion*, Martha Nussbaum and Saul Olyan, eds. (New York and Oxford: Oxford University Press, 1998).

"Anti-Blackness and Effeminacy," in *Black on White*, David Roedinger, ed. (New York: Schocken/Random House, 1998).

"Frederick Douglass as an Existentialist," in *Frederick Douglass: A Critical Reader*, Bill Lawson and Frank Kirkland, eds. (Oxford: Blackwell Publishers, 1998).

"Philosophy of Existence," in *The Edinburgh Encyclopedia of Continental Philosophy* (Edinburgh: Edinburgh University Press, 1998).

"Philosophy of Existence, Religion, and Theology: Existence and Faith," with James Marsh, in *The Edinburgh Encyclopedia of Continental Philosophy* (Edinburgh: Edinburgh University Press, 1998).

"A Tragic Dimension of Our Neocolonial 'Postcolonial' World," in *Postcolonial African Philosophy: A Critical Reader*, Emmanuel Chuckudi Eze, ed. (Oxford: Basil Blackwell Publishers, 1997).

"Fighting Master Covey: Frederick Douglass as an Existential Thinker," in *Frederick Douglass: A Critical Reader*, Bill Lawson and Frank Kirkland, eds. (Oxford: Blackwell Publishers, 1997).

"Africana Existential Philosophy," in *The Blackwell Companion to African-American Philosophy*, Tommy L. Lott and John Pittman, ed. (Oxford: Blackwell Publishers, 1997).

"Sex, Race, and Matrices of Desire in an Antiblack World: An Essay in Phenomenology and Social Role," in *Sex and Race: Comparing the Categories*, Naomi Zack, ed. (New York: Routledge, 1996).

Foreword to Joy Ann James's *Transcending the Talented Tenth: Elites, Gender, and Agency in Black Intellectualism* (New York: Routledge, 1996).

"Black Existential Philosophy," introduction to *Existence in Black: An Anthology of Black Existential Philosophy*, Lewis R. Gordon, ed. (New York and London: Routledge, 1996).

"Existential Dynamics of Theorizing Black Invisibility," in *Existence in Black: An Anthology of Black Existential Philosophy*, Lewis R. Gordon, ed. (New York and London: Routledge, 1996).

"Five Stages of Fanon Studies," introduction to *Fanon: A Critical Reader*, Lewis R. Gordon, T. Denean Sharpley-Whiting, and Renée T. White, eds. (Oxford: Blackwell Publishers, 1996).

"The Black and The Body Politic: Fanon's Critique of Psychoanalytical Human Science," in *Fanon: A Critical Reader*, Lewis R. Gordon, T. Denean

Sharpley-Whiting, and Renée T. White, eds. (Oxford: Blackwell Publishers, 1996).

"Frantz Fanon's Tragic Revolutionary Violence," in *Fanon: A Critical Reader*, Lewis R. Gordon, T. Denean Sharpley-Whiting, and Renée T. White, eds. (Oxford: Blackwell Publishers, 1996).

"Ruminations on Violence and Anonymity in Our Antiblack World," in *Soulfires: Young Black Men on Love and Violence*, Daniel J. Wideman and Rohan B. Preston, eds. (New York and London: Penguin, 1996).

"Can Men Worship?: Reflections on Male Bodies in Bad Faith and a Theology of Authenticity," in *Men's Bodies, Men's Gods: Male Identities in a (Post-) Christian Culture*, Björn Krondorfer, ed. (New York and London: New York University Press, 1996).

"A Lynching Well Lost." *The Black Scholar* 25, no. 4 (1995): 51–54.

"Sartrean Bad Faith and Antiblack Racism," in *The Prism of the Self: Essays in Honor of Maurice Natanson*, Steven Crowell, ed. Series: Studies in Phenomenology (Dordrecht, the Netherlands: Kluwer Academic Publishers, 1995).

"'Critical' Mixed-Race Theory?" *Social Identities* 1, no. 2 (1995): 381–95.

"Antirace Rhetoric and Other Dimensions of Antiblackness in the Present Age," Symposium on Racism, *Social Text*, no. 42 (1995): 40–45.

"Joint-Appointments from an African-American Faculty Member's Perspective," *The APA Newsletter on Philosophy and the Black Experience* 93, no. 1 (Spring 1994): 20–21.

"Racism as a Form of Bad Faith," *The APA Newsletter on Philosophy and the Black Experience* 92, no. 2 (fall 1993): 6–8.

[six]

Michele M. Moody-Adams

Michele M. Moody-Adams currently is associate professor of philosophy at Indiana University. She earned her first B.A. in philosophy from Wellesley College and her second B.A. in philosophy, politics, and economics from Oxford University, Somerville College. Her M.A. and Ph.D. degrees in philosophy are from Harvard University. She has also taught at the University of Rochester and Wellesley College. Her areas of specialization are moral philosophy, social philosophy, political philosophy, and the empiricists. Her articles and reviews have appeared in *Hypatia*; *Journal of Social Philosophy*; *Ethics*; *The Philosophical Forum*; *Character and Morality: Essays in Moral Psychology*; *Feminist Ethics*; *Public Affairs Quarterly*; *American Philosophical Quarterly*; *Women's Review of Books*; *Character, Dignity and Self-Respect*; and more. And she has also served on the editorial board of such distinguished journals as *Utilitas*, *Hypatia*, and *Public Affairs Quarterly*. (A more complete citation list of Michele M. Moody-Adams's published works can be found at the end of the interview.)

Michele M. Moody-Adams
Indiana University

George Yancy: When and where were you born?
Michele Moody-Adams: August 31, 1956, in Chicago, Illinois.

Yancy: What was it like growing up there?
Moody-Adams: Basically, pretty good. My parents were very middle-class professionals. They were both in education, employed as teachers in the Chicago public school system, at least when I was growing up. I lived in a Black neighborhood, but I didn't actually end up going to elementary school there. I went to school somewhat south of my own neighborhood in the Hyde Park area (right around the University of Chicago) and that was really pivotal for my intellectual and, I suppose, personal development in the end.

Yancy: What impact did your family have on your early intellectual growth?
Moody-Adams: Their impact was enormous. They would be the people that I would put at the top of the list. This is partly because of their involvement professionally in education, but also personally they pushed me to do whatever I was good at and to do it to the best of my ability. They gave me all kinds of freedom both intellectually and emotionally, and they were very unusual people. They introduced me to the sorts of things that a lot of people like me, particularly young Black kids growing up in the '60s, would not have normally experienced. My father, for instance, was a member of the First Unitarian Church in the University of Chicago area and this really made a big difference in my intellectual development. I read people like Martin Buber and Paul Tillich when I was very young.

Yancy: How young were you?
Moody-Adams: Well, I don't exactly remember but I guess I was about eleven or twelve. Not that I understood it all but it was there, it was on the shelf. My parents never told me that I couldn't read something, rather, they just said that if you think you can make your way through it then see if, in fact, you can. So that was important. I even remember during grammar school going to the school librarian when I was, I guess, in the fifth or sixth grade and asking for a copy of *Ulysses* and getting this very odd response. My parents actually got a note sent

home saying that I was asking for pornographic material. Then when they found out that this "material" was *Ulysses*, they were at least willing to let me consider it at a time when other people were not so sure about that sort of thing.

Yancy: Where did you go to elementary school?

Moody-Adams: I went to a public elementary school on the South Side of Chicago called William H. Ray. This school occasionally gets some national attention for being a public school with an Alumni Association which seeks donations from former students (and others) to keep special kinds of programs going—art, music, and certain kinds of gifted programs. They had a lot of these special programs when I was there and that was important. When I first went there, the school had a very stringent tracking system. But they would assume that if you were Black that you would not go into a gifted track. I'm not all that big on IQ tests, but I always did really well on them and my parents knew that there was something fishy about how I'd been placed. Because my parents were knowledgeable and fussy, however, I ended up being placed in the proper "gifted" classes all the way through the eighth grade. I also took "early involvement" high school classes when I was still in elementary school. So that made all the difference. I've since seen that person who put me in those other classes and she actually apologized for ignoring my test scores and assuming that because I'm Black that I could not have been capable of being placed within a gifted track program. But thank heavens that my father knew what was up and kept a watch on things.

Yancy: Where did you go to high school?

Moody-Adams: I went to a public high school called Kenwood High School. It was also on the South Side of Chicago. It was always basically a very good school. I mean, it sent lots of kids to college, and generally to pretty good colleges. Moreover, both Black and white students tended to do very well there.

Yancy: Were there any particular teachers during this period who influenced you most?

Moody-Adams: There were several. In particular, one teacher right before high school, an eighth grade teacher, Florence Stein, encouraged us to read very widely and to put on plays. I was in the Oscar Wilde play called *The Importance of Being Earnest*. It was the sort of thing where Black students and white students got together and did this and nobody commented on the fact that a Black student was playing a character from this late Victorian play.

Yancy: Which role did you play?

Moody-Adams: I played Gwendolyn. The role has stuck with me because there's actually a line about philosophy in the role. In high school, however, the single biggest influence would be my French teacher, Susan Key, who taught advanced placement French and had us reading Albert Camus and Jean-Paul Sartre in French. That really got me thinking about philosophy, though not thinking that I'd major in it.

Yancy: Do you happen to remember the philosophical line from the play?

Moody-Adams: Well, it's actually a line referring to something as a "purely metaphysical speculation that had no place in ordinary life." It was a very funny reference to something that really wasn't metaphysical at all. But while I thought it was a good line, I didn't know why it sort of resonated with me, even though I looked up the word "metaphysical."

Yancy: At what point did you actually realize that you wanted to study philosophy?

Moody-Adams: Well, to be frank, very early on. I knew in high school, but I never thought I'd actually go on and do it. It was partly reading Camus's novel *L'Etranger,* and reading up on his life, and reading about his connections with the existentialist movement. And although I didn't go on to study existentialism at any great length, it was very appealing to me at the time. Again in college I took philosophy courses and although I said to myself that I really can't make a living at this, I just kept coming back to it, especially in college.

Yancy: In high school, what was it about your own self-understanding that led you to believe that philosophy was the sort of thing that you thought you were interested in?

Moody-Adams: Well, you know, this is complex. A lot of it does have to do with growing up Black: Just this sense that you have to work a little harder to get a sense of yourself drives you to think philosophically. My parents used to talk a lot about identity. Indeed, early on, my father used to talk at length about the concept of race. People now talk about this all the time as though you needed some sophisticated philosophical reflection to realize it is a complicated idea. But my father used to talk about it all the time. I was taught to be proud to identify myself as a Black person. But my father always said, you know, deep down there is no such thing as race. He said there is just one race, the human race. Trying to put all of this together with awareness of discrimination, and differences in class and so forth, really made me want to investigate it in a way that was different from investigating something in a science class or in a sociology class. I felt that there was something deeper going on that I needed to think about. My first thought though was not to be a philosopher but to be, of all things, a Unitarian minister. So for a while I thought that I would go to Divinity School and then get a combination Ph.D. and divinity degree to be a minister. At the end of my sophomore year in college I actually had written to the dean of an important theological school, one of the two that you go to if you want to be a Unitarian minister. Now this Dean had actually said to me (and I actually believe that he did this for my own good and it shook me up) that even if I got all of these degrees and did very well in school that I'd have difficulty getting a church. And it is still relatively uncommon to find Black women, and Black people in general, who made their way in the Unitarian church. And then I thought, "Look, if philosophy is my first love then I might as well go ahead and do that."

Yancy: So the realization that philosophy was your first love occurred during your undergraduate days.

Moody-Adams: It did. The single biggest influence was a professor named Ruth Anna Putnam. Actually, her specialty and her early research had been with Hans Reichenbach. I think that she had actually translated some of his early works into English. But while at Wellesley College, which was my undergraduate institution, she taught a variety of courses, including some courses in moral philosophy. But she taught other courses as well. For example, I took a course on Ludwig Wittgenstein from her and it was then that I knew that I wanted to be a philosopher. I still have papers from that class: especially one on which she wrote that I really should become a philosopher. That really stuck with me. She's been one of my biggest champions. She's been a genuine friend and supporter all the way through my career in a way that just makes a difference between your sticking with a subject and quitting, if you know what I mean. Even when you're not talking with a person, your memory of their confidence in you makes all the difference.

Yancy: Is it correct to assume that your earlier reading of Sartre and others had given you a firm foundation for your later reading in philosophy?

Moody-Adams: It did. But that's not the reading that actually convinced me that I wanted to go to graduate school. It was John Rawls's *Theory of Justice,* which I read in one of my courses with Ruth Anna Putnam, that really made me want to be a philosopher. I really thought, "Wow, this is it!"

Yancy: So, was it that text in particular?

Moody-Adams: It was that text's attention to the problem of equality. But I ended up not working on Rawls when I went to graduate school. Even though I worked with him, I ended up not working on his theory because I could see he had moved away from the vision I had of it.

Yancy: So you decided to apply to Harvard to do graduate work because of Rawls?

Moody-Adams: It was Rawls and partly the urging of Ruth Anna Putnam whose husband, Hilary Putnam, was a faculty member of the department there.

Yancy: Besides Rawls, who else influenced you at Harvard?

Moody-Adams: Lots of people. Hilary Putnam would be one. Even though Putnam's main emphases, at least at the time, were not in moral and political philosophy, he was a major influence on me.

Yancy: Specifically, how did Hilary Putnam influence you?

Moody-Adams: Oh, in a variety of ways. He was a philosopher of mathematics, a logician, and a philosopher of science, yet he was very skeptical about contemporary insistence, at least in some circles, that inquiry was fully rational and fully objective only if it was "scientific" or looked just like science. His insistence that there's something fishy with that attitude is the single most important thing that anybody can say in philosophy. This fetishism of science is deeply embedded in popular culture. Putnam has pursued that theme throughout a variety of works over the last twelve to fifteen years.

Yancy: What about Quine?

Moody-Adams: Well, Quine was no longer teaching at the time. He was an emeritus professor. I did do some work on his writings, however. Largely as somebody to play my own views of ethics off against,

Quine ended up probably quite unwittingly being a very major influence. My first published article takes off from a criticism Quine made of the nature of argument in ethics. In *Theories and Things*, he stressed that you're always going to have a kind of infirmity of the methods of ethics, particularly when you look at the way in which there is continued disagreement in a way that there isn't in science and so forth. It was playing my views off of Quine's criticisms of ethics that really got me headed in the right direction in my own research. It moved me away from writing on historical topics, particularly David Hume, to the contemporary things I've been writing about since.

Yancy: Were you the only Black female presence at Harvard in the philosophy department?

Moody-Adams: In my first couple of years, I was the only Black person in the program. So, I was definitely unusual.

Yancy: Did you ever feel discouraged from pursuing philosophy, particularly at such a white male-dominated institution like Harvard?

Moody-Adams: At Harvard? No. There were so many other oddities about being in philosophy at Harvard at the time. First of all, being in philosophy, in the Ph.D. program, you're already kind of an odd being, whatever you are. And at Harvard I did have people like Rawls and Putnam who just took me for what I was. If I did my work and did it well they accepted that. I discovered after I got out of graduate school just how horrific people can be in philosophy toward people who are Black and female. I had to wait until I actually got employed in a department to experience this. The program at Harvard was very demanding. But I personally never experienced racial or sexual harassment from anybody, or at least I didn't know that I did, so I guess I didn't.

Yancy: What do you take an African-American philosopher to be and do you fall under that rubric?

Moody-Adams: Well, I think of myself as an African-American and I think of myself as a philosopher and as an African-American who does philosophy, that's the first thing. Secondly, many of the reasons for which I went into philosophy are inseparable from the fact that I'm African-American. I think it has made me more reflective, just about things that most people take for granted in everyday social life. There are also certain questions that probably appeal to me more, and I think even certain philosophical views, that I find more appealing. But

I have to be careful here. I don't see myself as doing something that I would call, strictly speaking, "African-American philosophy" and I'm not really sure why I think this. I don't start out with a set of questions that have been defined by people like Alain Locke or Du Bois, for instance. I do not start out taking the problems that I will pursue from a set of questions set down by other people who describe themselves as African-American philosophers. Now, that troubles some people. However, I have written about race and problems of self-respect, and I've had interest in equality and justice. I write about culture and about what certain kinds of arguments about culture mean for people of all sorts, including African-Americans. And so I like to be cautious in terms of how I answer that question. You know, sometimes I write about Hume and I never talk about race. Or, sometimes I write about certain problems in moral psychology, about moral responsibility, and I may never mention race but I know that deep down that what is egging me on intellectually is a set of problems that come out of my experience. But there are a lot of African-American philosophers who would be troubled by the fact that some of the things that I write about—including my dissertation where I barely even mention race, in fact, I don't even think I mention it—don't even mention African-American issues. That for some people means "Well, you can't really be an African-American philosopher." But I don't buy that. I just don't buy that and I think I am not alone in that.

Yancy: What advice would you have for a young African-American female intent on pursuing a career in philosophy?

Moody-Adams: That's a really good question. First of all, you have to have that fire in the belly (as it were). If you don't love it then don't even think about it. If you feel you can't live without it, then do it. But if it is just a kind of passing fancy then it's not worth it. It's too difficult a route to try to go. The second one would be, be prepared for people who may question your very right to be where you are and to study what you are studying. There is an intrinsic prejudice in philosophy against women as embodiments of emotion and everything that's anti-thetical to reason. That's something you have to contend with. It is compounded, however, against Black people. Occasionally, being Black and female there are things you can do that you couldn't do if you were Black and male. For all the difficulties I have had in my professional career, some experiences may have been even worse had I been male. I guess that the other thing I would say is that Black women shouldn't feel that allegiance to, or sympathy with, certain kinds of feminist arguments makes them traitors to their race. Black women sometimes feel torn when they find that some issues in feminist thought appeal to them. There may be room for enlightenment in terms of how we think about problems of race, social justice for African-Americans, and so forth, that may come from feminist thought. And there is a lot to be mined from feminist concerns. Black Americans, both male and female, can learn from these concerns. So, in summary, I guess there are four things. Make sure you love it. Be prepared not to be treated right, initially. Be prepared also to be forgiven for your differences, in some respects, because you are not Black and male. But then, fourthly, also don't be afraid to accept that there are certain allegiances you will feel to other women who are not Black and that there's nothing wrong with that. Even intellectually there may be something very important about pursuing those allegiances.

Yancy: Are there specific responsibilities that a Black female philosopher might be said to have that might be different from, let's say, a Black male philosopher?

Moody-Adams: Yes. There are certain problems embodied in African-American culture, in all kinds of complicated ways, involving men and women and how they get along, that I think philosophy could say something about. Maybe not in academic journals but certainly there are philosophical issues bound up with these problems. Certain kinds of attitudes that get filtered through popular rap music, for instance, are not always absent even at the highest regions of academic life when Black women and Black men encounter each other in certain settings. I think there are issues that Black women have to address if they're going to ever be able to assume their rightful place in American culture, American society, that maybe Black men aren't yet capable of addressing or maybe need a nudge to address. A few years ago I had a brush with punditry, which I backed away from. I wrote a letter to the *New York Times*'s letters column in response to something Tom Wicker had said about rap music being "quintessentially Black," claiming that people just didn't understand that to criticize rap music, this was back in 1990, was to criticize all Black people. It was to criminalize Black culture. I just wrote a letter in, and the kind of response I got to this would amaze you. I wrote Wicker and said "Look, please, whatever else you do, acknowledge that when somebody like the leader of 2 Live Crew, Luke Campbell, gets up and says things about women in his songs he does not speak for me. In fact, he is degrading me, he is devaluing and not listening to me." And I had some acquaintances, Black American male friends, who were deeply troubled, at least initially, by my saying this. Nobody else would say this at the time. And people like Skip Gates were getting up and saying "Oh, it's just poetry. You know, it's the modern equivalent of Shakespeare." But it isn't. When it's somebody trying to make money by doing things that demean women, particularly Black women, Black women have to speak against that. Some African-American males, even philosophers, still don't appreciate the extent to which they can be blind to the dangers of the way Black men sometimes view Black women. There is room to say it so that it's not about punishing people or about attacking or assaulting them; rather, it exposes some of the difficulties that women can experience even from Black people.

Yancy: I would like for you to talk a little more about your entry into ethics.

Moody-Adams: I suppose it comes in college, as I said, after reading Rawls's *Theory of Justice.* I had at first thought I would just be the kind of philosopher who talked generally about the nature of Being and meaning and essence and all that sort of stuff. You know, those metaphysical questions. Then I got intrigued more specifically by the moral dimension of human life. I suppose that was always there, implicit in my interest in being a minister. I suppose it was really a series of worries about social justice and then just about what it means to lead a good life and what kinds of things you do to be a person who leads a life worth living. It was very much a Socratic inquiry: the idea that everything we feel and think and do is properly something that should be subjected to rational self-scrutiny, to self-examination. The unexamined life is not worth living, in other words. And that started to hit home in more specific ways as I started to read Rawls's *Theory of Justice* and reflected on how American society had ignored the ways it had treated Black people and hadn't addressed, I thought, sufficiently, the wrongs that had been committed, not just in slavery but also in post-Reconstruction and into the twentieth century.

Yancy: I have a question in regard to your essay "On the Alleged Methodological Infirmity of Ethics." Briefly, what is the difference between a scientific theory and a moral theory?

Moody-Adams: There are lots of differences. The principle one is that a scientific theory purports to tell us what the world is like. It may enable us to predict future occurrences on the basis of the theory or to explain past occurrences but it is trying to tell us something about the way the world is. And a moral theory is trying to tell us, or to guide us, to an understanding of what the world ought to be like. And that's a very different enterprise from what one does in science. People like Quine, in the negative sense, are trying to say that ethics should look more like science. But ethics isn't (and shouldn't be) about trying to describe the world, because we want to tell people how they ought to act, often when they are not doing the right things. Ethics should be about what the world should be like in the future even irrespective of what it has been like in the past, especially when things have gone wrong.

Yancy: Would you say that Quine is guilty of committing a category mistake there?
Moody-Adams: Absolutely.

Yancy: Would you say that a correspondence theory of truth is inappropriate with regard to a theory of morality?
Moody-Adams: Well, I have to be careful here because a correspondence theory of truth, even in science, is not exactly what some of its defenders claim it is. Quine has this notion that in the end the best scientific theory you're capable of getting has links with experience outside of itself, that is, "corresponds" with something outside of itself. But it's never a one-to-one correspondence. It's always this theory taken as a whole. You can't take any single piece, any single sentence, of a theory of science and say this corresponds with some fact that's out there in the world. Coherence and correspondence aren't neatly separated even in science. In ethics they are probably more closely intertwined than in science. So I suppose correspondence is simply less important in ethics. But one thing I have to say, is that deep down, objectivity and truth, in both inquiries, are always a matter of our aspirations to something outside of human inquiry. Nobody, even Albert Einstein or whomever, can step outside their theory and say, "Look, I know that this is true because I've seen the other side," or "I've seen the facts that the theory corresponds with." You can't do that even in science. All that you have are certain circumstances, maybe, if you get lots of good predictions from your theory, that give you reason to hope or believe that your theory corresponds with something outside of itself. I think that kind of hope is also available in

ethics. For some people that is kind of a heterodox thing to say, but to me the same kind of aspirations to objectivity that are there for a scientist are acceptable in ethics.

My favorite example involves a great scene from the documentary *Eyes on The Prize* where they are talking about the early '60s when demonstrators in New Orleans, I think it is, were trying to get them to open up the lunch counters and so forth. A woman is being interviewed saying, "You know, they say they're coming down here as nonviolent demonstrators just trying to make us see, but I think it's really a kind of violence trying to *make* us rethink and *make* us see that something we're doing is wrong." It suddenly occurred to me that you wouldn't see what the demonstrators were doing as a kind of violence unless it was forcing you to see something that you knew was wrong about what you were doing. I thought, these people know that there is a moral requirement that they are not living up to. They don't care and they don't like having somebody come and force them, even in a genuinely nonviolent way, to confront that. And when I see that kind of thing happening, where people feel that there is a moral truth that they're being forced to confront, and they may never openly confront it, I think there's reason to believe in objectivity in ethics. I don't think that you're going to get a theory where you can sit down and say, "Here are the moral truths for all time." I don't think that's possible. But I think there are intimations in human experience that there is an objective moral truth that people can be made to see—but they can also run from. That same thing happens in science. You can get scientists to agree on things and they can say, "Yes, we see it and we can all agree that this is the truth and, boom, we suddenly see it." I think that there is an equivalent in ethics. You can't prove it and you can't write it down and you can't give a short list, but that aspiration to objectivity is as genuine and as, I think, defensible in ethics as it is in science. There are just different places in experience where we can confirm its value.

Yancy: In reference to Richard Rorty, what's your response to his claim that "The Good" is what we have historically carved it out to be and that there are no moral or ethical facts, as it were, but just communal solidarity? Does your essay "Theory, Practice and the Contingency of Rorty's Irony" at all deal with these problems?

Moody-Adams: It does. Could Rorty march up to a freedom rider in the South, or to someone in Tiananmen Square who stands in front of a tank, and say that there is no such thing as justice, and there is no such thing as equality and there is no such thing as political fairness, or whatever? Could the student or the freedom rider engage in these activities, if they accepted Rorty's view? Rorty wants to say they could and that all you need is solidarity, I want to say that that's just nonsensical. And it's not just a psychological mistake that Rorty is making here. I actually think that there is a conceptual flaw. I think that you need the idea that at some point human moral inquiry could be progressing closer and closer to the grasp of an objective truth. Could be, but not necessarily is. You need that aspiration, you need that hope in order to be able to carry out the activity. Rorty claims that he can do everything with his concept of solidarity. My argument is that he can't. And if you can't then you have the way into seeing what's wrong with Rorty's argument, at least as a political philosophy. And then I think there are independent reasons for thinking that it's rational to hold onto the aspiration to objectivity. But Rorty thinks because he can say that we can get along without this aspiration, and I don't think we can. At one point, Rorty tries to make some argument about civil disobedience as it was practiced within the Civil Rights Movement without understanding at all what it was rooted in. These were people who were rooted in the Black church who believed in a higher purpose for which they were living and acting and Rorty seems not to have understood this as a psychological phenomenon at all. And so that to me is the beginning of an argument against him. I'm thinking here particularly of Rorty's work *Contingency, Irony, and Solidarity.*

Yancy: Does your approach to moral theory include a conception of God?

Moody-Adams: Well, this is the problem that I am having. I think, and I suppose this is the Kantian side of me, that there must be room for a conception of moral action, the right thing to do, that makes it possible for somebody who is an atheist to do the right thing and lead a good life. However, as I've gotten older, I've started to wonder whether I can really make that work. And I've started to wonder if it works for Kant. Maybe it is *difficult* to make sense of what is required of us without something in the background that holds out the promise of an afterlife where things are made right or whatever. This is something that I'm of two minds about right now. But I do genuinely think that it's possible for somebody who not only doesn't have a concept of God, but just kind of denies that there is a God, to be a good person. I genuinely believe that. And I have always sought a vision of moral theory that worked on that premise.

Yancy: I'm wondering here if we don't work from the premise that there is a God, then where does value come from?

Moody-Adams: Okay.

Yancy: And then I'm thinking here of David Hume's is/ought distinction. And even Sartre has this notion where he talks about not being able to derive ethical imperatives from ontology's indicatives.

Moody-Adams: That's a good thing to recite. I want to say that it's possible for human beings, maybe it's not probable or maybe it's not even that common or that likely, to hold that out as a kind of open question as to where value comes from. One of the things that I argue in *Morality, Culture and Philosophy: Fieldwork in Familiar Places*, is that human beings, however they come to them, have articulated over time (and in a variety of cultures) a very complex set of moral concepts the richness of which is yet to be mined. I don't know where those concepts come from. For example, in a lot of cultures you'll find, expressed in a variety of ways, sometimes negatively and sometimes positively, something like the "Golden Rule": Do unto others as you would have them do unto you. Many different versions of this are floating about in all kinds of religious traditions, all kinds of historical eras and so forth. This seems to be a good candidate for one of the moral concepts. Where does it come from? I'm not sure I can say. Why should we care about it? Well, I think there is an argument that you can make that doesn't appeal to any theological conception. It helps make sense of the things we care about morally and helps guide us to do things that we can all recognize, however we do that, to be the right thing. Now, how you explain our ability to recognize it, how you explain where this concept, and as others like it, comes from, I'm not sure you need to. You might want to ask why as a philosopher I would want to stop here. Well, this is the Socratic side of me. Why do you need to know this in order to try to be a good person?

Yancy: Now, in your approach to moral and/or ethical issues is it important to assume the existence of mind as an explanatory category or is it enough that we are part of a sociolinguistic community capable of effectively using moral and ethical predicates to describe overt human behavior?

Moody-Adams: The second is enough. And even more than that, one of the most morally important manifestations of our existence as sociolinguistic beings is that we are capable of assenting and dissenting to various self-conceptions over time, various interpretations of what we are and what we are about. I think that's enough. You don't need any elaborate metaphysical theory. There is this capacity that human beings have to accept, to scrutinize, to rethink their self-conceptions and that is really all you need, I think. I think that's all philosophy needs. That is all you need to do what Rawls does or to do what Hume did. Maybe somebody will come up with some way to give an unproblematic account of the self or the mind or whatever, but I don't think you need it. You've got this fact that human beings can say that "Yes, I am this kind of person, or no I'm not." If you are a Rawlsian, for instance, you can say, "I do want a society where people pay to contribute to welfare, etc." If you are a libertarian you may reject that conception and you can get a debate going between these different positions.

Yancy: Running throughout many of your essays is the argument that responsibility for human action is irreducible, right?

Moody-Adams: Yes. You can try to run away from it but you have it whether you want to face it or not.

Yancy: Is human freedom also irreducible?

Moody-Adams: Yes, I think so because I think that responsibility presupposes freedom. But I don't think there's anything more to be said in virtue of why we are free. One footnote to a passage in Kant's *Groundwork of the Metaphysic of Morals* says that it's enough if we are the kind of beings who can't act except under the idea of freedom. That probably sums up my whole view about the relationship between responsibility and freedom. If you're willing to deny your freedom you don't actually become less than an agent, but you start to view yourself as something less than human. You can actually buy into someone's picture of you as fully determined and in that instance you begin to act as though you were not a fully human agent. I don't want to say that that means that you aren't human. I want to say that even the choice to see yourself as not free proves that you are free.

Yancy: How does your view here differ from someone like Sartre where there is this ontological conception of human freedom?

Moody-Adams: Well, in many respects I suppose it is similar to Sartre's view. The things that I have come to in my mature intellectual life are not that far from the things that sent me to philosophy in the first place. But I'm not interested in saying more about the nature of freedom. I'm not interested in making any richer, if you will, ontological claims.

Yancy: And that stems from your Socratic approach?
Moody-Adams: Very much so.

Yancy: Could there ever be a case where there is such a strong link between culture and agency such that this would lead to undermining the standard attribution of responsibility for a given action?

Moody-Adams: I think about this daily. I want to say no. I don't want to say that there aren't other influences on a person, maybe chemical influences in the brain, maybe some disease of the mind, or something that might undermine agency in the sense that you suggest. I do want to deny that culture can do that. And I guess it is largely the function of the following vision of what a culture is. It is the kind of thing that survives only when it creates individuals who are capable of choosing to perpetuate the culture. If you participate even to a mild extent in some practice, there is a degree to which you are sanctioning the practice in which you are participating. And I want to say "degree" because I want to be careful. I acknowledge degrees of responsibility for things people do in any walk of life but certainly as a function of their cultural upbringing. There are degrees of responsibility for perpetuating a practice. I'm very cautious about this too because the thing that got me going on this was looking at African-American people growing up in circumstances of oppression and where they are underprivileged and so forth. This has led me to ask, "Why do they act the way they do?" I mean, why, given the fact that there is so much oppression and so forth, look at a person and say you could "choose" not to do certain things? But then you look at people who may all grow up in the same housing project, for instance, and you can find some people who do not do the things that others in their environment do and then you ask, why? Is it something about their internal constitution? Possibly it is. But it also suggests that it can't be culture which itself overwhelms the person. There may be other things in addition, but I want to argue that it can't be culture that undermines agency. I also want to say, if you stop a kid in Chicago, for example, who's involved in drug trade and you ask them why they are doing this, you would find somebody who would say that they are in bad circumstances and that their circumstances limit the kinds of choices they have. But they have made choices and in fact sometimes you'll find some people who can very articulately say, "Look, I'm only acting rationally given the kinds of circumstances I've been confronted with. You know, I need money, I need this, I need that. So, it is rational, given the circumstances, for me to do what I'm doing." You misrepresent or misconstrue the capacities and the abilities of the people you are talking about if you assume that they are crippled by the culture they grow up in. Limiting the range of choices is one thing but limiting the capacity to choose I will not accept.

Yancy: So it is culture as an "entity," as it were, that you find problematic?

Moody-Adams: Right. Culture should not be construed this way. A lot of people want to treat a culture as though it were what Erving Goffman called a total institution: where you are beaten down and your capacity to think any thought that isn't determined by the institution is somehow taken away. Culture couldn't survive that way and any humanly designed or constructed institution that does that, in my mind, is not a culture. It's something else, a concentration camp, or it's a slave system, or whatever. Culture influences the kinds of things we're likely to see as alternatives. It does then place certain burdens on a person in a culture to be conscious of this tendency to limit the things one sees as alternatives. For instance, when we limit cigarette advertisements I think there is value in doing that for the following reasons. It is not a way of saying that people can't choose not to smoke, but it is a way of saying that we'll make it a little less difficult for you to choose not to smoke by not constantly dangling this as an alternative in front of you. There are circumstances under which you might mitigate your response to something somebody does by saying that some set of limitations made it harder to choose not to do something than another set. I fully acknowledge mitigating circumstances.

Yancy: Are you a methodological holist or a methodological individualist?

Moody-Adams: I want to say neither. To make sense of human beings in their collectivity, in societies, groups, cultures, nation-states, you have to recognize the existence of individual people whose choices to perpetuate or not perpetuate collective practices allow those practices to survive or to disappear. Neither is prior. You can't have one without the other. Sometimes when I talk about culture the way that I do some people say that I must be a methodological individualist. And I say no because I do acknowledge that to be a human being is to be encultured in some way, that is, to have a certain social and historical origin and that determines very important facts about you, though not all of them. But you can't have one without the other. Anybody who insists that one or the other is a requirement just doesn't understand the relationship between the whole and the part, or between the individual and the collective.

Yancy: You've served on editorial boards of major journals. How does race impact at that level?

Moody-Adams: When you get certain kinds of papers that might seem opaque to somebody else you can sometimes make apparent the philosophical merit of a paper. I recently received a paper on the topic of race, and the moral and political implications of the concept, that the person sending it to me didn't fully comprehend. It was really quite wonderful; and one of the best I've seen. I am still waiting to hear about the disposition of that paper, but I had some impact in just making it clear why it was an intellectually valuable thing to do. You can make a difference by simply being attuned to the intellectual value of things to which other people might not be attuned.

Yancy: Who is Michele Moody-Adams, philosophically?

Moody-Adams: An inquirer who cares very much about leading a good life and about helping other people think about leading good lives as well.

Yancy: And how does your philosophical worldview tie back into your identity?

Moody-Adams: In many respects the things I care about philosophically come directly out of the way I see myself in the world. And even when I don't mention race, even when the fact that I am an African-American woman is not uppermost in my writing or in my mind, it's clearly an important influence. I think it makes me even more able to care about what's hidden and what's beneath the surface.

Yancy: What would you describe as your overall philosophical project?

Moody-Adams: Mine is a Socratic project of encouraging people to scrutinize their own lives. Rational self-scrutiny is essential to my project. The unexamined life, I think, is not worth living. That is the single most important philosophical claim I would make, assuming that it is a philosophical claim, and I think it is.

A Selection of Published Works of Michele M. Moody-Adams

Books

Morality, Culture and Philosophy: Fieldwork in Familiar Places (Cambridge: Harvard University Press, 1997).

Articles

"Feminist Inquiry and the Transformation of the Public Sphere in Held's *Feminist Morality*," *Hypatia* 11, no. 1 (winter 1996).

Reprint of "Race, Class and the Social Construction of Self-Respect," *Character, Dignity and Self-Respect*, Robin Dillon, ed. (New York: Routledge, 1995).

"Theory, Practice, and the Contingency of Rorty's Irony," *Journal of Social Philosophy*, 25th Anniversary Issue (June 1994): 209–27.

"Culture, Responsibility, and Affected Ignorance," *Ethics* 104 (January 1994): 291–309.

"Race, Class and the Social Construction of Self-Respect," *Philosophical Forum* XXIV, nos. 1–3 (fall–spring 1992–93): 251–66.

"On the Old Saw That Character is Destiny," in *Identity, Character and Morality: Essays in Moral Psychology*, Owen Flanagan and Amelie O. Rorty, eds. (Cambridge, MA: MIT Press, 1991), 111–31.

"Gender and the Complexity of Moral Voices," in *Feminist Ethics*, Claudia Card, ed. (Lawrence: University Press of Kansas, 1991), 195–212.

"On Surrogacy: Morality, Markets and Motherhood," in *Public Affairs Quarterly* 5, no. 2 (April 1991): 175–90.

"On the Alleged Methodological Infirmity of Ethics," *American Philosophical Quarterly* 27, no. 3 (July 1990): 225–35.

[seven]

Albert Mosley

Albert Mosley is professor of philosophy at Ohio University. He earned both his B.S. degree in mathematics from the University of Wisconsin and later his Ph.D. in philosophy. He has also taught at the United States Air Force Instructional Services, Howard University, and the University of the District of Columbia. His areas of specialization are logic, philosophy of the natural and social sciences, social and political philosophy, African philosophy, and African-American philosophy. His articles and reviews have appeared in the *Encyclopedia of Philosophy: Supplement*; *Africa Today: Philosophy, Identity, and Social Transformation*; *Applied Social and Political Philosophy*; *The American Philosophical Association Newsletter on Philosophy and the Black Experience*; *The Review of Black Political Economy*; *Philosophy and the Black Underclass*; *Papers in the Social Sciences*; *Philosophy Born of Struggle: An Anthology of Afro-American Philosophy From 1917 to the Present*; and more. He is also coauthor of the books *Affirmative Action: Social Justice or Unfair Preference* and *An Introduction to Logic: From Everyday Life to Formal Systems*. He is also the editor of *African Philosophy: Selected Readings*. (A more complete citation list of Albert Mosley's works can be found at the end of the interview).

Albert Mosley
Ohio University

George Yancy: When and where were you born?
Albert Mosley: I was born October 28, 1941, in Dyersburg, Tennessee.

Yancy: Would you provide a sense of what it was like growing up there?

Mosley: Dyersburg is a town about eighty miles north of Memphis on Highway 51, which ran from New Orleans to Chicago. My father and mother operated a cafe, hotel (with about ten rooms), and a pool hall. This was during the heyday of segregation and all Black people who came through Dyersburg looking for a good meal, a place to stay, or a little recreation usually ended up at our place. It was like a neighborhood community room. People came there to eat, have a few beers when they got off from work, shoot a few games of pool, and just hang out. And on weekends, people came to town from "out in the country." The primary crop in West Tennessee at that time was cotton, and most of the people that lived in the countryside were sharecroppers who raised and harvested cotton for a living.

Yancy: Were your parents very instrumental in terms of your early educational experience?

Mosley: My father could neither read nor write, but he always liked to point out that he could count money "at the flash of an eye." He had been a gambler before he became a businessman. My mother got as far as the sixth grade. But she loved to read and had taught me to read by the time I was four years old. It was her influence that channeled me and my brothers to college. Most of the kids who came from my area didn't go to college at that time. If they graduated from high school, they went into the army or up North, to places like Chicago, Detroit, Milwaukee, and Cleveland, to find work. Most young people did not leave Dyersburg going to college. And without my mother's vision, it is much less probable that I would have gone either.

Yancy: What were your early educational experiences like?

Mosley: I started school at Future City Elementary School on the west side of Dyersburg. It was like growing up in a cocoon. Future City was a segregated school where we knew one another intimately. There was a lot of spirit in the school. Most of the children who went there lived on the west side, but after sixth grade we had to go to Bruce High School on the east side of town. It was also segregated, and Black kids from the outlying areas were bussed in. That's where all Black kids in the county went to school, from the seventh grade on. Bruce High had a big influence on me because not only were the teachers competent and devoted to their students, but my principal, M. L. Morrison, was a brilliant man. It was from him that I learned music. He was principal of the school and not only directed the band and choir but also at different times was the football coach, the basketball coach, the science teacher, and the French teacher. Each year Bruce High School produced a minstrel show, which our principal directed and performed in. He was a talented man with abilities in many, many areas. His wife, Julia Morrison, was the school librarian, the math teacher, my homeroom teacher, and the piano player for our dance band. After Bruce High was closed, Mr. Morrison went on to get his doctorate and taught at Alabama A and M until his retirement. I believe Mrs. Morrison is still living in Montgomery, Alabama.

Yancy: So did you demonstrate an early interest in music?

Mosley: Oh, yes. I was a good musician and still am. I started playing when I was about nine years old. By the time I was twelve, I was playing regularly throughout West Tennessee. Not only did we have a marching band, we had a dance band, and Dr. Morrison arranged all of the music for the dance band. We played a lot of standards like "Body and Soul," "Mood Indigo," and Ellington compositions like "Take the A-Train." We played dances for the V.F.W., the American Legion, area country clubs, and high school proms. We also had a smaller band we called the Combo that played for parties and teenage dances.

Yancy: What instrument did you play?

Mosley: Trumpet.

Yancy: I assume that you were also a voracious reader?

Mosley: Oh yes, I read all of the time. I read comic books.

Yancy: Which were your favorite?

Mosley: Superman, Batman, Captain Marvel, and all the superheroes. My brother and I had stacks of comic books. We also read the local newspapers: the *Dyersburg Gazette* and the *Commercial Appeal* from Memphis. My brother was also a major influence in terms of my reading. He was six years older than me and something of a dreamer.

Yancy: Would he suggest particular books that you should read?

Mosley: Oh yes, and especially after he had left and returned to Dyers-burg. He joined the army after graduating from Bruce High and served in Korea. He was always giving me heavy books to read, like Freud's *Interpretation of Dreams,* Camus's *The Myth of Sisyphus,* Bertrand Russell's *Why I Am Not a Christian,* Sartre's *Nausea,* and others. And he forced me to discuss them with him. I was not an eager participant.

Yancy: So, retrospectively, was there something about your own cognitive tendencies during this formative period that you feel predisposed you to study philosophy?

Mosley: Growing up in my family's business, I counted a lot of money and shot a lot of pool. I believe these activities may have helped develop my perceptual intuitions for algebra and geometry, and influenced my ability in mathematics.

Yancy: Provide a sense of the transition from high school to your having decided to attend an undergraduate college.

Mosley: Going to college was not something I thought a lot about. My mother had decided that we should go to college and my brother enrolled at Fisk University on the GI bill after leaving the army. On the other hand, most of the people going to college from my hometown went to Tennessee State University (TSU), which is also in Nashville and on the same street as Fisk. My brother was already a junior at Fisk when I enrolled at TSU in 1958 as a freshman. I had a great time there. I was a math major but that was not the focus of my efforts. I learned to play tennis and I played a lot of music. I played with a number of small blues bands around town and had my first exposure to serious jazz musicians. Though I had learned standards and how to improvise, I had never been where jazz was played. It was at Tennessee State that I met and played with jazz musicians and developed a more sophisticated level of musicianship. But I've never had a course in music or formal music lessons. I was taught the basics of the trumpet and how to read music by Dr. Morrison. Other musicians taught me about chord changes and transposing. The rest I did on my own by reading books and sitting in. I've always considered this way of learning to play closer to the way jazz musicians traditionally learnt their craft, even though that's seldom the case anymore.

Yancy: If one individual at Tennessee State influenced you most, let's say in mathematics, who would that be?

Mosley: That would be my algebra teacher, Mrs. Sasser. She was the first to impress on me the importance of rigor. I pledged a fraternity at Tennessee State, Alpha Phi Alpha, and her son was one of my big brothers. He became an airplane pilot and I believe was killed in Vietnam.

Yancy: I understand that you didn't complete your studies at Tennessee State.

Mosley: That's true. I transferred from Tennessee State in 1960 when my brother, Bill, graduated from Fisk. Bill warned my parents that after he left I might be tempted to drop out of school and go on the road playing music. And it's quite probable that I would have. I thought I was a good musician and others did too. And the prospect of touring with a band was exciting, even though I'd had enough experience to see that being on the road was no picnic. Bill convinced both me and my parents that I should transfer when he left, and so, I applied to a number of major schools and chose the University of Wisconsin. As it turns out, Wisconsin had one of the best math departments in the country, but I didn't know this at the time. Talk about a rude awakening! The pace, depth, and intensity of the way mathematics was done there was something totally novel to me. I had never imagined anything like it. My first year was quite difficult. I remember finishing it with a D average. I was minimally qualified and didn't know how to study. In a nutshell, I didn't know what was going on. My father was upset with my grades and we decided it would be best for me to leave. My plan was to join the Merchant Marines and see the world. I took a job as a dishwasher that summer (after my first year) in order to make enough money to get to Detroit and the Great Lakes. But while playing table tennis one day after work I met another Black student, Costello White, who was in astrophysics and is now an attorney. We became roommates and that's when I learned how to study. While I had thought studying a couple hours a day was doing a lot of work, Costello studied days at a time.

Yancy: Who there influenced you?

Mosley: In mathematics, one of the people that influenced me most was a professor named Ralph Bean who I took topology from and became close friends with. Then there was R. C. Buck, who was my advisor. He had written a very popular book on advanced calculus and his area was functional analysis. Steven Kleene is probably one of the most famous names of this century in the foundation of mathematics, and I was his teaching assistant in advanced calculus, even though at the time I didn't appreciate how renowned he was. I got my bachelors in 1963 and began work on my masters. But the civil rights battles of the '60s made it difficult for me to concentrate on mathematics. During my last year at Tennessee State I had participated in the Nashville sit-ins. And as the struggle for justice intensified, I felt a real need to be more involved. One of the major reasons I changed from mathematics was in order to have more time.

Yancy: So when did you definitively decide that you were going to study philosophy?

Mosley: I got my bachelors in 1963 and began work on a masters in mathematics. It was during that year that I decided I needed to do something else. So, I looked around. I took courses in history, the history of science, and philosophy. And of all of them I liked philosophy best.

Yancy: But why philosophy and not, let's say, physics?

Mosley: Well, I wanted something that would give me the greatest degree of freedom to be more directly involved in the social changes that were going on. And for me, philosophy allows one the widest range of possible interests. The fact that you can do philosophy of anything intrigued me. It provides an extraordinary amount of latitude in terms of legitimate professional interests and involvements.

Yancy: Which professors in the philosophy department at the University of Wisconsin influenced you most?

Mosley: The first course I took was from William Hay. I did a seminar on Plato with him, and that really hooked me on philosophy. But there were others: Marcus Singer, then chair of the department. And of course my major professor, Fred Dretske, who is now at Stanford University.

Yancy: But what was it specifically about this course on Plato that really hooked you on philosophy?

Mosley: First, I think Plato is one of the best introductions to philosophy because the dialogues are dramatic presentations of philosophical issues. Second, I was coming from mathematics and for Plato the study of mathematics was the best training for philosophy. Third, it's been said that all Western philosophy is a footnote to Plato, meaning that one can find within Plato almost every issue that has been raised in the history of Western philosophy.

Yancy: What did Dretske teach?

Mosley: Dretske's areas were in the philosophy of science and philosophy of mind. He became my major professor after the death of Julius Weinberg and directed my thesis work for the doctorate.

Yancy: What was the thesis?

Mosley: I did my thesis on the Kuhn-Popper debate in the philosophy of science.

Yancy: Briefly, how would you characterize the Kuhn-Popper debate and whose position did you side with?

Mosley: I was very much influenced by the work of Thomas Kuhn, as most academics have been. Kuhn clearly introduced a new perspective on science and on how science develops. He gave credence to what is now called an externalist view of scientific development. According to this view, science is not merely the product of truth-seeking individuals making inferences from theories and testing them by experimentation, but science is deeply influenced by social and aesthetic considerations. Sir Karl Popper had argued that science progresses, not by inductively proving theories to be true, but by deducing implications from theories which were experimentally proven to be false. Kuhn was one of the first to show that this is never really the whole truth of the matter when it comes to the historical development of science. Contrary to Popper's position, he stressed that no particular experiment ever conclusively disproved a theory.

Yancy: And what was it about Dretske? Was it his teaching style, was it his rigor?

Mosley: Oh, I think both factors. Dretske was very informal and personable, yet was and is solidly in the analytic tradition. But I decided on my dissertation topic only after I left Wisconsin and was studying at Oxford.

Yancy: What did you study there?

Mosley: Philosophy of science. When I was finishing the last part of my graduate work, Rom Harre came to Wisconsin as a visiting professor from Oxford. I took a seminar from him on logical positivism and he invited me to continue studying with him. He encouraged me to seek some means of coming to Oxford. So, I applied for a Fulbright, and got it. But 1966–1967 found me torn again between scholarship and activism. I almost refused the Fulbright scholarship because I felt guilty that I was not actively involved in the civil rights struggle. I was even considering not taking my preliminary examinations. I went to a grassroots conference in Washington, D.C. chaired by Queen Mother Moore, a lady who had long been involved in the movement, and I asked her advice. She encouraged me to follow through with my degree because, she argued, the movement needed committed people with advanced degrees and international experience. Not everyone should be working at the grassroots level. She encouraged me to take advantage of the opportunities I had and use them to enrich the struggle.

Yancy: Were you the only African-American in the Ph.D. philosophy program while at the University of Wisconsin?

Mosley: Yes. I was also the only African-American in the math department while I was there.

Yancy: How did this impact you at the time?

Mosley: Oh, it didn't bother me. At that time I was quite curious about white people because I'd lived all of my life in a segregated community in Tennessee, and Wisconsin was the first time that I'd been in an environment where it was possible to mix freely. Most of my friends at Wisconsin were white because most of the students there were white. I think that out of a school of about forty thousand at that time, there were about two hundred African-Americans, most of whom were athletes. So, there were very few African-Americans on campus. In terms of total population, African-Americans were a very small percentage. On the other hand, it was good having white friends, for it destroyed the idea that there was something peculiarly different about whites that made them special.

Yancy: I would like for you to say something more about your early experience of segregation in terms of how that may have impacted the formation of your consciousness.

Mosley: Segregation was something I was born into and simply took for granted. During that era in Tennessee, there were certain things you did and certain things you did not do, and there were serious consequences if you stepped over the bounds. You didn't look at a white woman. If you talked to a white man, you weren't supposed to look him directly in the eye. There were many subtle things that you learned to do. But I was fortunate because my parents were economically independent. We had our own business and my father had an extremely dominating personality with both whites and Blacks. He was what Southerners called "half-crazy," practicing a kind of "strategic irrationality" that kept both whites and Blacks off balance when they were around him. So, I never had to work for or depend on others, and was never in situations where I was ever directly threatened by whites. I was protected from the kind of abuse that many Blacks experienced living in the rural South during that era.

Yancy: Would you say that philosophy for you constituted a passion?

Mosley: I don't think so. I liked philosophy because of the intellectual freedom it allowed me.

Yancy: It was pragmatic?

Mosley: Yes, I think it was a pragmatic choice. Before I went to Wisconsin, except for readings suggested by my brother, Bill, I knew very little about philosophy and wasn't particularly attracted to it. But after I decided that I wanted to teach and discovered Plato and professional philosophy, then I appreciated that this would be something I wouldn't easily get bored with. In this sense, my choice of philosophy as a career was a pragmatic one. Philosophy wasn't the realization of a dream I'd preconceived. Recently I met an African-American woman who told me that she read a book by G. E. Moore when she was in the fifth grade and realized that philosophy was something she wanted to do. I'm always amazed by that story. She read G. E. Moore in the fifth grade and liked it! But it was nothing like that for me. I remember one of my professors asking me why I didn't do social and political philosophy instead of the philosophy of science. Besides feeling that African-Americans should not be ghettoized in one area of philosophy, the simple fact is that I came to philosophy from a background in mathematics and the sciences rather than the humanities.

Yancy: Would you describe yourself as an African-American philosopher?

Mosley: Oh, absolutely. I would describe myself that way in the sense that I believe I embody many seminal aspects of the African-American experience—having been raised in a pool hall in Tennessee during the segregation era and being a fairly accomplished self-taught musician. Those are experiences almost paradigmatic of how African-Americans are often identified. So, in one sense, I think I exemplify a certain aspect of the African-American experience and that no doubt has influenced the way I do philosophy and the direction of my philosophical career. When I left Oxford I had offers from numerous elite universities that were looking for Black faculty, but I chose to go to Howard University because it was a Black school. I taught at Howard for a year and then went to an open-admission school that had just opened in Washington called Federal City College. This was the predecessor to what is now the University of the District of Columbia. I chose those schools because I thought that my talents, my abilities, and my knowledge should be channeled back into the African-American community. I left Howard because I wanted to serve those who were among the least well off.

Yancy: Which other African-American philosophers were on the faculty at Howard University when you were there?

Mosley: Dr. William Banner, a graduate of Harvard, was there. Dr. Winston K. McAllister, chair of the department, I believe had gotten his Ph.D. from the University of Michigan. Eugene Clay Holmes, a Marxist philosopher of science, was there. And Joyce Mitchell Cook was on the faculty, though I believe she was on leave during the year I was there. Fortunately I came to Howard with the kind of credentials that they respected. As such, I was able to function as a kind of mediator between older members of the department and the radicals among the student body. I remember McAllister as a very robust and congenial man. I believe he was an ethicist. Dr. Holmes was nearing retirement and wasn't around the department very much. But he and I did talk on a number of occasions. At that time there was quite a lot of turmoil on Howard's campus, with student strikes, etc. But the students were mostly unaware of Holmes's early radicalism, particularly the significance of his having been a Marxist during the McCarthy era. Holmes often expressed his disappointment at being so little appreciated for what he had done. Banner was also a very active man and is still a productive scholar. But Banner was somewhat put off by the student emphasis on Black power, Black nationalism, and a separatist agenda.

Yancy: How would you define the nature of African-American philosophy?

Mosley: Well, I'm not an essentialist in terms of the nature of African-American philosophy. I don't think there is any one factor, or even a set of factors, that would define it. If I were to give a characterization I would say that African-American philosophy is philosophy that is by African-Americans or about issues of particular relevance to African-

Americans. This would not imply that one would have to be an African-American to be involved in or do African-American philosophy, anymore than one would have to be Greek in order to be interested in or do Greek philosophy. African-American philosophy has evolved around the situation of African-Americans, and anyone who made that a professional interest would be doing African-American philosophy.

Yancy: Provide a sense of the historical conferences held by African-American philosophers.

Mosley: The earliest conference I attended that focused in bringing African-American philosophers together was held at Chicago Circle, sponsored by Irving Thalberg around 1968 or 1969. The one I participated in after that was at Haverford College, sponsored by Lucius Outlaw. There were other efforts to support the development of African-American philosophers. Dr. Broadus N. Butler, former president of Dillard University and Ph.D. in philosophy from the University of Michigan, sponsored many activities supporting African-American scholars. He headed the Institute for Services to the Humanities and the Moton Foundation, which provided grants to African-American scholars to spend a year of research and writing at the Moton Conference Center in Capahosic, Virginia. I spent a year there and finished a book on logic, which was subsequently used at UDC for many years.

Yancy: Did you attend that particular African-American philosophy conference, in 1994, held at Rutgers University?

Mosley: I was there.

Yancy: Would you explore the conceptual rift that occurred there between Anthony Appiah and Lucius Outlaw?

Mosley: Anthony Appiah has argued that race is a fiction and has spearheaded a movement among philosophers to disavow race as a legitimate and useful concept. He's made a very strong case for this and I think many African-Americans have reacted negatively to his efforts. The fact of the matter is that the majority of African-Americans do identify themselves in terms of their race. This act of self-identification by race reinforces an important sense of historical continuity. Their parents and grandparents were classified in terms of race and most associate denying their racial identity as an act of self-hatred. But Appiah has argued that the very concept of race is a fiction. And within the literature of biology and anthropology this claim has been made by many others. Ashley Montagu has a famous book called *Man's Most Dangerous Myth: The Fallacy of Race* where he presents the many false beliefs that have evolved around the purported Jewish and Aryan races. Moreover, biologists have shown that there is no such thing as a race gene, something that makes every person who has that particular gene (or constellation of genes) Negro or Caucasian or Oriental. As a result of World War II, there was a concerted attack by scholars against the illegitimate use of racial categories, especially the idea that race determines a peculiar national orientation. Appiah has taken this orientation and applied it to the American situation in his essay, "The Uncompleted Argument: Du Bois and the Illusion of Race." There he argues that W. E. B. Du Bois used the notion of race in characterizing African-Americans, but was never able to define it adequately because it can't be adequately defined.

Yancy: What was Outlaw's response to that?

Mosley: I've written a response where I tried to show that biologists are divided on this: Some biologists believe that there are distinct human populations and other biologists do not believe this. Outlaw has a similar point of view. He argues that you can't deny that race exists simply because it's a historical construction. At the conference Outlaw was bemoaning the fact that he had to continue to comment on commentaries about his and Appiah's differences, and rather offhandedly characterized Appiah's position as a form of ethnic cleansing. Given what was happening in Yugoslavia at this time in terms of ethnic cleansing, Appiah was insulted by the analogy, and he walked out of the room. I think Outlaw used an inappropriate metaphor but had not intended his description in the way Appiah understood it, and I followed Appiah out and said so to him. Afterwards Outlaw and Appiah talked and I believe clarified their positions to one another. But the passions generated reflect the importance of the issue. One of the attacks on affirmative action is based on the idea that there is no such thing as African-Americans. Were we able to get rid of all references to race there would be no basis for affirmative action on the basis of race. Many African-Americans believe this is simply a ploy designed to consecrate the status quo and ignore the historical wrongs that have been and continue to be perpetrated against African-Americans. Restitution for opportunities denied because of race could not then be corrected on the basis of race.

Yancy: In your essay "Negritude, Nationalism, and Nativism: Racist or Racialist," you discuss the distinction between a racist and a racialist. Would you briefly define the two terms?

Mosley: A racialist position accepts the claim that there are races and that there might be differences between races, both physiological and even behavioral. A racialist wants to allow that possibility. There is physiological evidence of such differences and a racialist would not preclude the possibility of correlated differences in behavioral traits. In the article, I make the analogy between races and varieties of dogs, not in order to taint the notion of races, but in order to point out that if you segregate any population long enough they will develop distinctive traits as a result of assortative mating. This is how people create varieties of dogs. Pit bulls didn't exist three hundred years ago. They're a fairly recent breed created by mating bulldogs and terriers. But the fact that this variety is a historical creation is no reason to deny that the variety exists. A racialist would argue the same thing with respect to races. There has been geographical isolation between continents as well as social isolation within continents that has led to the existence of distinct groups of people. Now, this doesn't mean that those groups have always existed or should be preserved into the future. So a racialist need not believe that races are primordial groups created by God after the flood or the Tower of Babel. But there is no reason to believe that groups cannot legitimately be differentiated into racial varieties.

Yancy: And to that extent you are a racialist?

Mosley: I see no reason to deny racialism. Racism, on the other hand, would not only say that there are different races, but that certain races are superior to other races. That I would deny.

Yancy: How does your position differ, for example, from someone like Leopold Senghor? Should we conceptualize Africans as essentially an emotive people and conceptualize Europeans as essentially intellective?

Mosley: Senghor argued that Africans and African-Americans are physiologically inclined to be more emotive and kinaesthetic, and this accounts for the fact that their primary achievements have been in athletics and the arts. But it's very difficult to actually justify that claim. Are such achievements the result of an innate group predisposition or is it that achievements for Africans and African-Americans have been limited to those areas? In either case it remains true that there have been more famous African-American musicians than famous African-American mathematicians. Is that because African-Americans are "naturally" more oriented toward music than mathematics or is it because African-Americans have been limited by slavery, segregation, and other exclusionary practices to the development of entertainment skills as opposed to management and/or scientific skills? There is no clear way to determine this. But, whether the cause is genetic predisposition or social restriction, the fact remains that most African-Americans tend to cultivate the kinds of talents they have seen other African-Americans exhibit and profit from. Whether it's genetically or socially based, the influence still remains.

Yancy: Anthony Appiah as well as Jean-Paul Sartre have argued that the conception of race that grew out of the Negritude movement is actually a case of antiracist racism. I understand that you disagree with Appiah's contention here, right?

Mosley: That is correct. I don't think racialism is a form of antiracist racism. Senghor has been interpreted as taking the supposed inferior features of African-Americans, their tendencies toward aesthetic and kinaesthetic activities, and transforming them from a deficit into an advantage. In assessing the merits of affective and analytic tendencies, Negritude flips the value from negative to positive. A similar reaction occurs with respect to the question of whether women are more emotional than men. Many feminists have answered in the affirmative, and considered it an advantage rather than a disadvantage because it makes women in general more sensitive and nurturing. Likewise, Negritude argued that the emotional orientation of Africans makes them more oriented to the arts rather than the sciences. Now that might be true or false. But it's not a racist position, because there's no implication that the arts are superior to the sciences. It's only when there is a claim of superiority that you get racism, and Negritude has never made a claim of absolute superiority, only relative superiority. Ideally the racialist position is pluralist. It recognizes that every advantage is only relatively an advantage. In changing circumstances and situations what is an advantage here may be a disadvantage there.

Yancy: On your view, should we or should we not abandon the concept of race?

Mosley: Well, this question has to be considered historically. And given the historical reality, I think we certainly *should not* abandon it. It would preclude the possibility of restitution for exploitation and denied opportunities if at this stage race was eliminated as a legitimate means of identifying the victims of racism. I think this would be immoral and unjust. Again, even if race is an historical construction, the fact is that the identity of many people has been shaped (both positively and negatively) by that means of categorizing human beings. And those individuals unjustly injured as a result of racist exclusions have a right to have the injuries they have suffered acknowledged and corrected. I think many African-Americans see the position that Appiah and Naomi Zack and others have championed as being a means of wiping the slate clean and accepting the status quo as is without regard to how it came to be. Do you follow me?

Yancy: Sure. What got you interested in writing in areas of affirmative action?

Mosley: It is clearly a highly controversial subject and I felt that since I had the ability and opportunity to address it, I should. While I was still at the University of the District of Columbia in 1987 I was invited by Bob Ginsberg to give a paper on the topic at Penn State, Delaware County Campus. That's what started me writing on affirmative action and the debate on the issue has maintained its relevance.

Yancy: What's your response to some white males who argue that they are victims of reverse discrimination?

Mosley: I think that white males have inherited improved educational, employment, and investment opportunities as a result of restricted opportunities for nonwhites and women. The probability of their achieving certain kinds of positions in society has been enhanced because others have been denied those opportunities. Many white males have expectations that are the result of opportunities denied others and now that this advantage is being withdrawn, many feel threatened. Affirmative action involves giving underrepresented groups that were formally discriminated against improved opportunities, and this means that many white males no longer can expect to get what they otherwise would have gotten.

Yancy: In your essay "Preferential Treatment and Social Justice" you argue that the white male who claims reverse discrimination is really not being wronged against so much as it's really an instance of distributed justice for Black people.

Mosley: Yes, that's exactly right. If nonwhites and women as a group have been denied opportunities and that has enhanced opportunities available to white males, then when distributive justice makes these opportunities available to groups formerly excluded, that reduces the probability that white males will achieve what they traditionally would have expected. White males have developed expectations that if they achieve certain levels of merit then they should get certain kinds of rewards, but now those rewards are less probable because formerly excluded groups are now able to compete for those same opportunities. The white males' probability of getting those positions is decreased even though he has met all of the traditional require-ments for getting them. So, it's not unnatural that they would feel resentful. The question is whether they are morally justified in feeling resentful. And I don't think that they are.

Yancy: Why aren't they?

Mosley: Because they are the recipients of ill-gotten goods. Even though they have satisfied traditional requirements for receiving those opportunities, once it is determined that they no longer have a right to them then they can't morally assume that they should get them.

Yancy: What is your response to those who argue that affirmative action is ineffective because it primarily benefits Black people who are already skilled and does not benefit truly disadvantaged Black people?

Mosley: I argue in *Affirmative Action: Social Justice or Unfair Prefer-ence* that this is what affirmative action was intended to do. That is, it was intended to benefit those who had qualifications but whose qual-ifications were being underutilized because of discrimination. It was well-known and a common fact during the '40s, '50s, and early '60s that many Black people with advanced degrees could only get jobs in the post office. The best occupation that many Black people with M.A. and Ph.D. degrees could get was in the post office. And other Black people used to laugh at them saying, "Well, what's the good of all that education when you're here doing the same job I'm doing and I only finished the eighth grade?" Affirmative action was a recognition of and corrective for the fact that this country was underutilizing the talent that it had available among African-Americans.

Yancy: But affirmative action was never designed to specifically rem-edy or to do away with the so-called Black underclass, right?

Mosley: Never. When affirmative action was introduced the notion of a Black underclass hardly existed. We were just coming out of the economic boom of the '50s and affirmative action was designed to utilize qualified Blacks in positions that they had been denied access to. Affirmative action is unjustly criticized for not correcting a situation that it was never intended to address. I think it does give Blacks who are among the least well off hope that if they do become qualified they will find that positions are available to them. Another misconception is that affirmative action has only helped those who are highly educated into executive positions. This too is false. Most of the successes of affirmative action have been in blue-collar occupations: police and fire and sanitation departments. We now have policewomen and firewomen. Many of the major sources of discrimination were labor unions. Keeping Blacks out of the unions kept them from getting apprenticeships that could only be gotten through union membership, and from getting higher paid jobs and seniority. These were not white-collar occupations, but this is where affirmative action has had the greatest impact. But even for these kinds of jobs, applicants have to be qualified. They can't be uneducated, they can't be illiterate. But you don't need a college degree to be a good police[wo]man. Nor do you need to be able to bench press 200 pounds.

Yancy: In your opinion, what maintains the existence of a Black underclass in the United States?

Mosley: I think that it's due to the same developments that have produced an underclass in the rest of the world. As capitalism develops, more and more people become underemployed and unemployed. That's happening among whites here now. And this is why so many whites feel insecure. Jobs are being automated or transferred to places that have cheaper labor. Thus, there are more and more people in this country who, because they don't have the kinds of skills that are required by the new technologies, are out of work or who will never get the kinds of opportunities that their parents got. And if you look around the world, there is growing underemployment and unemployment as people move off farms and into cities. They just have no employment. A similar thing has happened in this country. Now, jobs have moved out of the cities leaving people trapped by racial disinvestment and stereotyping. The need for manual labor is falling and lower levels of human capital among Black people make them disproportionately vulnerable.

Yancy: In your opinion, how do we best eliminate the existence of a Black underclass?

Mosley: How? This is really two questions: How do you eliminate the underclass and how do you eliminate Black overrepresentation among the underclass? Marx predicted that there would be a growing lumpenproletariat. These would not be people who only have their labor to sell, but people who cannot even sell their labor. This is a class of people who are not needed in the economic system, and Marx predicted that this would be a growing part of the population. I propose no solution to this problem. But we can ask why it is that Blacks are more represented among the underclass than other groups? This would address the second question. And I think it is possible to ameliorate that overrepresentation.

Yancy: In what way?

Mosley: By eliminating the factors—institutional and individual—that make Blacks less likely to get opportunities than whites. That is, give Blacks the kinds of schools and opportunities for an education that whites have. Eliminate discrimination or at least introduce counter-vailing procedures or countervailing factors to offset discrimination. That's what preferential treatment does. It offsets the discrimination that exists. I think that people are not "irrational" in having many of the stereotypes they do of Blacks. More often than not, Blacks do not have the kind of educational background their white competitors have. It is thus easy for evaluators to see a Black person and assume that person is not well educated and doesn't have a work ethic. And they discriminate on the basis of such stereotypical beliefs. After four hundred years of segregation and slavery such beliefs have become conventional and commonplace. So, I don't think that it's irrational for people to discriminate against Blacks. But there needs to be some-thing to both discourage and offset that tendency.

Yancy: And when you say it's not irrational you mean, I guess, given the persistence of racism?

Mosley: Yes. In other words, given what most people know about Black people, they are likely to assume that any particular Black per-son is probably from the inner city, probably came from a very bad school, and probably has friends and family who are involved with the criminal justice system, probably has an attitude, etc. Relative to the frequency of such factors among whites, it may indeed be higher among African-Americans, Native Americans, and Hispanics. And for these reasons it is not irrational for people to make such projections. But such trends, though higher in one group than another, still need not characterize the majority of individuals in the group in which it is higher. Nonetheless, many who are qualified are not considered to be qualified simply because such trends become generalized into stereotypes.

Yancy: So, at least one way of addressing the problem of the Black underclass is by exploding these stereotypes?

Mosley: Yes. We must let people see that those stereotypes are just that, mere stereotypes. For any particular individual you have to deal with that person's peculiar historical development—which in most cases probably will not fit the stereotype. But in order to get to that stage people will have to get over their initial inclinations, and affirmative action forces them *not* to operate in accordance with the stereotype that most people would generally accept. Antidiscrimination laws makes discrimination based on racial and sexual stereotypes illegal. Affirmative action requires procedures that require outreach to such historically excluded groups. And preferential treatment acts to offset the reality of continuing individual and institutional discrimination against members of such groups.

Yancy: You've given a few papers addressing the issue of relativism: "Cognitive Relativism," "Paradigms In The Case For Relativism," and one called "Saving Kuhn from Paradigms." To what extent are you a relativist?

Mosley: I think I'm a relativist in the sense that I think that there are many different kinds of capacities and endeavors within which we participate that are in a sense incommensurable. And I don't think we should always be attempting to measure one against another or compare one to the other. Interests may be different, but equally important. As such, the advantage of one over the other is only relative. It's relative in that it makes certain kinds of accomplishments possible, but is limited in that it doesn't make certain other kinds of accomplishments possible.

Yancy: Talk about your relativist position vis-à-vis so-called scientific objectivity.

Mosley: Sure. The philosopher of science Paul Feyerabend emphasized that we shouldn't make science the paradigm of all knowledge. We should remain open to human traditions other than science, instead of believing that science is the paradigm by which every other kind of endeavor ought to be measured. I certainly agree with that. There are many kinds of human endeavors and human traditions that we have. There is a danger of them becoming extinct or atrophied simply because they don't fit the model associated with science. Many argue that even our view of science is jaundiced and misleading. Many philosophers deny that instrumental reason is the only form in which reason manifests itself. Jurgen Habermas, Martin Heidegger, and Hubert Dreyfus would fall within this critical tradition. There are numerous philosophers, and, in particular, philosophers of science, who warn against taking science as the epitome of human cognitive accomplishments.

Yancy: So, you were very much influenced by postmodernism?

Mosley: Yes. I think that doing my dissertation on Kuhn and following through on that debate has influenced me tremendously. Also, I think that it personally compliments my lifestyle, again, being interested both in music and mathematics, formally trained in the latter and informally trained in the former.

Yancy: In an essay entitled "Relativism, Rationalism, and The Sociology of Knowledge," Barry Barnes and David Bloor questioned the claim made by Martin Hollis and Steven Lukes that all cultures share a common core of true beliefs and rationally justified patterns of inference. Do you believe that there are certain common perceptual statements to which all rational persons cannot help but to give assent? And do you believe that there are so-called rules of coherent judgment which we cannot fail to subscribe to?

Mosley: I don't know about that. On the one hand, I think that it is possible for human beings to communicate across cultures. I think that if I was put in almost any culture then I would, over the years, learn to appreciate that culture and be able to communicate within that culture and within whatever set of beliefs that had developed within that culture. It's almost like learning another language, you see? And, of course, I could learn another language.

Yancy: Even if that language involved, let's say, a defiance of the law of the excluded middle?

Mosley: But of course. I mean, even contemporary quantum mechanics is often interpreted as denying the law of the excluded middle. That's one of the paradoxes of quantum mechanics. Is the electron here or there, wave or particle? Is it P or not-P? In many cases it's not possible to say either P or not-P.

Yancy: Would it be correct to say that within a quantum state, if you will, we may have a case of both P and not-P?

Mosley: That's simply the flipside of rejecting the law of the excluded middle. An electron is both a wave (P) and a particle (non-P). Neils Bohr argued that under different conditions we must conceive of quantum phenomena in different ways and I think we have to extend that approach to macrophenomena as well. All knowledge, in my humble opinion, is situation specific.

Yancy: And what about perceptual judgments? Are they also situation specific?

Mosley: Yes. Is x red? Well, it depends on the kinds of conditions that we're looking at x under. Scientists suggest that the color red is really reflected light waves of such and such angstroms. Well, under what conditions does x reflect light waves of the appropriate wave length? You can't leave such questions out of the picture, even though we tend to in trying to make objective statements and in acting as if bodies have properties that are independent of us as observers.

Yancy: Do we also find epistemological relativity in the area of mathematics?

Mosley: There are some who believe so. David Bloor argues that different cultures can develop different kinds of mathematics. He makes his case primarily from the fact that in the development of Western mathematics, mathematics has taken very different forms. Our concept of number, for instance, is very different now than it was, say, among the Greeks. He and Salomon Bochner (*The Role of Mathematics in the Rise of Science*) argue that the very way in which we conceive of mathematics is radically different now than it was two thousand years ago. If, within the same cultural tradition, mathematics has been different within different eras then it is easy to extrapolate that to different cultures.

Yancy: Is your focus within the philosophy of science more geared toward the problematics involved in the natural sciences or the social sciences?

Mosley: The kind of material I have been interested in shows that it is often very difficult to distinguish natural from social phenomena. And a central objective of the sociology of science movement has been to show that the development of the natural sciences is not independent of social interests and influences. Given the interplay between the two areas, I don't know if I would classify myself as primarily interested in the one or the other.

Yancy: Is there a way to talk about the nature of reality independently of a paradigm?

Mosley: I don't think so. I view reality as a construction that reflects our interests and our historical development. And for human communities that have a different tradition, who have developed different "technologies" and have different interests, then reality might be perceived in significantly different ways. So, I certainly do think that reality is a social construction. Is there something that exists independently of that construction? Well, there is something, but you can't say what because whenever you say what it is then you put it within categories that reflect your own tradition. In a way it's like asking, "Well, is there sound in the forest when no one hears it?" We can say there's no sound if there is no one who hears it, but there would still be pulses in the air, sound waves. Would there be sound waves if there were no human beings to conceive of them in that way? Well, no, there wouldn't be. Would there be anything? Yes, there would be something, but we can't say what it would be because you can only say what it would be from your perspective, a particular tradition that says what *is*. The categories that we use are historical constructions. So, as far as independent reality is concerned, all that we can say is that there is something there, but in order to say what is there we have to use the conceptual and technical tools that are the products of our peculiar historical evolution.

Yancy: How do we talk about the superiority of a given culture's ontology? For example, Western science posits the existence of electrons, leptons, muons, etc., as being casually linked to certain observable phenomena, but another culture may talk about observable phenomena in terms of the casual power of ancestors for example. How do we decide upon the superiority of these perhaps incommensurable ontologies?

Mosley: I wouldn't try to rank them in terms of superior/inferior. What could one possibly use as a standard of measure in order to say that this is better than that? One would have to in some sense stand outside of both systems in order to measure them against some independent, objective standard. I think one of the major points of agreement in contemporary philosophy is that there is no such "view from nowhere." You're always standing within a particular tradition. It's an illusion to think that it's possible to stand outside of traditions and measure them one against the other. Kuhn denies that the Copernican system is superior to the Ptolemaic, because the two conceptual systems are really asking different questions. They're not trying to do the same things. Moving from one conceptual system to another is not just a shift in ontological frameworks, but a shift in interests as well. People are trying to do things in one system that they aren't even trying to do in another one.

Yancy: I see. Jarrett Leplin interprets Adolf Grunbaum's essay, "Can A Theory Answer More Questions than One of its Rivals," as implying that there are no transtheoretic criteria for the legitimacy of questions. In other words, the legitimacy of a question is relativized to a conceptual system. Hence, the Einsteinian conceptual system answers more Einsteinian questions and the Newtonian conceptual system answers more Newtonian questions.
Mosley: Exactly the idea.

Yancy: How does your identity square with your overall philosophical worldview?
Mosley: I think it's quite consistent. You probably noticed that I make a lot of references to music and mathematics as relative conceptual orientations and I also talk about magic and science, again two things that I have been involved in personally. And so I think that in many ways my personal experiences have influenced the kind of philosophical positions that I have developed.

A Selection of Published Works of Albert Mosley

Books

Affirmative Action: Social Justice or Unfair Preference? with Nicholas Capaldi (Lanham, MD: Roman and Littlefield, 1996).
African Philosophy: Selected Readings (Englewood Cliffs, NJ: Prentice Hall, 1995).
An Introduction to Logic: From Everyday Life to Formal Systems, with Eulalio Baltazar (Needham Heights, MA: Ginn Press, 1984).

Articles

"The Philosophy of Science and African Philosophy," in *African American Philosophy*, Tommy L. Lott and John Pittman, eds. (Oxford: Blackwell, 1997).

"Are Racial Categories Racist?" in *The Significance of Race: African-American Philosophical Essays*, Maurice Wade, ed. (Philadelphia: Temple University Press, 1997).

"Racism," in the *Encyclopedia of Philosophy: Supplement*, D. M. Borchert, ed. (New York: Macmillan, 1996).

"Pluralism," in the *Encyclopedia of Philosophy Supplement*, D. M. Borchert, ed. (New York: Macmillan, 1996).

"Negritude, Nationalism, and Nativism: Racist or Racialist?" in *African Philosophy: Selected Readings*, A. Mosley, ed. (Englewood Cliffs, NJ: Prentice Hall, 1995).

"In Defense of Affirmative Action," in *Applied Social and Political Philosophy*, Elizabeth Smith and H. G. Blocker, eds. (Englewood Cliffs, NJ: Prentice Hall, 1994).

"Introductory Logic at a Predominantly African-American Open Admissions Urban University," *The APA Newsletter on Philosophy and the Black Experience* 91, no. 1 (spring 1992).

"Affirmative Action and the Urban Underclass," in *Philosophy and the Black Underclass*, William Lawson, ed. (Philadelphia: Temple University Press, 1991).

"Preferential Treatment and Social Justice," in *Terrorism, Justice, and Social Values*, Creighton Peden, ed. (Lewiston, NY: Edwin Mellen Press, 1990).

"The Effect of Logic on Subsequent Academic Performance," in *Papers in the Social Sciences* 5 (1985–86).

"Paradigms and the Case for Conceptual Relativism," in *Papers in the Social Sciences* 3 (1983–84).

"Negritude, Magic and the Arts," in *Philosophy Born of Struggle: An Anthology of Afro-American Philosophy from 1917 to the Present*, Leonard Harris, ed. (Dubuque, IA: Kendall/Hunt, 1983).

"The Metaphysics of Magic: Practical and Philosophical Implications," in *Second Order: An African Journal of Philosophy* (Ile-Ife, Nigeria: University of Ife Press, Ile-Ife, Nigeria, July 1978).

[eight]

Anita L. Allen

Anita LaFrance Allen currently is associate dean of research and scholarship at Georgetown University Law Center, professor of law and adjunct professor of philosophy. She earned her B.A. in philosophy, classics, and literature from New College. Her M.A. and Ph.D. degrees in philosophy are from the University of Michigan, and she earned her J.D. degree from Harvard Law School. She has taught at Harvard Law School, the University of Pittsburgh Law School, Carnegie Mellon University, and the University of Pennsylvania. Her areas of specialization are legal philosophy, constitutional law, the right to privacy, reproductive health, race law, and law and literature. Her articles and reviews have appeared in *The Philosophical Forum*; *The Harvard Journal of Law and Public Policy*; the *Encyclopedia of African American History and Culture*; the *Encyclopedia of Bioethics*; *Iowa Law Review*; *Harvard Women's Law Journal*; *Southern California Law Review*; *Stanford Law Review*; *The Philosophical Review*; *Ethics*; *Blackwell's A Companion to Feminist Philosophy*; and more. She is also author of *Uneasy Access: Privacy for Women in a Free Society*. (A selected citation list of Anita L. Allen's published works can be found at the end of the interview).

Anita L. Allen
Georgetown University

George Yancy: When and where were you born?
Anita L. Allen: I was born in 1953 at Fort Worden, Washington, a military installation.

Yancy: Provide a sense of what it was like growing up on a military post.
Allen: I lived at Fort Worden for only about a year. Thereafter I lived with my parents and siblings at Fort McClellan, Alabama; Fort Gordan, Georgia; Fort Benning, Georgia; Schofield Barracks, Hawaii; the Atlanta Army Depot; and the Indiana Ammunition Plant. I grew up believing that I was lucky to have a father in the army. For a long time I was afraid of the civilian world, which I associated with economic peril and racism.

Yancy: During your early educational training, did you experience the sting of segregationism?
Allen: To be perfectly honest, although my first experiences with formal education were in forcibly segregated schools, I was not aware of it. I had no consciousness of race at all until I was in the second grade, living in Hawaii. I remember the exact day that I learned the concept of race. I was playing out of doors on a sunny day with a German-American friend. She was a very fair skinned girl, with short strawberry blond curly hair. I was not wearing shoes, but she was. Noticing my bare feet, she said, "Oh, you don't have to wear shoes because you're Black and you can't get dirty." Her comment puzzled me. I knew that I got dirty and I knew that my skin was brown. What could she mean? I went home and asked my mother whether I was Black. My mother was standing over the kitchen stove straightening her hair. She paused and gave me a loving little lecture. She pointed to the knob on the stove and she said, "Now, that's Black and you're brown, but many people will call you names. You're a Negro." She didn't like the word Black, so she taught me how to say "Negro" and told me how some people would say "Nigra" or "Nigger," but that was a mistake because I was actually a Negro. "Knee," she said, pointing to hers, "grow." That's how it's supposed to sound. That's how I learned that people were classified by categories of race, and I belonged to a maligned category. While I was going to the Jim Crow kindergarten I

had no sense of race. I was just a little kid going to a school full of strangers, far from home.

Yancy: Did your parents assume an active role in terms of encouraging you to achieve educationally?

Allen: My parents, both of whom were born in Atlanta, Georgia, made sure that I went to school and Sunday school. They made sure that I went to school well fed and well clothed. Both of my parents were high school dropouts who earned diplomas and took college courses as adults. My mother became pregnant when she was about fifteen, and did not want her daughters to share her fate. While not having a lot of education, my parents placed a great emphasis on it. I was encouraged to do well in school. And I did.

Yancy: During elementary school and junior high were you showing any early signs of philosophical inquisitiveness?

Allen: I became interested in philosophy when I was about fourteen. It happened through religion. My parents sent me to Sunday school, church and, every summer, Bible school. I memorized many Bible passages and was fascinated by theological concepts. I eventually began to ask myself questions about the nature of God and the cosmos suggested by religion. I discovered secular philosophy and academic theology. When I was in high school I read books by Paul Tillich, the theologian; I read Søren Kierkegaard; and some of the medieval philosophers, like St. Anselm and Thomas Aquinas. From there I tackled the existentialists—Sartre, especially. I read a fair amount of philosophical poetry, too.

Yancy: Upon graduating from high school did you know that you wanted to study philosophy?

Allen: When I left high school I thought I would be a doctor. I wrote poetry, and I read philosophy but I did not know that philosophy was a living academic discipline on which one could base a career.

Yancy: When did you realize that this was the sort of thing that you wanted to study?

Allen: I went to a small liberal arts college, an experimental college called New College in Sarasota, Florida. In spite of the fact that they had a very weak science program, I could have done premed work there. My father's hope was that I would join the army and become an army doctor. But in order to enlist, one had to be eighteen. Since

I skipped a year of high school, I was too young at the time to enter the army's medical program. I was planning to enlist after my freshman year of college. Yet, once I got away from my parents the idea of becoming a doctor just disappeared and I pursued the humanities. I did literally no science at all in college. I indulged in the intellectual subjects that I liked best. Poetry, philosophy, and literature took precedence in my schedule over any potential science and math curriculum.

Yancy: Who there influenced you most?

Allen: B. Gresham Riley, who was a Charles Sanders Peirce scholar and a scholar of pragmatism generally. He took a personal interest in me. The other big influence was Bryan Norton, who also took a personal interest in my education. Bryan Norton's specialty was logical positivism and empiricism. Norton was my senior thesis advisor. He encouraged me to apply to the University of Michigan for my Ph.D. It was through his influence that I ended up in graduate school at the University of Michigan. I was also influenced by my Latin teacher, Lyndon Clough. To a lesser degree, I was influenced by philosopher Douglas Begrin. He taught phenomenology, existentialism, and European philosophy. I took several classes from him, but never got to know him well.

Yancy: Your senior thesis was on Rudolph Carnap's philosophy of language, right?

Allen: Yes.

Yancy: Why Rudolph Carnap?

Allen: Because Bryan Norton was a Rudolph Carnap scholar and because the big question for me at this time was "Is metaphysics possible?" Having spent my teenage years and early twenties looking at questions of religion and the possibility of metaphysics and religion, I found that Rudolph Carnap's rejection of metaphysics was vexing. My thesis was about the significance of the linguistic turn in Anglo-American philosophy and its significance for the possibility of doing ethics and metaphysics meaningfully.

Yancy: Within the framework of that thesis project, were you in agreement with Carnap or not?

Allen: The thesis was very descriptive and it was also a very immature piece of work. I do not recall whether I actually came to any position.

I probably described Carnap's project and compared it to the project of metaphysicians without really taking a definite stand. But I think I was pretty convinced by the pragmatists and empiricists that conventional beliefs about religion and ethics could not be established in any scientific or logical way. Since I was persuaded that ethics and religion were matters of bare faith, I went to graduate school with that bent of mind. I was puzzled in a way by the dominant view of ethicists at the University of Michigan that ethics could be made rational.

Yancy: Were you reading Wittgenstein at the time?

Allen: I read Wittgenstein in college. I wrote one or two papers on his work. I also read Martin Heidegger. I went to Germany for a semester and I made reading Heidegger's *Was ist Metaphysik?* my project. I read and studied that text. I read some Habermas, too.

Yancy: Were there other African-Americans studying philosophy at New College?

Allen: There were barely any other African-Americans. There were only about three of us on campus. There were never more than five of us on campus at one time and there were no other African-Americans studying philosophy.

Yancy: Now, who influenced you at Michigan?

Allen: There is not a single person at Michigan whom I could point to and say, "This person was my mentor." What I can say is that I enjoyed taking classes from William Frankena, the ethicist. I remember very vividly he taught a course that advanced the question: Why should I be moral? That was a very engaging course. I also enjoyed Jaegwon Kim under whom I studied metaphysics. If I'd been a little more courageous I would have written my thesis with Jaegwon in metaphysics, but I think that I began to panic about my future a little bit. I went to graduate school at a time when there were all these signs posted indicating that there were no jobs in philosophy and it was very hard to get jobs. So, I thought I needed to do a more practical dissertation and have a more practical set of career goals. I began to think that some day I might become an academic administrator. So, I concocted a thesis in philosophy of education and political theory that was about Hobbes's and Locke's theories of parental authority and children's rights. And I say "concocted" because it had little to do with anything I had studied in graduate school. I didn't have anyone giving me good advice. Although I was pretty well respected by my teachers and I got good grades in graduate school, no one exactly took me under their wing and made me their student. When it came to my thesis I was on my own and ended up taking as my thesis chair Richard Brandt. He was a very good philosopher in ethics and quite famous, too. I would not call him a mentor. I do not think that my dissertation, "Rights, Children, and Education," represented me at my most genuine, creative, or best.

Yancy: Say a little more about Jaegwon's course in metaphysics. What was so influential about that course?

Allen: I discovered in that class that I was pretty good at analytic manipulation. I remember reading David Wiggins's work on identity. I found analytic metaphysics fun. I liked taking tightly drawn arguments and poking holes in them. Yet as a Black person it felt odd to sit around asking such questions like "How do you know when two nonexistent objects are the same?" There you are in the middle of the era of affirmative action, civil rights, women's movements, etc., and you're sitting around thinking about nonexistent objects and how to tell when they are the same. On the one hand I was fascinated by these questions and Wiggins's version of metaphysics; but on the other hand, I was afraid of the uselessness of such inquiries.

Yancy: You went on to get the J.D. from Harvard Law School, right?
Allen: Yes.

Yancy: What's the genesis of your interest in the philosophy of law?
Allen: It is tied into my need to escape from the irrelevant that I encountered in graduate school in philosophy. Somewhere along the line, I began to feel that I was going to become an irrelevant, useless person. So I got my degrees, but I moved into more practical areas of philosophy, away from metaphysics, into ethics and political philosophy. When I took my first teaching job, which was at Carnegie Mellon University, I found that teaching the more detached versions of ethics and political theory made me feel bizarre. Sometimes students would ask me questions about the government or about history and I did not have a clue, I knew nothing. It's embarrassing for me to tell you how little I knew about the real world. I never read magazines; I never read newspapers; I rarely watched TV. I was completely cut off from the real world both in terms of my academic life and in terms of my ordinary personal life. I had no contact with the real world and I began to feel as though I might die teaching introduction to logic and

eighteenth-century texts. I decided to pursue law school with the idea that, at minimum, I would make my philosophy courses more relevant. I also thought I might want to become a judge or a lawyer and do something worthwhile.

Yancy: Were there any African-American woman who influenced you at Harvard?

Allen: There were no Black women on the faculty at Harvard between 1981–1984. There were five white women on the Harvard law faculty. I had two Black teachers at Harvard. There was Clyde Ferguson and Christopher Edley. Derrick Bell, whom I had met in Washington, was away from Harvard during my tenure there. He helped me make the decision to go to Harvard, though. I was initially more interested in going to Yale, until I met Bell through work at the NEH.

Yancy: Do you see yourself as doing African-American philosophy?

Allen: I have not given the matter much thought. I see myself as an African-American doing philosophy. The reason I say that is because I do not believe, or I am not convinced, that there's a distinctive African-American approach to philosophy. I am very interested in topics that many other African-Americans are interested in, such as civil rights, affirmative action, poverty, racial classification, and such things. This assures me that I have a connection with African-American thinking and values and culture. I cannot define "African-American Philosophy." The concept doesn't have any definite denotation for me. There are people who've made interesting efforts at carving out a kind of Afrocentric philosophy or Africana perspective. The number of people doing African-American philosophy is very small, and most African-Americans who write philosophy or teach philosophy do not write or teach topics that are related to African-American history or culture. I admire people like Lucius Outlaw and Tommy Lott and Bill Lawson and others who try to focus their work on slavery, etc. But I am not yet persuaded that something called African-American philosophy or an Africana perspective as such has emerged in a clear and salient form. I think it's very interesting to mine the culture for distinct perspectives, but I myself do not believe that a distinct African-American philosophy yet exists. It's not important to me that it exists. It doesn't matter to me if there's an African-American philosophy. What is important to me is whether or not African-Americans are a part of the intellectual life of the nation and whether or not African-American people are well treated by the nation. So, my work has been about, among other things, the treatment of African-Americans in American society.

Yancy: Assuming that there was something called African-American philosophy, would this entail that it would have a distinctive philosophical methodology, worldview, and so on?

Allen: It could be a methodology or it could be a worldview. I do not think that there is either a distinctive worldview or a distinctive methodology. Many African-American male philosophers are interested in issues related to race, politics, government, etc. But I don't think that means that it's distinctive African-American philosophy. I don't think that Bernard Boxill's methodology or his work, for example, is distinctly African-American. I think that any liberal could have written Boxill's work on social philosophy.

Yancy: How does race mediate your philosophical concerns?

Allen: One of the things that it does is that it makes me suspect about the power of logic alone to illuminate the world. I think that being an African-American I am extremely sensitive to and aware of the ways in which logic can be used instrumentally to achieve ends which may be unjust and ignoble. And so whereas I sometimes feel as if my white counterparts are trusting methodologically in a philosophy of what they've learned through logical analysis, I am more suspicious of what seems to be true as a consequence of the application of logical methods to real problems. So, that's one way. I think that the issue of race makes me methodologically skeptical. I also think that race affects the topics I find compelling and interesting. Particularly in the last six years, I have found compelling and interesting such issues that relate to the relative power of individuals vis-à-vis groups, identity, group identity, and selfhood. Gender may mediate my work in philosophy even more than race. With regard to my work concerning reproductive rights, birth control, abortion, and surrogacy, my race causes me to think about how policies might bear on certain racial groups more than on others, or might impact certain racial groups more than others. Issues about distributive justice, equity, and disparate impact are functions of race. ✓

Yancy: How do you understand the nature of race constitution?

Allen: Race is a social construct. Race is a way that our culture has come to sort people. Race is loosely connected to a person's history, their appearance, parentage, and social roles. And if you think very hard about race and try to be precise about it, you quickly end up in tangles and circles of webs of absurdity and contradiction. I think that race has practical utility for distributing public goods and services, today, but I don't think that race is real. I would ideally prefer a world in which there were not distinctions based on race, though there would still be distinctions based on something. It's hard to imagine a world in which people were not sorted according to some categories. I think that the problem with racial categories is that some of them are always deemed less good than others and that the purpose of race has been to divide people into categories of privilege and lack of privilege. Therefore, racial categories are inherently *bad* and it's hard for me to imagine that not being the case. In the last five years or so there has been an attempt to treat all of the races as multiculturally of equal value, but it's still the case that, despite our best efforts, there are negative stigmas and negative assumptions attached to nonwhite races.

Yancy: Do you think that there are some who reject race as a natural ontological kind for the distinct purpose of attempting to undermine the utility value of race in terms of distributive justice?

Allen: There are those who emphasize that race is not ontological with the very purpose of attempting to justify discontinuing discourse and policies that require us to divide people based on race. But there are others, like myself, who, on the one hand, say that race is not ontological and who, on the other hand, can see the practical utility value in continuing to talk about racial categories in order to undo institutions and practices that could have led to discrimination against people who have certain backgrounds and appearances. And, more affirmatively, though here I am less clear, there are those who deny ontological status to race, but who then celebrate race as a surrogate for culture, Black culture, Latino culture or Puerto Rican culture, Asian-American culture, Native-American culture, or Native-American group cultures, etc. Those who take this view feel threatened by any claim on ending discussions of race because they fear that it would also obliterate important cultural distinctions. One shorthand way of saying this is that if you love jazz then you've got to love race. For example, such people would fear the loss of the Black church and all of those spiritual traditions and practices if there was a deemphasis placed on race as a category.

Yancy: And do you see this as a non sequitur?
Allen: Yes.

Yancy: Over the years, how have African-American women fared in the field of philosophy?

Allen: Extraordinarily badly. I gave a talk to the Society for Women In Philosophy (SWIP), in New York, about these issues. As I'm sure you know, there are probably about four or five African-American women in this whole country who have doctorates in philosophy and who have taught, or continue to teach, in universities. I think that the numbers are very bad and that there are reasons for that and that it's an unrealized potential.

With all due respect, what does philosophy have to offer to Black women? It's not obvious to me that philosophy has *anything* special to offer Black women today. I make this provocative claim to shift the burden to the discipline to explain why it is good enough for us; we should be tired of always having to explain how and prove that we are good enough for the discipline. We can always talk about how prejudice and sexism keeps us from being mentored as undergraduates, admitted into graduate school, mentored as grad students, accepted as faculty, and so on, blah, blah, blah. But I think that a more interesting inquiry is whether the field of philosophy can help us achieve our goals. Any Black woman who has the smarts to do philosophy could do law, medicine, and politics with greater self-esteem, greater financial reward, greater visibility, and greater influence. Why bother with philosophy when there's so many other fields of endeavor where one can do better, more easily?

This is the question that must be answered.

Yancy: Specifically, in your opinion, why are there so few professional African-American women philosophers?

Allen: There are a number of factors. One is the lack of role models and mentors; that is, people who would exhibit for Black women the possibility of being a philosopher and secondly people who would encourage Black women to do it and stand by them and show them how it's done. Another factor, I think, is that a lot of Black women are very practical. In other words, we are raised to think that we have to take care of ourselves and to take care of our children and it's very difficult to face philosophy when you have those kinds of expectations put on you by yourself and by others. I do believe that it's not insignificant that the Black women in philosophy who have stuck it out have either delayed having children or who don't have any children, who have delayed marriage or who have gotten divorced. It's very hard to have a "normal" social life and be a philosopher. I think that for many

Black women those kinds of personal sacrifices are not possible. I think that my first marriage was difficult in part because I was a philosopher. I think that it's not an accident that Adrian Piper is unmarried and childless, that Michele Moody-Adams had her first child only very recently, that I didn't have children until I was in my late thirties and forties. We have all struggled mightily. The young women who were on the panel at the SWIP Conference made the point as well that being a philosopher may be just too hard. To have time for reflection, you have to have a certain kind of personal life. Caretaking roles may be obstacles to philosophical work. For a Black woman to not be a caretaker is almost an impossible dream. And so it takes quite a luxurious life, and a well-planned one, in order to avoid the kind of roles that would prevent philosophy, of all things, from being a live option. If you're going to get a Black woman philosopher she's probably going to come out of a very elite setting and a very upper-middle-class background. I haven't done any research on this, but I think it's not by accident that Adrian Piper, Michele Moody-Adams, me, Georgette Sinkler, and Joyce Cook went to elite schools and came out of middle-class backgrounds.

Yancy: I have a few questions concerning your essay "The Role Model Argument and Faculty Diversity." In the case of African-American women philosophers acting as role models, should they act, and I'm thinking specifically here in terms of the categories that you've generated, as ethical templates for the exercise of adult responsibilities, symbols of special achievement or nurturers providing special education services.

Allen: Traditionally, among Blacks, the idea of being a service provider has been the most dominant notion of what it means to be a role model, not just sort of being there, but to be there doing something positive and concrete. And this might well mean having special seminars, programs, office hours, etc. That idea of a role model is a very important one. My role modeling has been more on the lines of being a symbol of achievement, although recently I have become the advisor here at Georgetown for our joint degree in philosophy and law. And I have counseled and mentored a number of young women, and some Black, who want to pursue Ph.D.'s in philosophy. The reason I've been doing more hands-on kinds of special nurturing, and, indeed, I've become a very nurturing type of role model, is because in the past I was more of a symbol of special achievement. That's in part because I think that it's been a little difficult for me to find the right discourse to communicate with young people. I find that my military background, my having gone to white schools, my training in philosophy, these things in a way have made it harder for me to communicate with young people. It's taken a long time to find a comfort level as a means to be useful in a very direct way. The comfortable jargonistic style of speaking that philosophers and lawyers use can alienate poor young people who are coming out of more traditional African-American communities. So, we as professionals have to become, if we have become unilingual, bilingual again or bilingual for the first time and learn how to use a mode of discourse that is accessible to students who want from us the special insights we have to offer them.

Yancy: What are some of the adverse implications of "premising," as you put it, the recruitment of Black women philosophy teachers solely, or primarily, on their role modeling potential?

Allen: First of all, in philosophy the role model argument has not had much impact at all on the recruitment of women. There are so few Black women in philosophy that in so far as we're thought about as special appointments it is primarily in a general affirmative action mode. But in law school, where I have spent the last ten years of my life, the role model argument may have a bigger role in people's thinking. This is in part because law schools think about affirmative action in a much more open and positive way, for the most part, than philosophy departments where there are so few slots available that having the luxury of hiring "role models" simply does not exist. But in any event, the idea of hiring a Michele Moody-Adams or an Adrian Piper as a role model is a complex idea because such people have very busy, complicated lives and busy complicated sets of research priorities that make role modeling a very small part of what they do and can do.

Yancy: Given their complicated lives, perhaps they might be able to act as symbols of special achievement, but as nurturers it might be more difficult, yes?

Allen: Right, and I want to emphasize how few same-kind role-argument model opportunities there are going to be at a school like Indiana or Wellesley. How many Black women are going to come through Wellesley with an interest in philosophy? Not very many. It's almost beside the point to talk about the same-kind role-argument in schools like that, both because the nature of the profession is white, and also because of the nature of the institutions. So, until you get more people in the pipeline to these elite schools, the idea of being a special role model nurturer is a unique but uncommon opportunity. I've been here at Georgetown for ten years, and I've had one African-American student with a serious enough interest in philosophy to pursue a Ph.D. I'm thrilled to say that I did help this Black woman with her application and that she was admitted into Georgetown's Ph.D. program in philosophy.

Let me tell you a story which, to me, highlights some of the problems. Last year I had an interest in possibly applying for a job in a philosophy department and I had an idea of maybe starting a legal studies program through a philosophy department. So, I responded to an advertisement that appeared in *Jobs In Philosophy* and I sent my Curriculum Vitae and some writing samples to the chair of a certain department. I got back in the mail a little postcard saying "Thank you for your application. Please send in 'x' number of recommendations." I was stunned by the form-letter (postcard) reply. There seems to be no interest, or very little interest, by philosophy departments in really trying to attract top-notch people of color, women of color, to their faculties. If you're pointing to the question of what are our role modeling duties and how do we as African-American women or people perform, I think we have to go back and look at where we are and why we are where we are and what we could possibly hope to achieve in the settings in which we find ourselves. In these settings where we're there by a miracle or as a fluke or where there's no programmatic interest in cultivating African-American philosophers, we're lucky to have any students to role model for, as luck would have it.

Yancy: Briefly, what are some of the philosophical and political issues having to do with the concept of privacy in relationship to women?

Allen: I have written a lot about reproductive rights, about abortion, birth control, surrogate parenting, and, most recently, about genetics. Women have achieved a certain amount of autonomy and freedom and control of their lives through a legal ideology of privacy rights. On the other hand, feminists have been hostile to the idea of privacy in the private sector as being sort of a condition of confinement for women. So, a lot of my work is intended to praise privacy rights as useful tools while being sensitive to the fact that the private sphere has been a sphere of confinement for women. Through the surrogacy issue, I first began to think about reproductive rights and privacy in connection to Black women. I explored the whole idea of a surrogate mother and the idea of privacy rights protecting the right to be a surrogate mother or to hire a surrogate mother and the conflicts between ideals of respect for people and the noncommercialization of people coming out of my position about slavery. I was tying together concerns about slavery with concerns about commodifying babies. And so I've written about surrogacy, about adoption, and about genetics and about AIDS from a more racially self-aware perspective where I can see how to talk about women's privacy is important not just from the point of view of middle-class white women, but also from the point of view of poor women of color whose "privacy" is often even more compromised and impossible than the privacy of white women.

Yancy: In what way has your book *Uneasy Access: Privacy for Women in a Free Society* helped to contribute to clarifying the conceptual parameters of women's privacy issues?

Allen: This book has been a good thing for me. It has been a piece of writing that others have been able to use and to get some conceptual clarity about the concept of privacy. What it does is to present a definitional analysis of privacy that people have found useful, to provide some normative guidance on the value of privacy and then to provide some substantive recommendations about the way the law regards women and their privacy that would hopefully make women's lives so much better. I think the book has been analytically useful and also practically useful in shaping the way we can think about constructive reform of privacy-related fields. What I like about the book the most is that up until it was written, most of the feminists who talked about privacy thought about it solely in terms of choices and decisions and not so much in terms of the actual physical experience of being alone in solitude, of what physical and psychological seclusion can mean for a person. I talk about those things in my book. Those things are very important to me, as a person in being alone, and the fruits of creativity that being alone can bear have always been very important to me, and, I think, for a lot of people who are authors and scholars.

Yancy: At the end of the work you maintain that women's privacy has already acquired new and better meaning. Would you elaborate on that?

Allen: In the nineteenth century the kind of privacy that women were surrounded by and that was encouraged was basically the idea of modesty, of being at home wearing the "proper" clothing, of being seen but not heard, being in the private spirit, behind the walls of the private spirit in traditional roles. In other words, not making much of oneself. But privacy in the '70s came to mean something bolder and brasher; it came to mean having rights to choose and that those are positive meanings for women who have, again, needed to have some control over their reproductive and social lives. So, the new and better meaning of privacy, I think, would include the idea of choosing, but also the idea of shaping a lifestyle that enables one to have time for individual forms of solitude and seclusion.

Yancy: Why is it that in the mid-'90s, let's say, there is still cause for concern about the ascribability of legal rights to some Blacks?

Allen: Having a right connotes having something that is efficacious, and the failure of American society to solve the problems that slavery and segregation wrought in a context of declining economics of power and resources has meant that some Blacks lead lives that feel rightless. Having rights of equality by virtue of constitutional law or civil rights acts, for some Blacks, means very little at all. If you are a welfare mother living on three hundred dollars a month and your kids are going to school and you have leaky ceilings and there are drug dealers on the corner who threaten you at every turn, then those kinds of lives are really not lives in which people feel that they have rights, individual entitlements, and powers that enable one to shape one's own destiny. Because the '90s has been a period in which many people are still quite poor and have very little by way of security, I think that the idea of having a right seems to be a hollow idea. I have lived in and around Washington, D.C. for many years and almost half of the children are living in poverty. Something like eighteen of every one thousand babies die shortly after birth. The infant mortality rate is huge here, like a Third World country. Every year the public schools are delayed in opening because of the fire hazards and other code violations. Every day someone is murdered in an African-American neighborhood. In Washington, D.C., literally half of the boys never graduate from high school and the rate for girls is only slightly greater than that. So, around here, things are so bad for Black people that talking about rights, again, rings hollow. If there are rights, and we have them, they don't function to make us feel empowered, efficacious, and in control.

Yancy: In your essay "Legal Rights for Poor Blacks" you state that "the law serves to perpetuate the Black underclass when certain philosophical conceptions of what it means to have a right are cemented into the edifice of constitutional jurisprudence." Which philosophical conceptions of what it means to have a right are so cemented such that they perpetuate the Black underclass?

Allen: The best example is the notion that rights are only negative rights to be free from restraints as opposed to positive rights to something. There is no constitutional right to education. There's no constitutional rights to benefits that enable one to cope with poverty. There are no welfare rights that are a part of our constitutional tradition. People in the U.S. do not have rights to things they need. And that tradition of not linking rights to needs, of construing rights as negative and not positive, those two things together mean that there's no jurisprudential power to force the government and force one's neighbors to provide the things that one needs in order to have dignity. In the abortion context, for example, there's a right to obtain an abortion if you can pay for one, but if you're a poor woman on welfare and if you already have four kids and you do not want to have that fifth kid, Medicaid will pay for you to have that kid, but it won't pay for you to have an abortion. Why? Well, you have the right to have an abortion if you can afford one, but not the right to have the government pay for the abortion that you may choose to have. So your choice is not efficacious. It's there but it's not meaningful because you can't afford it.

Yancy: Is American law in the '90s a natural ally of the Black underclass?

Allen: No. The recent affirmative action cases have shown that. The cases which deny the existence of a right to at least a decent public education shows this. I think that fortunately we do have the civil rights laws to protect us against some of the more grotesque invasions of our liberties and our dignity, but we still don't have legal rights which enable private and public entities to construct meaningful remedies to past discriminations. We don't have a right to public education. We don't have a right to welfare benefits. We don't have a right to escape poverty. We don't have a legal system that makes it easy for us to construct solutions to our problems.

Yancy: What must be done legally in this country to bring about justice for Black people?

Allen: A couple things. We need laws that are responsive to needs. We need law enforcement officials who are not bigoted, prejudiced, and violent. It's not an accident that Blacks are suspicious of law enforcement authorities; just look at the police brutality all around the country. We need good laws, we need good people to enforce the laws, criminal laws, and we need a greater degree of understanding and toleration for affirmative action and for remedial remedies. We need to get rid of the notion that somehow we can, in a "color blind" fashion, solve all of our race problems. We need admissions policies to all of our public and private schools that give Black people an equal chance to succeed. We need to have public laws that make housing available on an equal basis and that makes medicine available on an equal basis. Justice within the framework of a libertarian philosophy is viewed in minimalist terms of not having government get in your way. That idea of justice is much too skinny to accommodate the realities of the African-American predicament. So, for me, justice means attending to people's needs and giving them meaningful opportunities to take care of themselves and to participate fully in self-government and the community. This broader notion of justice requires both procedural and substantive laws and law enforcement policies that are sensitive to the needs and deficiencies of our community. In the '60s there was a notion that it would just take a law saying you can't keep Black people out of your restaurant, your skating rinks, your swimming pool, your school, etc., and that those kinds of laws would equalize Blacks and whites. But we've discovered that's not true and so the kind of justice that the next century might provide would be a justice that was self-conscious about the inadequacies of formal equality and of so-called "color blindness."

Yancy: Rejecting any fictive construct like an innate aggressiveness on the part of Black men, how do you account for the statistic that in 1990 although Black men made up about 5.9 percent of the U.S. population, that they made up nearly 50 percent of prison inmates?

Allen: There are a couple of factors. Firstly, how is crime defined? I recently wrote a paper about drug policy. The paper is a response to the view of a couple of libertarian philosophers, Douglas Husak and Jan Narveson. They argue that drugs should be decriminalized and one of their arguments is that the way drug violations are defined has a disproportionate impact on Blacks. And this is true because we define possession of crack as a more serious offense than possession of white powder cocaine. So, you have more crack users being given worse sentences. You have more people who are involved with crack going to jail than you have people using cocaine, and the crack users are typically going to be the poor folks because crack is a cheaper drug and the crack business is a business which is more available to younger and less experienced drug dealers who are so often going to be African-Americans. So, one factor is the way crimes get defined. Behaviors of African-Americans are often defined as crimes, or defined as more serious crimes, requiring more serious punishments. The way we construct what it means to be a drug dealer or drug importer makes it easier for Black men to end up behind bars. So, the way we define and enforce the drug laws results in a very concrete way of there being too many Black men in jail. I have to agree with Narveson and Husak that drug laws disproportionately impact Black men badly, though I disagree with them about decriminalizing drugs. The other factor is that I do believe that law enforcement is more aggressive against minorities than against white people. Police officers go after Blacks, Native-Americans, and Hispanics more aggressively. They associate baggy pants, head scarfs, or feathers, or a tattoo, with criminal behavior, especially when they're sported by a Black person, or a brown person, or red person. Another reason why you have so many Blacks in jail. Also the life of crime may be more attractive, may be regrettably a more rational choice for people living in communities where opportunities for gainful employment that are not illegal are very few and far between. It may be as easy for a kid to get a job as a crack dealer as it is to get a job at McDonalds in the inner city. And so adult men who don't want to work making Xerox copies in a stuffy office could do much better for their families by dealing drugs. There are factors about the kinds of jobs that are available that may lead people into criminal activity. Poor women may find prostitution and other crimes appealing because such things are better than no job at all or better than low-paying minimum-wage jobs in office buildings or such places. So, the lack of good economic opportunities may be a factor that leads some Black men and women to do things which are in fact defined as crimes in our society. I don't think that Black men are inherently more aggressive or violent than white men.

I do, however, think that Black men may suffer from a high degree of frustration and anger that leads them to commit acts of violence because of their social place in our society. I say this because of my own experience with Black men. I have dealt in my personal life with more Black men than white men. I have never been struck by a white man. I've been slapped by an angry Black man, I have had my apartment trashed by an angry Black man, I have been sexually assaulted by angry Black men. I've always explained these occurrences as a matter of "short fuses" caused by too much frustration. So much disrespect comes to Black men from the wider society, they can stand little felt disrespect from a spouse, a sibling, or a classmate.

I remember in college having an argument with a Black male student about the relative advantages of a pacifist to a violent approach to solving disputes. This classmate got so angry with me when he couldn't persuade me of his point of view, that he slapped me in the face. My ex-husband, a very mild mannered, highly educated African-American man, could not deal with my level of self-assertion, my self-confidence, and my independence. The last time we were alone together, I was compelled to call the police. When I hear about Black women calling the cops on their boyfriends or husbands, or Black men going to jail for committing acts of violence, this resonates with me, not because I think that Black men are inherently violent, but because I know that Black men in my own family have used violence as a way of gaining dominance to assert their masculinity in a context in which they believe others have little respect for their masculinity.

Yancy: Two things. Firstly, of course, we don't want to say that all African-American men are like this.
Allen: That's right. But my point is that even educated, professional Black men may become violent. Why is this so?

Yancy: Secondly, we don't want to deny that there are also many white men who obviously slap and rape their spouses.
Allen: That's right, too. Mass murderers tend to be white men. White men blew up the Federal Building in Oklahoma. The Unabomber is a white man. Jeffrey Dahmer, the cannibal-murderer is a white man. If you take these four things together—(1) frustration with disrespect; (2) the criminal law enforcement policies of this country; (3) how crime gets defined; and (4) poverty and lack of education—it is not surprising that Black men would end up in jail in larger numbers.

Yancy: In your book on privacy you talk about prostitution and the good life. In there you maintain that prostitution is not a selection of the good life. What is the good life? That's an old philosophical question.
Allen: I actually have fairly definite opinions about what the good life is. I think that the good life is a life in which a person lives with a healthy mixture of solitary and group activities. It's a life in which there is a tremendous development of the mind, an active mind, a cre-

ative mind, that's cultivated, not just in childhood but throughout one's life. There are opportunities for cultivating one's life that are actually seized upon. So that the good life involves a continual series of creative and intellectual explorations that tax and challenge the mind. It is a life that's full of ethical self-awareness and moral self-awareness, and a life that involves bringing young people into the world which are healthy and happy. For me, the good life includes taking care of children and cultivating the next generation in a very positive way. The good life involves knowing the world, traveling. It involves having an appreciation of nature and being engaged with nature. I'm a gardener, and so for me, the good life involves having a relationship with Mother Earth. The good life involves minimizing divisions among people. Overcoming racial prejudice is a very important part of there being any hope for people in general in this country enjoying the good life. But, for me, education, thinking, traveling, creativity, whether it's poetry, or gardening, or singing, or playing an instrument, dancing, all those things are part of the good life. Prostitution is not part of the good life because prostitution is premised on economic urgency, on the objectification of the female body, and an overvaluation of sex relative to other human goods. So, it's not part of the good life.

Yancy: Which feminist thinkers have had an impact on your philosophical consciousness?

Allen: I was influenced by Charlotte Perkins Gilman. She was a late-nineteenth-century white utopian feminist who wrote a book called *Women and Economics.* She wrote about privacy in a way which I found remarkably contemporary when I first read it. Simone de Beauvoir also had an influence on me. When I was young I was very interested especially in existential philosophy. Catharine A. MacKinnon's work caused me to crystallize points of agreement and disagreement that I have both with traditional liberal thinking and feminist thinking. I was also influenced by Ruth Gavison, who is an Israeli philosopher who influenced my thinking about privacy. More recently Patricia Williams has been important. Her work emboldened me to think and speak publicly about my experiences. In a sense, I would say that the entire Northeast collective of women law teachers, as a feminist enterprise, during the late '80s and early '90s, greatly influenced me by making it possible for me, for the first time in my life, really to speak and to write openly about gender and race. Prior to this experience, a lot of my thinking on such issues had been quite private and personal and had never been published. And I think that if you look at my writing before and after that experience you will find more narrative, more personal expression, a livelier and more engaged style. All of this is due to the confidence that that group imparted to me.

Yancy: What's your overall philosophical project?

Allen: I would start by saying that I have spent the last ten years in a law school and I don't view myself as a philosopher in the same way that I suspect Lucius Outlaw views himself as a philosopher. I view myself as an intellectual who is interested in philosophy, law, culture, society, government, and all kinds of things. So, when you ask, "What is your overall philosophical project?" I hesitate because I don't normally think of my work in those terms. I have ongoing writing projects right now which are very important to me. My goal for myself is to continue to write about things that matter.

Yancy: So tie this back into how this reflects your identity.

Allen: My identity combines my roles as professor, dean, mother, wife, daughter, sister, and friend. All these things are who I am right now. So keeping a balance, keeping enough of the good life in my life right now is very difficult. I'm working hard at trying to live out my ideals of a good life in a situation in which I have so many competing roles that it is a challenge to do anything as well as I would like to do it. I am happy to have had some one or two splendid successes.

A Selection of Published Works of Anita L. Allen

Books

Privacy: Cases and Materials, with Richard Turkington and George Trubow (Houston: John Marshall Press, 1992).

Uneasy Access: Privacy for Women in a Free Society (Lanham, MD: Rowman and Littlefield, 1987).

Articles

"Reproducing Norms: Recent (mainly White) Feminist Perspectives," *Hypatia* (fall 1997).

"Genetic Privacy: Emerging Concepts and Values," in *Genetic Secrets,* Mark Rothstein, ed. (New Haven: Yale University Press, 1997).

"Privacy and Feminism," *A Companion to Feminist Philosophy,* in Alison Jaggar and Iris Young, eds. (Oxford: Blackwell, 1997).

"Forgetting Yourself," in *Feminists Rethink the Self,* Diana Meyers, ed. (Boulder: Westview Press, 1996).

"The Half-Life of Integration," *Reassessing the Sixties*, in Stephen Macedo, ed. (New York: W. W. Norton, 1996).

"The Jurispolitics of Privacy," in *Reconstructing Political Theory*, Molly Shanley and Uma Narayan, eds. (Cambridge: Polity Press, 1996).

"Constitutional Privacy," in *A Companion to Philosophy of Law and Legal Theory*, Dennis Patterson, ed. (Oxford: Blackwell, 1996), 139–55.

"Affirmative Action," in *Encyclopedia of African-American Culture and History*, J. Saltman, D. Smith, and C. West, eds. (New York: MacMillan, 1996), 31–40.

"Moral Multiculturalism, Childbearing, and AIDS," in *HIV, AIDS, and Childbearing: Public Policy, Private Lives*, Ruth Faden and Nancy Kass, eds. (New York: Oxford University Press, 1996), 367–407.

"Legal Aspects of Abortion," in *Encyclopedia of Bioethics*, rev. ed., Warren T. Reich, ed. (New York: MacMillan Publishers, 1995).

"Privacy in Health Care," in *Encyclopedia of Bioethics*, rev. ed., Warren T. Reich, ed. (New York: MacMillan Publishers, 1995).

Comment on Angela Davis's "Surrogates and Outcast Mothers: Racism and Reproductive Ethics," in *"It Just Ain't Fair": The Ethics of Health Care for African Americans*, Annette Dula and Sara Goering, eds. (Westport, CT: Praeger, 1994).

With others, *Women and Health Research: Ethical and Legal Issues of Including Women in Clinical Studies* (Washington, D.C.: National Academy Press, 1994).

"Do Children Have a Right to a Certain Identity?" 15 *Rechtstheorie* 109, (1993).

"The Role Argument for Faculty Diversity," 26 *Philosophical Forum* 267, (1992–93).

"Legal Rights for Poor Blacks," in *The Underclass Question*, William Lawson, ed. (Philadelphia: Temple University Press, 1992).

"In the Wake of the Abortion Decision: For Women, Some Solace, New Concern," *Legal Times*, 6 July 1992, 23.

"Legal Issues in Non-Voluntary HIV Testing," in *AIDS and the Next Generation*, Ruth Faden, et al., eds. (New York: Oxford University Press, 1991).

"Reading Afrocentric History," 9 *Law and Inequality Journal* 407 (1991).

"On Being a Role Model," 6 *Berkeley Women's Law Journal* 22 (1990–91).

"The Black Surrogate Mother," 8 *Harvard Blackletter Journal* 17–31 (1991).

"How Privacy Got Its Gender," with Erin Mack, 10 *Northern Illinois Law Review* 441 (1991).

"Surrogacy, Slavery, and Ownership of Life," 13 *Harvard Journal of Law and Public Policy* 139 (1990).

"Women's Privacy and the Law," *Washington Women's Bar Association Newsletter* (March 1989).

"Privacy, Surrogacy and the *Baby M* Case," 76 *Georgetown Law Journal* 1759 (1988).

"Why Does Bork Have Trouble with a Right to Privacy?" *Chicago Tribune*, Op-ed, 29 September 1987.

"Taking Liberties: Privacy, Private Choice and Social Contract Theory," 56 *Cincinnati Law Review* 401 (1987).

"Women and their Privacy: What is at Stake?" in *Beyond Domination*, Carol Gould, ed. (Totowa, NJ: Rowman and Allanheld, 1983), 233–49.

"Retribution, Justice, and Therapy," *The Philosophical Review* (July 1981).

[nine]

Tommy L. Lott

Tommy L. Lott is professor of philosophy at San Jose State University. He earned his B.A. degree in philosophy from California State University, Los Angeles and his M.A. and Ph.D. degrees in philosophy from the University of California at Los Angeles. He has also taught at Stanford University, the University of Massachusetts, Northeastern University, and California State University, Los Angeles. He was chair of the American Philosophical Association Committee on the Status of Blacks in Philosophy, 1993–1996. His areas of specialization are modern philosophy, social and political thought, and Africana studies. His articles and reviews have appeared in *Social Identities*; *Multiculturalism: A Critical Reader*; *Found Object*; *The Philosophical Forum*; *Black Women in the United States: An Historical Encyclopedia*; *History of Philosophy Quarterly*; *The Underclass Question*; *Philosophical Investigations*; *Hobbes: War Among Nations*; *Mind & Language*; *Thomas Hobbes: His View of Man*; *Revue europeene des sciences sociales*; *African American Review*; *Ethics*; *Radical Philosophy Review of Books*; and more. (A selected citation list of Tommy L. Lott's published works can be found at the end of the interview).

Tommy L. Lott
San Jose State University

George Yancy: When and where were you born?
Tommy L. Lott: I was born on December 17, 1946, in Shreveport, Louisiana, but I grew up in Alexandria.

Yancy: Would you say there was something about Shreveport that may have positively impacted your identity in some way?
Lott: I doubt it, because I hated it. I was so glad to leave that I doubt very much that it had any lasting influence. Except in one regard. My mother was a housekeeper for the priest. We were raised as Catholics. So, to the extent that I was an altar boy attending Catholic School, etc., I would say that was more of an influence than just being in Louisiana in a small town. So that's what continued up until my fifth grade, I think. Then we moved to Los Angeles.

Yancy: Did you hate L.A. as much as you hated Shreveport, Louisiana?
Lott: No, I didn't have the same experience. I much preferred living in Los Angeles only because in Louisiana it was segregated. It was the segregated South. We're talking about the '50s. And I can remember, even as a child, all the signs of segregation. And although a lot of people were no longer obeying any of that, it still existed. I can remember being told we couldn't sit in a certain section in the theater. One of the priests took us to the theater once when his sister visited and of course she was from the North so she just assumed we were all going to go in together. And she was quite disturbed, I still remember that, by the fact that we had to separate and sit in different sections.

Yancy: When you got to Los Angeles I guess that was sort of a cultural shock.
Lott: The most interesting thing about Los Angeles was that I experienced it as leaving the country because we came to a very remote section of Watts where there was a Mexican immigrant community. And they only spoke Spanish. And there was only one Catholic church in that part of Watts. San Miguel Parish was the name of it. And I remember being an altar boy. And at that time Latin was still used. So even in a Spanish-speaking or English-speaking congregation they were still using Latin. So I was able to just be an altar boy because of that. And the sermons and everything else was in Spanish.

Actually, I thought I was in Mexico. And it looked like Mexico. There were murals all over the church and later I was to discover that that was a cultural feature that had actually been transported from Mexico.

Yancy: Do you remember any teachers while in Los Angeles, particularly given that this was a formative period, that may have shaped your intellectual consciousness?

Lott: No, most of my educational experience was quite negative. I was deemed an incorrigible by the time I reached the end of the seventh grade and was sent to a reform school.

Yancy: Would you describe yourself during this period as an inquisitive child?

Lott: Yes, very much. I used to read all the books in the rectory. The priest had a library. And I used to just like going in there. It had leather chairs, which was nice and cool in the summer heat and I enjoyed it. My mother, who was very strong on education, taught us how to read almost at the same time I was talking. I mean, I remember being able to read two or three years before I went to school.

Yancy: Were there certain tendencies, certain temperaments that were salient for you as a child that still persist in your adult life?

Lott: I can't think of too much more other than the fact that I have always been outspoken, which has gotten me into a lot of trouble and I think that goes way back. I can remember in the third grade learning how to use profanity. For example, once we were punished by being placed in the hallway on our knees with our heads down lined up against the wall. I spent the whole fifteen-minute recess period cursing, just trying to invent new curse words which became a kind of amusement for the rest of the group. But what I didn't realize was that the teacher was standing over me the whole time.

Yancy: Retrospectively, is there anything in your youth that might act as an index that philosophy would eventually become your field of inquiry?

Lott: I would say that being raised a Catholic and developing a healthy sense of skepticism. I can never forget being told about pagans and then learning that that word was meant to apply to everyone who wasn't a Catholic. Now the funny thing about the school system in Louisiana was that it was based on race, not religion, and the Catholic schools were simply accommodating an overflow from the only other Black high school. This was in Alexandria, Louisiana. At that time they did not have enough room for all the Black kids in public school. The Catholic school was 50 percent non-Catholics and most of my friends were not Catholic so I always had a problem with this kind of Catholic identity I was supposed to develop. As a result, I think there was a questioning of the religion itself. You know, what does it mean to be a pagan, what does it mean to be a Christian, and a Catholic in particular? And that's where I think the skepticism began. I mean, here you have an all-white clergy in an all-Black parish making caste distinctions between Catholics and non-Catholics. And you know, there's this other thing going on in the world, racism. So, there was something to be figured out here. Even as a small child I was puzzled about that. You know, why would I prefer a group of Catholics who segregate? And the church had always taken the position that you had to have white Catholic churches and Black Catholic churches and that never made any sense to me, even as a small child.

Yancy: Talk about your contact with philosophy as an undergraduate.

Lott: Well, I started out at Los Angeles City College and while I was there I had Marie Reichenbach, Hans Reichenbach's wife, as my first philosophy teacher. She taught an introductory class that was very political. However, we read Hans Reichenbach's work, *The Rise of Scientific Philosophy*, which had to do with a logical positivist critique of everything else that was going on in philosophy. But I was immediately won over by reading his work.

Yancy: Besides her course, what other courses did you take?

Lott: I think I took a few other courses that were quite disappointing. I remember taking two other philosophy courses at LACC that were just absolutely boring. I had bad teachers, really bad teachers who couldn't discuss anything. Because anything that bordered on disagreement they were very uptight about and I remember that. But, I had a lot of other English classes where we read Albert Camus and a lot of interesting people who I later learned to identify as philosophers. I had taken a comparative religions class and we did Eastern religions, which was very interesting. So I always used arguments that I picked up reading Bertrand Russell and other people that Marie Reichenbach turned me on to. Even in my writing for other courses I think I had already become a philosophy student in terms of style and content but a formal commitment was not made until I transferred to California

State, L.A. as a psychology major. But I was dissuaded by being told at the time of registration that the degree required another year of statistics and that the statistics courses that I had taken at the community college were not adequate. And so I immediately went to the next table, which was for philosophy, and signed up as a philosophy major. I didn't take anymore statistics.

Yancy: So which four-year college did you eventually transfer to?

Lott: California State University, Los Angeles. So, this experience of being told about requirements in statistics happened when I registered as a transfer student at Cal. State, L.A. And that's when I became a philosophy major which was pure happenstance.

Yancy: Now, at California State University were there particular professors who influenced you most?

Lott: Oh yes, I had actually decided upon the dissertation topic that I eventually wrote at UCLA as a result of my work with my advisor Tom Annese. He had done work in philosophy of mind. He was a very good teacher. Very high level for a state college. I mean, he would teach classes that only four or five students would take. It was very intense. He had written a dissertation with David Kaplin on actions and the body at UCLA. And we did an independent study and several seminars structured around philosophy of mind. You know, central at that time, and you have to remember that that was late '60s early '70s, G. E. M. Anscombe's book on intentions was quite popular still. And Annese introduced me to that book and to Wittgenstein, through Anscombe actually. And that's where I decided to write on this notion of knowledge without observation that Anscombe had advanced. The title of Anscombe's book was *Intention*. In that book she argues for a notion of intention that turns on a discussion of what she calls knowledge without observation. That becomes a criterion for what constitutes an intentional act.

Yancy: So, Anscombe would reject B. F. Skinner's claim, which he makes in the book *Science and Human Behavior*, that first-person intentional announcements, for example, "I am about to go home," are based upon observations of some sort.

Lott: That's definitely something that she would reject. For instance, I need not observe my own behavior to know what my own intentions are. I need not observe anything to know what my intentions are. It's not like there is something that I have to find out about. Now,

Anscombe goes a step further as she maintains also that when I raise my arm as a consequence of some intention that I have I don't have to observe my arm, not only to know that I intended to raise it, but to know that the act was even performed. And see that's why I take her on in my dissertation because it always struck me that that entailed too much. You can't know the position of a limb, it has always seemed to me, without knowing something on the basis of observation. But she actually argues against that and she is following Wittgenstein in that regard. So, what I did in the dissertation is indicate Cartesian reasons for thinking that observations of some sort, kinesthetic sensations, are involved in the process that results in our knowing bodily positions. But I come out on her side. I think that from an epistemological standpoint, one need not be in a position to observe oneself in order to know, for instance, that one is standing up rather than doing a headstand. You don't have to look in the mirror to know that. So, to some extent I sustained her argument with some skeptical concerns about how much it entails.

Yancy: On this whole issue of the ontological constitution of mind are you an idealist, a behavioralist, or closer to a Wittgensteinian view?

Lott: I used to be a Wittgensteinian but I think now I am more of a functionalist. I'm kind of a Cartesian functionalist. I think there is kind of an epiphenomenon that is generated in these intentional systems which count as a substance. So that brings in Descartes, I think. Other than that I think I am a functionalist. You know, a physicalist of some sort.

Yancy: Many African-American philosophers have described their sense of pursuing philosophy as a passion from which they could not escape. Would you say that philosophy for you, at this particular juncture, was an inexorable passion?

Lott: No, I would say the opposite. My passion was music. I played the trumpet, and because it was such a dead end, philosophy became therapy for having to give up my real passion. So, I would say far from it. And philosophy just happened to be something that happened to be the easiest thing to do for me. It did not require the hard work with no payoff that I had experienced doing work in other areas. ✓

Yancy: Who did you work with at UCLA in terms of your dissertation?

Lott: I worked with Rogers Albritton who specialized in the philosophy of Wittgenstein.

Yancy: Was Albritton the most influential on the direction of your thinking at that point?

Lott: No. I had actually published three papers before I wrote the dissertation. And two were in political philosophy. I had written on Thomas Hobbes because I had been a student of Greg Kavka's. And at UCLA the system had just undergone a change when I arrived. We had a large class of first-year grad students that year. We had about sixty students. So they decided that the ten-year plan, the average length of time people were taking at UCLA to finish a thesis was ten years, should be curtailed to five or six. So they came up with this idea that they would let people write propositions rather than take these horrendous preliminary examinations. And they changed the exam system to a first-year exam after which you would just get an M.A. But even if you passed it sometimes they would decide to just wipe you out of the program. And you could not pass and still be accelerated in the program. It was a way to evaluate you after the first year. But your real work would start with the writing of propositions. You had to write several propositions in value theory and metaphysics and epistemology. Now, my work in value theory was on Hobbes.

Yancy: The three pieces that you had published were all on Hobbes?

Lott: Two on Hobbes and one on George Berkeley.

Yancy: Why the philosophy of George Berkeley?

Lott: Well, I had to write the other proposition in metaphysics and epistemology. I hadn't taken any courses from Albritton yet, though I eventually became his teaching assistant. But my first proposition was on Berkeley because I had taken a philosophy of perception course taught by a guy named Robert Yost. He eventually became my dissertation advisor when Albritton was sick. But I wrote a proposition that he and Robert Adams read and the proposition won the Rudolph Carnap Essay Award in the department. So I presented an excerpt from that. In total it was about forty pages and I presented approximately fifteen pages to the World Congress meeting, about ten years later. It had been written in '73. It was eventually published in Brighton, England, somewhere, but was written ten years earlier.

Yancy: And what was the main focus?

Lott: I was giving my take on Berkeley's theory of visual depth perception. So, it was on *The New Theory of Vision*. It was the philosophy of perception, literally.

Yancy: I am thinking here of William James's discouragement of Du Bois's pursuit of philosophy. Were there ever any professors who were discouraging of your pursuing philosophy?

Lott: Oh yes. All of the time. All the time. But, you know, that didn't really mean anything, because after being deemed an incorrigible there was nothing else they could say to me. I wasn't in college for them, so it didn't matter what they thought. So I was impervious to that. And that's still going on. I see that right now in the whole structure of the profession.

Yancy: I have questions around that but let me first ask, do you construct yourself as an African-American philosopher?

Lott: Definitely. It has to do with two things. One, it is very important that certain subjects get treated and that means subjects pertaining to race and African-American culture in particular. But also the critical stance that African-Americans have developed from their cultural base when studying and viewing and even appropriating European thought is a very important ingredient. Look, I was told that you have to write in value theory. I hated ethics. I mean, with a passion I hated ethics. But then I discovered Hobbes and he seemed to have embraced a view of morality that fit, more than anything I have ever studied, the African-American experience. And part of what I've attempted to articulate, as a Hobbes scholar, I believe, is that reading of Hobbes. I have also pushed that reading, in a lot of cases, without even discussing explicitly anything pertaining to race or culture or Black people, but I have recently written on Hobbes's notion of slavery and so on as a way to more or less bridge that gap. But even as I look at his theory of motivation or his theory of obligation, I'm looking at it from a Black perspective. So, one point is that the subjects themselves, for example slavery, should be discussed by African-American philosophers. You know, questions of economic justice or injustice should be discussed by African-American philosophers. You can just go down the list of issues that are quite philosophical that have a direct bearing on the welfare of Black people as a group. So, there is this notion of African-American philosophy as a discipline or an area that is devoted to examining those types of issues. But then there is also the study of European thought that is equally important, especially since it can be done by an African-American philosopher from what I consider a critical stance that's informed by our experiences, our history, our culture. So, I think in both ways you can be an African-American philosopher. So, in a sense, if I had just written and taught courses only on modern philosophy, Hobbes, Descartes, Spinoza, Leibniz, Locke, Berkeley, whomever, there would still be a way in which I could claim an African-American identity. But, in fact, I teach both. I teach Black studies courses and what we now call Africana and African-American philosophy. I mean, those are officially recognized disciplines and we are doing research in them.

And let me also add that as a grad student, I had Bernard Boxill as an instructor. He would teach seminars on Negritude, for instance. He taught a survey course on the history of Black intellectual thought, basically. But then I also had Angela Davis who was teaching Hegel. And she taught a course on dialectical materialism. So there is a sense in which they too have always been a major part of my educational experience. So, in my publication record I have stuff on Descartes, Berkeley, and whomever, that is just straight Eurocentric philosophy, but on the other side I am recognized as someone who does work in African-American philosophy as well, and Black studies, which is not even philosophy in some cases, it is more cultural studies. This was in the early '70s at UCLA. Angela came in '69 and Boxill taught there all the way up to '73 or '74. So, although my dissertation was in philosophy of mind, a lot of the courses I took and a lot of what I studied as a student was in fact African-American philosophy.

Yancy: Now you've served as the chairperson for the APA Committee on Blacks in Philosophy, right?
Lott: Yes.

Yancy: What is the purpose of the APA Committee on Blacks in Philosophy?
Lott: Well, if I understand it, it was a committee that was deemed necessary to promote the interests of African-American philosophers by ensuring that they're included in the program and that the concerns of the African-American community, you know, students in departments, professors going through tenure, get represented in the organization. So the idea was to have a proactive group that would, in fact, ensure that that happens.

Yancy: As a chairperson, how have you been able to personally affect the number of Blacks in the profession?
Lott: There are a lot of ways you can do this but I think the main one is to try to get policies and practices shaped so that there is an expectation on the part of the board of directors and the top brass in the

organization to sponsor activities that are germane to maintaining a Black presence in the discipline and in the profession. That's the kind of structural move I think is most important. But then there are other ways. As chair, you are in a position to affect things. For instance, I remember being brought into my very first role as chairperson which was to participate in a committee discussion regarding referees. The refereeing process was alleged to have been discriminatory against women and minorities. So there was a big committee meeting about that. I was stepping into that not knowing anything about the history of the discussion and finding out that there had been a complaint from minorities and women. And the committee had been apprised of the complaint and had taken it on as something that needed to be addressed only to discover when I stepped into the discussion that there wasn't much that could be done until people began submitting work. So, there was no rejection rate that anyone could point to but there was a general feeling that papers by Black philosophers or whomever were not welcome. But it was very difficult as an official to adjudicate a dispute of that sort because there is nothing concrete there. So, what I did was I made a deal to be a broker. I said, look, I'll find you people who want to submit stuff and you give me your editors and I'll send it to them. But that's not a structural change, that's just something you can do because you are in a position to talk to people. I can talk to editors of journals that are interested in doing special issues on race or African-American philosophy. Or I can set up a session with Black philosophers and Chinese philosophers, which I am doing, but that's all through personal contact, etc. You know, it is not as if the committee has in place something structural that we can rely on yet. So, part of my job has been to try, and that's happening gradually, I mean, we are beginning to put those things in place. But it is very difficult.

Yancy: In the face of racism in the academy would you suggest that African-American philosophers as a group ought to develop a concept of their own identity that would contribute to their development and progress as a group?

Lott: Well, you have to keep in mind that you are going to have a natural division among African-American philosophers. Now what I've tried to do, in my role as chair of the Committee on Blacks, is acknowledge this. So, for instance, when we put together panels should we only consider African-American philosophers who do work on African-American topics? And, how do you, under the auspices of the Committee, include people who just do philosophy of language, people who just do logic? What would be our entree into those subjects as a committee that represents the interests of Blacks? Well, the only reply is that they're Black people. Right? And it just seems to me that we have to acknowledge the fact that you have, especially in the second and third generation of African-American philosophers, I mean, I'm a senior person in the profession, a lot of people coming through the ranks who are in fact African-Americans who don't necessarily identify themselves as African-American philosophers just because there is this index of working on certain topics or approaching European philosophy with a certain perspective. And that's been literally rejected by a whole group of younger generation philosophers because they just want to be considered philosophers.

Yancy: Has that in any way affected this cadre or critical mass of African-American philosophers?

Lott: Oh yes, it has affected it quite a bit in the sense that there are actually two groups along those lines. The group of philosophers who are more focused on African-American topics tends to be more cohesive, whereas everyone else seems to be more of a rugged individual. And it just seems to me that we have to acknowledge that presence, you know, that is divided in that way. And as chair what I've done is simply tried to accommodate the rugged individuals as much as I can without imposing on them anything like an African-American identity as a philosopher. I mean, I just see that as not required. And that doesn't mean they don't have an African-American identity. It only means that as someone who works on Nietzsche why should they be treated any differently than anyone else who works on Nietzsche. So I think we are getting that much more than ever before. So, what's happening is that we're getting students now who will come in and want to specialize in African-American philosophy. That wasn't possible when I was a student. They can actually go to Ph.D. programs now and work with people on dissertations in areas where the primary readings will be readings by Black scholars and Black philosophers. For example, they can go to Purdue where Leonard Harris is part of a Ph.D. program in philosophy and it has a heavy Black studies emphasis. Or, they can go to Brown University where Lewis Gordon teaches Afro-American studies and religion. They could also go to Rutgers

University where Howard McGary and Jorge Garcia are. Or they could go to Hunter College and work with Frank Kirkland who teaches Africana philosophy amongst other things.

Yancy: What is African-American philosophy?

Lott: I think it is the study of issues and the kind of traditional thought that has been developed by African-American thinkers, to put it broadly. And that can include everything from music to religion to the Harlem Renaissance to Pan-Africanism, depending on which set of authors you choose to represent those topics.

Yancy: Do you see any trends developing?

Lott: Well, what's happening now is that we are at a level of canonization. You see publishers quite interested now in developing, not just publishing books, but developing a whole series of books on African-American philosophy. I mean, Blackwell Publishers is doing it. Temple University Press seems to be interested, and Westview. There are a number of major publishers now who are quite interested in race theory in general but African-American philosophy as well. And, a lot of this has to do with the hard work that was put in earlier by people like Bill Lawson, Howard McGary, Frank Kirkland, Bernard Boxill, and others, and it looks as if it is finally paying off. I mean, this is a blossoming field right now. And it has been catching on like wildfire.

Yancy: My question here stems from your own writings on Du Bois and Alain Locke. How important is Black folk culture with regard to the conceptualization of African-American philosophy?

Lott: That's a good question. You know, no one has ever explored that and I've recently been thinking about that in connection with African philosophy. There is a big issue about the status of what Africanists call ethnophilosophy, which is really the folk thought of Africans, the parables, the mythologies, the proverbs, etc. They're supposed to be modes of expression that capture African philosophic thought. When you rely on that as a source, the question arises: What's the status of the thinking that you develop from that source? Do you get theories that are comparable to the Europeans, for instance? And the arguments have gone a number of different ways on this issue. Anthony Appiah and Paulin Hountondji and a number of other people have developed arguments around this question but no one has considered the extent to which the elders in Africa have a parallel in peasant cultures in America. And perhaps even in urban centers where elders gather in somewhat traditional ways still. But it hasn't been studied as a source of philosophical thought. Only people who do folklore, people like Skip Gates at Harvard. But they have just barely scratched the surface. I mean, Gates's book *The Signifying Monkey* was an attempt to show that you have African retentions in folklore that have a rich history in West Africa. So, if ethnophilosophy applies to the mythology that Gates unearths in Africa as a source for the transformation of that mythology in Southern Black folk culture, and then later transformed again in relation to urban environments, why not see if there is an argument that would apply here about its utilization as a source for philosophical thought in the African-American arena. And no one has thought that through. I mean, we're busy adapting John Rawls, etc., to understand African-American culture. At some point we are going to have to make a break with that simply because it is limited. But it hasn't been done as far as I know. Now I have a theory about why. I think we have been thoroughly preoccupied with getting African-American philosophy legitimated, accepted in the discipline as a legitimate research area where students can come into a Ph.D. program and get a Ph.D. working on topics in this area. And it is very important that we do that. And in my role as chair I've worked very hard to make sure that all the books that come out get sessions at APA meetings and so on. So, I think that is why, with that emphasis on legitimating our work in this research area, the other approaches have been neglected. And it is better to legitimate the area first, in my opinion.

Yancy: Realizing of course that the level of legitimation is done within the framework of Western philosophical hegemonic power though, right?

Lott: It is an expression of the hegemony itself and it only reiterates that hegemony and that's why I think it is limited. Books on African-American philosophy that only aim to demonstrate the equality of our work seem to me to be limited. There should be more to what we do than that.

Yancy: Do you envision a time when there will be no need for a Committee on Blacks in Philosophy?

Lott: No, I don't. Because the younger generation of whites are divided. And it seems to me that the power is being transferred to that group of whites who will perpetuate the tradition that has basically kept Black people in their "proper" place in the APA. That's going to continue so there will be a need to continue to struggle to change that and I just don't see that happening because if any generation was going to change it, the '60s would have. And I don't see anything approaching what whites were willing to do in the '60s in the name of social justice. I don't see anything approaching that now. As a matter of fact, I see the opposite.

Yancy: Would you elaborate on the opposite?

Lott: I think we are moving in a direction where most of the white liberals who were committed to the goals of the Civil Rights Movement à la Martin Luther King, Jr., for instance, are more in tune with Shelby Steele and the whole neoconservative line. So I just don't see any future for any kind of cross-racial coalition that's going to bring about the demise of institutionalized racism, I'm sorry. Which is not to say that there are no cross-racial coalitions. It's just that they are not big enough and they're not strong enough and they're not effective. Because I think the hegemony is in place and has been maintained and will be perpetuated, that doesn't mean that we are not going to continue to struggle. It means there will always be a struggle as far as I'm concerned for that reason.

Yancy: Briefly, what is race identity and how does your view differ from someone like Naomi Zack or Anthony Appiah?

Lott: I focus on culture, so in a lot of ways I'm very sympathetic to the antiessentialists. But it seems to me that they have no appreciation for the role of African-American culture in shaping the identity of African-Americans in a very particular way. I mean, it is in a way that is tantamount to biological essentialism. So I would say that the main difference is that I see a role for biological differences for physical appearances in any notion of racial identity that applies in the American context simply because racism works that way. I just feel they don't have a well-developed notion of how African-Americans have employed racial identity to struggle against the particular form of racism that we face here. If we were in England, for instance, where the concept of a Black person could include Asians, and the kind of biological difference that matters in America doesn't matter anymore, I would be more than happy to accept the kind of notions that I think would be more congenial to their view. But, as it stands, it seems to me it doesn't apply here as well as it might apply to other circumstances where for the most part you have the same groups of people,

Blacks and whites. There is, I think, a need to discuss race from all of these different subject positions. I mean, Anthony Appiah has an African identity but he is very much in dialogue with African-Americans. So being a Black professor in America certainly has, I'm sure, impacted whatever African identity he brought here. And it seems to me that the cross-dialogue helps everyone arrive at a better understanding. I think Naomi Zack's subject position is mixed race, which is also very important to consider when you talk about Black identity. And I think all those subject positions need to be addressed much more fully. I think what happens is that there are these different subject positions but the cross-dialogue is where we are going to get the most interesting results. And that is starting to happen a little bit.

Yancy: Now getting back to Hobbes, what got you interested in writing about issues involving Hobbes and international relations?

Lott: Well, that came out of a realization that everyone talks about Hobbes without applying the argument to international relations. Now I've since decided that that's wrong. Since I wrote that article, "Hobbes on International Relations," I have learned that there are a lot of people who are aware of the problem that I raised, although no one has ever laid it out. But I am much more sensitive now to David Gauthier and other people who take themselves to be doing what Hobbes didn't do. At that time I didn't realize that I shouldn't have stated it that way. But Hobbes himself, I think, had a reason for not applying his notion of an absolute sovereign to international affairs as a way to resolve conflict in international affairs. And it is because Catholicism, in England, was such a problem, meaning, you don't want to suggest the holy Roman Empire as a solution to the problems of the world. But that is exactly the logical position he was in once he argued that that was the solution to domestic conflict, such as a civil war. And in fact I went to a conference on international relations in Helsinki where the question was "Can there be a Hobbesian theory of World Government?" So, they brought in twenty people and we all discussed whether Hobbes's theory would support a notion of world government, and you had people on both sides of the fence. And that's where the idea came up for the article.

Yancy: I would think that given Hobbes's negative framing of human nature, where he talks about man being a wolf to man (*homo homini lupus*), it would seem that internationally speaking it would be very

difficult to establish peace amongst nations just as it is difficult to
establish peace amongst individuals?

Lott: Well, you can do it by conquest. You see, Hobbes allowed sovereignty by acquisition, or force, as well as sovereignty by institution,
which is voluntary. So if a sovereign conquered the world à la Roman
Empire, or if the United States gained dominance over the Soviet Union
and became the world power, for Hobbes that would count as absolute
sovereignty that would be legitimate. In such cases, political authority
would be justified on his theory. But he couldn't argue that because it
would be really problematic to make that statement at that time.

Yancy: What relevance does Hobbes's work have for contemporary
issues of international relations?

Lott: Well, one of the things that came out of the conference was the
feeling of the urgency of the nuclear stalemate, because at that time
the Soviet Union was still going strong, and so the idea behind a lot of
the papers was maybe there was a Hobbesian solution to what's going
on with these nuclear weapons. And you had people like David Gauthier, Greg Kavka, Jean Hampton, and dozens of people using Hobbes
to argue the way out, whether we should get more weapons to win
this nuclear arms race, or whether we should get rid of all of them.
People have argued both of those views strictly using Hobbesian arguments. A lot of game theory is connected to the kind of problem you
get in *Leviathan,* chapter 13. Greg Kavka has a whole book on this,
the paradoxes of nuclear deterrence, and it is all informed by his reading of Hobbes, his work as a Hobbes scholar.

Yancy: Say a bit more about your interest in Hobbes.

Lott: Well, Hobbes's state of nature theory is very powerful because
most Black communities, especially now with the so-called drug
wars, have existed with those principles in operation. I will never forget reading C. B. McPherson who, as far I know, is the only commen-
tator on Hobbes who has pointed out that the state of nature for
Hobbes continues even into civil society. There wasn't a dichotomy
between what you had before and after but there was a transference
of power relations which allowed, as he put it, the invasions that
occurred in the state of nature to continue. People kept invading each
other in civil society, only now they have different power relations. It
seems to me that was the idea that motivated me to study Hobbes and
want to write about Hobbes.

Yancy: So are you suggesting that many African-Americans living within urban spaces can be described as living in a state of nature?

Lott: Oh yes, definitely, because it's a question of self-preservation.

Yancy: Besides philosophy what other things impact your identity?

Lott: Oh, as I said, I started out as a trumpet player in high school. I had a job that prevented me from playing in the school band, which had to go to football games. So I could only play in the ROTC band. I hated the military because I had been in reform school. So, I agreed to be in the ROTC band only if I didn't have to march or wear a uniform. When they practiced sometimes they practiced marching and I got the name "Sachmo" because of the way I would kind of profane the military in a different style of marching. Basically, my identity developed around jazz, even at an early age. I mean, all through high school I would go to night clubs. If John Coltrane or somebody like that came to town I would go every single night. And I graduated from high school when I was seventeen, so I must have been fifteen or sixteen and I'd be at the club every night at the back door if I couldn't get in.

Yancy: Does the jazz aesthetic in any way impact your philosophical writing?

Lott: Oh, totally. I remember reading a chapter by Cornel West in his book *Prophesy Deliverance*, which I always thought was his best, where he was discussing the oral tradition and the music tradition and the failure of Black intellectuals to live up to the standards set by those traditions. And I couldn't agree with him more. I think, what we haven't aspired to as a group of Black philosophers is to develop a system of thought that is comparable to the intellectual achievement of the music tradition. Our music tradition has far surpassed European music. I mean, just far surpassed it. And to some extent in certain areas of art such as sculpturing the Africans were far ahead of European masters who started borrowing all their concepts later. And the idea isn't to surpass anybody, but why get locked into something that isn't necessarily the highest level of aspiration that one could pursue? Why are we locked into that? It just seems to me that it is comparable to setting standards around be-bop, let's say, if you are a musician playing jazz, when the music has moved to all these other levels. And it seems to me that in philosophy we are doing that still. You know, we are doing big band swing stuff.

Yancy: When we should be doing what?

Lott: We should be doing post-John Coltrane.

Yancy: What on the contemporary African-American philosophical scene would constitute a post-John Coltrane form of philosophical thought?

Lott: Nothing. Nothing. No one has even aspired to that, it seems to me, and that is my basic complaint. And I think what is really interesting is whether it will happen with African philosophy first. They have a tradition of both this kind of ancient philosophy as well as now, in fact, they must have fourth generation Eurocentric philosophers, like Mudimbe, for instance. Think of Mudimbe in relation to Leopold Senghor. You would think, well, at some point there will be a break with the Eurocentric paradigm. Even the one that Mudimbe is locked into and struggling with. It's like he wears clothes that he can take off. I'm inclined to think that in some way they are ahead of us because they can take it off. And I'm expecting that two or three generations down the road of studying African-American thought, someone is going to get the bright idea that there may be a way to take off the clothes that we're constantly dressing it up in. We may not have to ask did Frederick Douglass read Hegel as a way to study Douglass. Now this doesn't mean that there is nothing fruitful in asking that, but at some point we may not need to ask such a question.

Yancy: Is there anything else you would like to add in terms of what shapes Tommy Lott's African-American philosophical identity?

Lott: I think that you have two things, and I think it is true for most Black people, and that is you have African-American culture. And as I've said, coming out of that musical background is very strong and influential and will always be the most important part. And then there is also institutionalized racism. I mean, there is no way to escape one's African-American identity, it seems to me. And to some extent it has to be acknowledged, and this is where I would agree with Appiah and Naomi Zack, and a lot of other people have argued this, that race is to some degree imposed from the outside. But I think there is actually the cultural identity that should be affirmed. We're all engaged in antiracist struggles and hopefully that will eventually be eliminated but there would still be a cultural identity that provides the fundamental basis for my African-American identity.

A Selection of Published Works of Tommy L. Lott

Articles

"Racism and Patriarchy," in *Sex and Race: Comparing the Categories*, Naomi Zack, ed. (New York: Routledge, 1997).

"Hobbes on Voluntary Motion," in *Hobbes Studies* IX (1997).

"Lichtman on Compensatory Justice," review essay, in *Radical Philosophy Review of Books* (spring 1996).

"Herman Gray, *Watching Race* (University of Minnesota Press)," review essay, in *Social Identities* (fall 1996).

"The Politics of Representation in Contemporary Black Cinema," in *Quarterly Review of Film and Video* (fall 1995).

"King Kong Lives: Racist Discourse and the Negro-Ape Metaphor," in *Next of Kin: Looking at the Great Apes*, MIT List Visual Arts Center Catalog, fall 1995, 37–43.

"Paul Gilroy, *The Black Atlantic: Modernity and Double Consciousness* (Cambridge, MA: Harvard University Press, 1993)," review essay, in *Social Identities* 1, no. 1 (spring 1995): 200–220.

"Black Marxist in Babylon: Bayard Rustin and the 1968 UFT Strike," *Educational Foundations* 8, no. 1 (winter 1994): 29–41.

"Nationalism and Pluralism in Alain Locke's Social Philosophy," in *Defending Diversity*, Laurence Foster and Patricia Herzog, eds. (Amherst: University of Massachusetts Press, 1994), 103–19.

"Black Vernacular Representation and Cultural Malpractice," in *Multiculturalism: A Critical Reader*, David T. Goldberg, ed. (Oxford: Basil Blackwell, 1994), 230–58.

"Slavery, Modernity and the Reclamation of Anterior Cultures," *Found Objects*, Issue 4 (fall 1994): 36–45.

"Black Cultural Politics: An Interview with Paul Gilroy," *Found Objects*, Issue 4 (fall 1994): 46–81.

"Du Bois on The Invention of Race," *The Philosophical Forum* XXIV, no. 1–3 (fall-spring 1992–93): 166–87; reprinted in *Social Justice in a Diverse Society*, Rita Manning and Rene Trujillo, eds. (Mountain View, CA: Mayfield Publishing, 1996).

"Alice Coltrane" in *Black Women in the United States: An Historical Encyclopedia*, Darlene Clark Hine, ed., (Brooklyn: Carlson Publishing, 1992), 365–66; reprinted in *The Facts on File Resource Collection on American Black Women*, Darlene Clark Hine, ed. (Brooklyn: Carlson Publishing, 1995).

"Hobbes's Right of Nature," *History of Philosophy Quarterly* 9, no. 2 (April 1992): 159–80.

"Marooned in America: Black Urban Youth Culture and Social Pathology," in *The Underclass Question*, Bill E. Lawson, ed. (Philadelphia: Temple University Press, 1992), 71–89.

"Anscombe on Justifying Claims to Know One's Bodily Position," *Philosophical Investigations* 12, no. 4 (October 1989): 293–307.

"Hobbes on International Relations," in *Hobbes: War Among Nations*, M. Bertman and T. Airaksinen, eds. (London: Gower Press, 1988), 91–98.

"Descartes on Phantom Limbs," *Mind and Language* 1, no. 3 (autumn 1986): 251–79.

"Hobbes's Mechanistic Psychology," in *Thomas Hobbes: His View of Man*, J. G. van der Bend, ed. (Amsterdam: Rodopi, 1982), 63–75.

"The psychology of self-preservation in Hobbes," *Revue europeene des sciences sociales* XX, no. 61, (1982): 37–55.

[ten]

Leonard Harris

Leonard Harris is professor of philosophy and director of the African American Studies and Research Center at Purdue University. He earned his B.A. in philosophy and English from Central State University. His M.A. degree in philosophy is from Miami University, and he obtained his Ph.D. in philosophy from Cornell University. He has also taught at Morgan State University; University of the District of Columbia; Rutgers University; the Oxford Center for African Studies, Summer Institute; the University of Maryland; and Tuskegee Institute as the Portia Washington Pittman Fellow. His areas of specialization are problems of explanation and justification in critical theory, philosophical anthropology, and the history of American philosophy. From 1991 to 1997, Harris was editor of *The American Philosophical Association Newsletter on Philosophy and the Black Experience.* His articles and reviews have appeared in *It Just Ain't Fair: Ethics of Health Care for African-Americans; Rethinking Masculinity; African American Perspectives on Biomedical Ethics; African American Humanism; Exploitation and Exclusion; The Journal of Social Philosophy; Transactions of the Charles S. Peirce Society; Quest; The Journal of Ethics; The Philosophical Forum; Social Science Information; Ethics; The International Philosophical Quarterly; Encyclopedia of African American Culture and History;* and more. He is also coeditor of *Exploitation and Exclusion: Race and Class in Contemporary U.S. Society.* He is editor of *The Philosophy of Alain Locke,* of *Children in Chaos: A Philosophy of Children Experience,* and of *Philosophy Born of Struggle.* The Philosophy Born of Struggle Annual Conference, Rockland Community College, Suffern, New York, is the largest annual gathering of minority philosophers in the world. Conference papers address themes in Harris's *Philosophy Born of Struggle*. Harris is also the executive director of the Alain L. Locke Society. (A selected citation list of Leonard Harris's published works can be found at the end of the interview.)

Leonard Harris
Purdue University

George Yancy: When and where were you born?
Leonard Harris: I was born April 12, 1948, in Cleveland, Ohio.

Yancy: What was it like for you growing up in Cleveland, Ohio?
Harris: It was wonderful. I had three sisters and a brother who were all older than me. Most of our life was spent on Forest Grove in Cleveland, Ohio. Forest Grove is off East 123rd Street. It was primarily Jewish and progressively became exclusively Black by the time I graduated from high school. I went to Chesterfield Elementary School, Patrick Henry Junior High School, and then Glenville High School.

Yancy: In what ways did living in Cleveland, Ohio, shape your identity at that time?
Harris: I guess it shaped me in various ways. I don't know if it was Cleveland as opposed to my family which shaped me because my life was essentially built around my family and then of course the external environment. My family on my mother's side was rather large and on my father's side was rather small. But we were fairly close knit. I had a lot of cousins, uncles, and aunts, and they were always sort of watching out for me.

Yancy: What impact did your mother and father have on your intellectual development?
Harris: They encouraged me to go to school. But as far as encouraging me to go into philosophy, well, that is a different question. They encouraged me to go to college. My mother, Agnes Chappell Harris, was very insistent that education was important for uplift and personal growth. My older brother had gone to college for a couple of years and then he went to the army. My sisters got married. One of my sisters became a nurse which in those days was impressive for a woman.

And then of course, there was me. Now with regard to college, the only college that the school counselor told me that I was eligible for was Central State University in Wilberforce, Ohio. So, my father, Eugene Harris, Sr., went to see a man by the name of John Busta-mante, who was a lawyer in Cleveland, to see what might be done to help to get me into college. I don't know what happened but I do know that I filled out an application at Glenville High School, and that my father and mother took me to Central State University.

Yancy: In the preface of your book *The Philosophy of Alain Locke*, you briefly mention that you were part of a gang culture. How did that impact your identity?

Harris: Oh, you mean the Del Amours? But that's not an identity question, it's a culture question. I mean it wasn't an identity, it was a group. And the Del Amours were hip. Me and a couple of my friends, Forest Gary and Billy Talbot, started the Del Amours over at Forest's house. We said, "Yeah, we're gonna call it the Christmas Savings Club. Yeah, call it the Del Amours, that'd be cool." So that sort of grew and we added more people to it. Supposedly, it was a Christmas Savings Club but it never saved us any money, although we had a bank account. Basically, it was a gang and we were a bunch of ruffi-ans and we would threaten people at the skating rink.

Yancy: During that time did you consider yourself as reflective?

Harris: Yes, I was the smartest one of the group. I had Cs. Gary Rosen-berry, another member of the Del Amours, graduated from high school at twenty years old and was like on level fourteen! He was the oldest. It went from level one, which was like the A level, and it went down to, you know, beyond hope.

Yancy: Were you reading many books back then?

Harris: No. I was reading enough to get by. Except for William Som-merset Maugham. He was a novelist, and my mother had some of his works in the house. He wrote travel stories which I enjoyed.

Yancy: What was it about the travel story that interested you?

Harris: What interested me about these travel stories was that the heroes were always searching for something and they found it. They were at peace with themselves. They lived interesting, exciting lives. They knew what love was.

Yancy: Again, in the preface of your book on Alain Locke you mention that you barely graduated from Glenville High School. Would you elaborate on this?

Harris: That's true. I graduated with about a C average. I was not in anybody's top echelon, that's for certain. And I was not your A student. I worked hard and certainly in my group I was considered fairly bright. But almost none of the others were getting out of high school anytime soon. And I was fortunate enough not to get in trouble. I wasn't in any school trouble because my parents wouldn't have tolerated that. Whereas some of my friends were in various forms of trouble because they didn't attend school. And the family situations were all very different. Billy's mom was a single mom and Forest was being raised by his father, a single father. Other than that, my one other best friend, Freddy Dunnigan, had both his mother and father at home.

Yancy: What was it like studying at Central State?

Harris: I enjoyed it. I was fascinated. I was very happy to go. I was flabbergasted when I saw the college gates. When my parents drove me up to Central I knew then that I would never leave.

Yancy: What did the gates symbolize for you?

Harris: It was a different world. It wasn't like Cleveland. I knew I had to get out of Cleveland. Cleveland wasn't where I was going to live my life. It offered me a different opportunity to have a different kind of life.

Yancy: Who at Central State University influenced you most?

Harris: The people who influenced me most at Central were William Harris, a poet who actually lived in Antioch, Ohio, but came to Central for classes; Marian Musgrave, who taught literature; and Francis Thomas, who taught philosophy.

Yancy: Before you go on, I'd like to move back to around 1966 when you find yourself within the midst of the Civil Rights Movement in Cleveland. Can you say something about this social matrix and your own militant consciousness at that time?

Harris: Yes, it was around 1965/66 in Cleveland. We were throwing bricks and stuff at the police. But that's not a consciousness, that's a reaction to a situation that you find heinous. I can't say that I had any consciousness then. Moving forward to Central State in 1966, well, that's a different question. There I had a consciousness. And my consciousness there was very different.

Yancy: Would you elaborate on that difference?

Harris: Well, in Cleveland, I was a teenager trying to survive. I was trying to socialize and make friends. And I was feeling so much disdain
for the reality of police in my neighborhood. I didn't particularly
enjoy that reality. On the other hand, it is the reality of a teenager trying to have a social life on the fringes of a ruffian reality. And so that
mental state, so to speak, is one of bolsterism in response to perceived
threats. Central State was a different ball game. I had some education.
I had the opportunity to listen to Amiri Imamu Baraka. There was a
fellow student there named Alton Patterson who was Muslim, a Black
Muslim at the time, a very radical fellow. You know, there was the
whole philosophy department. There were other students from different places who you would get a chance to meet and talk to. I was
interested in literature, that is, I became interested in literature once I
got there. And, consequently, I eventually became interested in politics. I was a parliamentarian for my junior class. So, that's where my
consciousness grew and I began to be aware of what it is that I was
doing. I was acting with awareness of why it is that I was acting.

Yancy: Was it also at Central State that you decided that you wanted to
study philosophy?

Harris: Yes.

Yancy: What led to that?

Harris: Well, I had been studying literature and had planned to focus
on English. In my senior year, Francis Thomas told me that I was pretty
good with prose and he asked me about going to graduate school at
Miami University in Oxford, Ohio, to study philosophy, and I said,
"yes." And Marian Musgrave had encouraged me to write more. She
used to tear up my writing something terrible. But she encouraged me
to write more, to write more prose. And so I did. At the same time, I
was also publishing poetry with William Harris in a little publication
called *Gem*, which he was editing.

Yancy: I understand that you still write poetry.

Harris: Yes. In fact, my daughter, Jamila R. Harris, and I just did a
poetry reading at a coffeehouse here.

Yancy: What's the connection between your philosophy and your
poetry writing?

Harris: That's a good question. My poetry is much more blues oriented than my philosophy. I like Langston Hughes so I like to do my poetry around Langston Hughes's work. My poetry is much less creative than my philosophy. My poetry does not portend to greatness, it portends to being adequately survivable and entertaining. It is a release.

Yancy: So, specifically why did you decide to study philosophy?
Harris: In addition to having been given encouragements, philosophy was also a subject that I understood and enjoyed. And it was also a subject in which I thought I could say something of relevance. It was a subject that I didn't find perplexing and confusing like many of my schoolmates. You know, in philosophy, there are a lot of conflicting opinions and claims that people have and I found that rewarding and enriching. I found it relatively easy to become immersed in it. So I would read it a lot.

Yancy: Were there many other Black undergraduates studying philosophy at the time.
Harris: No. I didn't know of any other majors.

Yancy: What was it like studying philosophy at Miami University?
Harris: I enjoyed Miami University. I taught my first course in Black philosophy at Miami University in 1970. The department allowed me to do it. A guy named Robert Harris was the chairman of the department. We used to call him Bubbling Bob Harris. I had a teaching assistantship and I said I wanted to teach a course in Black philosophy. And they said OK. So he had me teach it. Actually, I taught it under the auspices of another instructor named Carl Hedman. And so there I was. I taught my first course in Black philosophy. In fact, I still have the syllabus for that. What I did was that I would show slides of Black people being hanged. That's how I started off the course. Then I would play blues music. And I'd say, "We're studying Black philosophy here."

Yancy: Were there particular professors of philosophy who influenced you most while you were at Miami University?
Harris: No one in particular. I didn't become a follower of any of them. And as far as courses, I took the standard courses. I didn't take any special independent courses. Explicitly, there were no influential professors in my intellectual life, period. They were good people who I learned a great deal from but they didn't shape my mind. And I don't follow any of their philosophies, although I know what many of their

philosophies are. Martin Benjamin was a pacifist, Rick Momeyer was a Humean, Carl Hedman was a pacifist. These are not people that I agree with at all.

Yancy: At this stage in your intellectual growth, were there any particular philosophers within the Western tradition that you found yourself gravitating towards?

Harris: Karl Marx and Kwame Nkrumah, though Nkrumah wasn't in the Western tradition as such. I had to do a master's thesis. My master's thesis was entitled "Justification of Revolutionary Violence."

Yancy: Why Marx and Nkrumah?

Harris: They were socialists and so was I. They were interested in social revolution and so was I. I did a criticism of Bayard Rustin's integrationism and passivism, yet he was a strong working-class advocate.

Yancy: Talk about your move from Miami University to Cornell University?

Harris: I applied to two places, Cornell and The New School for Social Research in New York. With respect to applying to Cornell I said to a friend of mine, Alan Williams, who wasn't even thinking about graduate school, "We're going to go to Cornell." I applied there because it was a popular university, for that reason alone. And I applied to The New School for Social Research because I understood there were a lot of radicals there. I got admitted to both. But I had written to Cornell and said, "I refuse to take the GRE test" and gave a whole lot of reasons why. I had objections because I thought that it was culturally biased. It was racist and it didn't substantively provide students with a definition of aptitude which it was supposed to be measuring. And they admitted me anyway.

Yancy: Who did you primarily study under while at Cornell?

Harris: My main professor was Allan Wood. Wood taught some of everything. He taught Karl Marx, Immanuel Kant, and Jean-Jacques Rousseau.

Yancy: Do you construct yourself as an African-American philosopher?

Harris: Oh yes.

Yancy: What is the nature of this construction?

Harris: Well, it is a double-edged thing, you know. There is no social construction without a reality that helps pick it out. So, on the one hand you don't have a history of African-American philosophy without someone making a conscious effort to create it. So it is as much a created project as it is one that is already there. So I've helped create it. But I've helped create it out of some raw materials. So I think that both variables are operative. Just like there is no such thing as American philosophy existing in never-never land. People sit around and help produce it, maintain it, and create it. So I guess in that sense I have made a conscious commitment, among other things, to develop some raw material that was there. And I think that it has been a very valuable experience.

Yancy: What is African-American philosophy?

Harris: Well, it's not a *thing*. I mean, African-American philosophy is simply the history of African-Americans engaged in doing philosophy. It's the cultural matrix of doing philosophy within the context of America and also having an identity of being an African-American. It is the matrix of doing philosophy in America out of issues most popular on this continent, with conscious recognition of the African-American heritage and the kinds of issues and problems which that heritage emphasizes. That's what it is. It is a doing, it is a practice and it is a genre within American philosophy. As a genre, it is dominated by issues of practicality and struggle, which means that it is not committed to a metaphysics in the sense of having a singular true proposition out of which all other propositions arise. As a genre you have people who have fundamentally different philosophies, some of which may have a metaphysics, others of which may not. As a *thing* that's a different question. I don't know how to address African-American philosophy as a *thing* question that makes it fundamentally disconnected from the genre question.

Yancy: What does African-American folk culture have to do with an articulation of an African-American philosophical system?

Harris: On the one hand, nothing. It depends upon the individual. The assumption that there is a philosophy, call it epistemological realism or nonrealism, which is more or less right because it fits with the folk culture is seriously misguided. Because it sits with the folk culture doesn't tell you anything. It might be a horrible philosophy because it does. Sometimes folk culture is the worst place in the universe to locate oneself. For example, I'm talking about the folk culture of crime, violence, rape, murder, etc. So which feature of the folk culture are you talking about? Unless you want to engage in a certain kind of romanticism of cultural pretentiousness from the standpoint of a petty bourgeois intellectual, folk culture has its vulgar features. That there is nothing more substantive than folk culture is much like looking for a philosophy that really represents a "true Negro." You're not going to find one. So, I think the relationship is more one of showing respect in regard to folk culture and borrowing from it where you see it as relevant for your project and giving credence to it for that relevance. Blues, I think, is a classic music, far more so than jazz, and so to some degree I borrow from the blues to give it credence. But I do this without making the assumption that somehow I've got the essence of the blues, or that all of the blues artists who disagree with me must be wrong.

Yancy: What particular aspects of folk culture have you found useful for your own philosophical enterprise?

Harris: Well, I guess several things. One is the history and heritage of the struggle to overcome adversity. I think we find that in a variety of genres. I think we find it in the blues in its emotion and its dedication to love and yet its rugged sense of reality. I think that you find it in the sense of the overcoming of adversity that is so prevalent in the literature, in the poetry, and in the novels of African-American folk culture, and trying to find a sense of self-worth in a world that constantly denies you worth as a person. I think those are tremendous themes. I think the theme of overcoming slavery is crucial, overcoming that heritage. I think the theme of constantly making oneself and remaking oneself over and against the odds is crucial. So those are the things that I think are important.

Yancy: Does African-American philosophy constitute what David Hollinger refers to as "communities of discourse"? If so, then what are the shared values, questions, vocabulary, methodologies, rhetorical devices, etc.?

Harris: I don't know if there are. I think it is somewhat pretentious to think that there are. The community of discourse is also the community of survival, people connecting with one another. It's a community of a sharing of information in a society that always excludes you from information. The common language is more a language about common topics than it is a common vocabulary. So it is not that kind of community that Hollinger describes. It is not nearly as bounded and connected as that. It only appears so from the standpoint of race. But people have radically different positions and those positions bind them fundamentally to somebody else. For example, a Marxist, an existentialist, a pragmatist, in honesty, are bound to other Marxists, existentialists, and pragmatists first.

Yancy: So, is it correct to refer to the cadre of African-American philosophers as constituting a community?
Harris: A certain kind.

Yancy: What kind of community?
Harris: The kind that is engaged in the common project to defeat the heinous consequences of racism. That's the kind of community that it is. It is bound in that struggle whether the members of that community are Marxists, pragmatists, existentialists, or whether they have their own orientation in this whole regard. That binds them together regardless of their philosophy. So there is something common in the works of Laurence Thomas, Howard McGary, Bill Lawson, Adrian Piper, and others even though they don't share anything philosophically. There is almost nothing that they have in common other than their having been harmed by American philosophy and American philosophy's racism, their exclusion, and the insistence on dealing with certain topics. Otherwise they don't have anything in common. I don't think that African-American philosophy is a biological project.

Yancy: But it is certainly a cultural project.
Harris: Yes.

Yancy: You've argued that *The Encyclopedia of Philosophy* should be renamed *The Encyclopedia of Eurocentric Nationalism.*
Harris: Yes, that's what it is.

Yancy: Would you elaborate on this?
Harris: Well, basically, it is an expression of European nationalism. All of its characters are European, almost all male. The second group of characters are American and almost all male. All of its terms are the same and come from those individuals. That's it. If you wanted a foundation for nationalism, then you've got one. If you want to know what represents the essence of our nation, you would go to *The Encyclopedia of Philosophy.*

Yancy: Why is this fact so invisible to us?

Harris: I don't know if it is invisible. I think that the people who put it together knew damn well what they were doing. They knew that they were cheating all the time. They knew that when they put together *The Encyclopedia of Philosophy* that they were putting together an encyclopedia of Euro-American philosophy. They knew good and well that they didn't include anything from China, from Africa, or from India. They knew damn well that they didn't have anything from Latin America. They knew that. And yet they still use *The Encyclopedia of Philosophy* as if *this is philosophy* and this is the encyclopedia of it. These are not ignorant people. They knew what they were doing. It was an encyclopedia of European, Euro-American nationalism. It gives you a sense that, if you see these as philosophers, they have reached the epitome of knowledge and they are asking and answering the hardest possible questions. And there you have them. That's what it is in nationalist form.

Yancy: As editor of *The APA Newsletter on Philosophy and the Black Experience*, how has *The Newsletter* helped to combat white male hegemonic philosophical framings?

Harris: I think *The Newsletter* has provided a resource to combat white hegemony, period, both male and female. I think both exist. I think putting one on one side and one on the other is a little pretentious. The statistics don't give you justification to do that. So I think its impact is on how we see the possibility of having resources to do work that includes issues of ethnicity and racial identity. *The Newsletter* broadens the scope of works on and about Black philosophy and acts as a resource within the profession.

Yancy: In your essay "The Horror of Tradition," you suggest that a progressive tradition should be metaphorically a jazz tradition. What does it mean to develop an African-American conceptual scheme that is jazzed?

Harris: Well, part of what it means is to seriously take into account the jazz motif. The motif of syncopation, the motif of concentrated rhythm, the motif of allowing fallibilism, and alteration by new players.

Yancy: Are you a nihilist in the sense that you define nihilism in that same essay, where you talk about relativized principles and the perception of the past as invented?

Harris: Oh yes. I think that it is invariable that you need to destroy various kinds of traditions of the past. You don't hold on to them as essential and codified and internal. I think that it is just a lie to think that somehow you're supposed to just stay stable and make sacrosanct all traditions. I see the search for *essence,* the search for the *true Negro,* the search for the *existential being* of the good faith versus the bad faith as just nonsense. It's a hypocrisy. Philosophers are engaged in a construction process and they ought to at least admit it.

Yancy: I take seriously Alain Locke's understanding of philosophy as a derivation of life and as possible lineaments of a personality. How do you see your own philosophical work as linked in a derivative fashion to your life and as a lineament of your personality?

Harris: I just did a paper called "Revolutionary Pragmatism" and on the one hand it seems to me that if you have a philosophy which cannot justify revolution then your philosophy is seriously deficient. If your philosophy has to rely on somebody else to give you justification for revolution then something is wrong with your philosophy. It's inadequate. So, too, in terms of my own life, I think that it's an effort to make whole both the side that sees a justification in revolution and simultaneously the side that sees the need to be practical about life. I guess, on the one level, my personal life has been sort of a search for a compatible existence between the two. Having a life that allows you to see the limitations of your own actions and to see the possibility that your actions are not world transforming. They might influence the world but they may not necessarily be world transforming. At the same time, revolutionists do just that. They socially transform reality. Now, there isn't anything called human history without the history of revolution.

Yancy: What was the original intention behind your book *Philosophy Born of Struggle?*

Harris: To present a world that has been hidden.

Yancy: How was it received back then?

Harris: It wasn't. There wasn't anybody who was willing to publish it. Not a single publisher in philosophy. I went around to just about every one of them. I took it to one publisher and the one good thing about him, William Hackett, owner of Hackett Publishing Company, was that he was quite honest with me. He said, "I can't publish this because I don't think white people will use it." He told me that I had to find a publisher who doesn't care whether or not he makes any money off of it because white people won't use it. And it is white people who are in these classes. At that point I stopped going to the publishers in philosophy. I don't think he was being racist, I think he was telling me the truth. His position was that there was no way that he could publish it and stay in the business. I went to every publisher of philosophy that attended the American Philosophical Association, and none of them wanted to publish it. Howard University Press wouldn't even publish it but that wasn't because the book was radical but because it didn't fit within the Negro genre. There simply were no publishers that published works in philosophy by Blacks other than religious publishers and they published theology. So I eventually went to Kendall/Hunt Publishing Company and they published it as a trade book because the editor, Emmett Dingley, was in philosophy and yet he had never published a book in philosophy. And I was the first person to bring him a book in philosophy.

Yancy: How is your own philosophical project born of struggle?

Harris: It has all been a struggle to overcome, overcoming adversity, overcoming exclusion, overcoming a lack of opportunity, and overcoming the disadvantages that you didn't know you had. It is a certain kind of struggle that you are engaged in. I think my personal life has been on the one level an effort to overcome adversity of a certain kind. And that is linked to a whole variety of other kinds of people who also try to overcome adversity that is fundamentally different from mine. My M.A. thesis was on the justification of revolutionary violence; I spent part of 1993 in Tanzania; I helped establish and continue to support the Association for Caribbean Transformation, Trinidad, and the Radical Philosophy Association and its annual trips to Cuba.

Yancy: What initially got you interested in Alain Locke?

Harris: His work *The New Negro*, because he deconstructed and destroyed the Negro identity in many respects in the first couple of pages. He basically said that to the extent that a lot of the images of the Negro existed, they were fabrications. They didn't really reflect the person. They definitely could not reflect the diversity of kinds of persons. And also, if you read *The New Negro*, on the one hand, it is clearly a cultural project that he's trying to push, but it is also very unusual to have works on Africa, African art, white people, poets, and spirituals all within one anthology. This was weird to me. Who was this weird dude doing this weird stuff? All of this was in one anthology and called *The New Negro*. I came to Locke after I had gone through Karl Marx and Edward Blyden. Locke came later.

Yancy: Having read them first, how did this impact your appropriation of Locke?

Harris: In several ways. It was a critical appropriation of Locke because Marx provides a way of seeing the world as a certain kind of world of change through conflict. Locke doesn't always appreciate the terror of social revolution and class conflict. On the other hand, through Blyden's lens, Blyden does see the world in terms of kinds of people, Africans, Europeans, Asians, etc. Locke appreciates that the world is very often composed of communities and that it is only through communities that you can be a moral agent, but Locke sometimes doesn't see how crucial that fact is, how crucial collective moral agency really is in terms of group phenomena. So, you get on the one hand the critical approach to Locke from the standpoint of having read Marx and Blyden first. The standpoint of Marx is the role of class conflict and how terrible that conflict can really be, but yet it is through that conflict that we sometimes arrive at more radical social change. On the other hand, it is the crucial role of collective moral agency in a moral community and its role as a kind of separating and segregating phenomenon that is so very important to Blyden.

Yancy: What is your entry into philosophical issues revolving around the concept of honor?

Harris: I think honor is a crucial notion. One of the consistent criticisms of racism is that it doesn't allow for people to be honored. And this is the case whether you are talking about persons who are poor or rich. It doesn't allow for persons, on one hand, to be respected and most definitely never to be honored. It doesn't allow persons to be given deference by virtue of being of a certain status. That's on one level, in terms of the African-American stuff. On another level, it seems to me worldwide that the concept of honor is very operative in every culture that portends itself to civilization. There are codes of respect that command honor. And these are very much in contention, contestation, on the world stage. I guess naturally that one of the characteristics that makes persons interesting is their concern with this condition of how they can at least be the kinds of persons that are eligible for honor. I mean, there is a reason why honor and violence are always so closely linked because it is the kind of thing for which you should be willing to kill. It is something for which nations are willing to risk their existence. They do it all the time, even if they are pacifists. They are willing to risk the very existence of themselves and their whole population rather than have what they take to be their highest code of conduct violated. That's what honor is.

Yancy: Why hasn't the type of honor accorded Dr. Martin Luther King, Jr. been accorded to someone like Minister Louis Farrakhan?

Harris: Well, you have fundamentally different people. I mean, you don't just accord someone honor just because they exist, they are Black, and they have got a following. There are a whole lot of other sorts of things. And honor from whom? There is no reason whatsoever why people who fundamentally disagree with you should honor you. Why should people who define you as an enemy honor you? He hasn't done what King has done. He doesn't represent what King represents. He doesn't have the same kind of following that King had. His message isn't as universalizable in the same way. It is not intended to be. So, why should you expect the same kind of thing? "Oh, white people don't like him because he's Black." But that's silly, some Black people don't like him either.

Yancy: Is the differential honoring in this example possibly because of King's large white following?

Harris: No. I think for the concept of honor you've got a bad example. I mean, it's unanswerable. It is like asking why people don't honor the president of the Ku Klux Klan the way in which they honor Bob Dole. And then get mad because the answer has to do with the principles for which these people stand. So, well, is there something wrong with the people who don't honor both of them? There is something wrong with the way in which that is constructed. You are talking about two fundamentally different types of folks in two fundamentally different kinds of worlds. I think that the answer that one is looking for is that they do not honor Louis Farrakhan because they are racist and they honor King because he is palatable. They don't honor Jesse Jackson either. Is this a question of American racism or of honor?

Yancy: Then let me ask another question about honor vis-à-vis Farrakhan. Do you think the extent to which Farrakhan has been accorded honor has changed since the Million Man March?

Harris: By whom? Among Blacks it is probably the case that he got more honor. Among some whites it is probably the case as well. It depends which sector of the population you are talking about. I guess, lastly, the equating of the Million Man March with Farrakhan is rather problematic. The vast majority of folks there were not followers of Farrakhan and didn't think the march was about Farrakhan. The media did. I was there and I'm pretty certain that that is not what it was about.

Yancy: In your essay "Honor: Emasculation and Empowerment," you talk about lynchings, the horrible experiment where 399 Black men were the objects of a syphilis experiment, etc., and yet you don't suggest that such things are indicative of a larger conspiracy. Why?

Harris: It's a background assumption of a conspiracy that you suggest, namely, that there is this intelligent being out to get you as opposed to the whole array of class conflicts and structures.

Yancy: So you'd rather look at these issues in terms of class and race rather than postulate a conspiracy theory?

Harris: I think the conspiracy theory is just wrong. I certainly don't use it at all. I talk about how honor is not given to Black people, particularly Black men, and how it is that the traits associated with aggressiveness, assertiveness, self-confidence are in general denied Black people, especially Black men. I mean, these are traits for which those perceived as subordinate are not supposed to have anyway. So when Black men assert themselves they are already seen as illegitimate. That's what makes it, among other things, so difficult to achieve honor. And in one way that is how it is possible to honor King but not Malcolm X. You submerge a whole set of traits that in many others you applaud. You applaud these traits in presidential candidates and soldiers but if those persons are Black then there's a certain sense of uncertainty of how to applaud those traits and how to give credence and deference to them.

Yancy: How do we get more African-Americans into the field of philosophy?

Harris: Have more African-Americans in positions of authority and power. The ability to fire and hire people. Failure to have them in positions of authority creates obstacles to their admission. We need positions of authority to hire, to graduate, to grant Ph.D.'s. They have to be in positions of authority. It is that simple. And I think that's one crucial approach. I think another approach would be if you had better relationships between minority colleges and majority universities and graduate schools. Also it would be very helpful if you had graduate programs in philosophy at some of these predominantly Black colleges. And lastly, the African-American culture would have to be different.

Yancy: In what way?

Harris: Well, most persons interested in these kinds of questions, the questions that philosophers are interested in, are in theology. In fact, almost all of your popular intellectuals are persons seen as in some way religious or respectful of Christianity, unless they are Muslims.

Yancy: Why is this?

Harris: It has something to do with the history and culture of America. It has to do with a whole lot of variables. I don't think it is just some evil white man sitting around determining what Black people ought to worship. You know, as if Black people are really ignorant and don't have any sense. I think it's a long history of deeply religious people. Philosophy is not really seen as religious and it is not necessarily seen as honorific unless one is also in religion. I mean, there is a long history of Black humanism and people who are nonreligious. They are mostly in the arts but there is a long history of them. They're just not in the profession, that's all.

Yancy: How has the image of Cornel West shaped the way in which we understand African-American philosophers?

Harris: Well, I think Cornel has fundamentally changed the whole field, whether people like him or dislike him. He's part of the intellectual genre through philosophy. Only one of his many identities is philosophy. Nobody has as many identities as Cornel. He teaches in theology, you know. I think he has changed and encouraged the possibility of others to be public intellectuals and I think probably most young philosophers are trying to imitate him. So, they'll find fault with Cornel, or criticize him, trying to fundamentally imitate him. Or they will ask people to compare them with him. So, I think those are ways in which he has fundamentally changed the field.

Yancy: Do you see yourself as a public intellectual?

Harris: No. I am not a public intellectual. I doubt that I will become one. And that is for strictly personal reasons. I am a parent, a single parent, and as a single parent that is not a possible alternative for me. Even if I wanted it I couldn't have it. But I don't particularly want it.

Yancy: Concerning this issue of African-Americans in the field of philosophy, it is interesting to note that Joyce Mitchell Cook, who was the
first African-American woman to get a Ph.D. in philosophy, apparently encountered hostility impeding her advancement in the academy in the field of philosophy. Thomas Nelson Baker was the first
African-American male to receive a Ph.D. in philosophy. His was
from Yale and Cook's was, too, right?

Harris: Yes, she went to Yale and she received the Ph.D. in philosophy
in 1965. She went to Howard University shortly thereafter. She did
her doctoral dissertation on value theory. She taught at Howard for a
number of years. She went up for tenure under William Banner.
William Banner fought against her for promotion and tenure. When I
met her she was working on articles on Black philosophy. She then
went into administration and she was in senior administration at
Howard until she retired. So she left the field of philosophy in terms of
being an active agent in it.

Yancy: Was she embittered in terms of having not received tenure
while at Howard?

Harris: I think that she was embittered by the Banner experience.
William Banner was the chairman of Howard University's philosophy
department. He was the last chairman of the philosophy department
that Alain Locke hired.

Yancy: William Banner is an early African-American philosopher.

Harris: Yes. But he doesn't necessarily have that as a personal identity.
For example, he didn't want his publications listed in *Philosophy Born
of Struggle* because he didn't see himself as Black. He and I have
argued about some of these issues. He is on the other side of the spec-
trum from me.

Yancy: In terms of Cook having not received tenure, do you think it
was racial, ideological, or a question of gender?

Harris: Ideological. It wasn't racial, it was definitely ideological. I don't
know whether or not it was gender based. But he wasn't a favorite
member of her intellectual reality. There was a lot of bitterness there
because of what Banner did. You have to understand, these people
were struggling individuals. She was a first. And to be out of academia
because the chairman wouldn't really give you any regard and then to
go into administration and live the remainder of your working life in

administration is not a very happy experience. I first encountered Cook when I asked her to write an article for me for *Philosophy Born of Struggle*. At that time she was in administration and she was not very happy.

Yancy: So, at that time was there a Committee on Blacks in Philosophy?

Harris: Oh, yes. There has been a Committee on Blacks in Philosophy for many years. Alain Locke was a part of a Committee on Blacks in Philosophy. After Locke you get Eugene Clay Holmes. Then after Holmes you get William R. Jones and after Jones you get Robert Williams. That was the line of ascendancy of chairpersons. There was the informal organization first. That was with Locke and Holmes. It became formal under William R. Jones.

Yancy: Did they come to her rescue at any level?

Harris: No. Locke was dead and Holmes had retired and was living up in Martha's Vineyard. Winston K. McAllister was retiring or had retired, I'm not certain which. The chairperson became William Banner, and it is Banner who ends the era of philosophy at Howard in terms of being a source for Black intellectual activity. In terms of doing Black philosophy that ends the story. And in terms of having people coming in with that sort of willingness to deal with that approach, it ends with Banner. Banner's comment on the relationship of philosophy and Blacks is in the anthology called *African-American Perspectives on Biomedical Ethics*. That's where you get the clear and definitive voice of Banner. He is a classical Aristotelian.

Yancy: What is your overall philosophical project?

Harris: To radically transform reality, to participate in a fundamental transformation of reality. To be an active agent in the construction and destruction of all that exists now and help us to form something far more beneficial, profitable, and rewarding to humanity. I think that's what revolutions help to do, different kinds of revolutions help to do. It would be to destroy the idols of race, privilege, and prestige, which are unwarranted. And to encourage the negation and destruction of useless poverty and misery, starvation and death. To make the reality of misery present instead of the pretentious, cheap, phony, and fraudulent pop-dialogue that pervades the field. And that is to say whether it is Black or white.

A Selection of Published Works of Leonard Harris

Books

Exploitation and Exclusion: Race and Class in Contemporary U.S. Society, coeditor with Abebe Zegeye and Julia Maxted (London: Hans Zell, 1991).

Children in Chaos: A "Philosophy for Children" Experience, ed. (Dubuque, IA: Kendall/Hunt, 1991).

The Philosophy of Alain Locke, Harlem Renaissance and Beyond, ed. (Philadelphia: Temple University Press, 1989).

Philosophy Born of Struggle: Afro-American Philosophy from 1917, ed. (Dubuque, IA: Kendall/Hunt, 1983).

Articles

"Philosophy: African American," *Encyclopedia of African American Culture and History* (New York: MacMillan, 1996).

"African Philosophy in America," "African-American Philosophy," "Harris, Leonard," *Encyclopedia of African Religions and Philosophy* (New York: Garland, 1996).

Foreword to *Martin L. King Jr., and the Philosophy of Nonviolence*, by Greg Moses (New York: Guilford Press, 1996), 350–58.

Forword to *Fanon Reader*, coauthor Carolyn Johnson; Lewis R. Gordon, T. Sharpley-Whiting, Renée White, eds. (New York: Routledge, 1996), i–ix.

"Prolegomenon to Race and Economics," in *A Different Vision: African American Economic Thought*, Thomas Boston, ed. (New York: Routledge, 1996).

"Alain Locke," in *A Companion to American Thought*, Richard Fox and James Kloppenberg, eds. (Cambridge: Blackwell, 1996).

"Alain Locke," in *American National Biography*, Susan B. Monroe, ed. (London: Oxford University Press, 1996).

"'Believe It or Not' or the Klu Klux Klan and American Philosophy Exposed," *Proceedings and Addresses of the American Philosophical Association* 68, no. 5 (May 1995): 133–37.

"The Ways of Socialism," *Proceedings of the Radical Philosophy Association* (Des Moines, Iowa, 1995), 1–3.

"Postmodernism and Racism: An Unholy Alliance," in *Racism, the City and the State*, Michael Cross and Michael Kieth, eds. (London: Routledge, 1993).

"The Horror of Tradition or How to Burn Babylon and Build Benin While Reading *A Preface to a Twenty Volume Suicide Note*," *Philosophical Forum* XXIV, nos. 1–3 (fall-spring 1992–93): 94–119.

"Honor: Empowerment and Emasculation," in *Rethinking Masculinity*, Larry May and Robert A. Strinkwerda, eds. (New York: Rowman and Littlefield, 1992).

"Autonomy Under Duress," in *African-American Perspectives on Biomedical Ethics*, Harley E. Flack and Edmund D. Pelligrino, eds. (Washington, D.C.: Georgetown University Press, 1992).

"Agency and the Concept of the Underclass," in *Philosophy and the Underclass*, Bill E. Lawson, ed. (Philadelphia: Temple University Press, 1992).

"Epilogue," *It Just Ain't Fair: Ethics of Health Care for African Americans*, Annetta Dula and Sara Goering, eds. (New Haven: Praeger, 1991).

"Leonard Harris on the Life and Work of Alain Locke," in *African-American Humanism*, Norm R. Allan, Jr., ed. (Buffalo, NY: Prometheus Books, 1991).

"The Concept of Racism," in *Exploitation and Exclusion*, Abebe Zegeye, Julia Maxted, and Leonard Harris, eds. (London: Hans Zell, 1991).

"Chaos and Community: Exploration into the Visions of Dewey and Woodson," in *Children in Chaos: A "Philosophy for Children" Experience*, Leonard Harris, ed. (Dubuque, IA: Kendall/Hunt, 1991).

"Response to Anatol Anton," *Radical Philosophy Association Newsletter* 21 (winter 1989–90): 1–2.

"Rendering the Subtext: Subterranean Deconstruction Project," in *The Philosophy of Alain Locke, Harlem Renaissance and Beyond*, Leonard Harris, ed. (Philadelphia: Temple University Press, 1989).

"The Lacuna Between Philosophy and History," *The Journal of Social Philosophy* XX, no. 3 (winter 1989): 110–14.

"Identity: Alain Locke's Atavism," *Transactions of the Charles S. Peirce Society* XXVI, no. 1 (winter 1988): 65–84.

"The Characterization of American Philosophy: The African World as a Reality in American Philosophy," *Quest: Philosophical Discussions* 11:1 (June 1988): 25–36.

"The Legitimation Crisis in American Philosophy: Crisis Resolution from the Standpoint of the Afro-American Tradition of Philosophy," *Social Science Information* 21, no. 1 (1987): 57–73.

[eleven]

Naomi Zack

Naomi Zack teaches philosophy at the University at Albany, State University of New York. She earned her B.A. in philosophy from New York University and her Ph.D. from Columbia University. Her areas of specialization are seventeenth-century philosophy, social and political philosophy, and racial theory. She is the author of *Race and Mixed Race* and of *Bachelors of Science: Seventeenth Century Identity, Then and Now*. Her articles have appeared in *Hypatia*, *The APA Newsletter on Philosophy and the Black Experience*, and the *Locke Newsletter*. (A more complete list of Zack's publications can be found at the end of the interview.)

Naomi Zack

University at Albany
State University of New York

George Yancy: When and where were you born?
Naomi Zack: July 21, 1944, Brooklyn, New York.

Yancy: Did you grow up in Brooklyn, and if so do you have fond memories of having grown up there?
Zack: I was raised by my grandmother in Brooklyn, until I was two. My mother and my grandmother took a trip out to California and my mother took me back alone and we ended up on Suffolk Street on the Lower East Side. No, I don't have fond memories. We lived there for about ten years. We were extremely poor. My mother was a single parent and she was an artist. As our first means of support she had a

job as the janitor in the building in which we lived. I went back there a few years ago and I saw the building that we lived in had been torn down and I was relieved. The way I recognized it was that the Jewish mortuary next to it was still standing. We used to go downstairs—my mother was somewhat disorganized—to get the time from a clock among the tombstones that was in the window of this mortuary. A good beginning for a philosophical career.

Yancy:　How long did you spend in Manhattan?

Zack:　Until I was twelve. Then we moved to Westchester for three years and then I moved back to Manhattan. I finished high school at Charles Evans Hughes High School on 18th Street.

Yancy:　What was the racial composition like on the Lower East Side of Manhattan?

Zack:　It was a Jewish immigrant neighborhood until after World War II. Then there was a large Puerto Rican immigration. So, basically, Jews were moving out and Puerto Ricans were moving in at that time.

Yancy:　Where were your parents born?

Zack:　My mother was also born in Brooklyn. I think my father was born in Virginia.

Yancy:　Can you provide a brief sense of their cultural heritages?

Zack:　My mother was the youngest child in a Russian Jewish family that came here in 1903 from Lithuania. There were seven children. Her father was an herbalist and a Hebrew teacher and her parents had quite a struggle making ends meet. My father's father was born a slave and was six years old at the end of the Civil War. He married a Native American woman from Oklahoma and they settled in Virginia. My father had a gardening business and that's how he met my mother. But he was always married to someone else and had about ten legitimate children and also a number of illegitimate children. He was quite a patriarch in his own sphere, but was never a father to me.

Yancy:　I assume that it was fairly risky back then for a Jewish woman and a Black man to be romantically involved.

Zack:　Oh yes, it was a very illicit relationship.

Yancy:　In your book *Race and Mixed Race* you said that during your student years race was not an issue for you. Would you elaborate?

Zack: I had other problems. My mother was eccentric. Also, my grand-mother came to live with us when I was seven. She was senile and I looked after her, while my mother worked, until she died when I was fourteen. My mother sketched portraits in Macy's during those years. Race was an awkward sort of external issue because people were curious about my appearance. In New York, they thought I was "Spanish," which was the word for Puerto Rican at that time. My mother taught me to answer questions about my "nationality," which was the euphemism for race then, by saying I was Jewish. She did not officially admit to me who my father was until I was sixteen, although I had kind of figured it out years before. When we moved to West-chester, which was less racially diverse than New York City, I didn't fit in. People were more overt in suggesting to me that I was Black, the word for which was "colored," at that time.

Yancy: So, you found out that your father was Black when you were sixteen. How did this impact your early consciousness?

Zack: I didn't feel any different than I'd always felt, that is, I had a sense of continuity so that whatever that identity is that one continues with, that sense of being me, was still the same. But there was this fact about myself that I knew people had strong negative reactions to. The high school I went to had a large Black population and it also had a small, in effect, segregated, white academic fast track and I was in that. It was a commuter high school. Students came from all over the city. I didn't have any friends in high school that I saw outside of school, my friends were older.

Yancy: So it was your mother who primarily provided you with a sense of identity?

Zack: To the extent that she did. She had an identity because she was a Russian Jew who'd been born in Brooklyn, and whether she wanted to be observant or not that's what she was. She didn't go out of her way to provide me with an identity because she didn't think much about such things. She never went into a synagogue, not once.

Yancy: Had your father been a more permanent figure in your life, do you think that you would have begun to think differently about your identity?

Zack: I looked him up when I was twenty-eight. I was living in England at the time and I came back to the states on business for a week and I went to visit him, in Brooklyn. There were things going on with the

Black Panthers, there was turmoil about race, and this news was getting abroad. When I saw him I said, "You know, I think that in this country if I were to be Black, I would be so angry. I think I would try to be a revolutionary." He looked at me carefully and he said, "Well, you don't look Black to me." And I asked, "What do I look like to you?" He said, "You look like a pale shade of tan." I think he had a sly wit. I'm not sure where he stood on issues of racial identity.

Yancy: Were there any particular teachers in high school that influenced you most?

Zack: When I was a junior, my English teacher sent us to the 42nd Street library to do research, and my assignment was Aristotle's *Nicomachean Ethics*, the part about virtue being the mean. It was my first exposure to anything like it, and I took notes and presented the ideas in class. The teacher, Mr. Glanzer, was impressed by my oral report. He said that he was taking a course himself on the same subject and he wanted to use my notes. I didn't think he'd be able to read them but I gave them to him. I thought it was odd at the time, that's all.

Yancy: So can you take us to the point where you're leaving high school and you're deciding upon an academic career as an undergraduate?

Zack: Yes. I wanted to write novels like Fyodor Dostoevsky. But my mother wanted me to be a medical doctor and I modified that. I thought, "Well, actually, I'd find it more interesting to be a psychiatrist." And then I thought, "Well, I don't really want to go to medical school so maybe what I'll be is a psychologist." But what I really wanted to do was write these very deep novels about deep human situations; nevertheless, my major was psychology. I got put off by English because by that time its focus was not about stories or human beings, but about literary criticism. I was a psychology major for three years at New York University and then I switched to philosophy in my senior year. I found that I would raise questions in my psychology classes, which would make my professors really angry, and also there seemed to be a lot of tedious work as far as lab work goes and no result of any experiment was ever conclusive. There were always these other possible variables that hadn't been taken into account. What appealed to me about philosophy was that it was a field within which you could read, you could write, and you could talk, and nobody cared if you disagreed with them. You could just follow your ideas.

Yancy: Was it during this time that you felt that you had a talent for philosophy?

Zack: It wasn't so much that I had a talent for it; rather, it was something that I felt comfortable with, that I liked, because of the closeness
of the work where you could think things out on your own.

Yancy: After switching from psychology to philosophy, who did you
study with at New York University?

Zack: I had William Barrett's course on existentialism.

Yancy: Oh, yes, he is the author of *Irrational Man*. What was it like
studying under Barrett?

Zack: He was very breezy. He was very sophisticated. He had a literary
approach to existentialism. Well, I got hold of Heidegger's *Being and
Time* and I wrote a fifty-page outlined summary of that text and I gave
it to Barrett and he gave me an A or an A– on it, but I think it was a bit
too much for him. I mean, he was a literary existentialist. As a matter
of fact, it's funny, when you're young you can hear very superficial
stories about people, anecdotes about people and they can stick in
your mind as role models. Barrett was said to have left academia for
eighteen years and then returned after he was editor of the *Atlantic
Monthly*. When I left academia I used to think of Barrett. "Well, if Barrett did it," I thought, "maybe I can do it if I ever want to come back."
But I'll tell you my best story about Barrett. He was a big man. He was
pretty Irish in the mid-twentieth-century New York way of being Irish.
He wore some hats. He also wore a tan raincoat. You could see that
he was the sort of person who might have a drink. He came to class
one day on crutches. Here's this huge man and he's on crutches and
his foot was in a cast. So, he came hopping and lumbering in and I
was sitting in the front row and I laughed and I thought, "Oh God,
what have I done now?" But I thought very quickly: "Professor Barrett,
I was thinking of Thales of Miletus as you walked in. He fell into a
well gazing up at the stars." Barrett was very flattered. I avoided dis-
grace.

Yancy: Talk about the process that led to your going on to do graduate
work at Columbia University.

Zack: I found out that what you do with philosophy is become a college professor. That means that you go on to graduate school, and I
applied and was accepted by Columbia. I had a first-year Woodrow
Wilson Teaching Fellowship. Columbia was strong in philosophy of

science and history of philosophy. I got through my course work, did my comprehensives, did a year of teaching and chose a dissertation topic. I wanted to write an update on David Hume's theory of causation. Ernest Nagel was the original chair of my committee and he was not pleased with the development of the first chapter and so Bernard Berofsky became chair of the committee and he was not pleased with the development of the first chapter, and didn't know if he could support it. By then, I had revised that chapter five or six times. I was upset. I had been in school for a long time, for most of my life, and I really wanted this degree. I thought that I wanted to teach on a college level, I wasn't absolutely sure. But I took philosophy to be a place where you could do individual and creative work. They kept asking me to revise what I was doing for reasons that didn't seem to me to really get at the intellectual content of what I was doing. It was disillusioning. I really wasn't sure what the reasons were, but also there was a lot of stuff going on then. This was the late '60s. There was Woodstock. I was at Woodstock. I got married in graduate school. I married an English guy who was there from Oxford. When I came to that crisis with my dissertation I went to the chair of the department, Jim Walsh, and asked him what was going on and why I seemed to be caught in this awful Alice in Wonderland maze. He said, "Oh, you're trying to do original work. A dissertation is not supposed to be original work. It's supposed to be a discussion of the literature." He sent me to Sidney Morgenbesser. Morgenbesser said that I had a very good topic, but he thought that it would take about twelve years to finish, and I said, "Well, I don't have twelve years. I want to get my degree now because I'm not sure what I want to do." He said, "Well, if you want to get your degree, let me suggest a topic that you could get through more quickly." He suggested the epistemology of C. I. Lewis. And I had enough preparation for this given the history of philosophy and pragmatism that was stressed in my coursework. So, they liked it and they passed me. They offered me a job teaching at Barnard College but I said, "No thanks. I'm going to leave and write a novel."

Yancy: During that time did you feel that gender was an issue in terms of the intellectual "harassment" that you encountered around your first dissertation topic?

Zack: I'm not sure. Ti Grace Atkinson was there on and off. She was one of the founding members of the second wave of feminism and she was also doing activist/feminist things and really constructing feminism. It was called "Women's Lib" then. There were maybe three female students in the department. Philosophy has always had women, going back to the days of Plato, but very few. I don't think that philosophers are deliberately antifemale, but they don't go out of their way to accommodate the perspectives of women, either. I think that in philosophy, historically speaking, there has been a de facto exclusion of women, but I don't think that it's a fundamental exclusion.

Yancy: Concerning women in philosophy, I know that Hypatia, the Neoplatonist philosopher and astronomer, was staunchly rejected and brutally killed.

Zack: In my book, *Bachelors of Science,* I talk about the architects of seventeenth-century science and philosophy of science. And, yes, they were all male. They had some female correspondents, especially Descartes. But women were already excluded from most important spheres of activity and at least in the seventeenth century they did not yet have the kinds of constructions of female gender according to which women would be considered constitutionally incapable of doing philosophy on an intellectual level. I think that in a sense Columbia University had more of a seventeenth-century sensibility concerning women than a nineteenth-century sensibility. The nineteenth-century sensibility would say, "This is something that women are not good at and they can't do it and we don't want them to do it." The seventeenth-century view is, "Not many women can do this or even want to, but we have no objection to those who can and do."

Yancy: Were there any other people of color there in the philosophy department while you were there?

Zack: Not that I remember.

Yancy: Which teachers at Columbia influenced you most?

Zack: I learned more than I ever realized at Columbia, from all of them. Robert Cummings did existentialism there, but I didn't continue with my studies in existentialism at Columbia except for one course and then reading on my own. I focused more on the history of philosophy, metaphysics, and philosophy of science. And also epistemology given my dissertation topic. Arthur Danto was a very conscientious teacher. Morgenbesser was incomparable, a genius as everyone says.

Yancy: At what point in your philosophical reflections did you develop such a strong philosophical interest concerning the issue of racial identity?

Zack: In 1970 I left academia and stayed away for twenty years. I'll tell you what I did. I was married and divorced a number of times, I had two sons, I did freelance writing, I had a film company in London that wasn't successful, and I started a few small businesses. At forty-five I needed to settle down into something that I could do well for the long haul. Since I was trained in philosophy, I decided to go back. It seemed to me that the field had changed more than it actually had. People were talking about race, gender, etc., and it was acceptable to write about such things and to use your own experiences. I knew I had to do everything when I came back. I had to refresh myself on the standard stuff and then write for publication. I started thinking about race systematically in ways that I had never done before and that's how I got into it.

Yancy: At this juncture, did the issue of race present itself as an intellectual concern, or were there deep personal and existential issues at stake?

Zack: Anyone who has Black ancestry in this country has a constant awareness of race on different levels. You can't turn it off, but the volume varies depending on the situation. Writing about race is different, especially if you're applying the tools of philosophy. You get clarity on the subject that you can't get if you're just living it. When I came back, I started teaching as an adjunct. And I wrote about race from the standpoint of being mixed-race. Berel Lang who was chair at the philosophy department at SUNY, Albany, saw the first piece that Leonard Harris later published in *The APA Newsletter on Philosophy and the Black Experience.* He asked me if I would apply for a TOP (standing for Target of Opportunity) tenure-track line as an affirmative action candidate. I said, "Fine, so long as you realize that I'm not a paradigm African-American candidate." I also had two on-campus interviews in California. The result was two job offers, and I chose the SUNY position.

Yancy: What is the problem with the concept of race?

Zack: The problem with race is that it does not have the biological foundation that people in ordinary life assume it has. Most people think that there are three main racial categories. They don't know exactly how the categories are constituted or defined, but they think that biologists have the criteria. But biologists don't have such criteria. Race doesn't exist in biology.

Yancy: In your essay "Mixed Black and White Race and Public Policy," there is a constructionist understanding of the concept of race. Say more about the socially constructed nature of race.

Zack: Anthony Appiah has done seminal philosophical work in this area, and I found his work extremely helpful when I started. There is no set of necessary, sufficient, or necessary and sufficient traits that all members of any one race have in common. There is no general chromosomal marker for Blackness or whiteness like there is for maleness or femaleness, for example. The phenotypical traits that are used to define racial membership vary tremendously over time and from place to place. In the United States, this is the social construction of race: People are racially typed through the race of their ancestors. You're Black if you have Black ancestry. You're white if you have no nonwhite ancestry. That's it.

Yancy: Do you think that this way of tracing one's Black racial identity through ancestry is based upon the one-drop rule?

Zack: What else is it? If you say one thing about your ancestors and you're white and you say something else about your ancestors and then all of a sudden you're Black, and you look exactly the same—my appearance, for instance, is very consistent—then it's either a one-drop rule or a magical power of words. Actually they amount to the same thing in this case because there is nothing in biology to support a one-drop rule. I have a sixteen-year-old son who appears white. His father has four Irish grandparents. On the other hand, in terms of his ancestry on my side, he is not white. He is Black, according to the one-drop rule. I think he's going to identify as mixed-race once he sorts all this out. I have a twenty-two-year-old son, and his father is German and Swiss. He looks mixed-race, or maybe Chicano. Sometimes he identifies as Black, insists on it. They seem to have these choices but officially they don't. Officially, they are Black.

Yancy: So, assuming that race is a fiction, that there are no racial essences, no necessary and sufficient conditions for racial membership, what do you make of a fiction that has so much "reality"?

Zack: I take it very seriously. It has a great deal of social reality. It has become part of human bodily experience. People have visceral responses to what they perceive to be racial differences or racial sameness. It affects gender, it affects sexuality, it affects all kinds of spontaneous physical actions and reactions and that's where we all live. But it's an illusion.

Yancy: But even within the biological sciences there are scientists who also disagree.

Zack: There are schools of racialist scientists, some of whom receive funding from politically conservative—no, reactionary—organizations. They work from hypotheses about nineteenth-century hierarchical ideas of races. They're looking for proof of white superiority; they're looking for this Rosetta Stone of Black inferiority. As well, there are scientists who work with DNA in regard to race. But unless they start out with the groups that society has already picked out as racial and take care to choose "typical" members of those groups, they can't find any empirical foundation for the racial divisions. Within the socially constructed races, there are greater variations within races, than between or among races, according to all genetic measures of human traits.

Yancy: How do you propose then that we talk about similar and different identities between people?

Zack: We just have to talk them all out. I have an idea for a book called *The Dialectic of Race* and my thesis is that race is dialectical, not because there is some Hegelian Absolute that is working its way through history, but because race was never sufficiently thought out.

Yancy: What specifically do you find problematic with regard to the notion of a cultural identity? I am thinking of those theorists who reject the existence of a biological substratum underlying race, but who embrace a cultural identity based upon shared behavior, thought, and feeling patterns?

Zack: Walter Benn Michaels as well as Anthony Appiah have stated this problem well. In order to pick out culture you're going to use some antecedent racial marker to identify the members of that culture. So you can't use culture to define race without circularity. There are also problems with cultural sameness and cohesion within a so-called racial group.

Yancy: Given that you reject a specifically racial identity and indeed reject a specifically cultural identity, what constitutes identity for you?

Zack: I think that we have identities because they are useful for action and empowerment. We act through them and reflect upon them. They are media for social life. Identities are in fact fluid and they vary depending on our intentions and contexts.

Yancy: In terms of your identity, do you identify yourself as a Jewish person, culturally, racially, or religiously?

Zack: Probably only if you're marching me off to the gas chamber.

Yancy: But what if you're being marched off into slavery because of your Black paternal ancestry, would you then consider yourself a Black person?

Zack: Yes, absolutely!

Yancy: Doesn't the construction that because one's mother is Jewish then one is therefore also Jewish have conceptual problems similar to the one-drop rule?

Zack: Yes, because many Jews say that they are an ethnicity, or a religion, and not a race. Well, if they're not a race then how is it that Judaism is inherited through the identity of one's mother?

Yancy: So, you don't consider being a Jew to be part of a racial group?

Zack: No, I don't think so. I don't know that anybody does at this point. I think that most American Jews today, if you were to designate them as a racial group, would consider that to be a form of anti-Semitism. And I think that this is a lesson that Blacks might consider. It may be that racial designation opens the door to racist action.

Yancy: Do you think that the relinquishment of race as a primary designator of identity will resolve the fundamental maintenance of racism?

Zack: If it is really done. If people could un-think race and stop thinking in racial terms, then racism as we know it couldn't get started. Some writers think that racism, as a dominant group's us-versus-them mentality, is prior to and more enduring than ideas of race. I prefer a narrow reading of racism. I would say that if you get people to un-think race then their racism dissolves. I do believe, and this is a personal opinion, that that is a good part of the resistance against seeing how empty the concept of race really is.

Yancy: In terms of my previous question, why would we assume that whites would want to relinquish race given the fact that whiteness, as it were, is such a central designator of power and privilege. To ask people to relinquish race, particularly white people, is to ask them to relinquish their power. Are you also asking for the relinquishment of capital power and sociopolitical power as these are fundamentally linked to race?

Zack: I can only do so much. Of course, many people of color are leery about relinquishing race. Parts of their racial identities have been constructed in reaction to racism rather than positively and gratuitously for their own sake. However, they have, on the basis of those identities, gotten certain hard-won entitlements that they don't want to lose. So when you move this situation into a political context it gets very loaded in the short term. I'm not thinking in the short term. I'm thinking in a larger historical perspective.

Yancy: Do you think that there are some who desire to vitiate those hard-won entitlements by the very process of advocating the relinquishment of race? And if so, what's your response to such a stratagem?

Zack: I've heard about that nefarious position held by that species of racist. But I don't know where it exists. I think it's a straw man. Of course, some people call for color-blindness when they really want more freedom to discriminate. That's another matter, isn't it?

Yancy: In your book *Bachelors of Science: Seventeenth Century Identity, Then and Now* you argue that to refer to the early European colonizers as racists is an anachronism. Would you elaborate?

Zack: The idea of race that we are still beleaguered with right now has an historical beginning, and we are now somewhere in the middle to the end of it. It began in the eighteenth century and was fully conceptualized in the nineteenth. Much of that work was done by speculative scientists in the best American universities. They constructed theories of the hierarchy of the human races partly in response to a political need to justify slavery and then segregation. At the time that the slave trade began the modern concept of race was not in existence. There was no idea of a biological division of human beings into races that formed a hierarchy such that each contained a unique essence. Obviously, the people who were kidnaped and enslaved and brought to work in the colonies were considered different. The difference seems to have been based on religion and it was also a power situation. European technology was dominant over the technologies of the people who were exploited and destroyed. Obviously, all of this was the most extreme form of domination, persecution, and destruction. But in its inception, it was not driven by ideas of race that were fully conceptualized only later.

Yancy: And by this analysis I would assume that you're not attempting to mitigate the sheer horror of slavery.

Zack: No. Ideas of race were constructed to rationalize that horror.

Yancy: Let's assume that Europeans did not have this fully blown racist conceptual apparatus. Why didn't they look within their own communities and find differences and then proceeded to oppress and enslave?

Zack: They did where they could. The English enslaved each other during the religious wars of the seventeenth century. Some of the worst atrocities occur within so-called races—look at Irish history, for instance.

Yancy: But even so, the African was fundamentally conceived in nonhuman terms. This phenomenon of the European's sheer brutality toward Africans requires a deeper psychological analysis. For I would imagine that even during the religious wars that fellow Europeans, although considered enemies, would have maintained their status as human.

Zack: Africans were not considered nonhuman. However, there were different religious positions on the souls of heathens. You also had a very interesting phenomenon that I try to approach in *Bachelors of Science*, namely, self-deification of early Protestant capitalists. They took upon themselves divine characteristics of being the lord proprietors of the whole earth. You have this notion in the thought of John Locke where God originally gave the earth to mankind. It's good to work because God works, and you have to work in order to better yourself and you've got all of this material to work with. Not only did the early capitalists have an exploitative attitude towards heathens and people with lesser technology who didn't labor as they thought God wanted, but they saw natural environments as completely expendable and with no intrinsic value. They were very happy to posit a state of nature for rhetorical purposes and for the construction of political philosophies, but they had no concept of a state of nature as something that could support human existence as it was. The state of nature was something that one had to perform certain operations on as part of the divine, unnatural being that one was. And making money was a holy virtue.

Yancy: Why didn't Europeans simply go to some other place and enslave other Europeans on a large scale instead of the millions of Africans that were brutally deported from Africa?

Zack: They didn't have the technological superiority that would have enabled them to do it.

Yancy: Again, let us assume that race is a fiction. Now, the Civil Rights Movement was based on the struggle of Black people for Black people. How do we explain to millions of Black people that their struggle was held together by an intersubjectively held fiction?

Zack: Well, you can go back to W. E. B. Du Bois. In *Dusk of Dawn*, and throughout his career, he was aware that race was a fiction in any biological scientific sense. He has an interesting dialogue with someone who today we would call a white racist. And the white racist says to him at one point, "Well, if there really is no foundation for race, how do you consider yourself Black? What's the basis for that?" And Du Bois says, in effect, "Well, I'm Black due to Jim Crow." That says it in a nutshell. Race is a fiction that after the fact of domination was applied to large numbers of people many of whom could be picked out on the basis of skin color. (Not all but many of whom were also enslaved and who are today descendants of slaves.) So, that group has had racial categories ascribed to it in ways that they have not legally had the power to question. But even on the basis of that ascription, Black identity has not automatically sprung full-blown out of the heads of Black folk. It's been something that Black leaders have had to develop, work at, teach, preach, and everything else for a long time. Dr. Martin Luther King, Jr. and Malcolm X are both excellent examples of that, as was Du Bois and Frederick Douglass. The Black identity on the basis of which people who have been called Black resist white racism is an identity which is taken up because people have had racist identities ascribed to them. That is, the group that's been persecuted has formed its identity partly on the basis of the ascriptions under which they've been persecuted.

Yancy: Which are not *real* descriptions?

Zack: No, they're not real descriptions. They're ascriptions. They're not descriptions of things that exist. They are words that have been ascribed to people and by law mandated to be hereditary.

Yancy: Would you say then that our identity at the Million Man March was an identity dialectically linked to an ascribing Other?

Zack: Well, I'd put it this way. I'm preparing a paper about Lewis Gordon's book *Fanon and the Crisis of European Man*. I think that there are some real problems if you're going to take up existentialism as a way of dealing with race from a Black perspective. One of the assets of that project is that we can lay out in great detail the bad faith of white racists. However, if we're going to be existentialists, we've got an added burden of sophistication about our own bad faith. If you have a Black identity ascribed to you, that's a responsibility, that's a burden, and you've got to do something with it. You can't just fine tune the program by proving that what white racists say about Blacks isn't true. You have to interrogate what it means, literally, when they say you are Black.

Yancy: What is your response to a critic who says that your push for the relinquishment of the concept of race is just a form of self-denial or a way of avoiding the socially perceived negativity of Blackness and its consequences?

Zack: In other words, "She doesn't want to be Black, she's afraid." Well, that's a psychological statement. Psychology is a deterministic science. And I'm not in a position to make those evaluations about myself. In any case, we still have to deal with my ideas intellectually. So, the criticism doesn't matter.

Yancy: Do you think that what you're doing in terms of creating a paradigm shift in our conceptual understanding of race will have a bearing on the way in which African-American philosophers conceptualize Black philosophy?

Zack: I think that it already has. But look, if the paradigm shift has some input from my discomfort of being mixed-race, then this is not just an intellectual/philosophical shift. This is an historical shift. There are many other people who are mixed-race, and in many different ways. The mixed-race birth rate is a demographic fact. It has been increasing ever since they struck down the antimiscegenation laws. It is human existence and the conditions of human existence that will change the paradigm. I'm with Hegel where he talks about the owl of Minerva beginning her flight at dusk.

Yancy: What is the relationship between Naomi Zack's personal identity and her philosophical worldview?

Zack: I think that the fact that I'm doing this kind of work fulfills a sense that I've had ever since I was a child of having to find important work to do. Or maybe it has something to do with the fact that my mother was an artist, and I grew up valuing creativity. Having a worldview intersects with a certain kind of temperament. I'm fifty-two now and

I've gotten to know myself. I'm sort of introverted, though I interact with lots of people as necessary. I'm somewhat reclusive. I know I've got a philosophical bent. But whether this is a result of doing philosophy or whether it's a result of other social and psychological factors, I don't know. To have a philosophical worldview is something that suits me given the sort of person I am. In other words, I think that at this point I can say that I am a philosopher.

A Selection of Published Works of Naomi Zack

Books

Thinking About Race (Belmont, CA: Wadsworth, 1998).

Bachelors of Science: Seventeenth Century Identity, Then and Now (Philadelphia: Temple University Press, 1996).

Race/Sex: Their Sameness, Difference and Interplay, ed. (New York: Routledge, 1997).

American Mixed Race: Constructing Micro Diversity, ed. (Lanham, MD: Rowman and Littlefield, 1995).

Race and Mixed Race (Philadelphia: Temple University Press, 1993).

Articles

"On Being and Not Being Black and Jewish," in *The Multiracial Experience*, Maria P. P. Root, ed. (Newbury Park, CA: Sage, 1996).

"Race, Life, Death, Identity, Tragedy and Good Faith," in *Existence in Black*, Lewis R. Gordon, ed. (New York: Routledge, 1996).

"Locke and the Indians," in *The Social Power of Ideas*, W. Creighton Pedan and Yaeger Hudson, eds. (Lewiston, NY: Edwin Mellen Press, 1995), 347–60.

"Mixed Black and White Race and Public Policy," *Hypatia* 10, no. 1 (winter 1995): 120–32.

"An Autobiographical View of Mixed-Race and Deracination," in *Contemporary Moral Issues*, Larry Hinman, ed. (Old Tappan, NJ: Prentice Hall, 1995). Reprinted from *The American Philosophical Association Newsletter on Philosophy and the Black Experience*, fall 1992.

"Locke's Identity Meaning of Ownership," *Locke Newsletter*, no. 23 (1992): 105–14.

[twelve]

Joy James

Joy James currently is associate professor of ethnic studies at the University of Colorado, Boulder. She earned a B.A. degree in political science from St. Mary's University and her first M.A. in international politics from Fordham University. She earned her second M.A. from Union Theological Seminary, where she focused on Black theology/liberation theology and studied with Cornel West, James Cone, and Mercy Amba Oduyoye, the Ghanaian feminist theologian. Her Ph.D. in political philosophy is also from Fordham University. She has taught at the University of Massachusetts, Amherst, and at the New York Theological Seminary. James's areas of specialization are political philosophy/political thought, critical race theory, and feminist theory. Her articles and reviews have appeared in *Cultural Studies*; *The Black Scholar*; *Race and Class*; *Existence in Black: An Anthology of Black Existential Philosophy*; *Fanon Today: Readings and Confrontations*; *Skin Deep: Women of Color on Race and Color in America*; *Radically Speaking: Feminism Reclaimed* and *Marxism in the Postmodern Age*; and more. She is the author of *Resisting State Violence: Radicalism, Gender, and Race in U.S. Culture*, and *Transcending the Talented Tenth: Black Leaders and American Intellectualism*. She is also coeditor of *Spirit, Space and Survival: African American Women in (White) Academe* and editor of *The Angela Y. Davis Reader*. (A more complete citation list of Joy James's published works can be found at the end of the interview.)

Joy James

University of Colorado, Boulder

George Yancy: Where were you born?
Joy James: I was born in Frankfurt, Germany.

Yancy: What was it like to grow up there?
James: Well, I left when I was very, very young. I'm what some people would call a "military brat." But I would say I was in a family of people who were careerists in the military. So, we moved around quite a bit. I grew up on army posts, mostly in the South at Fort Benning, Georgia, Fort Bragg, North Carolina, Fort Belvoir, Virginia, and I spent some time in New Jersey at Fort Monmouth. When I was about eleven, we relocated permanently to San Antonio, Texas. My best memories were in North Carolina.

Yancy: Why North Carolina?
James: Partly because of the land. That's when I became very conscious about how comfortable you could be roaming around outdoors in a certain kind of environment. Also I think probably that's when my father first made officer and so the housing became different. It became more spacious. I had a lot of freedom at that time. I spent a lot of time outdoors alone. Those are my best memories.

Yancy: Given the degree of mobility, how were the formative years in terms of your schooling?
James: Well, that was an advantage. I guess everything is a trade-off. Military culture is pretty much self-enclosed. I think less so now in the '90s than it was in the '60s say, but once you are on Post everything is there. So you have your own school system, you have your own hospitals, you have your own stores. And the school tended to pay higher teacher salaries, particularly in the South, than other schools. So, the education turned out to be quite good. Basically you were well educated. It wasn't a private school or anything of that sort, but it was an alternative school to the schools in that particular region. Schools at military posts had classes that would be integrated, unlike other classrooms in the South during that period. The curriculum was more rigorous than that in the public schools at the time in that region. Even though you were indoctrinated into a certain kind of patriotism or loyalty because it was a military culture, there was another trade-off

that you got, a sense of self-confidence, that you belonged. That, obviously, in this military culture, was supposed to transcend race. And even though it didn't, it was supposed to.

Yancy: Were there particular teachers that impacted you intellectually?

James: Moving around every eighteen months there was limited ability for me to feel really nurtured until I was around eleven or twelve, when we stayed in San Antonio where my father retired. I do remember one teacher; I must have been in first grade. This was the time of Kennedy's assassination, which always struck me, but this is a symptom of what a military culture is like, right, that as a young child I can remember a teacher sobbing when Kennedy was assassinated. I remember all of us being sent home and being incredibly distraught because when you are in first grade (or kindergarten, I can't remember exactly what grade I was in), you know your teachers are this sort of bulwark of stability and emotional serenity and calm; and this was a woman who I felt emotionally drawn to. She was very maternal and was very good with children. And she was a white teacher. I was just totally distraught myself then to leave school and then to talk to my mother, "Well, my teacher broke down." I remember my mother being very angry, finding that to be very inappropriate behavior on the part of the teacher. But what struck me later was that I could not remember any kind of strong, emotional dissonance around the assassination of King or Malcolm X or other Black leaders in military or familial culture. So, there was a way in which the teachers themselves marked who you grieved for. And those figures tended to be state leaders; and they overwhelmingly tended to be white. And that shaped my consciousness; it was then that I started to pull away from military culture, at around the age of twelve or so, finding that the reflection it gave was just not me at that particular point.

Yancy: Were your parents instrumental in shaping your early intellectual growth?

James: Well, my parents, like a lot of Black parents at the time, were coming out at the time with the restrictions of Jim Crow—especially my mother who grew up in Mississippi. Her siblings, as soon as they became of age, all fled the state. You went to Chicago, you went to L.A., you went to Texas. You just didn't stay in Mississippi. I think their whole thing, as best as I can recall, not that they ever articulated it in a conscious fashion, was about assimilation, it was about acceptance. It wasn't really about thinking independently. But it was definitely that you don't allow people to disrespect you and that you stand up for yourself. But there was an emphasis on how far you had come, meaning themselves personally, out of that era. And, also once you become an officer, in that microcosm of a culture, that was a middle-class thing. I mean my mother, as far as I can remember, was at home until my parents divorced, when I was about twelve, and then she went back to work. But the intellectual growth was pretty much something that I found on my own. Obviously, they introduced me to the library, and I got a library card, and I would start reading, but we never really discussed what I was reading.

Yancy: What were you reading during that period?

James: When I was young I was reading what every "good American girl" reads, which was Nancy Drew and *The Happy Hollisters.* When I got older, meaning around eleven, I started reading *The Count of Monte-Cristo*, some Shakespeare, Jane Austin, what were considered "the classics." At that time I sort of branched off into them.

Yancy: At what point did you start to raise, even if unknowingly, philosophical kinds of questions?

James: I think my entry into philosophical questions came a lot from political reality.

Yancy: Elsewhere you have made reference to your father being in the Vietnam war as an impetus to your philosophical questioning.

James: Right. He first went to 'Nam when I was in third grade or so, and there was the juxtaposition of the culture; I've been talking about having been raised in this one culture, and then seeing its impact on your personal life. So, the absenteeism of fathers was one thing. The way they came back from 'Nam or the invasion of the Dominican Republic or the partition of Korea, serving tours of duty and the sort of strained relationships in the household had their impact. That became a real factor for me in terms of thinking about, although I didn't really have a language to call it, the "State," but I knew who our employer was—the government, the military, this culture itself. There was also this dissatisfaction with a certain kind of Black middle-class culture which we were a part of at the time. And even though we had become, when we moved back to San Antonio when I was about eleven, one of the few Black families on this white block that was pretty solidly middle class, and in some parts, upper middle class, there was this whole need to be respectable and an emphasis on appearance and acceptance vis-à-vis whites, but also vis-à-vis other Blacks. I remember at the time I started looking at E. Franklin Frazier and the Black bourgeoisie.

Yancy: How old were you then?

James: I was probably about thirteen. And a couple of years later, when I was around seventeen, I met one of the few Black Panthers in town. We are talking mid-'70s when there were a few Panthers in San Antonio. I also met people who were in the Communist Party, even though I never joined. I think I first met party people when I was about seventeen. I began reading some of the literature they had on Lenin and reading some of the revolutionaries in terms of African revolutionary thinkers at the time. So, it was not a structured approach to philosophy. It was very eclectic. I remember reading Machiavelli's *The Prince*. It was kind of like whatever I could get my hands on, particularly in a culture that did not talk about politics and a culture that did not talk about philosophy.

Yancy: When did you decide that you wanted to study philosophy formally?

James: As an undergraduate, I attended St. Mary's University, which is a Marianist school in San Antonio. This wasn't my choice, but I was under eighteen and the kind of alternative school I wanted to go to was St. John's (New Mexico). They had the great books program and you would study philosophy and there was this alternative curriculum, very open, and my mother kind of nixed that idea, and I didn't have the guts to rebel and forge my name on the application. So I ended up at St. Mary's, and in my first year with these Marianist brothers I started reading Bernard Lonergan's *Insight: An Understanding of Human Knowing* and studied Latin. Through political science I found Hannah Arendt's *The Origins of Totalitarianism*. And that hooked me. I was supposed to go to law school, but that was really my parents' (mother's) dream. Law school kind of turned me off because it seemed so competitive—cramming for this LSAT. I ended up applying for an American Political Science Association National Scholarship and getting it. You could take it to any school that you wanted to go to. And originally I think I was supposed to go to Arizona because it was still in the Southwest and you didn't move too far away from home. I graduated in December; so I had a couple of months to kill, so I ended up in New York hanging out with some friends, some musicians I knew. There was something about the city in terms of a critical mass, if you want to say that, of intellectuals, of artists, of people who didn't quite fit in conventional culture and who weren't asking conventional questions. And having grown up in military culture it was a complete change for me. So, I stayed for ten years.

Yancy: Were there particular professors who influenced you most as an undergraduate?

James: No. When I think about it, and, for me, it is a real tragedy, I think at that time a professor who would have influenced me greatly would probably have been one who had some sense or sensibility around African-American political thought, African-American culture, African-American politics per se. All my professors were white with the exception of Neftali Garcia who was Chicano. And his was the first course on "Minority Politics" that I took and the emphasis was on Chicano politics, which was, at that time, I think, a little bit disappointing for me because I wanted to learn more about Black politics. But definitely in terms of having faculty of color he was my first and only faculty of color. And I learned from others. I learned from Sister Anne Semel, who was in English, and I learned from other political scientists. It was a racist environment pretty much even with the most progressive people. You're talking late '70s, Catholic school, and San Antonio never had more than 8 percent Black population. The strongest cultural political force that was to the left would have been the Chicano, the Mexican-American culture. And I remember working on Henry Cisnero's first mayoral campaign when I was seventeen, which he lost. He was later elected San Antonio's first Chicano mayor in the '80s and became head of HUD in the Clinton administration in the '90s. I was involved in politics to the extent that there was a Black independent political base. I did voter registration and things like that. Critical consciousness was really something I was looking for because I always felt dissatisfied with being in San Antonio. That critical consciousness really came later from my being in New York.

Yancy: Where did you do your graduate work and why there?

James: Fordham University. I sort of got hooked up in the mythology of Catholic schools. And I probably felt comfortable in a Catholic culture. I mean, in certain ways, Catholic culture is probably like military culture. Maybe Catholics wouldn't agree, but at some levels, at least for me years ago, it was somewhat of a closed society. You had these hierarchies of Brothers and Sisters and Fathers. You had this false sense, for some people a real sense, of community as "family," something that bounds the collective you together to this faith. I was not Catholic myself but I still had a strong sense of being part of a Christian belief system. I knew Catholic schools from undergrad. I assumed that Catholics would have more of a focus on, and the word that comes to mind here is charity or *Caritas*. If I didn't frame it in that word, it was still a sense of a human service focus. When I was an undergrad I had worked with Brothers [Marianists] in terms of collecting meals for the poor and homeless people and doing food drives and that kind of thing. Although I didn't engage in that type of work when I got to Fordham, I just assumed that I knew the ritual of how to move around Catholic school, that there would be this larger mission of service, and that was something that I wanted as part of my education.

Yancy: At Fordham, who influenced you most in terms of philosophical criticality?

James: Well, you know, Fordham was full of male Republicans. Maybe I thrive on opposition. I would say nobody influenced me in terms of philosophical criticality. I had a dual educational system in New York City. I learned from people I worked with outside of the university. And then I learned a certain kind of skill, academic skill, and reading from inside of the university. So, in political science, particularly in political philosophy, the professors were conservatives, Reagan Republicans by and large. I would just say that one of the things that I appreciated from Fordham was the "traditional" education. I had to read Rousseau, Voltaire, and the Enlightenment philosophies. There was this groundedness even as I wanted to expand my critical thinking. Fordham wasn't about critical thinking; it was about indoctrination into what they considered to be the canon. The Jesuits felt that they knew the canon. And probably out of most Catholics in terms of education, they're pretty well grounded. But it's a conservative education.

Yancy: While taking philosophy courses at Fordham, were you often the only Black female presence in the class?

James: I was the only Black female in my department. Oh mercy. I was the only Black female in all of my classes.

Yancy: When did you first come into contact with feminist theory?

James: When I was a kid. I started baby-sitting around thirteen or fourteen for these white women who were pretty affluent; then I started reading Kate Millet and Betty Friedan, mainstream feminism. I began looking at these housewives who didn't work outside the home—this was after my mother's divorce so she has to go back to work, and their sort of alienation from themselves, and from their kids. They had maids. I had to make it very clear that "I am not your maid but I will baby-sit your kids." So, when I was thinking critically about race and class, I was also thinking critically about gender.

Yancy: Do you construct yourself as an African-American philosopher?
James: Well, I don't know what that is to tell you the truth. I under- stand, first and foremost, political commitments. And that's a product of my upbringing and also a part of my self-construction. I also under- stand critical thinking that has a relevance to people's struggles. When I was at Fordham; I would go over to the philosophy depart- ment and take classes; I know that there were certain books that "spoke" to me, like Ludwig Wittgenstein's *On Certainty.* That's a beautiful book. I was appreciating philosophy in different ways. But for me that became, on some level, a question of personal sensibility and taste. And there was this other level which was not sharply sepa- rated from that of personal sensibility. There was another level of accountability and political responsibility. And so whatever you appreciated in terms of the development of your sense of self, and of your intellect, however you nurtured yourself, on those levels that was fine with whatever it took. When it came time you also needed to be able to produce and contribute in a way that was very relevant, very incisive, very practical and also that was not in conformity with what exists just because it exists, just because it's the norm, if it doesn't allow you to go to the next stage in your being, as part of a collective.

Yancy: So, what is African-American philosophy?
James: Well, what's European-American philosophy? I mean there is no monolithic African-American thought. There have been ways in which our theory and philosophy have served in our liberation pro- ject and there have been ways in which it's resonated with particular aspects of culture, American culture and Black American or African- American culture. I see it though now splintering in a lot of ways. *Transcending the Talented Tenth: Black Leaders and American Intel- lectuals* takes a look at this construction of the Black intellectual, which has been debated quite a bit in recent years. So, there is a lot of this questioning of—and I'm not sure if people would use this term

"philosophers" anymore as they would intellectuals—who we are as Black intellectuals, what are our responsibilities, what are our intellectual abilities. I think that there is an incredible amount of insecurity running through a lot of this discourse right now that reflects the levels of performance and the lack of substance. There seems to be almost an ungroundedness in political thought and the ability to critique structure. And in this ungroundedness, there is a false performance. There is a type of vanity, the projection of the self as this Black intellectual self and a Black critical thinker, even though apparently the Emperor and Empress have lost some of their garments. This splintering of African-American critical thought (I do think there is a difference between philosophy and theory) has to do a lot with our low expectations and even lower levels of political courage.

Yancy: As a Black female intellectual, in what ways has the academy explicitly and/or implicitly militated against your occupying a space within its walls?

James: I believe that the academy is a corporation and practically all corporations like good functionaries for employees. There are people who function well within the structure, people who don't necessarily do stellar performances. I mean, that's not the point, it's that you can participate in your assigned slot and that there's a certain routine according to which you discipline yourself. I find that to be poisonous, toxic. I've seen some really good people, both undergrads and young faculty get kicked to the curb. One thing that really struck me when I was a graduate student was this token recognition for my "whatever" ability where they put me on this hiring committee in political science. And they had the chance to hire Cheryl Payer, an expert on the debt crisis. She had a Harvard Ph.D., had experience, and a number of publications. She was well known but they chose an ABD [all but dissertation] over her and the ABD was somebody who was very young and socially immature and didn't last for more than a year at Fordham. The male faculty wanted someone who could "get along" and who they could socialize into their idea of what a good academic is. Payer had a set politics that was progressive (left) and she was also incredibly bright, and yet that was irrelevant. That lesson of her rejection is one that I've seen played over and over again with its own characteristics shaped around race and around politics. I think that the academy has more hostility toward left-radicals than it does toward people of color.

Yancy: What must be done to demarginalize the activity of African-American philosophizing or theorizing with respect to its representation in the academy?

James: Well, see, that's an interesting point in terms of the multiplicity of African-American critical theory or African-American philosophy. I mean some of it isn't marginal at all. You go to Cambridge and check in with that crew there. The elites have managed to put African-American studies on the map in a certain way which we should all be grateful for, but at another level it feels like a Trojan horse. What exactly is it and who gets to define it and for whose service does it function? And this ability to deconstruct Black people and Black essentialism doesn't seem to be matched with the ability to deconstruct corporate settings and Black performance for middle-class, upper-middle-class consumers, and antiradicalism. As I see it, there is an emerging strain of antiradical thought. And so, what is not marginalized is the liberal African-American political thought or African-American cultural critique. The liberal and the neoconservative stuff is not marginalized. What's marginalized is the radical, the sort of critical left which says, "Let's talk about the State." You referred earlier to my dad in Vietnam, well, you come to consciousness with an awareness that there are these structures that shape people's lives, that cripple or set limits to their dreams. One story in our family is that my dad was drafted and then left the army but the only job that he could find was as a cook, so he reenlisted. When he died he died as a lieutenant colonel but very embittered. His story is very different from Colin Powell's story.

Obviously some African-Americans find this culture to be satisfactory in certain ways. Others find it to be devastating. But the ability of intellectuals who make claims to philosophy and theory to really examine the ceiling and the floor that we have, these sort of parameters that we share with this larger American culture, but also what it means to be racialized and too often stigmatized in this culture and what it means to resist, has unfortunately often functioned as mere performance. There is a perversion going on that resistance has been redefined as performance. And I can't for the life of me figure out how critical thinking is going to get back in the door with that kind of construct.

Yancy: Why do we hear so much about the works of say Carol Gilligan, Catharine MacKinnon, Drucilla Cornell, and other white women theorists and not about the works of Anna Julia Cooper, Angela Davis, Blanche Radford Curry, and others?

James: Well, there's a couple of reasons. There's the whole construction of "philosopher" as writer and academic which has been racialized in this culture. In a culture dominated by whites and in an intellectual environment dominated by European-Americans, their works will get more play and more privilege. The other thing, though, which is a bit problematic, is that the writings of thinkers who were engaged in very concrete struggle in their communities tend to be overlooked as philosophical or theoretical. I mean I really am happy that so many writers, and it seems to be mostly female writers, are recovering the works of say people like Anna Julia Cooper and Angela Davis. Blackwell Publishers has published a reader on Angela Davis, which I edited. There is this way in which particularly Black women have been typified as being "activists" rather than theorists or philosophers. So there is this false dichotomy between thinking and doing that has been constructed. And there is a racial irony, you know people don't dichotomize Hannah Arendt, who organized in Europe against Nazi occupation. Perhaps this is a generalization but it seems that whites are assigned, as part of their genetic construct, the ability to theorize and philosophize and so if they also happen to be engaged in political struggle on a very concrete level that doesn't throw their ability to think into question. But for a population that has had to prove that it is not mentally inferior and that has been encapsulated in the physicality of the body—we represent the body, the other culture represents the mind—for us to establish ourselves as political workers, as political activists, as political critics, means that we are often labeled as being anti-intellectual, or not intellectual, antitheoretical, you know, atheoretical. Incidentally, my dissertation at Fordham was entitled "Hannah Arendt's Concept of Power as Communication: A Feminist Critique" and my advisor at that time was William Baumgarth, who proved very supportive.

Yancy: Are the philosophical projects of Black feminist theorists different from those of white feminist theorists?

James: To the extent that Black feminist theorists have consistently talked about race; but increasingly white feminist theorists talk about race. So now the question is, "How well is this discussion going down?" People like bell hooks, Angela Davis, Toni Morrison, and Paula Giddings, as well as a number of Black feminists, have done incredible work in terms of putting the issues of race and gender on the table and there are more women obviously than the ones that I have mentioned. And this is a struggle that's gone back since before Ida B. Wells. OK, we are going to talk about violence, we are going to talk about sexual violence in relationship to racial violence, and we are going to talk about race. But at the same time as we are going into the next millennium, and people will call me on this, I think ideology is muting the differences that a Black liberal feminist will maybe talk about race in ways similar to a white liberal feminist who sees herself as an antiracist. But that means we could talk about "race" on levels that do not really offer a radical critique about the ways in which race is constructed and the ways in which people who are racialized as Black are punished in this culture.

Yancy: How do we get more African-American women in the field of philosophy?

James: Of course I have a recipe for this. This is interesting because bell hooks writes about this in *Breaking Bread* with Cornel West, about needing more Black people in this field, and my criticism of that particular piece that she wrote on Black women intellectuals is that it sounds like the intellectual is really the academic. And if the question is really how do we get more Black women into academia to get degrees in philosophy, postgraduate degrees or graduate degrees in philosophy, that's a separate question. That's really about how you are going to mentor and train people to get through what can be a very tortuous process, particularly because philosophy seems to have been contaminated with these biological notions of who can philosophize and who cannot. I would say that we need to build stronger support systems. We need to deal with the antiaffirmative action backlash. We need to make sure that philosophical works by African-Americans and people of African descent, it's not just African-Americans, right, by women, become part of the canon, part of the curriculum. We need to have more professors who are women, who are Black, you know, present, teaching these classes and so on and so forth. That's one thing. But there's a whole other part of philosophy and theory that is not professionalized and that, for me, is the exciting part. And the question is: How is it that we could struggle in order to change our conditions so that we even have more time to think?

In this culture, critical thinking is becoming, for some, a leisure activity. People are so pressed with meeting their daily needs and don't have this down-space for reflection. But the ability to have space for reflection in our lives, to have literature that we can engage in, and also to have these kind of associations with other people, is important. That does exist already, but maybe it is not well documented. So we don't know how much philosophizing actually goes on in Black communities among Black women. Nobody knows and nobody has really asked them. Patricia Hill Collins has done some important work on Black feminist thought, but when she talks about the "rearticulation specialist," as though you are supposed to go out and hear the story and resay what the sister said to make it theory, that's a questionable activity at best. But to recognize indigenous critical thinking, indigenous philosophy, and support it, create a space for it, document it, encourage it, and listen to it respectfully, I think that's a whole other project. And that may be more about what academics or professional thinkers need to be doing to change their and our outlook on what constitutes philosophy.

Yancy: In your book *Spirit, Space and Survival*, how do you distinguish theory from philosophy?

James: In that text I was thinking of theory as having this very clear focus around confronting political and economic conditions. That is the way Barbara Christian talks about theorizing in "The Race for Theory," where she says our people, we, have always been a race for theory. Because you're trying to figure out how to literally get from historical bondage, physical bondage, into freedom. And there is no greater philosophical question than what does it mean to be free. And today we have technical, legal liberation, yet you know what it means to be a subordinate group, culturally, economically, politically, educationally, and what it means to exist in this culture that is so pathological around race. Unlike theory, philosophy may not have such an instrumental focus, but still being in service because it has this idea of what is beautiful, what is good, ideas or ideals that people strive for. And to go back to what Black women do, like Black men, like other women and men, I think in our best moments we always ask ourselves these questions on these different levels.

Yancy: What role should the African-American philosopher play within the Black community?

James: Well, the African-American philosopher would be in relationship, which would go beyond that of what our degrees and our professionalization have given us, meaning that hierarchical notion and function. And to be in relationship probably means to be in struggle. And, to be in struggle means that you actually have to do some work. I'm going back to the organizing that I knew in the '80s. I know I've been out of it for some time and it has really dawned on me that just to survive academe becomes a "twenty-four-seven," you can get sucked in so much into this need to produce, to write, and to socialize or serve on committees. And I don't think it's bad to take breaks, to get involved in certain tasks, certain writings, certain thoughts, to work out ideas. But it's always important to touch base, particularly if you make these claims towards not being an isolated thinker but you make claims towards being representative and also claims to being informed, not about your own individualistic set of ideas but, in fact, the ideas of the people and the people in struggle.

So, one of the things that I learned, and this is what I got from Angela Davis and I'm very grateful, when I did this postdoc recently in California, was really to focus and begin to look at particular systems which become critical levels for entry. Not levels of entry for more discourse, but to actually work. And so, I'm in Colorado right now, I'm in Boulder, and there are not a lot of Black people, but they are in Denver. Also in Colorado there is this prison at Florence, Colorado, called the "Alcatraz of the Rockies" or "Super Max." This maximum security, really horrific, structure speaks to this whole criminalization process and punitive ideology that has infused parts of the U.S. right now. So, to start doing work around prisons means that I open myself to forms of education that I was aware that I needed to have when I was in grad school. But I had to balance the corporate, conservative atmosphere of Fordham with say organizing around antiapartheid or antiviolence against women movements in the city. But that's just not something that you do as a student. It's a lifelong process. And so now as an academic I need to go work in the community and not just talk about what communities need to do politically or intellectually but actually to receive knowledge and give back what I know. And that's what I mean by a relationship. A peer relationship doesn't often exist. If you read the works of some Black intellectuals you find that there's no peer relationship with working-class Black people. Unfortunately, they've become the objects of our discourse or they're the subjects of our lectures.

Yancy: From the essay that you have in the book *Marxism in the Postmodern Age*, how is it possible to continue to talk about Marxism within a postmodernist context where there is the whole notion of an incredulity toward metanarratives?

James: Well, you know, first, who's putting out the notion of incredulity in metanarratives? I mean, metanarratives should be critiqued, obviously. Any totalizing narrative should be suspect. OK, that's fine. So, we've agreed not to suspend critical thought. I don't know that we ever did.

Metanarratives were always being critiqued. The question is, is it useful? Are certain analyses that are put forward useful? It's not a point of fleeing from metanarratives because they are not in fashion anymore, it's a question of what are the tools. Well, Marxian thought is still a useful tool.

Lewis Gordon writes that for some thinkers (elites who don't find deprivation or poverty a critical issue) that it appears that the only thing to be liberated from is the liberation rhetoric itself. And, really, the rhetoric and the analyses are secondary to having an experiential connection.

Yancy: What do you think of the feminist critiques of so-called white male concepts of scientificity?
James: Objectivity as well?

Yancy: Yes.
James: Pat Hill Collins did a good job of critiquing the notion of objectivity and scientific gaze and stance. As you know, it's a stance that not all men share, not all whites share, and that some feminists share, including white feminists, and also we can customize variations of it. So, I agree that there are limited notions of how people think. That they are distorted. That the way in which these hierarchies of knowledge have emerged supports that they are racist, they are class biased, they are sexist, they are culturally biased. Not all cultures are embedded in this monolithic thought process. But, in the States, and in academia, everybody is socialized into thinking hierarchies.

Yancy: Have you been able to do more theorizing or philosophizing in the way that you would want to do it by working within academic spaces of a women's studies department or ethnic studies department as opposed to a traditional philosophy department?
James: Yes. I think so. You know, I remember when I was offered a job at the University of Tennessee, and that was after I finished up at Union, so I had a postdoc M.A. in systematic theology, and this was to teach philosophy as well as to teach philosophy of religion, and basically I was to teach the canon. And I went to U-Mass instead to do women's studies and this is less "traditional," conventional. But sometimes I think that if I had taken that job at Tennessee I would be much more different as a thinker.

Yancy: In what ways?
James: I was incredibly embattled at U-Mass and it was very difficult to

write there. It was not a hospitable environment. But there was a space there—because it was an "alternative" program, it wasn't part of the traditional disciplines—to experiment and to experiment in the classroom. I mention in *Spirit, Space and Survival* about where students, who did the tribunal for this course on "Women and the State," had a mock trial where they put the U.S. on trial for war crimes during the bombing of Iraq in the Gulf War. There was a way to watch other people theorize in this very creative manner, very gutsy, with a lot of heart. Using the tact, using the ideas, but also using their experiential knowledge and their moral commitment. And, traditional classrooms don't provide that kind of space. They're mostly clinical and antiseptic. It's so sanitized. It goes back to what you said about scientificity or objectivity. There is this sort of distance between the knower, the learner, and the text. There is this consumption and then you sort of regurgitate it, re-present it, as the authoritative person. And so, I learned something very important when I was at Fordham. This was over coffee talking to a faculty member who was progressive. He wasn't in philosophy, he was in international politics, but he was one of the few progressive people I found there. He said, "Look, there is a difference between philosophy and the history of philosophy, and what most people are taught is the history of philosophy." There is a difference between theory and the history of theory or memorizing the works of the key theorists. But most people don't know how to engage in philosophy or theory as an activity, where they create it. Not where they imitate it but where they create it.

Being in women's studies, trying all this experimental stuff in class, and some of it bombed, some of it went over. I still get letters from these students and this is years later and I'm really impressed by them. It was a multiracial group of students and they graduated and then they went out and did incredible organizing in the Bay Area or in New York. One woman from Germany went back and did work around the Neo-Nazi's persecution of Turkish immigrants. Others had dual citizenship and went back to do support work for the people in the occupied territories, for Palestinians resisting the state of Israel. So you get postcards, you get letters, and you sort of realize that as individuals and also as a group they brought that intellectual ability and that courage with them to this alternative setting where you've got to dance off away from the text. You know, keep the ideas but it wasn't about memorization, it was really about critical thinking, it was about self-awareness. They benefited from that, or at least they say that they did. Then they go on and they have an impact on other people's lives.

A Selection of Published Works of Joy Ann James

Books

The Angela Y. Davis Reader, ed. (Cambridge, MA: Basil Blackwell, 1998).

Resisting State Violence: Radicalism, Gender, and Race in U.S. Culture. (Minneapolis: University of Minnesota Press, 1996).

Transcending the Talented Tenth: Black Leaders and American Intellectuals (New York: Routledge, 1997).

Spirit, Space and Survival: African American Women in (White) Academe, coedited with Ruth Farmer (New York: Routledge, 1993).

Articles

"Black Feminism in Liberation Limbos," in *Existence in Black: An Anthology of Black Existential Philosophy,* Lewis R. Gordon, ed. (New York: Routledge, 1996).

"'Bread and Land': Fanon's Native Intellectual," afterword for *Fanon: A Critical Reader,* Lewis R. Gordon, T. Sharpley-Whiting, Renée White, eds. (Oxford: Blackwell Publishers, 1996).

"Experience, Reflection, Judgement, Action . . ." in *Radically Speaking: Feminism Reclaimed,"* Diane Bell and Renate Klein, eds. (Australia: Spinifex Press, 1995); reprint of "Teaching Theory, Talking Community."

"Politicizing the Spirit: American Africanism and African Ancestors in the Essays of Toni Morrison," *Cultural Studies* 9, no. 2 (spring 1995).

"'Gender, Race, and Radicalism': Teaching the Autobiographies of Native and African American Women Activists," *Feminist Teacher* 8, no. 3 (spring 1995); reprint in *Black Women in the Academy, Defending Our Name 1894–1994/Conference Papers,* Robin Kilson, ed. (New York: Carlson, 1996).

"The Politics of Language and of Law: Racism, Resistance and the UN Treaty on Genocide," in *Marxism in the Postmodern Age,* Antonio Callari, Carole Biewener, and Stephen Cullenberg, eds. (New York: Guilford Press, 1994).

"African American Women Writers, Activists and Interracial Rape Cases," in *Black Women in America,* Kim Vaz, ed. (Thousand Oaks, CA: Sage, 1994).

"Truthtelling: Community-Building and Women," in *Skin Deep: Women of Color on Race and Color in America,* Eleana Featherston, ed. (Freedom, CA: The Crossing Press, 1994).

"Ella Baker, 'Black Women's Work' and Activist Intellectuals," *The Black Scholar* 24, no. 3 (fall 1994).

"African Philosophy, Theory, and 'Living Thinkers,'" in *Spirit, Space and Survival: African American Women in (White) Academe,* Joy James and Ruth Farmer, eds. (New York: Routledge, 1993).

"Teaching Theory, Talking Community," in *Spirit, Space and Survival: African American Women in (White) Academe,* Joy James and Ruth Farmer, eds. (New York: Routledge, 1993).

"Anita Hill: Martyr Heroism and Gender Abstractions," in *Court of Appeal: The Black Community Speaks Out on the Racial-Sexual Politics of Thomas vs. Hill*, Robert Chrisman and Robert L. Allen, eds. (New York: Ballantine Books, 1993).

"Paradigms of Exclusion and the 'Integration' of Multiculturalism," *The Black Scholar* 23, no. 3 (fall 1993).

"Media Convictions, Fair Trial Activism and the Central Park Case," Z (February 1992).

"Reflections on Teaching: 'Gender, Race, and Class,'" *Feminist Teacher* 5, no. 3 (spring 1991).

"U.S. Policy in Panama," *Race and Class* 32 (July–September 1990).

"Panamanian Women and the U.S. Invasion," Z (February 1990).

"Havana: The Encuentro: The Commission on Women and Politics," report on the Third Encuentro Women's Meeting: "Latin American and Caribbean Women in the '80s," Havana, Cuba, October 1988, *The WREE-View of Women* 14, no. 1 (Jan/Feb 1989).

[thirteen]

Joyce Mitchell Cook

Joyce Mitchell Cook holds the distinction of being the first African-American woman to receive a Ph.D. in philosophy in the United States. Cook also broke the barrier against hiring female assistant instructors at Yale College to teach in fields other than foreign languages. Indeed, she was the first woman appointee to teach in the philosophy department at Yale College (September 1959 to June 1961) and the first African-American woman to teach in the philosophy department at Howard University (September 1970 to June 1976). She has also taught philosophy at Connecticut College and Wellesley College. Cook received her A. B., with distinction in philosophy, from Bryn Mawr College (1955). She also received her B.A. and M.A. from Oxford University (1957, 1961) with high honors in a double major: philosophy and psychology. She went on to receive her Ph.D. in philosophy from Yale University (1965). Between 1959 and 1961, Cook was managing editor of *The Review of Metaphysics* (Yale University). Her area of specialization is value theory. In the early '70s, during the early formative historical period when a handful of Black philosophers were attempting to define the discursive field of Black philosophy, Cook participated in a number of pivotal panel and conference discussions on the nature of Black philosophy. Cook is currently working on a book project examining the concept of the Black experience. (A selection of her writings and public lectures follows this interview.)

Joyce Mitchell Cook

George Yancy: When and where were you born?

Joyce Mitchell Cook: On October 28, 1933, in Sharon, Pennsylvania.

Yancy: Provide a sense of your precollege educational experience and which teachers were most influential in terms of your early intellectual development?

Cook: I was educated in the Sharon public schools through high school. Since I always liked school, I tended to like all of my teachers, and I cannot say that any one stood out more than others in the development of my intellectual interests. I liked every subject from the start as I still do today. When I was in the eighth grade, I believe it was, I came across the life story of Madame Curie, and from that time until my junior year in college, I committed myself to majoring in chemistry, but with a view toward teaching it. Teaching had been my goal from an early age, probably based on my observation of teachers in Sunday school. Of course I did not begin to study chemistry until my junior year in high school, but I stuck to the notion of chemistry for another four years.

Yancy: What impact did your parents have on your intellectual development?

Cook: My parents, particularly my mother, used to say that I could do anything that any one else did insofar as schoolwork was concerned. She was very much pro-education, meaning that she did not think that just because I was a female my destiny was determined. I think my father was more conventional in thinking that girls were supposed to get married after high school, although he supported my ambition because I seemed to be so determined.

Yancy: Did you demonstrate any early philosophical tendencies that you recall?

Cook: If philosophy is conceptual analysis, and I think that a good case can be made for the view that it is a great part, though not the be-all and end-all of philosophy, then yes, I suppose I did demonstrate an early penchant in that direction. However, in the early part of my life, up to college, my outlook was circumscribed to a large extent by religious categories, so I would not describe myself as having engaged in philosophical inquiry at an early age. On the other hand, I always had an ear for consistency, one of the cardinal philosophical virtues, and not infrequently stumbled onto what I would later learn to regard as philosophical issues simply by noticing and puzzling about inconsistencies.

Yancy: Were there any early experiences that may have impacted (negatively or positively) your early understanding of race?

Cook: Race was rarely explicitly mentioned in my household, though I suspect that when, for example, my mother would say that I could do as well as others, she probably had white people in mind. Sharon was, and still is, I believe, a largely white city in a largely white region of northwestern Pennsylvania. My neighbors were whites, a number of them of Eastern European background. In grade school and junior high, my best girlfriend was white, a girl who lived only a few doors away from me. We used to walk to school together. When it came time to go to high school, she no longer walked with me. She had found a new friend who had been in the parochial school system that went only up through junior high. They were of the same ethnicity and the same religion as well as the same race. In retrospect it makes great sense to me, but at the time I wondered that she did not bother to say goodbye.

I am convinced that the fact that my maternal grandmother (who lived close by), looked "passing white" accounted for the virtual silence about race in my home. Add to that my reluctance to generalize, and I think that goes far toward explaining why I did not see race as a "problem," until I was much older. But I was touched by it at the conclusion of eighth grade when I was denied the honor of being designated "high honor student," instead being acknowledged as having tied with three other persons. It was then I learned that two older brothers had been denied the same honor, which carried with it a year's free membership in a private boys' (or girls') club. My mother was afraid that I would be discouraged from educational interests, which is the only reason she told me about the earlier events. I reassured her that my interest was not in grades, that I worked because I liked school. I was not outraged moreover about the denial because I did not know then what I now know—that in academe one never rounds off grades for the purpose of assigning class rank. (Each of the tied persons was well known to me, and I am friendly with one even today.) If I had known academic ranking practice at the time, the experience to which I am referring might well have been the eye opener for me on race that it, mercifully I want to suggest, was not.

When I think of some of the things I pulled off, going to top schools in this country and England, for example, and my general cheekiness, as some would call it, I believe it was just as well that I was not aware of the "race problem," particularly of the widespread notion among whites that Blacks are intellectually inferior to whites (and perhaps I should include the fact that I was not aware that this same notion exists among Blacks).

Yancy: When did you first discover that there was a field called philosophy?

Cook: Well, when I was thirteen years old, I acquired a brother-in-law who had majored in philosophy and who later was to become a minister, like my father, who was largely self-taught. My father, however, used to mention Aristotle with some frequency, usually in the context of disparaging philosophy in favor of religion as, to quote him, "the panacea."

Yancy: What was it about your own self-understanding that may have helped you to decide that you wanted to pursue the field of philosophy?

Cook: I happened to have adored my father, though I distanced myself from his views while I was still in my teens. It was in college that I learned to appreciate philosophy as a breath of fresh air after having been encouraged to think that the truth was ready at hand. But it was not philosophy that turned my sights away from religion, it was the study of religion itself that did that. I took a course in textual or higher criticism during my freshman year—before I ever studied philosophy—and I began to understand religion as answering to a deep emotional need in humankind. I still understand it that way, and I am not opposed to it, because I believe that many people need an emotional crutch, a fail-safe support system in order to cope as best they can with the terms of existence that are beyond their control. ✓

Yancy: Where did you do your undergraduate years and why there?

Cook: I went to Bryn Mawr based on the description of it that I read in a brochure in the high school guidance counselor's office. It indicated that the school had the reputation of being the most difficult of the Seven Sisters, and although I thought it would be more exotic to go to Massachusetts to Radcliffe or Wellesley than to stay in Pennsylvania, albeit Bryn Mawr was some 400 miles from Sharon, I was persuaded by the description. To be sure, I did not know anyone in Sharon who had even heard of Bryn Mawr.

Yancy: Who influenced you most at Bryn Mawr, and what courses did you take? I understand that you wrote your honors thesis on the philosopher Benedictus de Spinoza. Why Spinoza?

Cook: In my first philosophy course I studied under Isabelle Stearns, the only woman philosopher there at the time. Initially I was not too taken with the idea of studying under a woman philosopher. My conception of a philosopher, ill formed though it was, was based on the stereotype of a white-haired man. But at that time I was a chemistry major and organic chemistry lab (five hours on paper—easily twice that in practice) interfered with my taking philosophy at other times when sections of the course were being offered by male professors. As it turned out, I greatly admired Miss (we tended to use the title "Dr." for the men only) Stearns and asked her to direct my honors thesis. I chose Spinoza in part, I am sure, because I was taken by the idea of his geometrical method. As my early papers in philosophy demonstrated, I was prone to present philosophical issues in a barebones style, or otherwise put, without any padding. I was later to discover the desirability of a more graceful style.

   Among other philosophers at Bryn Mawr I remember fondly Geddes MacGregor, a Scotsman who taught me medieval philosophy and who had a great sense of humor. For example, when, a year or so later, he had responded to my request to send a recommendation to Oxford, he told me that he was sure the recommendation he wrote would get me into heaven. Of course, he added, he couldn't be sure about Oxford!

Yancy: Were you the only Black female presence in your philosophy classes? And during this early period, how did you come to terms with the larger gender and racial implications of this?

Cook: Indeed, I was the only Black in my class, and one of only two Black undergraduates on campus when I entered. The numbers did not change very much during my four years. There had been one Black classmate in one class only in high school, and I had one class in common with the Black student at Bryn Mawr, a single semester of German, I believe it was. Subsequently through my student career up through my Ph.D., I never encountered any Blacks in my classes. You ask how I came to terms with gender and racial implications? I don't think I did come to terms; I don't think I realized sufficiently the necessity of coming to terms. Even when it dawned on me that not very many women were in the field of philosophy—in those days you hardly ever ran across a paper or a book by a woman philosopher— I still decided to pursue philosophy through the Ph.D. I was not concerned about making a living, I was concerned, hah!, about pursuing truth.

Yancy: Take us from Bryn Mawr to your decision to do graduate work at Yale. I understand that before Yale you spent time studying at Oxford University. What did you study there and with whom? Were there any significant influences?

Cook: Actually I had written to Harvard and they directed me to Radcliffe, but instead of following through with an application to Radcliffe, I applied instead to Yale and was accepted in 1955, the year I was graduated from Bryn Mawr. Meanwhile I had applied to Oxford and upon acceptance there had written to Yale asking them to hold on to my dossier, that I would reapply in two years, which is what I did. Oxford was very good for me insofar as its educational system emphasized writing essays. You didn't have to go to any lectures if you didn't want to, but you had to write essays every week. It helped me to have such a requirement imposed on me, for I learned to look at articles and books from the standpoint of how they were put together instead of concentrating merely on what they said and what my criticism ought to be. At Oxford I adopted the standard of knowing so well how to write that I would spend 90 to 95 percent of my time reading and reflecting and only 5 to 10 percent writing. I learned, I believe, that theretofore elusive lesson about grace in writing, and in my subsequent career outside academe, I functioned largely as a writer and editor, thanks in part to the experience I had at Oxford.

As for my course of study, I elected to do the undergraduate degree in psychology and philosophy, having been persuaded by my adviser that Oxford thinks more highly of its undergraduate degree than of any other of its degrees. It must be recalled that in the '50s Oxford had not yet widely embraced the German model of doctorate degrees. Most of Oxford's dons or professors had the M.A. degree (which I also have); it used to be that you could not be awarded an M.A., which is honorary, unless you had an Oxford B.A.; I don't know if that is still true. (I remember a row when I was there because the university with great controversy had voted to give an honorary degree to Harry S Truman, who not only did not have an Oxford undergraduate degree but had approved the use of the atomic bomb as well.)

I suppose I should mention that I had the wonderful opportunity to study with Peter Strawson, who was one of the leading analytical philosophers in the movement away from the positivist ideology in philosophy. I can remember his challenging my repetition of the Wittgensteinian formula, newly discovered by me, to be sure, that the meaning of a proposition is in its uses, not to be confused with the pragmatist criterion of usefulness.

I will mention also the informal lectures given by John Austin, who introduced me to the ethics side of the analytical school of philosophy. I will never forget the first time I attended one of his sessions (even before I studied with Strawson) along with an overflow of students hanging from the rafters, so to speak. For what seemed like a very long time the issue was debated, Austin taking pro and con, whether the sentence "This is a dumpy teapot" was evaluative or descriptive. I could not believe my ears—accustomed as they were to contemplating only traditional philosophy—especially when it turned out that one had good reasons for accepting either or neither side of the debate. My other tutors were Mary Warnock (now Dame Mary Warnock) and B. A. Farrell, in philosophy of mind. It was Warnock who sent me to Strawson, which itself, I soon learned, was a vote of confidence in my work.

Yancy: What year did you attend Yale and what was it like studying there? And who did you study with while there?

Cook: In 1957 I went to Yale, where I was one of perhaps a handful of women students in the graduate school studying philosophy. Today people tend to forget that Yale was then exclusively a college for men at the undergraduate level; women were visible in the graduate and professional schools but hardly numerous. As a token of their permanence, nonetheless, Yale built a graduate women's dormitory that opened my second year in New Haven. I lived there for one year before agreeing to share an apartment with a Canadian studying for a Ph.D. in English, who is after all these years my best friend. Our other roommate, an American who was graduated from Bryn Mawr two years behind me, and whom I did not know at Bryn Mawr, I have lost touch with. I stayed at Yale for four years, during the last two of which I was a teaching assistant and also managing editor of the *Review of Metaphysics*. In addition, I worked at Yale University Press. Needless to say, I did not finish my dissertation during those years in New Haven but only later after I had left academe.

I studied with most of the well-known people in philosophy then at Yale, which was, I understand, more eclectic in its faculty appointments than Harvard. Among others, and I mention them in no particular order, were Wilfred Sellars, F. S. C. Northrop, Rulon Wells, John Smith, and Paul Weiss. Of course my association with Paul Weiss has been continuous since 1957, albeit contact in later years was sometimes no more frequent than once a year. Shortly after his mandatory retirement from Yale in 1969 Weiss came to Washington to teach at Catholic University, so I have been able to see him upon occasion ever since, and especially on his birthday. In recent years I take him a cake with candles, which I have promised not to light anymore. I sat in on a summer "course" he led on Plotinus a few years ago and although his advanced age was beginning to show—he was born in 1901—it was still a very stimulating experience, with some sessions unbelievably brilliant.

Probably I have learned more from Paul Weiss than from any other teacher; I observed at close hand his extraordinary industry, his astonishing level of dedication to philosophy as well as to his children, both of whom I got to know in New Haven. One summer when I was at Yale he hired me to type a manuscript; this was before I could type really well, but he tolerated my lack of speed in exchange for faithful adherence to his meticulous editing marks.

Weiss hired me my first year at Yale to be a reader in his undergraduate philosophy of art course. I learned under his tutelage how to grade papers, since by prior agreement he would read all As (in the years before grade inflation there were not many) and Fs (again, not many). He would spot-check the papers with grades in between A and F, and then share with me his reasons for differing from my evaluations, which was very beneficial especially considering the grading system was in numbers not in letters. During two years of being a grader, he never differed with me on the letter equivalent of grades, only occasionally on the numbers. This gave me a sense of confidence since I never had compared any student's work with my own, so I had no idea of the intricacies and relativities of grading systems. And I will always remember his remark that one paper to which I had given a 94 was worth less because the writer had not been sufficiently responsive to criticism from oppositional points of view. This is the type of comment, among others, that I readily took to heart in my own work. When it came to philosophical orientation, however, I was not

Weiss's disciple, having learned how to separate appreciation for the teacher from the teaching. No doubt the Oxford view of philosophy had made me less than receptive to Weiss's brand of metaphysical speculation. But he helped me understand that when you kick metaphysics out the front door, so to speak, it sneaks in the back. For that reason, I became wary of the attempt to identify the aim of philosophy with an allegedly metaphysically neutral conceptual analysis.

Yancy: What was the direction of your dissertation and who directed it?

Cook: I was always primarily interested in ethics, but my choice of a topic I later realized was misguided in that it put an extraordinary burden on me to try to be fair to a position with which I could not, however much I might have wished otherwise, to agree. I had noticed that people tend to become disciples of whatever philosophy they specialize in. The trouble with that is that you have to choose what you will specialize in before you have had an opportunity to explore equally well all the options. To avoid that trap, I decided to explore an approach that was opposed to my own leanings (toward a Kantian deontology), and as it happens about the time I was looking for a dissertation topic there appeared a new work in ethics by Stephen C. Pepper that caught my attention because of its naturalist presuppositions, diametrically opposed to my own. I then formulated a prospectus based on my reading of that work and perhaps an earlier one, *World Hypotheses*, but I had not looked at Pepper's monumental *Sources of Value* at the time.

I began my dissertation work under Sellars, whose methods I much admired. He helped me to prepare my prospectus, but he left Yale for Pittsburgh before I made any real headway in developing the dissertation, and I also made some changes in my personal situation that resulted in my dissertation's being put off for a few years. In resuming the project under the threat of a deadline I turned to Paul Weiss, and through him, to Rulon Wells, under whom I had studied the history of logic. At the time I finished my dissertation I was working in the State Department in Washington as an analyst for African affairs.

Yancy: What is the genesis of your interest in ethics and value theory?

Cook: I would suspect that it was a spinoff from my early religious orientation. But as well it was a consequence of my refusal to separate philosophy from life itself; hence I cannot interact with other people without reflecting on ethical issues and bringing to bear theoretical considerations. I do not compartmentalize what I think I know from what I do or how I behave. For this reason I have always appreciated the enormous variety of my experience, the interaction I have had with people of all sorts of backgrounds, from English aristocracy to Haitian peasants. It has helped to strengthen my conviction regarding the centrality of the moral integrity of the individual. Of course, it is difficult to specify in what that integrity consists. And by no means do I take any one model of integrity to be a fixed target for all human striving. But when push comes to shove, if I may coin an expression, I believe that your moral integrity is all you can have that is inalienable.

As far as value theory is concerned, I look upon it as much broader than an interest in ethics. It includes even branches of logic insofar as logic is interested in what constitutes good argument. Like philosophy itself, value theory requires enormous acquaintance with factual matters, acquaintance with what Descartes referred to as "the book of the world," albeit as a starting point.

Yancy: What were some of your teaching experiences after graduating from Yale?

Cook: Well, I did not graduate from Yale until 1965, if you put it that way. Meanwhile I had taught at Wellesley and worked as an editor in New York and, as I mentioned, had also joined the State Department for what turned out to be a year and a half or so. After leaving State I worked for the now defunct Office of Economic Opportunity and left government in 1966 (returning for four years in 1977) to teach at Howard University in Washington. My teaching at Howard was interrupted by a two-year appointment at Connecticut College, after which I returned to Howard for six more years. It is ironic, I think, that my experiences at a predominantly Black institution would help convince me to abandon the teaching of philosophy for good, as it turns out.

Yancy: As the first Black woman Ph.D. philosopher, how were you received by students and colleagues? Were any of your students/colleagues "shocked" to find a Black woman teaching courses in philosophy?

Cook: I began teaching at Yale in 1959, before affirmative action I might add, and before women's liberation. The presumption was completely in my favor; I had students (all of whom were white; someone told me that Yale had some twenty or so Negroes campuswide, none of whom was my student) tell me that they wanted to be in my section because they figured that if Yale would appoint me I must be really good, even better, than the others. From what I hear, today the presumption would likely be against me, for there are those who would think that if Yale (or some other predominantly white institution) appointed me, it must be because of affirmative action. I must admit that I looked nothing like the stereotype of a philosopher I myself had once entertained; so I am more generous than I otherwise might be when I run into the stereotypes that others entertain. For one thing I looked extremely young at the time, even younger than my twenty-five-going-on-twenty-six years of age—an incredible representative, when you stop to think of it, of the wisdom of the ages!

Yancy: When it occurred to you that you were the first Black woman to receive the Ph.D. in philosophy in the United States, how did you understand the gender and racial implications of this?

Cook: It did not occur to me that I was the first Black woman to receive the Ph.D. in philosophy in the United States or even in the world, as it has been suggested to me by more than one person. How could such a thought occur to me—as uninformed as I was at the time in regard to Black history and indeed, American history? On the contrary, I believe that it was Eugene Holmes, my onetime senior colleague at Howard, who first imparted this thought to me. As I recall he mentioned that I was the first Black woman to teach in the philosophy department at Howard, not the first woman, mind you, but the first Black woman. But he went on to make the broader "first" claim, which I am not able to substantiate even after studying Black history for the better part of the present decade. I have seen written references (in *The New Negro*, for example) to Dr. Anna J. Cooper as having received a "doctorate in philosophy" from the Sorbonne, but I have reason to believe this is misleading, a judgment the new *Norton Anthology of African American Literature* also challenges by pointing out that her doctorate was in French.

Yancy: Did you ever experience any difficulty in terms of race and gender while teaching?

Cook: That is a hard question because one cannot tell what difficulties are due to race, or gender for that matter, unless one has a reference point. I have already alluded to this difficulty in talking about the class rank problem at the end of my junior high years. This point is also illustrated in a line I shall adapt from a shaggy dog story: to refuse to lend someone your toothbrush is not to exhibit racial or gender discrimination against that person. Whoever claims otherwise does not have a reference point, in this case, a point that establishes what is reasonable to expect by way of cooperation from others. And so it is, it seems to me, in the context of racial or gender relations, not that the two are the same in every respect. As it happens I was not looking for racial or gender slights and so I may have overlooked some. I believe there was and still is some discrimination of both kinds in white institutions and in Black institutions. I am not sure which is worse: race or gender discrimination, nor am I sure whether such discrimination is worse in white or Black institutions.

While at Howard, I began to reflect on the relation between philosophy and race for the first time, and to appreciate many problems that needed to be addressed before I could make the kind of relevant pronouncements students in the midst of a revolution were seeking. It struck me that nothing short of a totally dedicated effort would suffice to address those problems. I cannot say, however, that I received unmixed departmental encouragement to pursue those interests, and I was unwilling to ignore them by immersing myself in the traditional curriculum I otherwise was committed to teach.

Even now, after working in academic administration for a number of years before embarking on a new career of working for myself, that is, after some years of independence from all academic, institutional restraints on the direction of my professional efforts, I cannot see myself as effectively functioning in any environment in which political considerations predominate over others in my thinking. I am not nor do I aspire to be a political adviser, and I do not accept the notion, in the absence of more cogent argument than I have seen, that I have a responsibility to save the race or humankind or anything of the sort. As a matter of fact, it is contradictory for me to hold the view that philosophy is context-bound, that there are no absolute truths in morals, politics, science, and whatever, moreover that competing interests deserve equal consideration, and then to turn around and hold up my personal convictions as commendable to others *on philosophical grounds alone.* To be a missionary, after all, one must presume to know the truth—and also know that the intended recipient does not.

Yancy: When did you first begin to give philosophical attention to the Black experience as a more focused aspect of race? And what are some of your reflections on this notion of the so-called Black experience?

Cook: I suppose it was in 1970, when at the friendly insistence of my chairman, I agreed to represent Howard at a conference on philosophy and the Black experience at the University of Illinois, Chicago Circle. In my paper simply and, I might add, presumptuously, entitled "A Critique of Black Experience," I attempted to explore three hypotheses regarding Black experience with a view toward understanding what it is. For example, I considered and rejected the claims of Negritude, and I endorsed a modified statement of Franz Fanon that emphasized feelings of racial inferiority. Of course there are problems with defining Black experience in negative terms, as critics are quick to point out. Perhaps only the Black nationalists who discover white superiority to be the root of racial problems can agree that the attitude of white superiority in the dominant group fosters the reciprocal feeling among Blacks of inferiority. I am not talking about all Blacks, of course, but only about those who have not experienced what Charles Wesley the historian used to refer to as "second emancipation."

My later work in this area continues my interest in the definition of Black experience, which, to be sure, is not the same as the description of Black experience. As I see it, it is the task of sciences to describe, and it is the task of philosophy to analyze, i.e., define. The two are not entirely separate since Black experience, I believe, is a historical concept.

Yancy: How would you define Black philosophy? And is there such a thing? Have you come to think of Black philosophy differently since your days in academia?

Cook: Black philosophy, according to the American Philosophical Association, is a recognized subspecialty within the diverse tradition of American philosophy as a whole. As a practical matter, it has become what practitioners, mainly Black professors of philosophy, say it is. It tries to address certain issues that some Black philosophers regard as central to their interests as philosophers while at the same time having a bearing on the lives of Black people. Some of its adherents claim that it uses the language, the techniques, and approaches of analytical philosophy in service of the liberation of Black people. But without further analysis I am not convinced that we can identify something as Black (especially Black American) philosophy just because Black people write it or just because Black people focus their analytical tools on problems of especial interest to Black people, anymore than I would be convinced that we can identify a book as a book on Black logic because the examples of arguments used in the book call attention to subject matter of interest to Black people.

The authors of a 1974 textbook called *Logic for Black Undergradu-*

ates make this very point in denying that there is a separate logic for whites and Blacks. "All men are equal. John is a man. Therefore, John is equal," is in the form of the Barbara syllogism, but it does not prove that there is Black logic. Incidentally, this quotation is from a Black graduate student I met back in the '50s who said that she learned this in a logic class at a Black university. As I recall, she seemed not to have heard (or to have quite forgot) the standard version of the argument, "All men are mortal. Socrates is a man. Therefore Socrates is mortal." The moral of this anecdote is that as Black philosophers, ourselves the products of cultural pluralism, we have to take care that our statements about Black experience not turn out to be mere paraphrases like "All men are equal."

Now conceivably there could be Black philosophy in some other sense—quite like the sense we deny to the expression "Black logic." That is, we might want to insist that above and beyond the fact that its practitioners are Black, and the issues it pursues are important to Black people, the philosophy itself, understood as a body of results rather than methods, is Black. If such were possible, then Black philosophy would have the status of, say, scholastic philosophy, or perhaps existential philosophy, or more problematically, Greek philosophy. In short, Black philosophy would be a school of philosophy. I doubt such a claim can be sustained about Black philosophy in its present state of development at any rate.

Yancy: Since the time that you were active in academia, do you sense any changes in terms of the direction of Black philosophy?

Cook: I think that philosophers who are Black had not had opportunity to pay sufficient attention to the definition of Black philosophy back in 1976 when I left teaching. This meant, among other things, that we did not know who our audience was. If we attempted to communicate with other Blacks on social issues of the day, we were forced to abandon our professional mode of expression and techniques of analysis in favor of a looser language more suited to a general audience. There was no "universe of discourse" for Black philosophy, and terminological confusion proliferated. It is a problem that I think exists to a much lesser extent today. The volume entitled *The Underclass Question* is a good example of what I mean. In the climate of the mid-1970s as I remember it, the tenor and philosophical professionalism of this collection of essays would not have been possible.

So it seems to me that Black philosophers feel freer now to develop in technical ways their positions on Black-related topics without worrying about carrying along a general audience, although, in my opinion, there is still a price to pay for going against the prevailing perspective collectively referred to as political correctness. Having gained professional recognition, they now take for granted such basic issues as whether there is or can be a Black philosophical perspective, a question I still think is unsettled after having considered a number of their arguments.

Yancy: What advice would you have for a young African-American interested in pursuing a career in philosophy?

Cook: I don't know that I should venture to give career advice to anyone, let alone Black philosophy students. The best advice I can think of is to become as financially independent as you can so that you will be free to pursue and express your thoughts without unwelcome interference or without unwelcome consequences of unwelcome interference! I also happen to think that philosophy is a hard taskmaster that requires dedication beyond the call of duty of many other pursuits in terms of breaking new ground. If life is unthinkable without pursuing philosophy, by all means pursue it. Otherwise, do something else.

Yancy: During what period were you managing editor of the *Review of Metaphysics*? What was this experience like?

Cook: It was at Yale, the same year that I was appointed to teach, that I also became managing editor of the *Review*, thanks to Paul Weiss's confidence in my ability. I had worked for him, as I have indicated, and I also had contributed some book reviews to the *Review*, I think. Certainly, I had done minimal work on the *Review* when I was asked to be managing editor. It's a good experience for me to recall in the present debate about affirmative action, because it was brought to my attention by another graduate student that someone else who had worked a lot on the *Review* was more deserving of the appointment than I was. I answered that that was not my concern, that I had asked myself two questions: Was I qualified to do the job and did I want to do it? My answers were both affirmative (I had been editor of my high school newspaper and had occasionally contributed to the college newspaper. I have long felt that I have printer's ink in my blood, another irony in view of the paucity of publications under my signature).

The experience was educational as it was intended to be. For example, I was responsible for investing any surplus funds of the *Review* and in order to make a good recommendation I for the first time in my life had to consider the stock market. The treasurer of Yale was very supportive in giving me advice. I was also responsible for the quality of the printing, and I am told that the typographical errors were fewer than ever before. So all in all, I think that my selection was well acquitted.

Yancy: How does your identity as a Black woman philosopher mediate your philosophical concerns?

Cook: The fact that I have been absorbed for some eight years now in a project that focuses on Black experience, a project I conceived in the '70s, well before I was in a position to attempt to carry it out, is probably inexplicable if I were not Black. But it would be simplistic, I think, to regard my project as mediating my philosophical concerns, which are broader than Black issues. For example I am interested in cosmology and theories of physics. The problems I have identified in the area of Black philosophy reflect most of my philosophical concerns that are summarized under the heading of value theory, particularly ethics. My identity as a "Black woman philosopher," as you put it, already presupposes some construction on my part. And in giving this reply, I am passing over the gender part of your question, that, at first glance, might well call for a completely different answer. Many people ask me if I teach English, which is compatible with their idea of professions open to women, but no one ever takes me to be a philosopher. I myself have begun only recently to think of myself as a philosopher by way of justifying my interests as being different from the interests of most people I know—of whatever color.

Yancy: What are some of your thoughts on the contemporary debate in the area of critical race theory? Do you see race as a social construct? Would you elaborate?

Cook: I think that race is in part, but only in part, a social construct, just as race is in part but only in part an objective (natural) condition. To speak to the first part is to respond to a question about the arbitrary, historical, social relations that have grown up around race, while the second part answers the question of the basis of racial classification. These different questions, indicative of different uses to which the concept of race can legitimately be put, have been confused with disastrous consequences. We sometimes forget, for example, that the earliest occurrence of the word "race" in English comes in 1508, according to Michael Banton, well before the Atlantic slave trade to North America, and that it is used in a religious poem reflecting the Biblical view of Adam as the common ancestor of humankind even as it refers to followers of the sin of envy as "backbiters of sundry races." (If Adam is not the common ancestor, then how came sin into the world of the others?) It seems to me that these two senses of race cannot be reduced to a dichotomy of, on the one hand, a nothing-but-social construct and, on the other, nothing-but-physical characteristics.

Viewed as a social construct, race is a historical concept that changes in its social significance from society to society and from time to time. But as an objective condition (also subject to historical variation), race depends on certain characteristics—never mind these characteristics don't uniquely determine destiny and keeping in mind that they are variable, both diachronically and synchronically. Moreover, as anthropologist Vincent Varich has pointed out, it is easy for any mature-sighted individual of whatever background to sort out on the basis of their racial characteristics alone a combined group of individuals composed of one hundred persons each taken respectively from sub-Saharan Africa, Europe, and Southeast Asia, these individuals having been divested of all cultural or ethnic clues, such as distinctive clothing. With only a small margin of error, the combined group can be sorted out into the original three groups of one hundred each. All the discussion in the world does not render race in this latter sense an illusion, contrary to what some theorists seem to argue. Theorists seem to accept the Wittgensteinian view that definitions are clustering devices, yet they seem often to get hung up at the boundaries.

In short I regard the effort to ignore race as misguided. The concept of race was supposed to have been consumed in the analogous flames of phlogiston more than a half century ago, thanks to Ashley Montagu's widely acclaimed critique; that reports of its death were premature testifies not only to the testimony of common sense but perhaps also to strong biases in favor of a metaphysical doctrine of natural kinds.

But I see that possibly a lasting value of the current debate may be that racial pride, humankind's potentially most dangerous emotion, when given free rein, will yield ground in the socially motivated process of conserving group differences that, being cultural or ethnic rather than natural, will increasingly place more emphasis on choice rather than biology.

Yancy: What got you interested in writing on the nature/nurture debate in the area of human intelligence?

Cook: It was at a time when William Shockley and others were making too much of the disparities between Black and white scores on IQ tests, and a number of Black people of my acquaintance were attempting to refute Shockley by suggesting that since his Nobel prize was not in genetics his arguments should be overlooked. I was teaching logic at the time and, always in search of apt examples, I found this one could be interpreted to demonstrate an informal fallacy. But in truth I was embarrassed that students and even some faculty were hard-pressed to find a better argument against Black intellectual inferiority. So I began to research the topic of IQ tests, about which I had learned something in psychology some years before, and the paper to which you refer was the result.

Yancy: Yes, in that paper you state that "in the absence of further research in the area of measurement of Black intelligence, the IQ controversy will not abate. Driven underground temporarily it is likely to rear its head anew." What are some of your reflections on Richard J. Herrnstein's and Charles Murray's *The Bell Curve*?

Cook: Well, I am not a prophet but these authors certainly perpetuate a theory of reoccurrence, so to speak. There is a volume of essays, *The Bell Curve Debate*, that I think effectively exposes unfounded assumptions of Herrnstein and Murray. But you know, just as there is an objective condition that roughly defines races while stopping short of determining any objective purpose for racial distinctions, so there is an objective condition (call it what you will; Herrnstein and Murray call it inferiority as measured by the tests) that enables, not the man on the street, but some psychometrists to sort out individuals, again by race, who perform less well than others on IQ tests. However, the difference, or one difference, is that such tests arguably do not possess the predictive power they profess to have. And of course Daniel Goleman and others contend that emotional intelligence is more influential than IQ in determining success in the marketplace.

Yancy: In terms of the major philosophers of the past, who has influenced you most?

Cook: I suppose it's a toss-up between Kant and Plato. I would add Kierkegaard also but I am not convinced that he is a major philosopher although he certainly is a major theologian, whom I like to quote at times at the risk of being thought to agree with his major premises (I do not). Of all the existentialists, I noticed that my Black students were very sympathetic to Kierkegaard. It was as if they interpreted his emphasis on subjectivity as truth in opposition, not to scientific truth, which is what Kierkegaard intended, but to the truth of the white man. I have to admit that some analogies are striking. For my own part, I owe it to Kierkegaard to have reminded me of the importance of the claims of existence over the claims of theory. It was he who remarked that philosophers build castles but live in shacks nearby. To me this is an admonishment to put your life where your mouth is. Of course, Socrates would agree, and I suppose the latter's insistence on examining one's life is ground for regarding him as the first existentialist in Western philosophy.

Yancy: Talk about your nonacademic work experience in the State Department and how this experience helped, as I believe you have suggested, to illuminate the task of philosophy?

Cook: Philosophers today, as always, debate what philosophy is, but I cannot agree with the postmodernist view that philosophy has no special task and therefore should merge with other disciplines, in effect, disappear as a separate discipline. It is easy enough to understand some of the thinking that leads to that position, considering how difficult it is for philosophers to survey, let alone master, the vast bodies of knowledge some acquaintance with which is not only desirable but necessary in order to support the notion of philosophical relevance to practical affairs. But being difficult and being impossible are two different things. There are many difficulties in my own conception of philosophy which tends to draw, among other nonphilosophical sources, upon a model I saw in action when I worked in the State Department.

At my level as an analyst covering the affairs of a few Black African countries, I periodically assumed briefing duty which required me, having been alerted to possible breaking news by my counterparts, to read overnight cables from all the posts in Black Africa at six a.m. in the morning and then brief the assistant secretary on important developments at, say, eight (who, along with the five other assistant secretaries representing other parts of the world, would brief the secretary at nine, who would brief the president at ten). (I am not confident of the exact times.) Along with the secretary of state at the president's briefing might be individuals who headed other agencies also concerned with aspects of the countries in question.

Now this model, not a theoretical model but a working model, I should emphasize, is also widely used in the corporate world. The person at the top makes the hard decisions based on information gathered and evaluated at lower levels. No doubt the persons at lower levels may have greater knowledge and depth in their particular areas than the persons up the line, while the persons up the line presumably have broader knowledge. In this real world of which I speak, decisions are made, after this fashion. For example, a decision is made about some matter in Africa but not without considering its likely impact in Europe, and vice versa. The same person who specializes in Europe does not also specialize in Africa, and so on. What seems to be the greatest objection to such a model for philosophy in relation to other disciplines has been not the question of whether or how well it can work, *mutatis mutandis,* but whether philosophy has any right to dictate to other disciples. I am puzzled by this objection, since it would seem to me to be warranted only if we press the paradigm too far thus reaching the conclusion that philosophy in turn would issue directives concerning how and what is to be done in the other disciplines. But on the contrary it seems to me that the critical question ought to be whether philosophers can comprehend certain results (and problematics) of these other disciplines and interrelate them any better than the specialists in these other disciplines can comprehend the philosophical implications of their results (and problematics) and interrelate them. For my money, the jury is still out on this one.

When it comes to postmodernist views toward the theory of knowledge—if I may be permitted to leap—they demolish castles but live in the debris that falls out. On the one hand, they liberate knowledge from the foundational criteria that have driven modern Western philosophy; but when it comes to philosophy itself, they hold it to the standards of knowledge they themselves have proscribed.

In other words, it is only under the criteria of knowledge that they themselves discredit that the activity of philosophizing itself should be banished from the collective domain of intellectual inquiry. Under less privileged criteria, philosophy would have full rein to try to illuminate relations between key concepts that hypothetically characterize kinds of reality. In this connection, and at the risk of being another footnote to Plato, I think it would profit philosophers to resuscitate the original meaning of philosophy, i.e., the love of wisdom, not love of knowledge, mind you. Of course it will turn out, I also think, that wisdom is most severely tested in the uses it makes of knowledge.

Yancy: As the first Black woman philosopher to receive the Ph.D. in philosophy in the United States, who is Joyce Mitchell Cook?
Cook: Here we go again! I demur from the description since I have not

researched the question of who is the first Black woman philosopher, etc. But Joyce Mitchell Cook is, for better or worse, currently trying to understand (note not "know" but "understand") certain problems pertaining to Black experience that require her to study what a great many people have to say in a number of fields before she puts together a picture of the world as she sees it, a picture based on her own atypical experience as well as on reflection with due consideration, it is hoped, to what others have thought as well. Those enriched experiences, coupled with what she, rather I, recognize to be philosophical virtues, make me very wary of many of the claims I refer to collectively as Black romanticism—the project of venerating an African past that is not demonstrably one's own past, while at the same time refusing to come to terms with the ever-changing present and beyond. As I have indicated, I am suspicious of claims to bolster racial pride at whatever cost, including the sacrifice of sound scholarship. For one thing it overemphasizes the importance of the remote past in the motivational system of present-day Blacks. There is ample evidence, I think, that many Black Americans, no less than white Americans, aspire to goals that were impossible for their forebears to conceive, let alone attain. Each example of this—each Black "first" as well as subsequent pathfinders—confutes the claim that one must have racial pride in order to achieve if, indeed, racial pride is not identical to self-respect.

Almost a half century ago, Black American philosopher William Fontaine wrote that Black intellectuals were predisposed to be environmentalists in the debate between nature and nurture. But long before the lines of the debate were being drawn up in terms of IQ tests, in a point of view usually attributed to the father of behaviorism (American John B. Watson), two of the cofounders of the African Methodist Episcopal Church, Richard Allen and Absalom Jones, cast their vote in favor of environmentalism, and their view of the matter, stated in language that is remarkable in its anticipation of Watson's "give me ten healthy young infants, and I'll turn out adults of what profession you choose" was published in 1794! Fully to appreciate environmentalism, it seems to me, is to be liberated from the necessity of claiming Beethoven (I choose one of many examples) to be Black in the absence of reliable evidence simply, it would appear, for the purpose of enhancing self-respect.

Today it is not so much environmentalists as Black vindicationists with their fixation, one might say, on Black history that are driving trends in Black philosophy, to which support is given, for example, by

Lucius T. Outlaw's recent efforts to conserve and develop Black differences in what may be described as a resuscitation of W. E. B. Du Bois's turn-of-the-century view embracing the idea of a race spirit and always being careful, of course, to distinguish "racialism" from "racism." Black vindicationists are also responsible for the drive to discredit the alleged foundations of Western philosophy in Greece. Some Black philosophers have joined these endeavors, despite the specialist knowledge required to decide the factual issues, granted a paucity of evidence. In their defense I might add that my reading of *Not Out of Africa,* classicist Mary Lefkowitz's recent addition to the controversy, tells me that it takes more than classical knowledge to commandeer superior arguments against the vindicationists, just as it takes more than superior logic to establish the facts of the case put forward by the classicists.

I have a rule of thumb: If any particular conclusion is favorable to my case (my hypothesis, my race, etc.), it needs at least one more review, and perhaps the evidence of another book or two, before I can be satisfied that I have done justice to all the facts. At some point, however, I recognize that one has to take the dilemmas (or paradoxes or ironies) by the horns.

Yancy: What are some of your future directions in terms of your philosophical work?

Cook: Well, I hope to dig myself out of the mound of note cards and other memorabilia I have collected during my prolonged journey to understand and become immersed, I almost said "mired," in the concept of Black experience long enough to finish writing a book in progress. Not surprisingly, after six or seven years of research I have material for many books, and I hope in the future to follow through on some of them, not to forget an autobiographical account I started in the summer of 1969 under the onslaught of the Black revolution in an effort to convince myself that I knew who I was. Regrettably the press of other commitments made me abandon the narrative at the point I was entering college. But I am very grateful to have covered the early period at that time, and I look forward to allowing myself a peek at it when I shall have opportunity to carry it forward.

Public Lectures and Published Works of Joyce Mitchell Cook

"The Nature and Nurture of Intelligence," *The Philosophical Forum* (Boston University, January 1979).

"Black Scholars in Philosophy," a panel of Black philosophers in a radio broadcast sponsored by the Johnson Foundation (Wisconsin, February 1976).

"The Concept of Black Experience" (address to the American Philosophical Association, Western Division meeting in Chicago, April 1975).

The Search for Personal Identity (address delivered at convocation, Tuskegee Institute); published by Tuskegee Institute, November 1974.

"The Concept of Black Experience" (address delivered in December 1974 presenting an overview of book project inspired by work initiated in November 1970 paper listed below).

"Prolegomena to a Black Philosophy" (address presented at Springhill College, Mobile, Alabama, December 1974).

"The Nature and Nurture of Intelligence" (address delivered at Tuskegee Institute, April 1973).

"Classical Theories of Knowledge" (a series of eight lectures presented to teachers of philosophy in the Summer Program sponsored by the Institute for Services to Education, July 1973). These lectures took place in Chestnut Hill, MA.

"The Examined life," *Bryn Mawr College Alumnae Bulletin* (October 1973).

"A Critique of Black Experience" (address delivered at the Conference on Philosophy and the Black Experience, University of Illinois at Chicago Circle, November 1970).

[fourteen]

Laurence Thomas

Laurence Thomas is professor of philosophy at Syracuse University. He also teaches in the political science program and the Judaic studies program. He earned his B.A. in philosophy from the University of Maryland. His M.A. and Ph.D. degrees in philosophy are from the University of Pittsburgh. He also received an honorary L.L.D. from New England College. He has taught at Oberlin College and the University of Notre Dame. His areas of specialization are moral psychology and ethical theory. His articles and reviews have appeared in the *Journal of Philosophical Psychology*; *Midwest Studies in Philosophy*; *The Monist*; *The Philosophical Forum*; *Ethics*; *The Encyclopedia of Ethics*; *Philosophical Books*; *Law and Philosophy*; and more. He is the author of *Vessels of Evil: American Slavery and the Holocaust* and *Living Morally: A Psychology of Moral Character*. (A selected citation list of Laurence Thomas's published works can be found at the end of the interview.)

Laurence Thomas
Syracuse University

George Yancy: Where were you born?
Laurence Thomas: I was born in Baltimore, Maryland.

Yancy: What was it like growing up there for you?
Thomas: It was crazy, but lots of fun. I lived in a relatively nice and comfortable neighborhood. I think that I'm just young enough to have missed all of the fights and struggles over the Civil Rights Movement.

I never participated in any of that, but I was always kind of a book-worm. My earliest memories involve memories of my having read books on animals and insects. I had my own library card by the age of six and was a regular visitor to the public library. By the time that I was seven, I had gone beyond thinking about being a physician. I wanted to be a biologist. Though I was particularly fascinated by ants, animal life in general interested me greatly. It is an interest which remains with me today.

Yancy: Talk about your early educational experiences.

Thomas: First I went to Edgewood Elementary School. At this school I got away with murder because I assume that they thought that I was smart. I did get As on the material that I handed in. There were two teachers there, Mrs. Gross and Mr. Owens, whom I admired very much. They were very bright people who allowed me to deviate from the norm, and I admired them for that. With Mr. Owens, I participated in a lot of science projects. I wasn't very good at following rules just for the sake of following the rules. My view was that if the rule didn't have a point then why follow it. So, as you can see, I was meant to be in philosophy, right?

In this regard, I blame my parents because they were excellent at explaining things to me and trusting me to do things that called for responsibility. When I asked them a question, I got an appropriate answer. I was never just dismissed. So from a very early age, I took myself seriously in the sense that I regarded myself as capable of being a responsible person and expected people to treat me in that way. And, for better or worse, this trait of character stays with me to this day. I was profoundly trusted by my parents. It was a trust that I never abused in any serious way; and it is that parental trust that has so remarkably shaped my life even until this day.

I was deeply and majestically loved by my parents, and although I have no children of my own, I believe that some of my best philo-sophical work draws upon the parental fountain of love laid by my parents. Although they died when I was only a teenager, they bequeathed to me, among other things, the gifts of self-love, good will, and determination. They fortified me to live well!

I eventually went on to attend Garrison Junior High School, where I studied German in the eighth grade and French in the ninth, and this peaked my interest in languages. In the seventh grade I studied Judaism and I did research on the history of Jews in Baltimore and on anti-Semitism in the South. Garrison was predominantly a Jewish school. And while at Garrison, I can remember writing lots and lots of essays. But I still thought, up until at least the tenth grade, that I wanted to do research in biology, particularly genetics.

Yancy: So, at this juncture, you had no interest in philosophy?

Thomas: No. I was definitely committed to biology. There was no interest in philosophy. I didn't get into philosophy until I went off to the University of Maryland.

Yancy: Talk about that process.

Thomas: Well, I took a philosophy course at the end of my sophomore year from a woman named Wesley Piersol and that was my downfall. I mean, here was a guy who for so very long had an interest in biology, it was all about animals, and suddenly, out of nowhere, came this desire to do philosophy. Mrs. Piersol had written her Ph.D. in France and was very impressive. She had us write two essays, ten pages each. I wrote one on John Stuart Mill and one on God. I was very good at writing, but there was something about wrestling with those questions that was very exciting and Dr. Piersol thought that I was good at it. I then majored in philosophy. I dropped biology with a passion. ⌐

Yancy: Do you have any early memories of having engaged in what you would retrospectively call philosophical reflection?

Thomas: You've really hit a nerve here. One of the things that my family did was to meet once a week and discuss the Old Testament. It was kind of spontaneously generated, but with great regularity. And as far as I remember, you kept the floor as long as you could hold the floor. That's my earliest memory of hard discussions and we would really go at it. Someone would ask, "What did Abraham mean by so and so?" I would sit around the table and listen to all of these old folk fight it out. "This is what the text says!" They really went at it. As a kid you would try to jump in, and I did. I guess that's how it all began. It was this questioning, this raising and pushing questions that did it. It was an issue of not settling and being happy with any answer. When I asked a question, I received a really big answer. Parents have a way of giving stupid answers to questions asked by children, but what they need are really good answers. As I have indicated, my parents were very good at giving me good answers. So, I was always skilled at asking thoughtful questions because I was encouraged to ask questions and because I got good answers at home, I expected to get good answers at school.

Yancy: Where did you do your graduate work in philosophy?

Thomas: I went to the University of Pittsburgh. I went there because I wanted to study ethics with Kurt Baier.

Yancy: What specific philosophical impact did Kurt Baier have on your philosophical development?

Thomas: To this day, Kurt has been a phenomenal influence. He was a very insightful individual. I remain deeply influenced by his work on responsibility, authority, and the nature of reasons. I regard his essay "The Justification of Governmental Authority" to be one of the most brilliant essays written in modern philosophy, although little attention is paid to it. To have worked with him shall remain one of the highlights of my life.

Yancy: Besides Kurt Baier, who influenced you at Pitt?

Thomas: Well, most certainly Annette Baier, though I was already writing my dissertation by the time that she arrived. However, I sat in on a number of courses that she taught. I also sat in on a course taught by Wilfrid Sellars. I also took a lot of courses in philosophy of science with Larry Laudan and others who were there at the time. I also took a couple of logic courses, which I really liked, with the logic duo Alan Ross Anderson, who is now deceased, and Nuel Belnap. They were two superstars and it was fun. There was also Gerald Massey. I finished at Pitt in four years. I went from B.A. to Ph.D. in four years. I didn't waste any time. Those were four good years. I got a lot done, learned a lot, and worked hard. It was exciting. I arrived at Pitt in '71 and in '75 was teaching at the University of Notre Dame. I had a definite view about what I wanted to do. The one thing that I had going for me, and I suppose that this still holds, involved a pit bull mentality. When I really set my mind to something, you really have to pry me away from it. So, I was zipping through graduate school. I'd found Kurt Baier and he and I hit it off at the outset. And because we hit it off from the outset, I was able to avoid much of the angst that people experience in graduate school. I mean, at the beginning of the second semester we knew that we would work together. And that was good, though there are certain disadvantages because there is a certain exploration that you don't make. On the other hand, it allows you to just focus and that's what I did.

For the record, I would like to say that I have known McGary, Boxill, and Outlaw since the beginning of my career. Their personal influence upon my life and career has been boundless. Later, Adrian Piper,

Michele Moody-Adams, and Martha Nussbaum have each had a significant influence upon my career.

Yancy: Moving forward, are your philosophical reflections primarily
informed by the fact that you are an African-American philosopher?

Thomas: My answer to that question is, I would say, no. But I want to
say something else. Annette Baier did a lot of work on trust and that
seems to have been richly informed by the fact that she is a woman.
But she didn't think that she was just talking about trust for women.
She thought that she had an account of trust that was on target. It just
so happened that being a women helped her to get some access to it.
You know, I just finished a paper on Jean-Jacques Rousseau and I
would not say that that essay is informed by the Black experience in
any interesting way whatsoever. So, in reference to your question, I
think that Lucius Outlaw, for example, would tell you that when he
does philosophy he thinks "Blackly." I think that is how Lucius would
see himself and I think that that is wonderful, but I don't think that is
how I see myself.

Yancy: So, in terms of Laurence Thomas's philosophical identity, you
don't see it as somehow being inextricably linked to Laurence
Thomas *the* African-American.

Thomas: No, I think not. I think there is one more distinction that I
would like to make. If you look at my writings, my public persona, the
matter is more complicated. I write about trust, sometimes self-
respect, abuse, and a host of other things. I don't think that Blackness
or African-Americanness gets showcased in those things at all. It
might inform them in various ways, but I don't think that it's being
showcased. Now as a person, that's a whole different ball game
because that's a question of how people respond to you in public
space and all of that. But even then it's more complicated.
     I think that Outlaw is a good juxtaposition because there's no ques-
tion that whatever I'm doing it isn't energized in the way that Blackness or African-Americanness energizes what he's doing.

Yancy: What do you take African-American philosophy to involve?

Thomas: Well, there are a host of things. My version of it is really analogous to the lines of thinking suggested by Carol Gilligan and picked
up on by Annette Baier. When you look at feminism, you notice a set
of sensibilities. A man can have them, but you are more likely to have
them if you are a women, they sort of come with the territory. And

when you push these sensibilities, they can give rise to some very interesting insights. I think that there are a similar set of sensibilities that come with being Black. W. E. B. Du Bois talked about double consciousness and Ralph Ellison talked about invisibility, etc. I think that those are insights that come with the Black experience.

I also think, and I don't know how to completely say this yet, that speech is a very interesting phenomenon in the Black experience. This is partly because I think that if you started with oppression and gave people fewer words you might find that the way they spoke came across much more colorfully. For if you have fewer words to express yourself then intonation and voice will compensate for the absence of a vocabulary and I think that you get this in the Black experience. I mean, if you listen to Dr. King's "I Have a Dream" speech, what is significant is the Black preacherly quality to the speech. If you take that away, then you get a whole different speech with nice words, etc., but nothing beats the deliverance with that intonation and cadence.

Yancy: Relate this back to African-American philosophy.

Thomas: Yes, well, we need to extract and tease out those subtle ways in which there are philosophical insights here. This may have telling implications for someone like Paul Grice, a very famous philosopher who died recently and was known for his theory of language and what it meant to utter something intentionally. Take nonverbal behavior. Theoretically, one of the aspects of nonverbal behavior is intonation. A Gricean model of success or uptake says, "I communicate it to you effectively if and only if blah, blah, blah." Suppose that had to do with intonation, voice, and all of that stuff? Well, culturally, intonation is doing lots of work and might have a lot more to say about that, and might be more insightful about that than a culture where intonation isn't doing as much work. So I think that it's interesting when you look at Grice's analysis you get almost no reference to nonverbal behavior. I think that if you listen to Black people speak, you couldn't begin to talk about the speech practices of most Blacks without reference to nonverbal behavior where this includes intonation.

Yancy: Do you think that African-American philosophers see themselves as constituting a community?

Thomas: I think more so than ten or fifteen years ago. I think that this is interesting because back then we had all been taught by whites and we had all been so used to being validated by whites until the idea of us looking to another Black for validation made almost no sense. In fact, each of us had sort of been told that he was the best Black in philosophy. Therefore your attitude toward other Blacks was like, "What are you doing here? I got it from authority that I'm better." That has actually gotten some of us into trouble. I think that now there is more of a community, though there are still some Blacks in the profession who really distance themselves from Blacks in philosophy, but I think that there are others right in the center of it doing African-American philosophy. And then there are those like Michele Moody-Adams, for instance, who doesn't distance herself, but, clearly, African-American philosophy is just not the thing that is energizing her thinking as such. I think that I'm more like Michele or she is more like me. And then you get someone like John Pittman who, though he phenotypically looks white, is right there kicking and screaming and writing on Malcolm X. I'll probably be in my grave before I write on Malcolm X. So, I think that there is more of a community now than ever before, but I think that it is a touchy community because we are still very fragile. There remains the issue of being well placed; and I believe that no philosophy department in America would hire a Black who would trouble the waters.

Yancy: In terms of your occupation within the public space of the academy, have you found it difficult to work within that space given that it is prefigured by white male hegemony?

Thomas: I think that it's difficult. I've done very well. I think that it's difficult because you're dealing with people who are persuaded that they don't have an ounce of racism in their body. Now my own view about that is I still have some racism in my own body. And I see myself as having attitudes towards other Blacks and I say, "Boy, that's not a good attitude, where did that come from?" Well, it comes from the world in which I live. And I doubt there is any Black person who can tell me that they haven't had biases toward other Blacks operating upon occasion. You know, "If you haven't done this, or that, or if you sound like this or walk like that, then you can't be this or you must be that." And so, I don't deny that whites are well intended, but I'm tired of being told that they're beyond any misconceptions because that would be implausible in this world. And I think that the difficulty that one comes up against in the academy lies in the fact that you come up against people who are persuaded that there is no room for correction on the issue of social justice. That's the problem.

I also find that there is the prevalent mind-set that if you're Black then you can't deserve to be doing well. In other words, your doing well is viewed as out of place. As I have said, I think that it's no accident that Harvard University hired Anthony Appiah. He is surely good. But I suspect that it was relevant that he is not an American Black. Second, he's got as much royalty as most Americans will ever hope to have. In general the thought seems to be that if one is a Black American, then one really can't be deserving of such things; and this view shows itself in subtle ways. For example, take the process of footnoting. You can count on one hand the number of Blacks, in philosophy, who are referenced in footnotes by other philosophers. If you don't believe me, then go to the library and just look at the number of times a Black person is referenced. When John Rawls wrote his new book, *Political Liberalism*, I wrote him and I said, "Nothing pains me more than that after twenty years later you don't reference a single Black philosopher. Can it be that none of us, not one of us has written anything on justice that was of interest to you? Even worth disagreeing with?"

Yancy: Did he respond?

Thomas: Rawls is a very gracious person. He wrote a very gracious letter, but that doesn't change the fact. I think that the footnoting example is a good indication of a certain kind of invisibility of which Ralph Ellison spoke so eloquently that continues to prevail in philosophy. Footnotes are a sign of gratitude. And I suggest to you that there is no better indication that we fail to see people as human than the extent to which you see almost no gratitude shown towards them. The absence of a reference to any Black philosopher in *Political Liberalism* by one of the nicest thinkers in the profession will remain as one of the most poignant instances of invisibility, in the Ralph Ellison sense, that I have witnessed and experienced in the profession.

Painfully, I have seen Blacks not cite one another in philosophy. And one of my most profound pains in this regard is that I have not seen either West or Appiah cite some other Blacks in Philosophy. No one is so brilliant that her or his work does not build upon others. West and Appiah have had very illuminating things to say about race. But Boxill, McGary, Lawson, and Outlaw have been major philosophical conversationists who need to be acknowledged, not only whites.

Yancy: Is there then a tendency in the profession of philosophy to participate in what you in fact refer to as the "downward constitution" of others, Blacks, women, etc.?

Thomas: Not directly, but indirectly, yes. The footnoting example is a wonderful example of downward constitution. I've spoken to Thomas Nagel who said, "Oh, footnotes aren't relevant, nobody really matters who pays attention to them." But people do pay attention to them. Footnoting is a way of expressing gratitude, and a person does not have to make a brilliant observation in order for one to feel a measure of gratitude towards her or him.

I think that another way that downward constitution occurs is with regard to speaker's programs. The number of Blacks who have been invited is very small. People often cite economic reasons for this. Yet, these very same economic reasons do not seem to be barriers to inviting whites to speak, sometime very unknown whites.

Then in departments themselves, you have the view, "If we've hired one Black, then we don't need to hire another. And we're not racist." I think that if white folks could be comfortable being the only white amongst Blacks as they are with only one Black amongst them then we would have a certain equality. This suggests to me that whites think that Blackness is a stigma and that good quality attracts whiteness. I think that one of the greatest mistakes in the world that we make is to think that because something has made a small difference on today that it is thereby trivial, but if you keep making a small difference over infinity then you've got yourself a major difference. I think that we underestimate the cumulative effect of these small things and that's absolutely painful. So, in that sense, I am not very hopeful.

I think that you also have to remember that the academy is full of deadwood, but most of that deadwood is white. And you hear no discussion about whether whites deserve to be there. You don't hear any talk about these folks being stupid, neither among students nor among colleagues. A Black person need only make one mistake and suspicions, concerns, and worries abound. If people had that same wondering, that same suspicion, with like speed about whites, the academy would be full of self-doubt. And I think that all of these things together constitute a social pattern that in the end gnaws at Black folk in the academy. And one way of dealing with this is just to sort of not be Black at all, to just have this veneer. Another way of dealing with this, of course, is to become remarkably successful and most of us have not been.

I also have another example which is very poignant. I've seen whites up for tenure at some of the most distinguished places in the country, being treated with a kind of dignity that has never been accorded to a Black. For instance, when Warren Goldenfarb (a very wonderful person, indeed) was up for tenure at Harvard, the University of Chicago made him an offer on the off chance that he wouldn't get tenure at Harvard. They were hoping that he wouldn't get it. When David Velleman was up for tenure at the University of Michigan, Ohio State made him an offer. Again, they were counting on him not getting tenure. However, when the Black philosopher Bernard Boxill didn't get tenure at UCLA, not a single place made him a tenure offer. He hit the ground starting as an assistant professor. I shall go to my grave with that in my memory. He ended up at the University of Kentucky without tenure, although he had published a number of very seminal and highly regarded articles in *Philosophy and Public Affairs*. Boxill, of course, is now at the University of Carolina at Chapel Hill with tenure as a full professor, but that took nearly seven years. It was supposed to be that if you didn't get tenure at one of those schools in the upper echelon, then one of the other schools below you would catch you and you would get tenure. That's how it has been in the profession, but, to my knowledge, this has never happened with a Black.

Yancy: What attracted you to philosophical issues around morality and psychological development?

Thomas: I think that this goes back to what we talked about earlier. I've always been interested in nonverbal behavior, and there is a connection here with my interest in animals because with animals I've always been intrigued by what makes them tick, what motivates them, and how they behave. And really I'm interested in how human beings behave, and moral philosophy is a natural vehicle for that. I like to watch the reactions of people. I often present myself in public places in ways that require people to think. I like people to think about what they are doing. For instance, my latest tendency has been if I'm walking down the street and I've got a lot of bags, my shoulder bag and some others, and I see a white woman walking towards me and she grabs her purse, I grab my bags right back so that she can see that maybe I'm worried about her. I think that these small social ways of interacting make all the difference in the world. And it's that fact about the world that intrigues me enormously. If enough people grab their bags when you walk down the street this will have an effect no matter how much you pretend that it won't.

Let me give you another example. I'm intrigued by the extent to which my graduate students think that I have no clue concerning what they think about me. My colleague, Michael Stocker, who is very well regarded, and I do roughly the same thing. The only difference, ironically, is that I teach stuff on Judaism and he teaches stuff on racism, but other than that we're both interested in emotions, we've published in similar journals, etc. Let us assume, for the sake of argument, that he's better than I am. Graduate students love him and none of them think that what he does is not philosophy, but they systematically think that what I do isn't genuine philosophy. This simply does not make any sense. What plausible explanation could there be? Even if I do it badly, since Michael and I do the same thing, it still ought to be philosophy, just bad philosophy. The students, however, are prepared to say that I don't do *real* philosophy at all, yet Michael does. So, to tie all of this together, I'm interested in the reactions of people, how people behave, etc. As a Black person, one of the things that one learns is to distinguish between what people say and what people think. Much of my work is really about bringing all of those things together and that's why I talk a lot about nonverbal behavior or I talk about the circuitous references. So, in the above case, what makes the difference in the two judgments? One proposition is race, dare I mention it. I relayed this story to Stocker and he was shaken by it because he saw how powerful it was.

Yancy: What is moral deference and why does the majority of whites fail to show it?

Thomas: I think that it's very simple. On this issue of sexism, you would not dream of telling women what it is like to be a woman or what their experiences are like without listening to them first. Roughly speaking, as far as I can see, many white folks do not think they have to listen to Black people. They seem to think that they understand who we are, what we're about, what our needs are, and where they come from without listening to us. I don't understand how that can be. I can put this to you very poignantly. I've just ended my twentieth year of teaching and if I tell you that I understand white folks it is because I've been around them, working with them, supporting them, and listening to them. Most white folks will think they have just as much understanding of Black people after having interacted with Black people far, far less. It is this that I find terribly intriguing and I don't think that it's going to change. I don't see any indications of it changing.

Yancy: What's the difference between moral deference and empathy?
Thomas: I think that you can have empathy from afar. In fact, to have

empathy you really need not listen to someone. You can be concerned about someone, but not be interested in earning their trust, and I think that moral deference is really about listening to someone with the aim of earning their trust, and most white folks aren't interested in earning the trust of Black people.

Yancy: Why do so many white women and Jews, both of whom constitute minority groups, engage in analogical reasoning to the effect that their pain and suffering are so much like the pain and suffering of Black people?

Thomas: I think that it partly has to do with what I call the contest in America for who has suffered the most. I also don't think that Blacks have been as careful about articulating our pain as we should. My own view is that we did brilliantly up until about the '60s and then we lost it. I think that the pain of racism really hasn't been fully articulated yet. We talk about various changes and all of that, but we've underestimated the psychological damage of racism in our society. In fact, I think that the reference to our identity as "African-American" is an indication of how much psychological damage American slavery and its legacy has wrought upon the lives of Blacks in general. I don't think that there is any evidence that we have a greater identity or affinity to Africa. I mean, you're an American and will almost certainly die an American. The move to "African-American" was about what? Was it about showing that our identity is tied up with Africa? I certainly don't think that my identity is more tied up with Africans than the identities of Blacks in Jamaica, Blacks in France, or Blacks in England. I think that that tells you something about the extent to which slavery really did shake at the very core of the self-identity of Black people. So now we have so many Black people running around wearing these colors and sporting the braids as if now they're really African, that their identities have been finally anchored. That has to be the best indication of a lie gone wild. And you will notice, with regard to the braids, that they are always long and flowing, not short and kinky.

I think that one reason why other groups have been able to make the analogy that you've asked about is because we haven't richly enough expressed the nature of the pain that's there. I think that one reason why we haven't done this is because we have been unwilling to acknowledge the psychological damage of slavery. When I've taught my course on American slavery and the holocaust I've had to fight with Blacks over whether or not slavery had any psychological damage. I don't think that you can have 400 years of anything as wicked as slavery and not have enormous psychological damage. And until we are willing to properly address that, we will allow our history to be co-opted by others. The fundamental difference has to be located in the psychological damage of slavery and not located on the basis of all of these other things, which is not to say that there aren't deep African influences.

When Jesse Jackson introduced the term "African-American" in 1991, I don't recall him ever asking anybody. He just decided that's how we should go about it and unthinkingly here we are. I went from being Negro to Black while I was in college, but the move from Black to African-American didn't bring about a similar change in self-identity. The latter has been a lot of fanfare. Jews and women have been able to use the Black experience as they have very artfully carved out their own identities. And no people have been able to flourish in the absence of having a very secure identity. And I'm almost confident that our identity will not be secured in Africa because the differences are extraordinary. This is not a question of shame, don't misunderstand me; rather, there is a limit to how long you can hold on to your parents and their identity. There comes a time when you have to become yourself. I think that Blacks here in America have enough richness right here. We don't need Africa to somehow make things richer.

Yancy: How then should we anchor our Black identity?

Thomas: I think that we have to undercut the sting of Blackness, that is, where it is negative and pejorative. We have to sort of reconstruct history on this soil so that we can undercut the very sting of slavery. This is why I think that people like Douglass, Harriet Jacobs, and Du Bois are so important. Leap frogging over to Africa will not undo slavery and its pain. Our identity will be constructed out of that melding and anything short of that will leave us with a kind of emptiness.

Yancy: I sense that you're suggesting that there is a redemptive process involved.

Thomas: That's precisely what has got to happen. And the redemptive process may draw its inspiration from what is going on in Africa, but it won't leap frog over the 400 years of slavery here in America. We need to wrestle with it quite pointedly right here. And until we do that our identity here will not be secure.

Yancy: In your philosophical writings you draw upon the work of

David Hume. How do you reconcile the value of Hume's moral psychology with his own contribution toward the downward constitution of Blacks?

Thomas: I'm very open about this. I simply think that Hume and a host of others, Aristotle, Rousseau, Kant, etc., were wrong about their view of Black folks. And, it seems to me, that their moral psychology was such that it applied to persons and the mistake involved refusing to acknowledge Blacks as full-fledged persons. The mistake is not about the moral psychology as such. The moral psychology was not logically tied to it being false that Blacks were full-fledged persons; rather, the range of the moral psychology just so happened to have stopped at the borders of whiteness. So, if that's true, then what you want is the proper range of the moral psychology and that's simply a matter of getting the facts right.

Let me also add that I think that the more vicious the argument gets I suspect the less innocent the moral psychology becomes. So, one might ask: How vicious is their reference to whatever group it is in question? My view is that if it is particularly vicious then that may be a reason to go back and look at the moral psychology on the grounds that when one's opposition to a *kind* is hard driven then that suggests that one's moral psychology is going to be informed by that motivation. My sense is that Hume expressed an observation about Blacks rather than a hard opposition to Blacks and that distinction is important to me.

Yancy: In your essay "The Morally Beautiful" you take issue with Kant where you maintain, "The Kantian framework makes free choice an ontologically prior aspect of the moral landscape." Would you elaborate on this?

Thomas: I don't think we're that free quite often. Look, I'm going to prove to you right now that you're not as free as you think you are. I have two cases. Let's say that you've watched an amazing movie filmed in Japan. If you've got enough money you might say to yourself, "That was a brilliant film, the wonderful landscape and all. Well, I think that I'll go to Japan." Now imagine that you've watched another film, equally brilliant, but it's a murder film. It's almost unlikely that you're going to say to yourself, "I've never committed a murder before, but I want to try this one." I don't think that is going to happen. And I'm not sure in what sense you are free when you claim that you're free to commit it. So part of what I want to say is that we are much more historically situated than Kant thought. We can't leap frog over our entire historical self.

The analogue to this in sociological theory is Erving Goffman's observations that people talk as if our lives are but social roles such that once we peel away all of the social roles that there will be the *real* self. Goffman's point is that there is no such thing as peeling off all of the social roles. There is always something that you're doing. In a similar way, I don't think that there is a way of getting beyond all of our historical self. I don't see how we can do it and that's what I had in mind.

Yancy: If there is no noumenal subject which morally legislates, from a nonempirical sphere, then what sort of conception of the self does your approach to morality presuppose?

Thomas: I presuppose something like this. I think that we are quite frag-ile, and I think that what makes human beings so remarkable is getting it right. A way to see this is by looking at children. A child, long before it has a command of the language, knows whether or not it's being loved by its parents. I think that children have a beautiful mastery of nonverbal behavior. My view is that when a child is loved out of pure innocence that this innocence properly arouses the right sorts of emo-tions in the child. And when those emotions are properly aroused at the right level, from love, to affection, to kindness and all the rest, that shapes how we respond to others. Much of how we respond to others is really affected by the ways in which the kinds of feelings—and I'm very much like Joseph Butler in this regard—that our interactions with them produces. And whether or not the feelings that others call forth out of us are good or bad has a lot to do with whether the foundations of the formation of our feelings are proper in the first place. But once the foundations of emotions are properly laid, I can respond to an other as a person with value, not too little and not too much value.

Yancy: Does your approach to morality presuppose an epistemological foundation to our moral and ethical reasoning behavior?

Thomas: One might question whether there is anything *right* out there at all. I hold that there is something right because I take seriously that there is a human nature and I take seriously that one couldn't raise a child just in any manner. You've got to love that child, show it affec-tion, etc. There is no culture on this planet where you can just brutally beat your child, knock it down, and it will develop just fine. That suggests to me that there really are strong limits, but they are limits that allow for rich expression. So one way in which there are strong epistemological considerations here has to do with the fact that there is a right with respect to how we can flourish. You might think of Kant as a top down person. Well, I'm a bottom up person. I start with the subject and ask, What is the subject like? I then argue that our conceptions of the good must be driven by its very psychological makeup.

Yancy: Moving on to issues of justice, why should Black people engage in just acts towards whites when Blacks themselves are the victims of such systemic injustice?

Thomas: That's a nice question. The simple answer would be two wrongs don't make a right, but there is a better answer, I think. If we dull our sensibilities to being moved to do what is right, then what becomes of those, whites in this case, who haven't done anything to us? Take my white students. What have they done to me? Strictly speaking, nothing. And some of them are poor whites so they don't have any power over me. And if I just allow whiteness to inform how I act so that I thereby wrong all these white folks, then one has to ask: What will prevent me from wronging other Black people? If that approach allows me to start wronging other people who haven't wronged me, then those people could turn out to be Black. But presumably the whole point was supposed to be that Black people shouldn't be wronging one another. My view is that we are very fragile and that we can't go around wronging other people without in some sense damaging our own sensibilities. So it's really a mistake to think that we can do damage to others, Black or white, but that we won't do damage to people of our own kind. What easily happens is that we discover that our ability to narrow the range of people who are *our kind* becomes increasingly greater, and the circle becomes increasingly smaller, and it's that worry that we have to become concerned about.

Yancy: How does your philosophical worldview relate to your identity?

Thomas: Well, that's where we started. Much about who I am, me, has been about trying to understand my feelings, sentiments, and wrestling with a complex array of things that are presented to me. It also has to do with the fact that people have one perception of me. So I ask myself, "What would I have to do in order for someone to have the right perception of me?" In other words, that perception that is correct in my own eyes. But my identity is very much of a person who has lots of friends. I have friends who look white but are Black. I have some friends who are white but look Black. So my friendships encompass a broad range. I situate myself as a person with a certain historical identity that gives me certain insights. I don't think that any of us could have all of the truths, but I do think that each of us could have an insight about the truth. With respect to my identity, Blackness is there and Jewishness is there. I think that those two things come together nicely and they've not been the major tension that the world makes them out to be. On the other hand, they're not overarching in my life and I don't want them to be because I think that in the end I have this stupid view that we are human beings first and I think that's the way it should be.

Yancy: Do you privilege your Jewish identity over your Black identity? And are the two identities ever in conflict? If so how do you resolve such conflict?

Thomas: No. We all have multiple identities. After all, what about a Jewish woman? It just seems to me that negotiating multiple identities is a fundamental aspect of maturation. To be sure, there will be contexts where one aspect of one's life is more salient or relevant than another. But that, too, is a part of life.

A Selection of Published Works of Laurence Thomas

Books

Vessels of Evil: American Slavery and the Holocaust (Philadelphia: Temple University Press, 1993).

Living Morally: A Psychology of Moral Character (Philadelphia: Temple University Press, 1989).

Articles

"Evil and the Concept of a Person," *Midwest Studies in Philosophy* 20 (1996): 38–58.

"Erogenous Zones and Ambiguity: Sexuality and the Bodies of Women and Men," in *Rethinking Masculinity: Explorations in Light of Feminism*, Larry May, Robert Strickwerda, and Patrick Hopkins, eds. (Lanham, MD: Rowman and Littlefield, 1996).

"The Matricies of Malevolent Ideologies: Blacks and Jews," *Social Identities* 2 (1996): 107–33.

"The Soul of Identity: Jews and Blacks," *People of the Book*, Jeffrey Rubin-Dorsky and Shelly Fisher Fishkin, eds. (Madison: University of Wisconsin Press, 1996).

"Power, Trust, and Evil," in *Overcoming Racism and Sexism*, Linda Bell and David Blumenfeld, eds. (Lanham, MD: Rowman and Littlefield, 1995).

"Must We Care About Morality," *Journal of Philosophical Psychology* 7 (1994): 383–94.

"The Logic of Gossip," in *Good Gossip*, Robert F. Goodman and Aaron Ben-Ze'ev, eds. (Lawrence: University Press of Kansas, 1994).

"Group Autonomy and Narrative Identity: Blacks and Jews," in *Blacks and Jews: Alliances and Arguments*, Paul Berman, ed. (New York: Delacorte Press, 1994), 286–303. Other contributors include: Cynthia Ozick, Julius Lester, Norman Podhoretz, Richard Goldstein, Henry Louis Gates, Jr. and Cornell West. Reprinted in *Color, Class, and Identity*, John Arthur and Amy Shapiro, eds. (Boulder: Westview Press, 1996).

"The Reality of the Moral Self," *The Monist* 76 (1993): 3–21.

"Moral Flourishing in an Unjust World," *The Journal of Moral Education* 22 (1993): 83–96.

"What Good Am I," in *Affirmative Action and the University: A Philosophical Inquiry*, Steven M. Cahn, ed. (Philadelphia: Temple University Press, 1993), 125–31. Other contributers include: Alasdair MacIntyre, Philip L. Quinn, and Tom Beauchamp.

"Moral Deference," *The Philosophical Forum* 19 (1992–93): 233–50. Reprinted with revisions in *Theorizing Multiculturalism: A Guide to Current Debate*, Cynthia Willett, ed. (Oxford: Basil Blackwell, 1998).

"Morality and Psychological Development," *A Companion to Ethics* in Peter Singer, ed. (Oxford: Basil Blackwell, 1991), 464–75.

"Reasons for Loving," in *The Philosophy of Erotic Love*, Robert C. Solomon and Kathleen M. Higgins, eds. (Lawrence: University Press of Kansas, 1991), 467–76.

"American Slavery and the Holocaust: Their Ideologies Compared," *Public Affairs Quarterly* 5 (1991): 191–210. Reprinted with revisions as "Characterizing the Evil of American Slavery and the Holocaust," in *Jewish Identity*, David Theo Coldberg and Michael Krausz, eds. (Philadelphia: Temple University Press, 1993), 153–76.

"Trust, Affirmation, and Moral Character," in *Morality, Character, and Identity: Essays in Moral Psychology*, O. Flanagan and A. Rorty, eds., (Cambridge, MA: MIT Press, 1990), 235–58.

"Religion as Cultural Artifact," in *Mind, Value, and Culture: Essays in Honor of E. Maynard Adams*, David Weissbord, ed. (Atascadero, CA: Ridgeview, 1989), 346–53.

"Moral Motivation," *Midwest Studies in Philosophy* 13 (1988): 367–83.

"Christianity in a Social Context: Practical Reasoning and Forgiveness," in *Moral Theory and Moral Judgments*, Baruch Brody, ed. (Dordrecht, The Netherlands: Kluwer Press, 1988), 157–68.

"Rationality and Affectivity: The Metaphysics of the Moral Self," *Social Philosophy and Policy* 5 (1988): 154–72. Reprinted in *The New Social Contract*, Ellen Frankel Paul, et al., eds. (Oxford: Basil Blackwell, 1988).

"Jews, Blacks, and Group Autonomy," *Social Theory and Practice* 14 (1988): 55–69.

"Ethical Egoism and Psychological Dispositions," *American Philosophical Quarterly* 17 (1980): 73–78.

"Capitalism versus Marx's Communism," *Studies in Soviet Thought* 20 (1979): 67–79.

"Rawlsian Self-Respect and the Black Consciousness Movement," *Philosophical Forum* 9 (1978): 303–14.

"Morality and Our Self-Concept," *Journal of Value Inquiry* 12 (1978): 258–68.

"Human Potentiality: Its Moral Relevance," *The Personalist* 53 (1978): 266–72.

fifteen

Lucius T. Outlaw, Jr.

Lucius T. Outlaw, Jr. is T. Wistar Brown professor of philosophy at Haverford College. He earned his B.A. degree, magna cum laude, from Fisk University, and he earned his Ph.D. in philosophy from Boston College. He has also taught at Spelman College, Morgan State University, and Fisk University. His areas of specialization are African philosophy, African-American philosophy, continental philosophy (phenomenology and hermeneutics), and social and political philosophy (Marx and critical social theory). His articles and reviews have appeared in *Cultural Hermeneutics*; *Man and World*; *UMOJO: A Scholarly Journal of Black Studies*; *Praxis International*; *Social Science Information*; *Journal of Social Philosophy*; *The Philosophical Forum*; *Multiculturalism from the Margins: Non-Dominant Voices on Difference and Diversity*; *Encyclopedia of African Religions and Philosophy*; *The Review of Metaphysics*; and more. He is the author of *On Race and Philosophy*. (A selected citation list of Lucius Outlaw's works can be found at the end of the interview.)

Lucius T. Outlaw, Jr.
Haverford College

George Yancy: When and where were you born?

Lucius T. Outlaw: I was born December 28, 1944, in Starkville, Mississippi, and lived there until I went off to college when I was eighteen years old.

Yancy: Talk about racism and how the brutal murder of young Emmit Till impacted your early consciousness.

Outlaw: The murder of Emmit Till had quite an impact on me, so much so that I characterize myself as being part of the Emmit Till generation: that is, I lived in Mississippi, the state in which Emmit was killed, and I was about the same age as he was when he was killed. Such a murder certainly strikes a chord when you're a Black male teenager living in Mississippi, particularly in terms of impacting my thinking about the brutal extent to which some white males were prepared to go to deal with what they took to be violations of the rules prohibiting relations between Black males and white females that in any way might involve sexuality. The racist murder of Emmit Till thus solidified firmly in my mind (and soul) certain notions regarding relationships with white females—about how and why not to be involved in relationships with such females—notions that conditioned my approach to white women for many, many years, even today. The saga of Emmit Till certainly conditioned my thinking about race, racism, and sex in America.

I also spent a lot of time in churches as I was growing up. Since churches were racially segregated, I thus spent a lot of time around and with Black folk. My father, however, was a janitor of a large white Baptist church, so I was in and out of that environment in various ways over the years. But one had to understand the rules and dynamics of race relations. In that formally and informally segregated society, white supremacy was the order of the day. There were, though, some respects in which as a Black person you just didn't give a damn. But as long as you stayed on the proper side of legal authorities that enforced racial segregation, particularly the police or various incarnations, life was pretty normal, under the conditions. But, again, you had to understand the dynamics of race, race and sex and all of that. Otherwise, you could get into serious trouble or end up dead. It was a part of your upbringing to be assisted in achieving this understanding since your survival and well-being depended upon knowing the formal and informal rules governing interracial social intercourse.

Yancy: What impact did being an only child have on you?

Outlaw: Well, it's hard to give a complete account, but one of the most memorable impacts is that there were a lot of periods of loneliness and, as a consequence, early on I came to cherish friendships with both males and females. I didn't like being an only child. I didn't like being lonely when it rained, when we kids ran to our respective homes and usually I was forced to be in the house alone while my friends were elsewhere. That wasn't much fun for me. So, I learned to find pleasure and solace in reading and listening to music to compensate. However, the upside was that my paternal grandfather's and both grandmothers' attention, as well as the attention of my parents and other relatives, was lavished on me since I had no sibling competitors.

Yancy: So, you were a voracious reader?

Outlaw: By the time I was in junior high, and all through high school, I read quite a bit. There were a couple of teachers who pushed me and encouraged me to read this or that particular book. During my high school years I went to the school's library and checked out lots of books. (The public library was segregated, thus off-limits to Black folk.) But most of my reading was pretty much outside of the established school curriculum. I used to read books in the Hardy Boys series, every one I could get my hands on (mostly by buying them from a store in town). I was in the Boy Scouts a number of years, so I subscribed to *Boys' Life Magazine*, a publication that was devoted to scouting, and I read the monthly issues. I also read lots of novels, from *Pinocchio* to *Tom Sawyer* and *Huckleberry Finn*.

But regarding my teachers, most of them influenced me one way or another. Miss Stewart, my eleventh-grade and twelfth-grade English teacher, was especially influential on the development of my writing skills, emphasized my doing well, and devoted substantial effort to getting me and other students ready for college. Also, my math teacher, Mr. Manning, was also quite influential. Virtually all of my teachers were influential in terms of trying to make sure that we stayed in line, that we not be disrespectful and unduly smart-mouthed and that we did what we were supposed to do.

Yancy: What influence did your parents have on your early intellectual growth?

Outlaw: My parents always encouraged me to grow and do well. As typical Black folk, they were big on education. My father (who was born in Starkville and has spent his entire life there except for the years when he was in the army during World War II) was often given books by white folks attending the church where he worked as custodian that were intended for me to read. I read them. My mother, who was born in St. Louis, Missouri, but raised in Starkville, was very hell-bent on learning more and more and was very concerned about finishing school herself: She and my father got married when she was in her teens, consequently she was able to complete her schooling only as far as the eighth grade. That was a big sore spot for her, and she talked about it a great deal throughout my years in school. So, I knew what education meant to her. My father also talked a great deal about the value of formal education, to a great extent because it was something that he had not been able to acquire. This, in large part, is why he wanted me to get as much formal education as I possibly could. Therefore, the influence of my parents was enormous. Also, my father was a principled man and was influential on me in terms of the way that he carried himself: as a man of integrity, honesty, and decency. He was my role model in these ways, though at the time I didn't quite think of him in that way. I thought that I would be different from him, but ended up being quite like him in many respects (as my wife and one of our three sons frequently remind me). He was very firm about the way that I was to conduct myself, and it was very clear to me that he wasn't going to tolerate my straying very far away from that line that he was laying out along which I should walk in going about my life.

Yancy: When did you decide that you wanted to study philosophy?

Outlaw: Before I went to Fisk University I decided to major in religion and philosophy. During my sophomore year at Fisk I made a momentous decision to study philosophy only. Initially, I got on to the road of studying philosophy because I was committed to studying religion as preparation for a career in ministry. But during that fateful sophomore year, for a number of weighty reasons I decided that I liked the study of philosophy more than the study of religion—in large part because I gave up the idea of becoming a minister. Also, though, the desire to *understand* was a major drive for me, but that wasn't limited to my interest in philosophy. I was taking lots of courses ranging across all of the divisions of the curriculum at Fisk. Once I decided that the ministry was not the sort of thing that I was going to spend my time doing, I decided, since I really liked academic life, that I was going to become a college teacher, and philosophy the subject I would teach.

Yancy: Why did you attend Fisk?

Outlaw: Well, one very important reason was that I didn't want to go to school in Mississippi. A second was that a young minister that I knew, who had attended a seminary for Black folk in Nashville, told me that if I really wanted to study religion in a serious way, since I didn't want just a seminary degree, that Fisk would be the place rather than Tennessee State University, the Black institution I was planning to attend. I wanted a broader, liberal arts degree, and the broader—and to my mind much richer and more fun—experiences of a coeducational college. Thanks to the advice of this friend (who also told me that Fisk was widely known for having a large number of the most beautiful Black women in the country), I became very interested in Fisk, applied for admission, and was accepted.

Yancy: Who influenced you at Fisk, and which courses did you take?

Outlaw: Well, a lot of people influenced me at Fisk: fellow students, some of whom became (and some who remain) good friends, faculty members, support staff, deans, a dormitory director, classmates, and various professors whose courses I took. For example, there was Chike Onwachi's anthropology course in which, for the very first time in my life, I had to actually sit down and give serious attention and consideration to Africa, to think positively about Africa, about my own relations to Africa and its peoples. And there were lots of courses that were quite interesting. For example, I really liked the honors colloquia, courses, and seminars that I earned entry into during my freshman year and every subsequent year while at Fisk. While pursuing my major, I took courses in existentialism, analytic philosophy, and philosophy of science along with courses in the history of philosophy, though I wasn't that fascinated with some of the history of philosophy that was offered at the time. In addition, I took courses on various subjects and figures in philosophy and literature; art appreciation (taught by famed artist of the Harlem Renaissance, Aron Douglass); introductory courses in psychology, sociology, history, biology; and an advanced course in biology (taken on the advice of my major professor to better prepare me to pursue my interest in philosophy of science).

As a philosophy major I initially planned to focus on analytic philosophy and philosophy of science. I was reading Ludwig Wittgenstein, John L. Austin, and other philosophers of their kind, during my junior year especially when I participated in the exchange program through which I went to Dartmouth College, where I took courses in logic, philosophy of education, and a team-taught survey course in the Judeo-Christian tradition (fall semester of my junior year, 1960). But eventually (most poignantly after I was in graduate school at Boston College), I found the analytic stuff pretty boring and dry. Given everything that was going on in the country and in the streets—the

Civil Rights and Black Power Movements, the Anti-War Movement—I thought that the focus in analytic philosophy on analyzing sentences was not what I was going to spend my time doing.

Yancy: Why did you do your graduate work at Boston College and who were some of the influences there?

Outlaw: I had applied to a number of schools. I was also nominated for a Woodrow Wilson Fellowship and a Danforth Fellowship that resulted in my being ranked as Honorable Mention in both cases. Announcements of Woodrow Wilson and Danforth Fellows, as well as of the Honorable Mentions, were circulated around the country. The chairman of the Department of Philosophy at Boston College, Joseph Flannagan, S.J., read the announcements and called me at Fisk to inform that he and the department were interested in having me come to Boston College to do graduate work. (Father Flannagan contacted a number of persons listed in the announcements and persuaded several to come to Boston College.) At the time I had already been turned down by a number of the graduate programs to which I had applied, and was waiting to hear from several others. There was the prospect of going to graduate school in the Midwest thanks to offers of admission I received from at least two institutions, but after persistent discussions with Father Flannagan I received a very nice offer from Boston College. Since I had friends and a roommate from Fisk going to Harvard's law school, and preferred Boston and New England to the more southernlike Midwest, I decided to go to Boston College. ✓

And concerning influences, there were some people with whom I worked closely, especially David Rasmussen who directed my dissertation work. I had very good seminars with a number of people: Tom Owens, with whom I studied phenomenology and existentialism; Richard Murphy for Kant; Jacques Timeneuix for Hegel; Flannagan's course on Bernard Lonergan's work; and Edward Makinnon's seminars on philosophy of science and analytic philosophy. I also took independent reading projects on J. Piaget, Alfred Schutz, and other subjects and figures with Rasmussen and other professors.

Though I took courses with a number of people, the direction that I took I carved out on my own, particularly in the independent reading projects. I was pretty eclectic and gradually began to shape my own agenda. So, for me, a very important question was what kinds of issues, subjects, and figures, among the seminars available, and, those I studied, were of particular interest and value in terms of helping me to get at such things as sociopolitical matters, especially those of racial injustices, etc. The primary question that influenced the setting of my philosophical direction was what studies and resources would help me to meet my agenda.

Yancy: Do you construct yourself as an African-American philosopher and what is African-American philosophy?

Outlaw: First, I am an African-American, and I am a philosopher. Among other things, then, I am an African-American philosopher. (So, in an important sense, to a significant degree it is not a matter of my constructing myself because I am already constructed as a Black person, though there are, nonetheless, very important ways in which I can, I have, I continue to reconstruct myself.) Second, "African-American philosophy" does not refer to a single *anything*, but rather to a collectivity. "African-American" is a term that can be used to identify persons by race and ethnicity. Now, after having so identified them, one can then go on to ask about their philosophizing. "African-American philosophy" is thus a descriptive, identifying phrase for philosophizing efforts, but "African-American" does not immediately and necessarily identify anything particular about philosophizing other than the raciality and ethnicity of the persons doing so.

Yancy: But African-American philosophy certainly has some specific properties, yes?

Outlaw: That remains to be determined if what you mean is specific properties by virtue of being the philosophizing of African-Americans. When I speak of African-American philosophy, I'm referring to the philosophizing of persons who are Americans of African descent. Now, what that philosophizing is about, how it is conducted, are additional questions. Once you've specified "African-American philosophy," you haven't said anything in particular so far about the philosophizing other than that it is the philosophizing of people who are African-American.

Yancy: Does African-American philosophy have its own distinctive metaphysics, ontology, and epistemology?

Outlaw: You would have to survey all of the people who are African-Americans who are philosophizing and ask what constitutes their metaphysics, epistemology, etc. You would then have to bring all of the surveying together to see what the similarities and differences are and then compare all of these to other metaphysical systems, epistemologies, etc. produced by persons who are not of African descent. Again, my point is that there is nothing automatically conveyed about their philosophizing when we say that there are African-Americans who philosophize. I mean, there are all kinds of European philosophers who philosophize about all kinds of things, but just because they're European this does not mean that they think the same way about all kinds of things. There are similarities and differences among them in their philosophizing.

I think that too often when we hear "African-American philosophy" the presumption is that the phrase works to signal something unique and distinctive about the philosophizing of people who are African-American. My point is that this phrase does not do this; rather, it picks out and gathers together the philosophizing of persons on the basis of their distinctive ethnicity and raciality. However, if it turns out that after examining the philosophizing of persons who are African-American that there is something distinctive about it, then fine. But this would only come after having examined the philosophizing closely. For me, it is not even *necessary* that it be distinctive, though it may be (and in actual cases is). When you say "European philosophy," are you requiring that it be different from some other philosophies by saying it is European? Well, if in some instances it is, fine. If in others it isn't, fine.

Yancy: Concerning African-American culture, do you see any value in the utilization of the modalities of jazz, blues, or rap music vis-à-vis African-American philosophy?

Outlaw: Sure. If we have a fairly broad definition of philosophizing as rather systematic thinking about life, existence, etc., well, then, it has never been the case that such conceptualizing, or philosophizing, has been limited to people who have formal degrees in philosophy and work in academic institutions. There are academic versions of philosophizing that play by various sets of rules to govern credentialing and professional activities and thereby work to reserve the title "philosophy" for the professionalized versions of philosophizing. But if you just take the broader notion of philosophizing, people involved in certain explorations of thought and concern, then you find this in rap music, blues, jazz, R&B, spirituals, etc. But do we want to come along now and argue that such explorations of thought and concern can be enhanced by developing criteria and norms that would make this thinking more rigorous and valid? Well, I am persuaded, to a certain point, to answer "yes." Nevertheless, what is going on in a number of other modes of intellectual endeavor engaged in by Black folk—literature, social science, religion, the arts, jurisprudence, medicine, among others—certainly reveals very sophisticated thinking and serious concerns that should be attended to.

Yancy: Western philosophy has this image of being culturally elitist. Have African-American philosophers attempted to consciously combat this image or have they uncritically accepted this image?

Outlaw: You don't come along, as did my generation of African-American philosophers, trying to make an argument for what we once referred to as "Black philosophy" and now "African-American philosophy" ("Africana philosophy" we use to refer collectively to the philosophizing of African and African-descended people) without already deconstructing—or at least rejecting—a great deal of what has been involved in elitist notions of Western philosophy. Now, our earliest encounters with a significant number of professional philosophers not of African descent involved a great number of them rejecting anything termed Black philosopher or African-American philosophy, rejecting, even, the very idea of qualifying philosophy by color codes for raciality and ethnicity. Since, it was argued, there is no white philosophy, so there can't be a Black philosophy. Since there is no such thing as white physics or Black physics, why qualify philosophy with a color term? But once you get into the business of talking about Black, African-American, or Africana philosophy, you are already working against certain elitist and otherwise restrictive notions of philosophy. For philosophizing had been defined literally as reserved for a certain elite class of civilized people—white people—and among them the most civilized and capable of strenuous rational activity. So, once you entered into the arena, you were already working against the grain, so to speak.

Yancy: I have two related questions. Why haven't African-American philosophers developed something comparable to the Black Arts Movement, and why haven't they created something comparable to *Presence Africaine?*

Outlaw: Well, the thing about movements is that the accounts of them tend to be written after they are over. So, we'll have to wait to see the historical accounts of the last twenty-five years regarding the efforts in behalf of African-American philosophy. Concerning publishing ventures of the likes of *Presence Africaine,* there hasn't been anything comparable to that produced by African-American philosophers. But,

again, it remains to be seen whether we shall. I can relate to you stories from the last ten or fifteen years of efforts, on my part and others',
to try to get stuff published as African-American and African philosophy and being turned down summarily and repeatedly by publishers.
Recently, I received an e-mail message from an African-American
philosopher who had alerted me to the fact that a publisher had asked
him to do a volume on African-American philosophy, and I just
chuckled. For this was a publisher with whom I once had direct contact because I was the managing editor of an internal philosophy journal that they published. On one occasion, for example, while on my
way to a conference in Kenya, I stopped by the publisher's headquar-
ters in England to take care of a number of matters involving the journal and, during the meeting with a senior official of the publisher,
raised the question of their publishing some works involving African
and African-American philosophy. The official responded, "No. There
is no market. We can't publish it." I was turned down repeatedly by a
number of other publishing houses afterwards. However, almost all of
those publishers are now publishing books of African-American and
African philosophy.

Yancy: Why has African philosophy created such a critically discursive
field and yet African-American philosophy appears to be slow in this
regard?

Outlaw: Well, for a number of reasons, I think. One reason has to do
with Africa as a continent and with African people being in some
quite important ways distinctively different from Europeans and
Americans of European descent. For many years there's been a kind of
legitimacy to the otherness of Africa for many Europeans and Euro-
Americans that is complicated with respect to African-Americans: For
example, only a few decades ago, African dignitaries could enter the
U.S.A. as such, to engage in activities at the United Nations, for example, and have access to public accommodations and facilities from
which Negro Americans were barred. Also, Africa is an entire continent with lots of countries, institutions, and organizations of African
philosophers who have launched a number of journals and produced
a significant and still-growing body of literature. Even the sheer number of philosophers in Africa is much larger than the number of
philosophers of African descent in the U.S. They have graduate programs in philosophy in a significant number of institutions across
Africa that have produced several generations of students who are

now helping to sustain and enlarge developments in academic philosophy. And in some ways they've also been more prolific with regard to organizing and hosting local, regional, and international conferences, publishing, etc.

With regard to the over one hundred historically Black colleges and universities in this country, only one or two have graduate programs—Howard University being one of them—and those are only programs which offer the master's degree. With no Ph.D. programs in philosophy in Black institutions, we are without a necessary means for really intensifying and advancing developments in Africana philosophy. And of all the graduate programs in predominantly white universities in this country, it is only quite recently that we have had more than one Black philosopher on the faculties after a very long period of having only a small handful teaching in graduate programs. Consequently, we haven't had the development of significant curricula involving African-American and African philosophy. Sure, there are now a few courses of this kind being offered in a number of institutions (many more than was the case even fifteen years ago), but until recently we had very few places where people were producing masters' theses and Ph.D. dissertations that became scholarly books and articles on subjects that build up the body of literature of Africana philosophy. That's only now beginning to happen very slowly. So, the demographic, intellectual, institutional, and sociopolitical bases that support philosophizing have been much more substantial, in many important respects, in Africa than in the U.S.

Yancy: How can African-American philosophers teach Kant, Hume, and others, and yet consider themselves critically engaged, explicitly or implicitly, in the project of creating an African-American philosophical discursive field?

Outlaw: It depends on how you're teaching Kant. Also, for me, in order to have a flourishing and legitimated context of discourse of African-American philosophy doesn't require that Kant's works not be taught, nor required that I not know Kant, nor, even, that I cease to read or even teach Kant. Rather, in some cases, I might even be required to know Kant rather well, especially with regard to raising questions about Kant's racism. But in order to engage Kant on this issue carefully and fairly, I would have to read him more thoughtfully and closely than I might have to otherwise. It would not do at all simply to call him a racist and dismiss him.

Yancy: Does the deconstructionist attempt to de-essentialize the concept of race impact the way that African-American philosophy is done or how African-American philosophers see themselves?

Outlaw: Well, I think that such efforts should. Whether they do, and how, are two different, though related, questions. It depends on what we mean by "de-essentialize." Efforts of this kind have already impacted us in some respects, one consequence of which is the variety of positions taken on the viability of *race* as a concept: from the position taken by Anthony Appiah, on one hand, to my different, and opposing position, on the other. Further, out of deconstructive, anti-essentializing efforts, there have come some important clarifications that, I think, it behooves all concerned to take into account in wrestling with the complex and highly charged notion of race.

Yancy: Briefly, on this issue of race construction, what is the nature of your opposition to Appiah's position?

Outlaw: Briefly, it is Appiah's position that, epistemologically and ontologically, the concept *race* is very much the same as the concept *witch*: That is, though there are persons who believe that there are witches and use the word "witch" to refer to persons they believe to be witches, *realistically* (that is to say, on the terms of scientific empiricism or realism) there are no such things as witches. The term "witch" has no real referent, no matter a speaker's beliefs to the contrary. Likewise, Appiah has argued, "race" has no real referent that fulfills all of the conditions—that is, embody all of the biological, characterological, psychological, etc., characteristics—that would have to be met in order for a group of persons to be properly called a race.

Now, to an important extent I agree with Appiah. In other respects I don't. I remain convinced that it is important to get clear about deficiencies in older conceptions of race, particularly those that improperly mixed or conflated biological, cultural, and characterological characteristics. After having done so, I think it then possible to reconstruct the notion of race such that it refers appropriately to relatively distinct, more or less complex population groups that are also more or less complex cultural groups.

Yancy: With respect to this issue of race, do you see it as a social construction?

Outlaw: The short answer to that question is "yes," but it is very important to take care in how we understand and speak of social construction. One of the most influential texts that I ever read in graduate school, one I found and studied on my own, was Peter Berger and Thomas Luckmann's *The Social Construction of Reality*. This remains one of my principal guiding texts. It helped me to understand that human beings must basically construct virtually all of their meaning systems about everything. As a species we don't have any choice since we don't come into the world with any preestablished meaning-systems repertoires for surviving, adapting, and flourishing. We humans have to construct all that we have (though in relative stable, long-lasting societies successive generations enter worlds already constructed for them). Now there certainly have been long and rich traditions of naturalistic accounts of human species-being, accounts that, in quite important respects, have been different from and opposed to social construction accounts. And there are those who have argued against the viability of concepts of race by holding that there are no *natural* races (by which they tend to mean *race* is not a tenable concept by the terms of contemporary biological science), only individuals who have been *constructed* as races, that is, had an untenable complex of defining characteristics attributed to and imposed on them, almost always for pernicious reasons.

Well, I think that there is much in this argument that is correct, but that there is also a way in which some who take this position become facile and dismissive, particularly when their argument takes the form "Well, so and so is not real, it's *only* a social construction." I think that in many cases this is a really dumb and inappropriate way to go about making an important distinction: that is, between things that are socially constructed and things that are *real*. I just think this approach is wrongheaded.

In so many ways, what is real for us is by way of constructions that have social groundings. Language is a social venture in and through which we designate the real and the unreal. Perhaps if you're talking about what we might call the materially real, then some of the things of this kind do not owe their reality to social activity. Mountains, for example, don't tend to come about because you and I, nor any other humans, have wished them into being, or brought them about otherwise. Other materially real things are very much social constructions, such as automobiles produced in factories by way of highly coordinated social labor. A car is not a natural object, it is constructed socially, but it is real.

Yancy: But even in looking at something as a mountain as opposed to a hill, in terms of language as a mediational process, is a highly sociolinguistic constitutive affair. The raw visual data does not in and of itself announce itself as "mountain."

Outlaw: There is no conceptualization of it as "mountain" except through some social venture of language use in the form of communication conditioning conceptualization.

Yancy: Yes, but getting back to this issue of race, do you think that Afrocentricity as propounded by Molefi Asante reconstitutes a form of Black essentialism?

Outlaw: Well, not in his better moments of articulating his notion of Afrocentricity. In his better moments Asante makes a real effort, with notable success, to avoid any inappropriate racial essentialism. But there are times when his articulations lapse into precisely that.

Yancy: Does Asante's Afrocentric perspective make for the inability to talk across paradigms? That is, does he help create an incommensurability between Afrocentrism and Eurocentrism?

Outlaw: Not if you read him seriously and carefully. In a number of places, he quite explicitly tries to contribute to the opening spaces for dialogue within a healthy, humanistic pluralism. (This was reinforced for me recently when I participated in a symposium that included Molefi Asante, Maulana Karenga, Mary Lefkowitz, and Martin Myers, devoted to a discussion of Lefkowitz's *Not Out of Africa*.) Repeatedly Asante has been insistent about the need to create more democratic and humanistic spaces for intellectual and scholarly work within which to consider Africa and African-descended people. His goal, ultimately, is not to create some new, hermetically sealed, paradigmatic racialized space within which only African and African-centered people can operate. I think that there are people who do not read Asante carefully and who do not take him seriously on the basis of having done so. Rather, I think, unfairly to Asante, they fail to read enough of his works to get a fuller picture of what he's up to and/or they latch on to incomplete or distorted articulations that go by the name of Afrocentricity and attribute the lack of completeness or distortions to him.

Yancy: What's your thoughts on Lefkowitz's *Not Out of Africa*?

Outlaw: In some ways it is a commendable and courageous endeavor to take up and confront some important issues. I commended Mary

Lefkowitz publically for calling attention to the need to maintain respect for and adherence to certain scholarly standards, etc., and supported some of her criticisms of some of the works which she discusses in her book. However, I also think that, in some ways equally important, she is irresponsible in terms of the way in which she characterizes "Afrocentricity" and what she calls "extreme Afrocentricity." She uses these terms almost interchangeably and in the process makes no nuanced distinctions among those persons who have been called and/or identify themselves as Afrocentrists. In *Not Out of Africa*, Lefkowitz never sets out an account of what she means by Afrocentricity. She seldom, if ever, directly engages works by Asante or Karenga, two of the leading scholars elaborating and working out of the context of Afrocentric paradigms, to explore what they have meant by Afrocentricity.

Lefkowitz also doesn't take up the serious challenges that have been raised by a number of Afrocentrists to standards of scholarship that have been racist and exclusionary. I think that's a very glaring and irresponsible failure on her part. When we were together for the symposium on her book, I offered to her that if I went around saying that all Jews are racist because there were some Jewish persons who are racist, well, she would likely take very serious issue with my doing so. It is on the basis of works by George G. M. James, Ben-Jochannon, to some extent Cheikh Anta Diop, and in some cases Asante that she takes Afrocentrists to court. However, she never gives an account of a lot of people committed to an Afrocentric posture toward knowledge-production and justification who raise some very interesting, challenging, and important questions. I consider that irresponsible and inappropriate on Lefkowitz's part, and I have told her this both in public and in private.

Yancy: What is your entry into the Frankfurt school of critical theory?

Outlaw: My entry was really through attending a lecture by Herbert Marcuse at Boston University during the turbulent period of '67–'68 and being very impressed and inspired by what he offered. I found it provocative, interesting, and insightful. In response I turned my attention to first one, then others of his published works, starting with his *One Dimensional Man*. (Eventually I would go on to teach courses on, or others that involved, some of his writings.) What was striking about *One Dimensional Man* was the account he gave of what he called advanced capitalist society. Also, for me, it was the nature of the rhythm of his logic and writing that I found also attractive. In reading through his works and commentaries on his works, I learned that Marcuse was one of a cohort of intellectuals. I found out who they were and I devoted myself to learning more about them and to studying some of their works, as well.

Yancy: What about your entry into the works of Carlos Castaneda?

Outlaw: Well, for me, they were very interesting. You can call them fictional, but they were purported to be anthropological studies and reports of actual lived experiences. To me, it was fictive literature to be taken seriously. But when taken seriously, the works certainly stretched the bounds of credulity. Still, they became for me interesting test cases for ideas and concepts I was encountering in some reading that I was doing on phenomenological accounts of life-worlds and reality. So in one of my early essays I tested some of the phenomenological, theoretical stuff on what Castaneda was presenting through his texts. His books were fascinating reading, and I read all of them. Metaphysically and epistemologically they presented interesting challenges, as does good science fiction literature that takes you into well-constructed imaginary new worlds.

Yancy: Castaneda talks about a new system of glosses where this involves a total system of perception and language. How do we avoid a new system of perception and language from deteriorating into just another typifying scheme?

Outlaw: All language, to the extent that it is employed to describe things, must provide a means for typifying. Very few things in the world are identical, even if they are of the same type. So, we're always talking about things of the same kind in terms of their similarities, while disregarding, on those occasions, certain dissimilarities among them, and referring to those similar things by a single, typifying term. That's the economizing aspect of language that allows us to go about the business of daily life without becoming bogged down by all of the minutia of detail and difference in everything we encounter. Otherwise, we wouldn't be able to get very far. We'd be paralyzed since virtually everything is in some sense unique. For example, when we go to buy a pair of jeans, we ask for jeans of a certain size. Well, are all the pairs of jeans in that size category *exactly* the same size? Well, no, not quite. But for all practical purposes they are and thus there's no need to be concerned. Minute differences are irrelevant. But if we had to deal with all of the differences among the jeans such that we couldn't refer to them as "jeans of so and so size," then we would have to treat each pair of jeans as uniquely sized. Buying a pair of jeans would then become a major chore. And if this were the case for many or all of the objects, persons, and situations we encounter daily, very quickly we would become completely overwhelmed by quotidian life.

On the other hand, typifying some pants as jeans of size so and so, or a car as one of a certain make, etc., is economical and allows us to get on with routinized, customized living until the generalizations and typifications fail us in some way such that we have to deal with details. We need the typifying power of language.

But what is going to prevent the new glosses from being taken for granted? Well, there is a certain kind of watchfulness that results in our developing new terms. What we hope to do is to constantly renew the ways in which we look at the world. One of the things that Castaneda stressed was being able to look at the world freshly. This is one of the ways in which we try and prevent ourselves from growing staid and taking too much for granted. For Castaneda, a great deal of doing so has to do with how one perceives the world out of one's own position in the world, out of one's being in the world. It was very crucial for Castaneda that those who would live as warriors cultivate and practice ways in which to "stop the world" so as to really see it in new kinds of ways.

Yancy: On your view, how open is Being and how fluid is knowledge?
Outlaw: I'm not sure about "the openness of Being." I sort of gave up on Martin Heidegger's explorations of Being years ago. Pursuing the openness of Being has never been something that I was persuaded to do, certainly not on those terms. But as for the fluidity of knowledge, human beings are animals of evolution and knowledge acquisition, and the production of knowledge is a crucial, species-specific part of the pragmatics of human existence. We don't have any choice about this if we intend to survive, adapt, and flourish. We can't build up knowledge, make it part of our genetic code, and reproduce knowledge while producing offspring. Knowledge is always contextual and conditional. It is always subject to atrophy, and all kinds of fluidities, impediments, changes, etc. The business of producing, validating, mediating, and acquiring knowledge are never ending endeavors.

Yancy: In his book *Cultural Materialism*, I think that anthropologist Marvin Harris would say that Castaneda's work is obscurantist.
Outlaw: If you've got a model of knowledge-validation which depends

on some kind of empirical verification, then that's not what's going on with Castaneda, not if what you want is a form of social scientific validation. And if you say that forms of experience involving knowledge-claims [that] do not meet these norms for validating knowledge-claims are obscurantist, you might be right by the terms of your norms. But then what? Does this mean that you can dismiss all of the other possible experiences and claims? Well, it depends on how you want to stand on such things. If you ask me whether I have to choose between these two stances (empirical verification and the knowledge of Don Juan), well, for certain important purposes, yes I do, and most of the time I choose the former. I cannot take Don Juan's teachings as a way to go about trying to live in the world. I couldn't make that work for me. But as a thought experiment for raising other kinds of questions, to think about things in other kinds of ways, the teachings are very fruitful.

Yancy: Lastly, how would you characterize your overall philosophical project?

Outlaw: Trying to make sense of the world and of how we can organize it better and live better, particularly where matters of race and social justices are concerned.

A Selection of Published Works of Lucius T. Outlaw

Book

On Race and Philosophy (New York: Routledge, 1996).

Articles

"Africana Philosophy," in *The Journal of Ethics* (1996).

"'Conserve' Races? In Defense of W. E. B. Du Bois," in *W. E. B. Du Bois on Race and Culture: Philosophy, Politics and Poetics*, Bernard Bell, Emily Grosholz, and James Stewart, eds. (New York and London: Routledge, 1996).

"Marcus Mosiah Garvey," in the *Encyclopedia of African Religions and Philosophy*, V. Y. Mudimbe, editor-in-chief (Dordracht, the Netherlands: Kluwer Publishers, 1998).

"Africana Philosophy and The History of Philosophy in the West," in the *Encyclopedia of African Religions and Philosophy*, V. Y. Mudimbe, editor-in-chief (Dordracht, the Netherlands: Kluwer Publishers, 1998).

"On Race and Philosophy," *Graduate Faculty Philosophy Journal* (New School for Social Research) 18, no. 2 (1995): 175–99.

"Africa, Identity, and the American Experiment," in *African and African-*

American Sensibility, Michael Coy, Jr. and Leonard Plotnicov, eds. (Pittsburgh: University of Pittsburgh, Department of Anthropology, Ethnology Monograph no. 15, 1995), 1–19.

"On W. E. B. Du Bois's 'The Conservation of Races,'" in *Overcoming Racism and Sexism*, Linda Bell and David Blumenfeld, eds. (Lanham, MD: Rowman and Littlefield, 1995); and, in an earlier form, in *SAPINA Newsletter* (A Bulletin of the Society for African Philosophy in North America) IV, no. 1 (January–July 1992): 13–28.

"African, African-American, Africana Philosophy," *Philosophical Forum* XXIV, nos. 1–3 (fall–spring 1992–1993): 63–93.

"Against the Grain of Modernity: The Politics of Difference and the Conservation of 'Race,'" in *Man and World* 25, nos. 3/4 (November 1992): 443–68.

"Hortense Jeanette Spillers: Reading and Re-Writing 'The American Grammar Book,'" in *Notable Black American Women*, Jessie Carney Smith, ed. (Detroit: Gale Research, 1992).

"The Future of 'Philosophy' in America," *Journal of Social Philosophy* 22, no. 1 (spring 1991): 162–82.

"Life Worlds, Modernity, and Philosophical Praxis: Race, Ethnicity, and Critical Social Theory," in *Culture and Modernity: East-West Philosophic Perspectives*, Eliot Deutsch, ed. (Honolulu: University of Hawaii Press, 1991), 21–49.

"African 'Philosophy': Deconstructive and Reconstructive Challenges," in *Contemporary Philosophy: Chronicles, Vol. 5: African Philosophy*, Guttorm Floistad, ed. (Dordrecht, the Netherlands: Martinus Nijhoff, 1987), 9–44; and in *Sage Philosophy: Indigenous Thinkers and Modern Debate on African Philosophy*, H. Odera Oruka, ed. (New York: E. J. Brill, 1990), 223–48.

"Towards a Critical Theory of 'Race,'" in *Anatomy of Racism*, David Theo Goldberg, ed. (Minneapolis: University of Minnesota Press, 1990), 58–82.

Philosophy, Ethnicity, and Race (The Alfred P. Stiernotte Lecture Series in Philosophy, Quinnipiac College, Hamden, Connecticut, 1989).

"African-American Philosophy: Social and Political Case Studies," *Social Science Information* (London, Newbury Park, Beverly Hills, and New Delhi: Sage) 26, no. 1 (1987): 75–97.

"The Deafening Silence of the Guiding Light: American Philosophy and the Problems of the Color Line," *Quest: Philosophical Discussions* (Department of Philosophy, The University of Zambia, Lusaka) 1, no. 1 (June 1987): 39–50.

"African and African-American Philosophy: A Contribution to Efforts in Deconstruction and the Critical Management of Traditions," *The Journal of The New York Society for the Study of Black Philosophy* 1, no. 1 (winter/spring, 1984): 27–41.

"Philosophy, Hermeneutics, Social-Political Theory: Critical Thought in the Interest of African-Americans," in *Philosophy Born of Struggle: Anthology of Afro-American Philosophy from 1917*, Leonard Harris, ed. (Dubuque, IA: Kendall/Hunt, 1983), 60–67.

"Race and Class in the Theory and Practice of Emancipatory Social Transformation," in *Philosophy Born of Struggle: Anthology of Afro-American Philosophy from 1917*, Leonard Harris, ed. (Dubuque, IA: Kendall/Hunt, 1983), 117–29.

"Philosophy and Culture: Critical Hermeneutics and Social Transformation," in *Philosophy and Cultures: Proceedings of the 2nd Afro-Asian Philosophy Conference* (Nairobi, Kenya: Bookwise Limited, 1983), 26–31.

"Critical Theory in a Period of Radical Transformation," *Praxis International* 3, no. 2 (July 1983): 138–46. Reprinted in *Critical Sociology*, Larry Ray, ed. (Brookfield, VT: Edward Elgar Publishing, 1990).

"Philosophy in Africa and the African Diaspora: Contemporary African Philosophy," *Proceedings of the 6th Annual National Conference of the National Council for Black Studies* 3, Gerald A. McWorter, ed. (Urbana: Afro-American Studies and Research Program, University of Illinois, 1982), 1–21.

"Black Folk and the Struggle in 'Philosophy,'" *Endarch* 1, no. 3 (winter 1976): 24–36; and, in a revised version, in *Radical Philosophers' News Journal*, no. VI (April 1976): 21–30.

"Beyond the Everyday Life-World: A Phenomenological Encounter with Sorcery," *Man And World* 8, no. 4 (November 1975): 436–45.

"Language and Consciousness: Foundations for a Hermeneutic of Black Culture," *Cultural Hermeneutics* 1, no. 4 (February 1974): 403–13.

[sixteen]

Bernard R. Boxill

Bernard R. Boxill is professor of philosophy at the University of North Carolina, Chapel Hill. He earned his B.A. in mathematics from La Salle College. He obtained his M.A. in philosophy from the University of New Brunswick, and his Ph.D. in philosophy was earned at UCLA. He has also taught at the University of Kentucky and the University of South Florida. His areas of specialization are African-American philosophy and political philosophy. His articles and reviews have appeared in journals such as *Social Theory and Practice*; *Philosophy and Public Affairs*; *Ethics*; *The Journal of Ethics*; *Proceedings of the Charles S. Peirce Society*; *Law and Philosophy*; *Social Philosophy and Policy*; *The Philosophical Forum*; and *The Philosophical Review*, and in collections such as *The Underclass Question* and *Existence in Black*. He is also the author of *Blacks and Social Justice*. Boxill serves on the editorial board of such distinguished journals as *The Philosophical Forum* and *Ethics*. (A selected citation list of Bernard Boxill's published works can be found at the end of the interview.)

Bernard R. Boxill
University of North Carolina, Chapel Hill

George Yancy: When and where were you born?

Bernard R. Boxill: I was born December 8, 1937, on an island in the Caribbean called St. Lucia. St. Lucia at the time was a British colony. My parents were also from the Caribbean, my father from Barbados and my mother from Martinique. My father was a hard taskmaster.

Perhaps this was because he had studied so long on his own to eventually earn an external degree (first class honors) from London University. At the time he was one of the few people on the island who had a university degree. His degree was in French, but his favorite subject was Latin. The Latin language was a big thing in the Islands in those days. The way to prove yourself intellectually was to be good at Latin. I suppose we thought this showed we were as good as our English masters. My father started my brother and myself studying Latin and geometry before we went to high school. My mother did not have a university degree. Actually, I can think of only one woman on the island who had gone to a university. Don't misunderstand me. Looking back, I realize that it was great growing up in St. Lucia. But I left there and came to the United States when I was nineteen.

Yancy: Provide a sense of your educational experiences while in the Caribbean.

Boxill: Well, I attended a high school called St. Mary's College and it was run by the Presentation Brothers which was an Irish religious order. But the best teachers, those I remember with the greatest affection, were local people. These were people who had done well in high school and had been recruited to teach after graduation. None of them had a university degree. As I mentioned earlier, in those days very few people had university degrees. Perhaps because there was as yet no university in the British Caribbean. But it was these local teachers who were the best teachers and the ones we most loved. I remember especially Harold Haynes and Parry Husbands. Some of the teachers went on to make names for themselves like the novelist Garth St. Omer, the author of *Shades of Gray,* who now teaches at the University of California, Santa Barbara, and the poet and Nobel Laureate Derek Walcot.

Yancy: So what was your academic direction in high school?

Boxill: It was science. I wanted to get out from under my father's domination, his emphasis on Latin, and so I concentrated on science, mainly chemistry and biology.

Yancy: What sorts of things were you reading during this period? And did any of these works impact you philosophically?

Boxill: I read a lot and I suspect that my father was responsible for that too. Early on I read Charles Dickens, Robert Louis Stevenson, Alexander Dumas, and H. Rider Haggard. Later on I read mainly mysteries.

I don't think that these books had had any philosophical impact on me. If there was any philosophical stimulation during this time I would say that it was from religion. There were no nonbelievers, but the Catholic and non-Catholic boys in the high school (it was an all-boys school) argued endlessly about the virgin birth and the immaculate conception. A question that much exercised us was God's benevolence given that so many bad things happened. I remember vividly how shocked we all were once when an intellectual "street person," called Joey, interrupted our debates and gave us a lecture on what I have since come to know as Deism.

Yancy: So when did you first come to consciousness that there was a field called philosophy?

Boxill: When I came to the States. Before that I did not know that there was such a field at all, especially a field that one could do a degree in. I came to the States to study biology and then I changed to mathematics, but one of the required courses was in philosophy, and I said, "Oh, my God, there is this other thing!" During this discovery I was attending La Salle College.

Yancy: But why such an attraction to philosophy?

Boxill: At the time I didn't see philosophy as having to do with political philosophy, which, of course, is now my area. I then saw philosophy as providing a more systematic way of investigating questions concerning the existence of God, free will and determinism, death and the afterlife, the goodness of God and those kinds of theological concerns. I remember believing that the philosophers had actually solved these questions, and the only thing for me to do was to understand what they were saying. We mainly studied St. Thomas Aquinas. I think that I realized that philosophy involved more than these questions when the teacher in one of my math classes told us about Bertrand Russell's paradox. Russell was the first twentieth-century philosopher I studied. I read many of his books, the first half of the first volume of *Principia Mathematica*, *The Principles of Mathematics*, and others. For many years I thought that philosophy of mathematics was the area that I wanted to seriously study.

Yancy: Alfred North Whitehead collaborated with Russell on *Principia Mathematica*. Were you also reading his works?

Boxill: No. I looked at one of his books and quickly decided he was not for me.

Yancy: Why did you decide to do your undergraduate training at La Salle?

Boxill: Well, my father was the first Black man to have the job of head of education in St. Lucia. This position had always been held by an Englishman, but around the '50s there was a great deal of decolonizing and withdrawing and so these type of jobs were opening up for local people. So my father got this job. Now Saint Jean Baptiste De La Salle is the Catholic patron saint of teachers, and my father was very interested in all of this and so he got connected with the people at La Salle College. And years before I actually went there he had been corresponding with them and arguing about educational questions and exchanging papers, etc. So that by the time I was old enough to go to college they sent me a tuition scholarship.

Yancy: Who influenced you most at La Salle College in terms of philosophy of mathematics?

Boxill: I would say it was brother Aldan, who told us about Russell's paradox. He team-taught an honors class with another man, O'Brian, I believe his name was, who was teaching at Princeton University. O'Brian was a philosopher and he taught Wittgenstein's *Tractatus*, but I didn't understand it. After I finished my math degree, I went back to the Caribbean and taught math in the high schools there, first in Guyana in South America and then in Barbados where my father had retired.

Yancy: So when did you actually decide that you would pursue philosophy formally and get a degree in the area?

Boxill: When I was back home teaching. I guess I actually decided that I wanted to do philosophy while I was in college, but I wanted to finish my degree in mathematics because I couldn't afford to change in the middle. So I brought about a dozen or so philosophy books back to the Caribbean with me. I brought back an early paperback edition of a part of the first volume of *Principia Mathematica*, and textbooks on logic and by Alonzo Church and W. V. O. Quine. And then there was a lucky thing that happened. My brother, who was teaching at a university in Canada, the University of New Brunswick, alerted me that somebody had, at the very last minute, turned down a fellowship in the philosophy department and that it was too late to advertise the fellowship. So I quickly applied for it. And I guess I got the fellowship because he was a faculty member at the university. Anyway, I went there and received my master's degree in philosophy. I wrote my thesis on Quine entitled "Quine's Philosophy of Language," based mainly on Quine's *Word and Object* that had been published a few years earlier. It was there that I worked with two great guys, Neil Macgill and Frazier Cowley, both of whom were Scottish and very helpful and encouraging.

Yancy: So where did you go for your Ph.D. in philosophy?

Boxill: I went to UCLA because it was a place where logic was big. After all, I had done my earlier degree in mathematics, and my thesis was on Quine. But when I went there, there were the riots, Black Power, and so on. The year that I got there was the year right after the summer of the Watt's riots and so on. And, you know, I got completely turned on to these instead of logic.

Yancy: So how did you move from Quine and problems in mathematical logic to the social and political philosophical sphere?

Boxill: It wasn't easy as, at that time, I had never had a course in ethics or political philosophy. All of my classes were in logic, epistemology, and philosophy of language. I hadn't taken many classes in the history of philosophy either. I took a course in ethics the first semester I was at UCLA, but that course was really boring. What really got me interested in political philosophy was what was going on at the time. Also the woman who would eventually become my wife was doing a degree in political science. So between that and because of everything else that was going on in L.A. and the country, within months it seemed like this logic was not as important as politics. And I knew very soon that these political and ethical questions should be more important to me than what I had been doing.

But my previous training in philosophy didn't provide me with a good way of getting about in political philosophy. I didn't know anything about political philosophy or the history of political philosophy, though I read the books that were coming out at that time, like Carmichael and Hamilton's *Black Power* and Fanon's *Wretched of the Earth* and *Black Skin, White Masks*. And I felt that these were the sorts of things that I should be concerned with, but I didn't have any background to relate them in any intelligent way to the great issues in political philosophy.

Also, at the time, about thirty years ago, there was a general way of thinking that ethics and the history of philosophy was peripheral. I don't think that anybody believes this now, but at the time that was the feeling. Political philosophy especially was thought to be peri-

pheral. Actually one well-known philosopher declared political philosophy dead.

Yancy: So you were not very attracted to Russell's writings either on the
history of Western philosophy or his writings on ethical, social, and
political matters?

Boxill: He was writing on these things and he had written *The History
of Western Philosophy,* but that book was a very shallow book. The
first person for whom I was a teaching assistant used that book. It was
the first time that I had been really exposed to the history of philosophy, but, as it turned out, the book was not very good. He made it
seem that most of the philosophers before him were muddled. Also,
as I have said, at the time there was the feeling that political philosophy was dead. It revived and came alive only with John Rawls's
Theory of Justice in 1971. It was around '65 when I was around
UCLA. So all of these political upheavals, discussions, and arguments
were going on all of the time. And you could read about the things
that were being said, but I had not read them or heard them discussed
in any systematic philosophical way. However, I did feel that this was
something that I should know something about. In fact, I eventually
decided that I wanted to write my dissertation on these matters, and
Tom Hill was my dissertation chair and was the biggest influence on
me.

Yancy: Say more about this.

Boxill: At UCLA the logicians were interested in political questions, but
they didn't seem to think that they raised serious philosophical issues.
At any rate, political philosophy was not their field. Later on UCLA
hired political philosophers like Richard Wasserstrom, though he was
in the law school more than he was in the philosophy department,
and Arnold Kauffman, the author of *The Radical Liberal* who was
sadly killed in a plane crash. The great thing about Tom Hill was that
while he insisted that I rigorously explore the issues I was interested
in, he did insist that I know a lot about the history of political philosophy.

Yancy: What was the direction of your dissertation?

Boxill: In general, it was a discussion of the issues raised in the Black
Power debates that were going on at the time. For example, I dis-
cussed Fanon's views on violence in his books *The Wretched of the
Earth* and *Black Skin, White Masks.* My article, "Du Bois and Fanon

on Culture," which I believe was my third published article, came out of my dissertation. My first article, "Morality of Reparations," also came out of my dissertation. It was prompted by James Forman's book *Black Manifesto.*

Yancy: Does Fanon continue to be a source of philosophical inspiration for you? If so, in what ways?

Boxill: I stopped reading Fanon seriously about twenty years ago. This is not because I found him uninteresting; I found him fascinating; as I said a lot of my dissertation was based on his work. But when I tried to publish some more stuff on him no one seemed interested. So I began writing on other things and brought in Fanon only occasionally. I see now that thanks to people like Lewis Gordon that Fanon has caught on. Maybe I gave up too easily.

Yancy: Was philosophy, during this time, something you found impossible *not* to engage in?

Boxill: Yes, at first I couldn't think about doing anything else. Once the bug has bitten you there's no turning around. It is true, however, that after you get into philosophy, especially when you become a professional philosopher, you tend to lose that original wild enthusiasm for everything philosophical. But something of it remains, almost like a neurosis, for your specialty, which for me was philosophy concerning the racial issues. These issues were too close to home for me to ever lose interest in them.

Yancy: Was it the case that you were the only Black presence in your philosophy classes?

Boxill: Absolutely! I was the only Black graduate student there for a long, long time. I think that the next Black person there after me was the African-American philosopher Tommy Lott. I think that he came when I was finishing my thesis. So he probably came six or so years after I had started. But when I got there in 1965, I was the only one there. I remember thinking with only slight exaggeration that the Black students at the university were athletes and foreign students. Of course, that was not strictly true. Houston A. Baker, Jr., the African-American literary critic currently at the University of Pennsylvania, was there, though he was a graduate student in the English department. I remember him only slightly. I also knew Molefi Asante in the rhetoric department slightly. My best friend was Winston Van Horn, who is now at the University of Wisconsin. Although he was in political science, he was intensely interested in political philosophy, and I learned a lot from him.

Yancy: Do you construct yourself as an African-American philosopher?
Boxill: Yes. The first few years of my professional academic career I wrote about affirmative action, protest, desegregation, and assimilation. As I went along, it seemed to me that it would be important to study the history of African-American political thought as represented in the writings of Martin Delany, David Walker, Frederick Douglass, Alexander Crummell, W. E. B. Du Bois and others. I had read their books unsystematically to justify positions I had already taken, but gradually it began to be clear to me that these books contained arguments and positions that were important in their own right. Some of us speak of creating a tradition of African-American philosophy, but I think that tradition has already been started, and it is in the works of the people I mentioned. I don't think that it is philosophically explicit yet. But I believe that when we have it that it will be drawn from those political writings of David Walker to the present. These men and women were trying to make sense of their predicaments and to understand themselves, and it is from efforts such as these that philosophy is born. We are part of their tradition because we face essentially the same challenges to our humanity that they faced and tried to meet and to understand. Challenges like apparent powerlessness, disrespect and downright insult, injustice, and so on. My research convinces me that in trying to meet these challenges these men and women encountered the great and enduring questions of political philosophy and answered these questions in their own unique way. In this respect, there is not a whit of difference between Plato, Aristotle, Hobbes, and Locke, and Delany, Douglass, and Du Bois. Surely we would be the losers if we ignored their efforts.

Yancy: Why are African-Americans students so underrepresented in philosophy departments around the country?
Boxill: First of all, generally speaking, there simply aren't enough Black undergraduate students, and I think that this has to do with the many problems located at the high school and primary school educational levels. And I'm not sure things are not getting worse. In terms of the population of Black students going to college, I am told that the best of them go into law, medicine, business, and social work and so on. I think that at this point there should be a push toward getting more Black students into college. Concerning philosophy specifically, I

think that when what African-American philosophers are doing becomes better known and is taught in the general classes in philosophy that this will attract more Black students to philosophy; that is, when classes in political philosophy and ethics are taught from works by African-American philosophers. When this happens Black students will find things that are near to them and things that speak to them.

Yancy: Books like Richard Herrnstein's and Charles Murray's *The Bell Curve* in many ways militate against the notion of Blacks in philosophy. Indeed, the philosopher Michael Levin has, I think, propounded a very ridiculous and harmful line of reasoning which moves from low achievement on standardized tests by some Blacks to the negative implications of this for the capacity of Blacks becoming philosophers or doing philosophy.

Boxill: Well, I understand from people who know the genetic argument that the claims about Black intelligence in books like *The Bell Curve* are not well supported. They're saying that Blacks are genetically inferior and nothing can be done to improve their lot in this regard. These ideas have been around in America for a long time, but I speak carefully and literally when I say that I never heard anyone mention them in the Caribbean when I was growing up there. I suspect that this explains the fact that some conservative Black economists like to mention that West Indians who come to America generally do better than native Blacks. People in the West Indies took their education seriously. I do not mean that they put a lot of money into education. This is impossible because these are very poor islands; as I mentioned earlier, the people who taught me didn't even have degrees. I mean that Black people simply assumed that they would learn just like any other people. They did not have to deal with the barrage of criminal propaganda that they could not learn. This propaganda is distracting at best because students have to push it out of their minds, and at worst it can make Black students believe that they can't learn. I know that Black students don't read *The Bell Curve*, and few have even heard of it, but their teachers hear about it and some of them may actually read it. And they go into a class filled with Black students and believe that these students can't learn. These kinds of things are harmful. I feel that these things are destroying whole generations of students.

Yancy: A great deal of your philosophical corpus involves critical reflections on issues concerning affirmative action, preferential treatment, etc. How do you respond to a white male who argues that he has always fought against discrimination toward Blacks, that he has marched on their behalf, and that he is innocent of any oppressive or discriminatory acts against them and that therefore it is not ethically just that he should suffer and not get a particular position because of affirmative hiring?

Boxill: Well, he's got the benefits of other people doing it.

Yancy: In other words, he benefits from the oppressive and discriminatory acts of other whites?

Boxill: Yes. Throughout his life, he has received the benefits of discriminatory treatment that has given him a huge advantage over Black people. Also, don't forget that he has had the benefits of not having had to deal with the propaganda that he can't learn. Of course, he may not be guilty of any acts of discrimination or oppression, and no one is trying to punish him as if he had been guilty of such acts. Affirmative action is not punishment! It's an attempt to make the race for jobs and positions fairer. On the other hand, he would be guilty if he insisted on taking advantage of his unfair advantages. To use a crude example, if there is a race and you put one of the contenders twelve feet ahead of everyone else, then it is unfair and he shouldn't insist upon getting the prize even if he crosses the finish line first. However, though I can't think of a single case where this has happened, it would not be fair to hire a Black person, where he/she is not even qualified, over a white person.

Yancy: In your essay "Morality of Reparations" you refer to white people as a corporation or a company. There you maintain that "it seems not unfair to consider the present white population as members of a company that incurred debts before they were members of the company, and thus ask them justly to bear the cost of such debts." Would you elaborate on this claim?

Boxill: The claim is more complicated than I realized when I made it twenty-five years ago, but I still think it is true. Crudely it relies on the idea that white people act as if they think they are joint owners of the wealth of the country. Through their representatives they decide how the wealth of the country should be disposed. So they should pay the country's debts. Relevant and respectable objections are: If the country is like a company, when did they join? (Remember people join companies freely.) And even if they received benefits from the country, does it follow that they have to pay its debts when they could not avoid receiving the benefits? But they can be answered. The powerful intuition that drives these objections is the individualism that came to the U.S. via the writings of John Locke. According to Locke, no one has any obligations, besides those required by the law of nature, that she has not consented to, or incurred by her own voluntary actions. This, of course, led to the doctrine that the only legitimate government is government by consent. And it seems to support the objection that the present generation of white citizens is not obligated to pay the debts incurred by previous generations of white citizens; for the present generation of white citizens did not incur by their own voluntary actions the debts of previous generations of white citizens, and have not consented to paying off these debts.

Notoriously, however, Locke did not follow through consistently on his own individualism. Only the most famous of his lapses is his claim that mere residence within the boundaries of a country is tacit consent to that country's laws. Since this amounts to saying that residence in a country is tacit consent to the laws laid down by previous generations, Locke's claim seems to entitle me to the claim that the fact that present generations of white citizens reside in a country implies that they tacitly consent to paying off the debts incurred by previous generations of citizens.

The obvious rejoinder is that since Locke's claim is false and the result of a failure to follow through on his individualism, it cannot entitle me to the claim that I want to make. I concede this, of course. But now we must follow through consistently on Locke's individualism. This was attempted by Thomas Jefferson, Locke's ambivalent but in many ways more consistent student. According to Jefferson, all laws and natural debts should lapse after nineteen years. His point was that every nineteen years there is a new majority, and it should not be saddled with the laws or debts of previous generations because it neither consented to those laws nor incurred those debts. Jefferson's more consistent use of Locke's individualism than Locke himself may thus seem to raise even greater problems for my position, but before leaping to this conclusion we should pause to see some of the other claims Locke's individualism led Jefferson to make.

The most important of these claims is that "the earth belongs in usufruct to the living." What this means is that if persons do not inherit debts they do not inherit benefits either. Each generation should receive the earth free of the claims and debts of past generations to be divided among its members according to the laws of nature, or in Jefferson's better formulation, to be divided among its members so that each has a fair chance to be independent, well educated, virtuous, and upright. Are those who object to present white generations paying the debts of past generations willing to accept and to act on this conclusion? They cannot have it both ways. If they want to be Lockean individualists they must accept Jefferson's conclusion and procede with a radical redistribution of the country's wealth. If they take a more Hamiltonian view of the state they must allow that present generations may have to pay the debts of past generations.

Yancy: What qualifies Black people as eligible for reparations and affirmative action?

Boxill: Well, they suffer so many unfair disadvantages. There are disadvantages in the high schools. There is the fact that their parents are poorer than most white parents and therefore can't help their children as much. And I think that more important than any of these things is this pervasive negative attitude that is shown toward Blacks. Some try to make the argument that "Well, I know a Black person whose parents make more money than this white person's parents and that because of this the white person should receive affirmative action." But what about the other disadvantages? Black people are constantly reminded that they can't do such and such, treated like they are dumb, etc. I mean, there are a lot of white people who are poor, and whose parents are poor, who don't get a very good education, but they don't have such ideas drummed into them that they can't succeed or that they are naturally inferior. This is probably the most decisive reason why I would say that Blacks are eligible for reparations and affirmative action. In addition, of course, and the points are related, you have to remember the precariousness of Black success. Even successful Blacks teeter on the brink of being pushed back down into poverty because everyone else is so ready to push them back down, or at least to let them fall, and say, "I told you so."

Yancy: Is it enough to look at the pervasive amounts of poverty that exists within the lives of the vast majority of Black people on an axis of racism alone?

Boxill: That's a William Julius Wilson type of question. Well, I think that he's right that there is more to it than racism, but I've always disagreed with his argument that racism has little or nothing to do with it. Actually, he tends to say that and then to take it back in a complicated way. I've discussed these points in several essays and in my book. There have certainly been studies that have shown that you can have two equally qualified candidates, one Black and one white, where both are equally credentialed, well dressed, etc., and the white candidate in the majority of cases will get the position. There are many studies on this sort of thing. So, it seems to me that you can't eliminate this, though I think that Wilson is also right in terms of looking at the economy, expanded opportunities, more jobs, etc. After all, it is not going to work if you have a shrinking economy.

Yancy: How does your Caribbean identity square with your African-American identity? Are there differences and similarities? Are there ever any tensions?

Boxill: One thing that strikes me is that I seem to be slower to see insult and discrimination in what white people say and do than many, though certainly not all, African-Americans. Sometimes I think African-Americans see insult where there is in fact no insult. Mind you, I am not saying that they are being unreasonable. Given their experiences they are probably being very reasonable. Nevertheless, what is reasonable is sometimes mistaken. On the other hand, maybe I'm still not attuned to things here and my early experiences in the Caribbean prevent me from seeing things as they really are. But we should not overstate the difference between West Indians and African-Americans. Time and again, for example, I am struck by the similarities in the humor of the Caribbean and the humor of Black America. Perhaps these can be traced to our common heritage; or maybe they are a legacy of the very similar slavery our ancestors endured. In any case, it seems to me that a people's humor is an important indication of their character, so that my Caribbean identity fits rather well with my African-American identity. Besides, I suspect that a persons profession or vocation plays as great a part in creating his identity as his "race" or the place he grew up. I hate to seem disloyal to the Caribbean, but I fear that I am now more at ease with African-American philosophers, people like Howard McGary, Laurence Thomas, Lucius Outlaw, Bill Lawson, Leonard Harris, and Frank Kirkland, than my former schoolmates.

Yancy: How would you describe your overall philosophical worldview and how does this relate to your identity?

Boxill: That's a hard one. I'm an empiricist, and I'm skeptical of what powerful and influential people say, especially if they are philosophers. Politically, I am a left of center liberal. I feel that Marxism is mistaken and too optimistic about human nature; but I also feel that the free market must be strongly curbed and qualified. Government should interfere to make things fairer, but since we know how evil governments can be, we must also keep a bridle on government. I certainly do not believe that racism is permanent, but I am equally sure that the disposition to racism, and to most other evils, is permanent. Therefore people should trust in others' good will, but not too much. They must also be prepared to defend themselves. So, deliberative democracy is right only up to a point. It would be great if everyone was willing to talk honestly, but sometimes people won't, especially if they have the upper hand. Or they keep talking and talking and give up nothing. Talk can be a deliberate distraction. I'm also opposed to vulgar self-exposure, people demanding that others applaud them for what they have done, no matter what they are! Much of what a person is, apart from her basic dignity as a person, is her own business. It's a sign of immaturity to insist that others have to applaud whatever you make of yourself.

A Selection of Published Works of Bernard R. Boxill

Books

Blacks and Social Justice (Rowman and Allenheld, 1984); 2d. ed. (Lanham, MD: Rowman and Littlefield, 1992).

Articles

"Washington, Du Bois, and *Plessy v. Ferguson*," in *Law and Philosophy* (Dordrecht, the Netherlands: Kluwer, Summer 1997).

"Populism and Elitism in African-American Political Thought," *The Journal of Ethics* (fall 1997).

"Black Liberation, Yes," in *Liberation Pro and Con*, Michael Leahy, ed. (New York: Routledge 1996).

"Du Bois on Cultural Pluralism" in *W. E. B. Du Bois on Race and Culture*, Bernard Bell, Emily Grosholz, and James Stewart, ed. (New York: Routledge, 1996).

"Fighting with Covey," in *Existence in Black: An Anthology of Black Existential Philosophy*, Lewis R. Gordon, ed. (New York: Routledge, 1996).

"Separation or Assimilation" (chapter 8 from the book, *Blacks and Social Justice*), in *Campus Wars: Multiculturalism and the Politics of Difference*, John Arthur and Amy Shapiro, eds. (Boulder: Westview Press, 1995).

"Fear and Shame as Forms of Moral Suasion in the Thought of Frederick Douglass," *Transactions of the Charles S. Peirce Society*, no. 4 (fall 1995).

"The Culture of Poverty," *Social Philosophy and Policy* 11, no. 1 (winter 1994).

"The Case for Affirmative Action" (chapter 7 from the book *Blacks and Social Justice*), in *Morality in Practice*, 4th ed., James P. Sterba, ed. (Belmont: Wadsworth, 1994).

"Two Traditions in African American Political Thought," *Philosophical Forum* (fall-spring 1993).

"On Some Criticisms of Consent Theory," *Journal of Social Philosophy* (Spring 1993).

"Racism"; "Civil Rights"; "Martin Luther King," in *Encyclopedia of Ethics*, Lawrence Becker, ed. (New York and London: Garland, 1992).

"The Underclass and the Race-Class Issue," in *The Underclass Question*, Bill E. Lawson, ed. (Philadelphia: Temple University Press, 1992).

"Human Rights: The Dispute about the Underclass," in *Exploitation and Exclusion: Race and Class in the Twentieth Century*, Abebe Zegeye, Leonard Harris, and Julia Maxted, eds. (London: Hans Zell Publishers, 1991).

"Wilson on the Underclass," *Ethics* 101, no. 3 (April 1991).

Introduction to *Race: Twentieth Century Dilemmas-Twenty-First Century Prognoses*, special issue, *Ethnicity and Public Policy* (Madison: University of Wisconsin Press, 1990).

"The Race-Class Issue," *Philosophy Born of Struggle: Afro-American Philosophy from 1917*, Leonard Harris, ed. (Dubuque, IA: Kendall/Hunt, 1983).

"Sexual Blindness and Sexual Equality," *Social Theory and Practice* 6 (1980).

"How Injustice Pays," *Philosophy and Public Affairs* 9 (1980).

"The Morality of Preferential Hiring," *Philosophy and Public Affairs* 7 (1978): 246–68.

"Dubois and Fanon on Culture," *The Philosophical Forum* (winter/spring 1977–1978): 326–38.

"Self-Respect and Protest," *Philosophy and Public Affairs* 6 (1976): 58–69.

"Morality of Reparations," *Social Theory and Practice* 2, no. 1 (1972): 113–23.

[seventeen]

Robert E. Birt

Robert E. Birt currently is assistant professor of philosophy at Morgan State University. He earned his B.A. degree in history and philosophy from Morgan State University and his M.A. and Ph.D. degrees in philosophy from Vanderbilt University. He has also taught at Texas A&M University. His areas of specialization are phenomenology, existentialism, social and political philosophy, theories of alienation, and philosophical anthropology. His articles and reviews have appeared in *Quest: Journal of African Philosophy*; *International Philosophical Quarterly*; *The Philosophical Forum*; *Social Science Information*; and more. (A more complete citation list of Robert Birt's published works can be found at the end of the interview.)

Robert E. Birt
Morgan State University

George Yancy: When and where were you born?
Robert E. Birt: I was born October 7, 1952, in Baltimore, Maryland.

Yancy: What was it like growing up in Baltimore, Maryland?
Birt: Well, I grew up in a working-class family of modest income. The period in which I grew up gradually began to impact my social consciousness. The questions that began to burn in my mind when confronted with certain social contradictions and social experiences were, I think, part of the motivation for my development of an intellectual vocation.

I grew up in East Baltimore, which had a locally notorious reputation in those days, though it wasn't as difficult as Cabrini Green. The area where I grew up would more politely be described as the inner city. However, during the '60s it would simply be called the ghetto. In short, the general population was poor, though the type of poverty then is different from the poverty that you see in those areas now. Large numbers of people were not expelled from economic activity altogether, but we were relegated to the bottom of the economy even though our parents were employed. Currently, I think that there is a certain rawness about some of the poverty that you see now. During my youth, poverty stemmed from the fact that segregation ordinances circumscribed where we could live and what we could do. There was explicit discrimination or color barring in the workplace. Ironically, the poverty during that time allowed for a modicum degree of stability. For example, I don't recall chronic unemployment in my family. There were only low-income jobs. My father, who comes from a family of agricultural laborers, worked in rural North Carolina and you can imagine what rural North Carolina might have been like in the '40s.

Yancy: In terms of your early consciousness, how did seeing the segregational ordinances in this way influence you?

Birt: One experience which I recall must have happened when I was no older than eight because it happened before 1960. There was an amusement park, though it's gone now, called Gwyn Oak Amusement Park. It was advertised and I was interested in going. And so eventually my mother had to explain why I and my little sister couldn't go. And that was the first confusing experience with the racial system. It's hard for a child to be made to understand why he is excluded from a facility for children just because he is Black. I began to understand a little better as I got older. It takes some growing up to comprehend (let alone critique) the adult insanity of racist reason.

Yancy: Talk about your early educational experience. And were there any particular teachers that influenced you most?

Birt: I attended Mergenthaler Technical Vocational High School. Concerning teachers, I can't say that they really influenced me, but it was after I got into high school that something like a social consciousness really began to develop. The teaching staff at Mergenthaler was ridiculously conservative. During the time that I was there it was predominantly white. It has since become predominantly Black. It was very vocational and technical and I just floated through. I was taking printing shop and was training to be an electrician. However, the courses that interested me most were history and literature, and I would just read a lot of the history books from the library. In fact, it was during this time that I first encountered works by Du Bois and James Baldwin.

Also, there were a few politically conscious students. There were some white students there who were inclined toward Students for a Democratic Society (SDS). There were also developments among Black students who had leanings toward nationalist movements or the Black Panthers, though this was not comparable to what was going on at Berkeley.

Yancy: So, would you describe this period as discovering your reflective side?

Birt: Yes. I began reading even more during this time. I was just about fifteen. The courses at Mergenthaler simply bored me. I began reading African authors and African-American authors. I also began reading about the history of religion and various religious writings. This actually had the effect of disenchanting me with religion. This was before I looked at religion philosophically. The role of Christianity, for example, in the slave trade, the conquest of indigenous populations of North and South America, and the iniquities of the Inquisition, and so forth resulted, for me, in a kind of disenchantment with religion, though I wouldn't say that I was an atheist. And, again, I became skeptical that someone was trying to hide something. I mean, you would get your regular Sunday sermons. But why wasn't anything said about these other heinous matters? I actually began to suspect that maybe it was the job of teachers to mystify you while you actually think that you're being educated. To get the unofficial story you had to do some digging. And I was not only curious about the things that I did not know, but I was curious about why I didn't know them.

I actually ended up for a while at a school called Cardinal Gibbons here in Baltimore. There were some neighborhood missionaries who had said: "Well, look, you're a bright kid so you ought to go to this place." And so I got financial assistance and went there for a couple of years and eventually graduated. Their library was much better, but the Black student population was even smaller, though they were more politically conscious than the Blacks at Mergenthaler. Also, a larger part of the white population was politically conscious. Cardinal Gibbons encouraged greater freedom to engage in certain intellectual pursuits. During this time my two areas of interest tended to be history and philosophy. Though there were no philosophy courses, there were literary courses in which many of the authors were actually philosophers. I encountered Albert Camus, Friedrich Nietzsche, Martin Buber, and Frantz Fanon.

Actually, there was a rather straight-laced English teacher at Mergenthaler. He got very angry when someone distributed SDS literature in his class, but he apparently was not very conventional on matters of religion. And though I'm not sure why he did this, one day he used the entire class period talking about some writings of David Hume. It was only later that I came to identify these as Hume's essay on miracles and his criticisms of natural religion. And these things actually made some students angry, though it didn't upset me as much; for, as I've suggested, I was becoming disenchanted with religion for other than philosophical reasons. I had more social concerns. Why is it that religion is always on the side of those who were in power? I eventually, of course, discovered that the relationship between the philosophical, the social, and the political are not, strictly speaking, separate. But during this time I was not interested in systematic theology or the cosmological argument or the design argument for the existence of God. In fact, I'm not interested in these things now. I was interested in the morally questionable record of religion. Hence, Frederick Douglass and Malcolm X, as far as concerns their critiques of religion and how it was used to support slavery, seemed extremely relevant.

Yancy: Why undergraduate training at Morgan State?

Birt: Well, there were a number of reasons. One reason had to do with the fact that Morgan, then and now, is accessible, especially for a person of limited means. Secondly, given that Morgan is a predominantly Black university, I wanted to be around socially conscious and serious young Black people like myself. Morgan also had a certain prestige in the Black community. A large part of the leadership elite of the Black community was produced by Morgan. And a good number of student activists, who were challenging segregation in public accommodations, were Morgan students at that time. I should also add that Morgan's philosophy department had the notorious reputation for being perhaps the most left-wing department on campus. And at its height it may have had around twenty-five Black philosophy majors.

Yancy: Who was teaching there in the department at that time and who influenced you most?

Birt: There was Robert A. Cheemooke, who was a Trinidadian. He had studied at Howard University and was a friend of Stokely Carmichael.

He was also rather popular with a number of students. He taught courses in the area of social and political philosophy and, of course, this was the area in which I was interested. In continental European philosophy, there was Otto Begus. Actually, Begus is now the chairman of the department. He is a product of the Frankfurt School. He apparently studied in Latin America. I believe he did his licentiate on Martin Heidegger and Max Scheler. And then I believe he did some work on the Neo-Kantians with Theodor Adorno and that group.

Yancy: So, at this juncture, were you interested in continental philosophy?

Birt: Yes. I eventually wrote my dissertation on Jean-Paul Sartre.

Yancy: Before we go on to your graduate experience, what got you specifically interested in existentialism and Sartre in particular?

Birt: Well, I actually noticed an unusually large number of African-American writers who seemed to find something of value in the existentialist movement. There were even certain activists who would talk about rebellion and they would make reference to Albert Camus. At some point I would wonder about this and would take another look at *The Rebel*. I would also notice certain influences in Richard Wright, Ralph Ellison, or Harold Cruse. In fact, Cruse talks about the notion of revolt, including metaphysical revolt, and I wanted to really look at this because it seemed to challenge something that I had read or something that Sartre had said. In *Anti-Semite and Jew*, Sartre suggests that metaphysics tends to be the cultural privilege of ruling classes and dominant castes or racial groups. But Cruse suggests that the notion of metaphysical revolt might have special significance or relevance to the experience of Black Americans. The whole notion of absurdity has probably a poignant relevance to the Black experience that exceeds anything familiar to the French existentialists. Cruse doubts that anyone has had a greater experience of the absurd than the Black peoples of the United States.

When I read the literature by African-Americans, I found an affinity with existentialism. There is the concern about freedom, responsibility, anguish, situatedness, as well as the existential engagement of the thinker or the intellectual. Given my own history, a history in which my social consciousness was awakened by the movements of the time, Sartre's *What is Literature* had an appeal to me. And in that text, Sartre actually cites Richard Wright; for Wright is correctly seen as historically situated in such a way that he is a member of a radically oppressed group and he gives voice to the aspirations of Black people and informs and clarifies the consciousness of these people. In fact, Sartre writes as if he is envious of Wright, because as an old bourgeois French writer Sartre himself is uncertain for whom he is writing. Sartre wants to see the craft of writing involved with the emancipatory project of oppressed classes. And he sees Wright as contributing to an enlightenment of the consciousness of Black people and aiding in the emancipation of the dispossessed. And Sartre realizes that Wright knows the audience to whom he is writing. But Sartre himself wonders to whom he is writing.

I first read Camus after hearing his name mentioned by some of the more intellectually oriented activists during my early period of social consciousness. And Camus captured my imagination immediately with his description of the rebel as one who says "No!" and for whom consciousness is born after each act of rebellion and resistance. I was struck by similarities, though not exactly in Camus's metaphysical terms, when I read about Frederick Douglas's contention with the slave driver Covey. And what interested me is the fact that what these existentialist philosophers described in metaphysical terms actually keeps occurring, though in more concrete or social terms, in African-American literature. Douglass does not speak of *the rebel* as such. He speaks of *his* confrontation with Covey. It is a life and death situation. It occurred to me that there is something to Angela Davis's claim that the experiences of Black people in the United States and perhaps the world is an as of yet unexplored gold mine. The interesting thing is that the existentialist tends to describe these experiences in ontological or even metaphysical terms. But I think that there is a more concrete experience of these things in terms of the experiences of Blacks in America. There is a meeting, as it were, of the whole lofty metaphysical description of freedom and the historical struggle for freedom.

Yancy: Now, where did you do your graduate work in philosophy? And in terms of your eventual philosophical direction who influenced you most?

Birt: It's kind of interesting. I finally decided on Vanderbilt University around 1976. I tried The New School for Social Research, but they said that they didn't have any money for financial assistance. And I also applied, I think, to either Boston or Georgetown and received a similar response. Vanderbilt offered something that was very slim. It allowed me to live very frugally. I was accustomed to living this way so it wasn't insufferable. But I didn't enjoy living this way.

Also part of what decided the matter concerning my choice of Vanderbilt had to do with my wish to avoid the type of university which required you to follow a certain philosophical line. But Vanderbilt, in terms of this whole debate in the late '70s over analytic versus pluralistic approaches to philosophy, was pluralist. In other words, "pluralistic" meant that you did something besides analytic philosophy and was able to have some chance of getting successfully into the program.

Now, in terms of influences, I would have to say it was Charles Scott and John Lachs. If nothing else, I simply took more courses with them. With Scott I studied the work of Heidegger, Kierkeggard, and Sartre. I also took a course entitled "The Philosophical Foundations of Psychoanalysis." This course consisted of an exploration of existential psychoanalysis. As for Lachs, he directed my dissertation and was interested in pragmatism and particularly in German philosophy. I studied Kant, Hegel, and Schopenhauer with Lachs. But I also took courses in phenomenology with John Compton. In one of those courses we read *Cartesian Meditations* and *The Transcendence of the Ego*. And in an advanced course of his we read Maurice Merleau-Ponty's *The Phenomenology of Perception* and Edmund Husserl's *The Crisis of the European Sciences*.

I should also mention that the African-American philosopher Robert C. Williams, who died in 1987, was also teaching at Vanderbilt while I was there. And though he was on leave most of the time, I did manage to take a course with him entitled "Philosophical Issues in Imaginative Literature." Literature was my other love and I would imagine his also. There was another course that he taught that I wasn't able to take at the time. It was a course on Ludwig Feuerbach, Hegel, and Marx, but because of his leaves of absence, I was never able to take the course. I knew that he had an interest in religion so I was wondering how he would handle Feuerbach and Marx. And though I didn't get a chance to study the work of Feuerbach formally, I was particularly interested in him and so decided to read his work on my own.

Yancy: In your essay "The Negation of Hegemony: The Agenda of *Philosophy Born of Struggle*" you discuss Leonard Harris's *Philosophy Born of Struggle*. How significant was this text in terms of reshaping previous philosophical discourse?

Birt: That text pulled together for the first time a substantial number of essays by Black philosophers. To my knowledge, that had not happened before, though this is becoming common now. Harris's text may have pioneered this trend. I'm not sure, however, in what way philosophical discourse has been reshaped by his text. In other words, I'm not sure to what extent the things done in that text requires us to think about things differently. But I do think that his book provoked a trend, in terms of doing African-American philosophy, whereby it is not only acceptable but it is increasingly now expected to be the sort of thing that should happen. So, it is this trend that can be said to be in some sense a contestation with the previously established hegemony whereby philosophy is implicitly understood as being essentially white and male. *Philosophy Born of Struggle,* the text itself, presented us with certain kinds of perspectives and orientations that were overlooked, dismissed, or just not known to exist. Harris's book brought these things to the surface so that it has become less and less possible to talk about philosophy as if there were no African-American presence in the field. So that now I have to think about philosophy differently. One shortcoming of Harris's text was the paucity of female philosophers in the text. Angela Davis perhaps being the singular notable female philosopher in that text.

Yancy: Do you feel that racism is very much alive in the profession of philosophy in America?

Birt: Yes, but I think that it is discreet. It doesn't present itself with the bluntness of a Willie Horton campaign. That is, it's a matter of exclusion; a question of not raising certain issues. One speaks of philosophy as being able to see things *sub species aeternitatis.* And, of course, this is still a patriarchal, elite, Eurocentric model of the enterprise of philosophy. I mean, you don't find a philosophical George Wallace standing at the doors of the halls of philosophy barring your entrance. It's like you're just not there. And if you are there, then it's like you're not. So, the racism that I see in the profession of philosophy is of a very discrete kind and it doesn't see itself as such. I remember when I taught at Texas A&M University there was this guy, an older guy, who said that during the period of segregation he didn't know that there was segregation. He thought that it was a matter of coincidence that all Black people just seemed to want to sit in the upper part of the movie theater. It's just remarkable that people can have eyes that just don't see. So, there's no particular reason why there are no Blacks in philosophy. I guess they just sing and dance, but have no interest in intellectual pursuits.

Yancy: Do you see African-American philosophers as creating a new morphology of philosophical questions and methods?

Birt: I'm not really sure yet, but I think that perhaps in the next fifteen years I'll have a better view of this. Besides a few periodic exceptions, the halls of philosophy have been pretty much painted white. I think that it's fairly recent that you have something that's beginning to develop into a small Black philosophical community. This is also beginning to manifest itself through the circulation of texts. But what will be the outcome of this? I'm beginning to wonder how these things are going to impact discourse. Perhaps the texts themselves will not explicitly delineate a new morphology of questions and so forth, but they may, by their sheer influence, suddenly begin to rework philosophical discourse in such a way that this new morphology of questions eventually happens. When I was in undergraduate school, I was told that there were a little under twenty Black professional philosophers in the United States. There were hardly as many Black philosophers as I was old at the time. But perhaps we have now reached the numbers where we can have something like ongoing communication and a community of discourse that may have the practical result of helping to reinvent the philosophical enterprise.

Yancy: Why is it that African-American philosophers are principally preoccupied with issues in value theory, social and political philosophy and not with metaphysics or grand epistemological questions?

Birt: Well, I think that the reasons are similar to those provided by Sartre where he responds to a question concerning why among Jewish intellectuals in Europe you find so few metaphysical thinkers. And he says that the primary concern of the Jewish thinker is the relation of man in society as opposed to the place of man in the universe. Sartre says that people who are rooted belong to the dominant group and that they enjoy a certain kind of security about their position in society. This is true even of some of those who belong to the dominated classes. I mean, they've been French for two thousand years. The social and psychological security of an Aryan aristocracy affords the leisure and liberty to dwell on metaphysical concerns with Olympian composure. That isn't so easy for an outcast and denigrated people. But it isn't true that metaphysical or epistemological concerns don't deeply interest Black people; rather, it's that the social question tends to be a predominating concern. This, it seems to me, is the case with regard to African-American philosophy. There's a tremendous number of African-American philosophers who are interested in ontological and metaphysical questions, but as they think and rethink such questions they do so in social terms.

I was reading Huey P. Newton's memoir, which has a very unhappy title, *Revolutionary Suicide*. There he discusses his encounter with Nietzsche. He talks about his concern with the notion of the will to power, the concept of the transvaluation of values, and he begins thinking about the possibility that there is something in Nietzsche's metaphysics that would be helpful socially and politically. So even where there is an addressing of metaphysical questions, the social concern is often predominant. There are, I think, some Black philosophers who are primarily epistemologists, but still very few. Nevertheless, the philosopher is an historical person in situation. So that when the philosopher engages certain questions and concerns, he/she is already a socially informed being.

Yancy: How do we get more Blacks in the field of professional philosophy?

Birt: This is something that I've been worrying about for a long time. Well, just on an institutional level, there is the whole question of how to best make high-quality education available to larger numbers of Black people. There are two things. One has to do with the expansion of opportunity for education. And part of this is financial, especially in the light of the worsening economic state of the majority of Black America. The worsening of educational circumstances is tied to the worsening of economic circumstances. How to attack that, of course, is no easy matter. Racial barriers that remain would have to be contested.

But there are dual issues here. There are the external obstructions which, if you please, the white world presents. And then there are internal problems that, for better or worse, involve a kind of pragmatic, anti-intellectual attitude which, though affecting the larger American culture, tends to have a greater impact on the culture of Black America. This is intensified in relationship to the greater economic and social insecurity of the Black population. One of the things that has to be done internally, and I'm not sure how, is that those of us who are philosophers and intellectuals in the Black community have got to find ways of getting people to see that philosophy is not simply a white thing. That's a notion that must be eliminated. There must be some collective effort of trying to find ways of influencing the popular culture of the Black youth in such a way that they see intellectual pursuits as some how vital to their well-being as individuals and vital to the well-being of their people.

After all, among Black youth you get the attitude that says, "Look, I'm sort of coming out of nothing and I need a job that will quickly get me an income."

Yancy: And philosophy may not do that.

Birt: Right. We can't lie to people about jobs in philosophy. But obviously you don't find a majority of Ph.D.'s subsisting on welfare. People have to also understand that the philosophical vocation, despite the problems, is a noble vocation in and of itself. Moreover, people have to understand that there is a need for the kind of leadership, in relationship to the progress of the community, provided by people like Du Bois. And philosophy is one of those areas of study that prepares one for that kind of leadership. And it's not that everyone must be committed to this, but the community should see to it that some of its members are committed. Just as there are concerns for more businesses in the Black community, there must be a concern for intellectual life that is beyond pecuniary concerns. But there is an emphasis in the culture of Black America going back to slavery which sees enlightenment as a contribution to emancipation. If the emphasis on that point, which you find in Frederick Douglass and others, can be made big in the popular consciousness then this may help us reorient Black youth into pursuing philosophy as an intellectual vocation. I told my students who were reading about some of the spokespersons of the '60s that Martin Luther King, Jr., Stokely Carmichael, and Angela Davis are all philosophers. Indeed, that a considerable deal of the progress of the movement is due to the leadership people who were philosophically informed. To say nothing about Ellison or Wright, who were seriously influenced by philosophy and had inclinations toward Hegelian and existential thinking which were important influences on their reinterpretations of their experiences and reality.

Yancy: You spoke earlier about some links between existentialism and some Black literary figures. What do you understand by a distinctively *Black* existentialism?

Birt: This involves Black writers who begin to interpret their experience through an existential lens. In Sartre, there is a description of the absurd, talk about bad faith, etc. But what experiential context gives us an understanding of these phenomena? Lewis Gordon has written a book entitled *Bad Faith and Antiblack Racism* in which he looks at the whole phenomenon of racism as a form of bad faith and he talks about how this is experienced. Gordon also takes issue with certain views that Sartre puts forward in his *Black Orpheus*. Sartre seems to suggest that Black people can't really engage themselves in bad faith in terms of race. Gordon, of course, sees this as nonsense. What Sartre had in mind is that even the Jew who is despised and persecuted is still a white man among white men and it's easier to try to claim that he is simply man, not Jewish, Gentile, just man. Now Sartre wants to say that Blacks aren't allowed the privilege of that type of inauthenticity because of the physiological character of racism. And, of course, Gordon argues that we can engage in acts of bad faith.

Yancy: And also acts of inauthenticity.

Birt: Oh, yes. We most certainly can and do. But he's mainly describing the bad faith that is involved in the racial attitudes toward Blacks by others. He also talks about the tendency of Blacks to try to hide from reality. There are some Blacks who simply say, "Well, I'm just an individual and although things happen they really won't happen to me because I'm just an individual. I'm not Rodney King. That couldn't happen to me." I think that there is a certain kind of self-deception that any human being can engage in. There is self-deception and bad faith that the dominant group engages in and there is bad faith that the dominated group engages in. What Gordon is trying to do is examine the phenomenon of bad faith from the consciousness of this historical experience. This may be an example of Black existentialism in which you're examining a certain phenomenon from the historical situation in terms of which you know it. So that he may not talk about bad faith in exactly the way Sartre does, but he might talk about it as it is shaped by the American context in terms of racial polarization and so forth.

Yancy: So as a Black existentialist, how do you reconcile the language of man as metastable, transphenomenal, or even Sartre's other notion of man as being-for-itself (*pour-soi*), with the use of the delimiting language of race?

Birt: Well, first of all, I don't necessarily cling to vocabulary too intensely. In other words, I'm not deeply concerned with trying to fit everything into a little pigeonhole that may have been developed by any particular European thinker. What interests me, as a thinker, is an existential critique of the concept of race itself. I'm enough of an existentialist not to believe that there is a Black essence. For example, I'm not very sympathetic to certain Black ideologies, if you please, which desire to essentialize race. That is, to essentialize race differently from the way that whites do it. So that what happens is that they usually end up inverting the terms of the essentialization. In a very crude way this happens with the Nation of Islam where an essentialist racial identity is accepted pretty much without question. That is, where the valorization is inverted, but this seems to me to be a kind of dead-end. It's important to recognize that race exists as an historical reality. For example, the whole of my identity isn't defined by race, though there is a tendency in the United States to engage in what Sartre calls an overdetermination from without which attempts to fix you, as Fanon would say. But the reason there is a racial identity at all is that it is part of a praxis of domination. At least this marks the historical origins of the concept of race.

Now why is it that I have a racial identity at all? Well, it's largely because of historical reasons. And it won't do to simply pretend that it doesn't exist because this is a social reality and it does affect one's identity. I mean, you can imagine at the age of seven being told that you can't go to this or that particular place. That certainly begins to affect your identity and yet I want to avoid an essentialist identity. I see race as a social creation. Africans, as far as I know, would not have had a racial identity two thousand years ago. Romans and Greeks did not know that they belonged to something called a white race. A Roman would probably be shocked to be told that he belonged to the same race as those *barbaric* Germans. It's not enough for me to pretend that race doesn't exist, because there are the social realities to be dealt with. People are historical and they come into existence under historical conditions. I regard myself as an African-American to the extent that I am situated within a certain historicity. I don't know whether there will always be a Black race or a white race. I'm not completely sure that there should be. But present reality is racialized, and we must struggle against racial oppression and alienation rather than simply dismissing race as an essentialist myth or pretending that it doesn't exist. Indeed such pretentious dimissals are indications of bad faith. Our task, as Sartre suggests in *Black Orpheus*, is to form "a more just view of Black subjectivity."

In the final analysis we have to regard the human being at least potentially as a field of possibility. And, of course, an existentialist thinker tends to be skeptical of a fixed nature of any kind. But my opposition to the racist would not take the form of an inverted valorization. It would take the form of an existential and historical critique of racial domination and identities based on domination and reinforcing domination. My approach would ask how we, as bell hooks would say, can create a space in which you could have a *radical* consciousness. She talks about a radical Black subjectivity. So, how do we rethink things in such a way that the world can become, as Ralph Ellison would say, a world of possibility?

Yancy: Within your existentialist framework, does the concept of God play any part?

Birt: Not in the way that it would play for a Christian existentialist. To be quite frank, I'm not committed to any theistic worldview. The notion of God does have some significance. Aside from the question as to whether there is a God, the idea of God is real in terms of its effect. Millions of people invest in the notion of God. I don't seek any deliverance through the agency of any supreme Being and I guess that death, for that reason, has a very different significance for me than it does for someone for whom death involves the notion of an afterlife. I guess in that sense I'm Sartrean.

Yancy: Do you think that life and the universe have meaning a priori?

Birt: I don't think so.

Yancy: And this is consistent with your particular existentialist bent, yes?

Birt: Well, yes. Meaning emerges out of the human world. Now if there is a meaning beyond the human world, and I guess that I'm like Camus on this point, I'm not in a position to know *that* it is or to know *what* it is. You see, I have no reason to believe that it does exist and if it does exist then I can say that it must be out of the range of human understanding.

Yancy: How does your Black existential bent square with your interest in phenomenology?

Birt: I haven't been able to pursue this as I would like, but you know that Frantz Fanon among others engages in this sort of thing. Fanon, of course, does an existential phenomenological examination of the deformation of the Black psyche under colonialism. I have an interest similar to that in many ways. I suspect that Fanon may have had a bigger influence on me than Sartre in that respect. Fanon, in fact, may have been the first phenomenologist that I encountered in my intellectual development. He's probably still the greatest one. To a large extent I see myself as working within the tradition of Fanon. The same kind of existential and social critique and the same kind of engaged commitment to intellectual work in the interest of human emancipation. I don't exclude the option, however, that philosophy can be pursued out of a sense of wonder.

There are two things that Sartre says that are of interest here. He suggested that once there is no longer an oppressor and oppressed that perhaps all human beings would become interested in metaphysical questions. And in his *The Search For A Method*, Sartre says that once there is real freedom beyond the production and sustenance of life, a philosophy of freedom will emerge. And I suspect that in the event that that happens everyone will be engaged in intellectual inquiry out of a sheer sense of wonder. A part of what motivates my intellectual interest, to be frank, like every philosopher or intellectual, is that I do this because it is exhilarating. But as a member of a disadvantaged group, an essential part of my intellectual processes is attuned to the feeling of this need to make some contribution to the emancipatory quest of the people themselves.

Yancy: So, how does your interest in phenomenology work in there?

Birt: Well, phenomenology, at least in terms of the framework within which I tend to look at things, has to do with an examination of human consciousness and the development of the human being as a subject. I wouldn't say that I have a fixed program that I offer as a phenomenologist. It's just that phenomenology offers a better way of looking at human experience from the standpoint of the human being as a subject as opposed to looking at the human being strictly as an object. And with respect to Black people as human beings, as conscious subjects, the phenomenological approach is more satisfactory.

Yancy: Is this because it examines consciousness as an *intending* consciousness in the world?

Birt: That's definitely it. I'm not sure about Sartre's critique of Edmund Husserl. I do find his own thesis especially interesting; that is, Sartre's notion that consciousness is *in the world*. And it is in this relation with the world that I'm in some sense formed and form myself. I think that Sartre's phenomenological approach dovetails, at least indirectly, with certain kinds of social concerns more so than the egological phenomenological approach found in Husserl's *Cartesian Meditations*.

Yancy: How does your overall philosophical project relate to your identity?

Birt: I think that I have been involved in this for so long that it has become an integral part of my identity. It's not that I think of myself as *only* a philosopher, but to the extent that I do think of myself I always still think of myself as a philosopher who does a lot of things. However, the philosophical project is always present in whatever I do. Some people get angry with me. They say that I can't sit and watch a movie without having to subject it to unnecessary scrutiny, but this actually makes the movie more enjoyable. Actually, bell hooks makes an interesting comment in one of her works where she relates how a Black female friend had gotten upset that bell had dared to take her to a movie where she had to read subtitles. And as if that wasn't enough, bell then subjected her friend to intensive critique of the movie after it was over. So that even though bell hooks critically engaged the film, she was, nevertheless, quite fascinated by it. Maybe there's something to Cornel West's claim that choice of becoming a Black intellectual is a choice of self-imposed marginalization. But I'm not sure that there aren't certain joys of existence even in marginality.

Published Works of Robert E. Birt

Articles

"Existence, Identity and Liberation," in *Existence in Black: An Anthology of Black Existential Philosophy*, Lewis R. Gordon, ed. (New York: Routledge, 1997).

"Identity and the Question of African Philosophy," *Philosophy East and West* (January 1991).

"A Returning to the Source: The Philosophy of Alaine Locke," *Quest: Journal of African Philosophy* (December 1990).

"The Prospects for Community in the Later Sartre," *International Philosophy Quarterly* XXIX, no. 2, issue no. 114 (June 1989).

"Negation of Hegemony," *Social Science Information* (Paris and London, March 1987).

"Alienation in the Later Sartre," *Man and World* (fall 1986).

"America's New Enlightenment: Philosophy Born of Struggle," *Philosophy and Social Criticism* (fall/winter 1983).

"A Critique of James Cone's Conception of God," *The Philosophical Forum* (winter/spring 1977–78).